Handbook of Religious Conversion

Handbook of
Religious Conversion

edited by
H. NEWTON MALONY
and
SAMUEL SOUTHARD

Religious Education Press
Birmingham, Alabama

Library of Congress Cataloging-in-Publication Data

Handbook of religious conversion / edited by H. Newton Malony and Samuel
    Southard.
    Includes bibliographical references and indexes.
    ISBN 0-89135-086-1
    1. Conversion.   I. Malony, H. Newton.   II. Southard, Samuel.
BL639.H35 1992
291.4'2—dc20   92-5640
                                               CIP

Religious Education Press, Inc.
5316 Meadow Brook Road
Birmingham, Alabama 35242
10 9 8 7 6 5 4 3 2

Religious Education Press publishes books exclusively in religious education
and in areas closely related to religious education. It is committed to enhanc-
ing and professionalizing religious education through the publication of
serious, significant, and scholarly works.

PUBLISHER TO THE PROFESSION

Contents

v

85776

Foreword

As far as the human sciences are concerned, conversion has been a prime focus of study throughout the twentieth century. William James relied heavily on Edwin Starbuck's seminal study of adolescent conversion in the 1904 writing of his still-in-print *The Varieties of Religious Experience*. G. Stanley Hall devoted a significant part of his 1917 two-volume treatise *Jesus the Christ in the Light of Psychology* to conversion. The topic evoked such interest that it was no surprise that De Sanctis brought together many of these ideas in the first full-length book devoted to the subject, *Religious Conversion: A Bio-psychological Study* in 1927—the very year in which Sigmund Freud published his brutal analysis of religion entitled *The Future of an Illusion*.[1]

It is to G. Stanley Hall's theory of conversion that we would like to pay particular attention in this foreword to the *Handbook of Religious Conversion*. Hall's was a noteworthy early attempt to combine perspectives from a variety of theories—a goal to which we, too, have aspired. Although he was writing with Christian conversion in mind, his ideas could be re-conceived to fit a number of other religions.[2]

Hall was convinced, along with Augustine and other fathers of the church, that deep inside each person was a spiritual dimension. Theologians have termed this the "image of God." There was a built-in intention in the creative process that persons mature to the point where they actualize this inner spir-

---

1. References for these early works are as follows:

De Sanctis, *Religious Conversion: A Bio-psychological Study* (London: Kegan Paul, Tranch, & Co., 1927); Sigmund Freud, *The Future of an Illusion* (Garden City, N.Y.: Doubleday, 1957); G. Stanley Hall, *Jesus the Christ in the Light of Psychology* (New York: Appleton, 1917); William James, *The Varieties of Religious Experience* (New York: Longmans, Green, 1929).

2. A more extensive review of Hall's thinking can be found in H. Newton Malony, "G. Stanley Hall's theory of conversion," *Newsletter: Psychologists Interested in Religious Issues: Divsion 36. American Psychological Association* (Fall 1989): 3-5.

1

itual potential and, thereby, become altruistic and loving in their relations with each other, according to Hall. He had deep faith in the evolutionary process and felt that just as humans progressed through lower forms of life *prenatally,* so, after birth they progressed through earlier historic/cultural stages *postnatally.* However, whereas the evolutionary process usually progressed unabatedly before birth, something seemed to happen after birth to stunt and frustrate human progress toward unselfish concern for others, i.e., altruism. The realization of this human potential for loving others was obstructed by laziness, fear, selfishness, guilt, and inferiority. Conversion was the way by which this obstruction was overcome and people were freed to become who they were intended to be.

According to Hall, faith in Jesus Christ transforms persons and gives them the strength to love. Thus, faith was the essential process in conversion. Hall contended that this transforming faith did not occur by appeal to rational arguments about Jesus. Reason easily turns to pragmatism and pragmatism returns people to self-interested functionalism, according to Hall. Nor does the transformation of conversion occur as a result of telling people to look to Jesus as a moral example. Martyrdom might inspire some folk, but most will simply look on in admiration but feel the cost is too great for them to follow. Further, fear will not provoke faith, in Hall's opinion. The satisfaction of God's wrath by substitutionary atonement will appear out-of-character for God and will not be inspiring. Only the story of a God who loved humans enough to die for them will be powerful enough to transform persons and awaken in them the memory of who they, too, were created to be. The transforming faith of conversion is a response of amazement to God's love which results in love for others.

To illustrate this principle, Hall used the image of geodes, those ugly crusted rocks which reveal beautiful inner crystals when broken open. Humans are like that. By adolescence, people have forgotten the altruistic, loving core of their lives, i.e., the *imago dei* (image of God) and have become crusted over with defensive self-centeredness. Hall's conviction is that only by faith in the truth of a God who loved humans enough to die for them could people be transformed. Like geodes which are broken open and reveal crystals, through faith people are broken open and their beautiful spiritual natures are revealed. Then, and only then, will transformation have occurred and the possibility of living unselfishly will have become possible. Hall called this a process of genetic development guided by recapitulation.

Hall is an example of our intention to combine a variety of perspectives on conversion in this handbook. We hope that this will enhance an understanding of the conversion process and perhaps lead religious educators and professionals in more informed ministries. Thus, we hope this will be a practical book. In a deeper sense, however, our intent is that this will be a theoretical volume. We are convinced, along with many others, that the most practical thing in the world is a good theory. Hopefully, we have not shied away from sound principles in our effort to provide functional ideas.

Another feature of this handbook is its intent to be comprehensive, but not exhaustive. Perusing the table of contents may tempt some readers to feel we have left out one or more dimensions of conversion. Some of these neglected themes are addressed as sub-themes within those chapters we have included. Nevertheless, readers will readily recognize that the writers themselves have been selective in their treatment of the various topics. A handbook is not an encyclopedia. The writers have been encouraged to be thorough yet perspectival. It is our hope that readers will take the chapters as springboards for their own reflection and feel free to add, subtract, and interact with the material.

The handbook is divided into several parts. Part I, *Conversion in Comparative Religions,* includes chapters dealing with Hinduism, Buddhism, Judaism, Christianity, and New Religions. Some readers may wonder how a volume on conversion could pay attention to religions such as Hinduism and Buddhism which teach respect for all faiths and seemingly have no need for the idea of conversion. Unlike Christianity and some of the newer, non-traditional religions, they are not exclusive in their emphasis on absolute truth. It will be apparent, however, when one reads the chapter by Paul Hiebert that both Hinduism and Buddhism spread through missionary effort and developed reform movements that can be compared to Christian emphases on enlightenment and escape from this world. There are also similarities in such methods as proselytizing and evangelism whether by preaching, teaching, or political coercion.

This does not imply that conversion means the same from religion to religion. As Dudley Woodberry shows in the chapter on Islam, there is no formal rite of conversion and no references to conversion in the earliest pages of the Koran. But there are terms and procedures in Islam that are similar in intention and behavior to those used in Christianity. Also, the interaction of Islam with other religious structures produced some mass conversions that had less to do with military force and more to do with social status. There are parallels in the history of Christian expansion.

Comparisons of thought and method not only show diversity among religions; there are also variations within one religion. Beverly Gaventa demonstrates this in the chapter on conversion in the Bible. There are varying images, emphases, and contexts of the biblical passages associated with conversion. Yet there is one dominant motif, particularly in the New Testament, namely, "transformation." The debate within the early church over whether non-Jews should be encouraged to become Christians seems to be have been resolved by Christianity in favor of a worldwide imperative to evangelize.

Although Judaism in the past was explicitly evangelistic, in more recent times it has resisted converting persons to its faith and has, instead, emphasized its cultural separatism. Arthur Glasser notes these historical changes and reflects on them in light of the universalism of the eighth-century prophets. Of particular interest in the contemporary scene are feelings among many Jews that Christians have inappropriately tried to convert them. Glasser discusses the justification some Christians feel in these efforts as well as unusual movements within Judaism itself to convert Jews to Christianity.

James Richardson discusses an issue that has concerned many persons over the last quarter-century, namely, the conversion practices of new and non-traditional religions. In American culture, the joining of such groups as the Moonies, the Hare Krishnas, the Children of God, and the Maranantha Fellowship has provoked great consternation. Richardson describes some of these practices and considers them in light of theories of social influence as well as accusations that these groups engage in "brainwashing" or coercive influence. He notes that some of these conversion practices may be less socially deviant than simply unfamiliar or different from customary religious habits.

Part II is concerned with *Theological Perspectives on Conversion.* With the demonstration of the diverse meanings and procedures of conversion in the previous chapters, readers may wonder if there is any systematic way to approach conversion from within one of the world's great religions. There is. This section of the handbook considers how conversion has been approached by a variety of Christian traditions. More particularly, conversion is herein reviewed as a part of the theological systems of western Europe and of North America.

Part II begins with the systematic study of biblical themes by Frederick Gaiser. In the midst of the diversity of scriptural approaches he finds a unifying theme, namely, conversion means "life transformation." This is a similar conclusion to that reached by Gaventa in the previous section. The context of conversion is highlighted by discussions of God's involvement in the world as creator, redeemer, as well as convicting and guiding Spirit. Alongside an examination of these divine themes, Gaiser discusses the biblical understanding of human nature and the way in which the human response to God's initiative in Christ leads to salvation.

How can this biblical evidence be organized into comprehensive systems of thought about God and creation? This is the task of systematic theology and the following three chapters consider these issues. Approaching the issue from a Roman Catholic viewpoint, Deal Hudson notes that conversion is centered in the turning of the individual heart to God. St. Augustine's report of his conversion in his *Confessions* has become the paradigm for this tradition. Hudson shows, however, that later scholastic preoccupation with metaphysical analysis came into tension with the Augustinian model. The unifying theme for contemporary Catholicism has become the mystical body of Christ operating through the church.

Donald McKim considers these same issues from the viewpoint of mainline Protestantism. While his analysis does not include attention to all the historical variations within this tradition, he does provide an overview of the ways in which conversion concerns have played both a major and a minor role in the development of current Protestant theology. Initially, McKim considers the Reformed focus upon conversion as part of the broader plan of God in the calling of the elect to receive salvation. Next, he notes the nuances of conversion themes in Lutheran, Calvinistic, and Armenian dogmatics. Each of these involves a slightly different model for redemption.

A unifying ecumenical approach can be seen in David H.C. Read's conversion sermon which concluded Part II. Read speaks from a lifetime of parish ministry about the conviction of sin that prepares a person for conversion. His is a call to evangelism which leads to conversion. Read provides a meliorist position in which the sharpness of theological differences and the precision of dogmatic formulations are mellowed and, to some extent, unified. This sermon is an example of how conversion themes might be communicated to congregants. It represents the application of conversion emphases to the life of the local church.

Part III is entitled *Conversion in the Social/Behavioral Sciences*. As Luke 10:27-28 implies, conversion includes love of God and neighbor with one's mind as well as one's heart and soul. Warren Brown and Carla Caetano examine the psychophysiology of mental life. They consider conversion as it relates to epilepsy and mystical experience. Various models of cognition are discussed in relation to the changes in identity that result from conversion. This discussion includes a description of how memory fits into self-understanding.

Closely related to Brown's and Caetano's chapter is Lewis Rambo's discussion of the psychology of conversion. He distinguishes four approaches to the study of conversion: the psychoanalytic, the humanistic or transpersonal, the social, and the holistic. Although he favors the transpersonal approach, Rambo includes contributions from all the approaches in proposing a heuristic stage model for conversion. Perception, emotion, and behavior are all considered in addition to cognition.

At times, psychological studies of conversion have been so introspective and individualistic that love of God seems to completely overwhelm love of neighbor. An opposite omission is sometimes found in sociological studies of conversion, for, as William Bainbridge notes in his chapter, the social sciences have no tool with which to study the supernatural. He details the advantages and limitations of emerging sociological theories that are used to explain conversion. The "strain" theory emphasizes a need for deprived people to satisfy their social anxiety through conversion. The "social influence" theory concentrates on the attraction of attachments that persons have with others in religious groups.

In the chapter on "The Cultural Anthropology of Conversion," Alan Tippett considers conversion from the viewpoint of acculturation. Using the example of New Guinea, he demonstrates how cross-cultural conversion experiences are related to people movements. He proposes a model of four periods of time (awareness, decision, incorporation, and maturity) which are punctuated by critical points in time (realization, encounter, and commitment) to explain the conversion process. This model applies to all types of radical cultural change.

The last section of the handbook, Part IV, is entitled *Conversion in Church and Culture*. Beatrice Batson reviews imaginative literary themes in fiction, poetry, and autobiography that have influenced American and English concepts of conversion from the time of Dante to the present. She gives vivid examples of how authors have probed the experience through their writings.

Both fiction and autobiographical writing are replete with reports of how conversion has changed self-understandings and perception. In "The Phenomenology of Conversion," Lewis Rambo utilizes a case-study example to illustrate the phenomenological approach to an intuitive and perspective understanding of conversion as it extends over a significant period of a person's life.

Writing from the viewpoint of a missionary anthropologist, Charles Kraft approaches conversion from the viewpoint of worldview. He makes practical the themes introduced by Tippett and shows how attention to group processes are crucial for effective conversion both within and across cultures. Allegiance to family and to clan must accompany personal decisions for conversion to be incorporated into identity and daily life.

Unfortunately, this emphasis on group identity, while not entirely lost in Western culture, is often ignored. When group influences are not recognized social manipulation often occurs. Eddie Gibbs avoids this danger in his chapter on "Conversion in Evangelistic Practice." He offers safeguards against manipulative programs through an insistence that pragmatism is not enough. Theology and culture are primary considerations. Subsequently, practical issues can be addressed through a study of the context in which conversion takes place. Evangelism should include procedures that deepen and stablilize the conversion experience.

In conclusion, some have suggested that conversion as known in the past is now the exception, rather than the rule, in religious life. Our conviction is that while the form may change, the substance does not. No doubt, there is a constant need for religion to adapt itself to change. However, there is a parallel imperative for religion to continue to call persons to alter their lives in light of transcendent truth. Conversion, whether quick or gradual, group or individual, is here to stay. Our hope is that a handbook such as this will serve the church in its ever-present desire to be faithful to its call to evangelize the world.

Not all the names of those who bring such a handbook as this to fruition appear in the contents page or on the book cover. Such is the truth in this case. Without Lynelle Bush, our efficient and faithful secretary, we would still be bogged down in endless and fruitless minutae. She kept us on schedule. She monitored the chapters. She typed the final manuscript. We owe her a deep debt.

Part 1

Conversion in Comparative Religions

Some may wonder how comparisons of great religious belief systems could include a study of conversion, for both Hinduism and Buddhism teach respect for all faiths. "Conversion" sounds like an emphasis which is unique in Christianity and Islam, both of which emphasize absolute truth and avoid syncretism.

Yet, as Hiebert shows in the first chapter of this symposium, both Hinduism and Buddhism spread through missionary effort and developed reform movements that can be compared to Christian emphases upon enlightenment and escape from this world. There also are similarities of method, with proselytizing either by preaching, teaching, or political coercion.

This does not imply some basic unity of understanding when the term "conversion" is used for comparative study. For, as Woodberry shows in the following chapter on Islam, there is no formal rite of conversion and no references to conversion in the earliest passages of the Quran. But there are terms and procedures in Islam that are similar to the goals of changed intention and behavior in Christian converts. Also, the interaction of Islam with other religious structures produced some mass conversions that had less to do with military force and more to do with social status. Parallels can be found in the history of Christian expansion.

Comparisons of thought and method not only show diversity among the great religions; there are also variations within one religion. Gaventa demonstrates in chapter three the challenge to respect and learn from the varying images, emphases, and contexts of biblical passages that are usually associated with conversion. Yet in all these there is one dominant motif—transformation.

In chapter four, Glasser notes the error in presuming that all of the masses of persons who followed Moses out of Egypt were consciously identified as a chosen people in covenant with Jehovah. The appeal to convert has been a feature from the time of the Exodus all the way through to the post-

7

exilic period, as can dramatically be seen in the call of the eighth-century prophets. These themes are traced through the Enlightenment to the present. Glasser notes the reluctance of modern Judaism to encourage conversion because of the history of persecution which Judaism experienced. Many Jews feel that Christians have inappropriately tried to convert them. Many leaders of mainline denominations argue that evangelism of the Jews is in bad taste, holding that all Jews, by virtue of their covenantal linkage with God, should be regarded as already saved. Glasser discusses the biblical reasons currently being advanced by Jewish believers in Jesus to support the thesis that the Christian call for conversion applies as much to Jews as to gentiles.

In the following chapter, Richardson discusses the recruitment processes which have been utilized by new religions, largely within Western culture. He details the ways in which the Unification Church, the Hare Krishna movement, and a Jesus movement have changed their appeals and used persuasive techniques in efforts to recruit members. The adjustments these groups have made to more church-like techniques and organizational formats is of particular interest as an illustration of how nontraditional religious movements have sought to covert others to their points of view.

Chapter One

Conversion in Hinduism and Buddhism

Paul G. Hiebert

The word "conversion" is primarily a Jewish, Christian, and Muslim term symbolizing a radical change in personal religious beliefs and behavior. In its broader sense, however, it refers to both personal and communal changes, and to changes both in beliefs and behavior, and in community affiliation. It is in this latter sense that we will use the term here.

With a few notable exceptions, such as Hindu mendicancy, conversion in Hinduism and Buddhism is communal in both senses of the term. It often involves group conversion, and it means joining a religious community by birth or by choice. Moreover, in line with Eastern thought, conversion in these religions is more often a process of change than a moment of radical conversion.

We will examine conversion in Hinduism and Buddhism on two levels. The first has to do with changes in beliefs and practices. Here we will look at beliefs and practices involved in conversion. The second has to do with assimilation into a religious community. Here we will discuss Hindu and Buddhist rites of initiation used to incorporate outsiders into various levels of participation and rites of reincorporation used to restore those who have left the faith.

Well before the birth of Christianity and Islam, Hinduism and Buddhism spread their gospels throughout Asia and the Pacific islands. Hinduism absorbed local peoples as it moved south across India. Buddhism sent out missionaries and spread across South, Southeast and East Asia. Both split into many different branches, each with its own doctrinal beliefs, organizational patterns, and views of conversion.

Today Hinduism makes up 13.3 percent of the world's population, and Buddhism 6.3 percent.[1] Their heartlands are still found in South, Southeast, Central and East Asia, and Sri Lanka. In recent years, however, their followers have spread their beliefs to the other parts of the world.

CONVERSION IN HINDUISM

In a sense, Hinduism may be regarded as the first example in the world of a missionary religion. Only its missionary spirit is different from that associated with the proselytizing creeds. It did not regard it as its mission to convert humans to any one opinion. For what counts is conduct and not belief.[2]

Hinduism is not a fixed set of beliefs—a doctrinal creed. In it are found dogmas ranging from materialistic atheism, pantheism, and polytheism, to monotheism and abstract monism. In such a diverse religion what does "conversion" mean?

CONVERSION AS CHANGES IN BELIEFS AND PRACTICES

On one level, conversion involves fundamental changes in the beliefs and behavior of a person or group of persons. This is true in Hindu views of conversion.

Conversion as a Change in Worldviews

At the deepest level of beliefs, to convert to Hinduism is not to adopt one specific set of doctrines. Rather, it is to accept a particular meta-theological view of doctrines themselves—in other worlds, a Hindu worldview. It is not our purpose here to examine that worldview in detail, only to note two assumptions that are essential to what Hindus mean by "conversion."

Personal Spiritual Pilgrimage

In the first place, religion in Hinduism is defined as a personal spiritual pilgrimage, and its goal (*moksha*) is the realization of the purpose of each individual. This does not mean Hinduism ignores the good of society or of human well-being on earth. It claims, however, that these are transitory and that the final realization of perfection must transcend history and this life.

Conversion, therefore, must be defined not as a radical change in beliefs but as an evolutionary progression of beliefs that lead a person to self-realization. Underlying this view is the fact that the Indian worldview sees reality not in terms of sharply defined categories, as modern Western thought

---

1. David Barrett, ed., *World Christian Encyclopedia* (Nairobi: Oxford University Press, 1982), 6.

2. S. Radhakrishnan, *The Hindu View of Life* (New York: Macmillan, 1964), 28.

does, but in terms of "fuzzy sets," or continua between poles.[3]

Conversion must also be defined, not as deliverance from sin, but as progressive enlightenment in which the ignorance and desire that keep us trapped in our human dilemma are expelled. Since the center of religion is the self and the root problem is ignorance, we cannot speak of "sin" in the Western Christian sense. Error of judgment is not a moral offense, and weakness of understanding is not depravity of heart.

Salvation (*moksha*) consists of learning to know the true nature of reality. This comes, not as intellectual knowledge, but as a deep inner conversion— a radical "ah ha" feeling that comes as an inner light that suddenly makes sense of what we "see," but have not really seen until now.

Conversion, then, is to begin one's pilgrimage toward the light. It is to begin to seek God, truth, light, and good, however one understands these concepts.

Many Roads to Salvation

Tied to this view of religion as self-realization is a second Hindu assumption, namely, that there are many roads to *moksha* or enlightenment, and ultimately all of them lead to the same place. In one sense, the pilgrimage of each individual is wholly personal, in another they all are the same.

Commonly, Hindus speak of three types of roads. The first is *karma margas,* or paths of duty. Everyone can at least make offerings to the gods of one's caste, observe times of impurity, and make pilgrimages to holy shrines. These are the first steps toward a spiritual transformation. Conversion here is to begin performing the rituals prescribed by Hinduism for one's status in society and one's stage in life.

The second is *bhakti margas,* or paths of devotion. This offers immediate, unconditional salvation to those who throw themselves on the mercy of God. Since all gods are manifestations of one God, it does not matter which god one chooses. A person must worship the god of his or her caste. He or she also has the right to choose a personal god (*ishta devata*).

Conversion in the path of *bhakti* is similar to that in Christianity. A person must choose a god or goddess and surrender totally to this deity. The god then saves all those who call on him or her. Because this choice is totally personal, the god may be Hindu, Muslim, Christian, or any other deity. Conversion here may be a radical transformation that involves leaving one god to worship another. Even here, however, the either/or-ness is blunted, for ultimately these different gods are, in fact, one.

The first steps of conversion are to sing the praise of the deity, to remember and salute him or her, and to worship him or her as master and friend. The final step is to dedicate one's self totally to the deity.

There are many schools of *bhakti,* each claiming to be the highest road to heaven. Many seek publicly to convert people to the worship of their own par-

---

3. Paul G. Hiebert, "The Category 'Christian' in the Mission Task,"*International Review of Missions* 72 (July 1983):421-27.

ticular god through preaching, distribution of literature, and public festivals. An estimated 90 percent of all Hindus are *bhaktis*. Most are worshipers
of one or another manifestation of Vishnu or Siva.

The third path to enlightenment is *jnana marga,* or way of wisdom. The
road is metaphysical, not theological. Conversion is to enter a life of strict
physical and mental discipline (*yoga*). The goal is not heaven, but enlightenment. This is not merely the knowledge that all is one and all is God. It is
the direct inner experience of that oneness with the universe and God. This
is the ultimate conversion that raises one above the plane of this world and
its sensory perceptions to a higher level of consciousness.

Because all roads lead toward *moksha,* however this is defined, we cannot say that this road is right and that one wrong. We can only claim that
this road is better for us than the others. Individuals must choose the road
that is best for them. They may seek guides who know one path or another. In the end, however, each must find his or her own way to self-realization.

We must not mistake this tolerance for indifference. Hinduism affirms
that all religions refer to reality, but denies that all are equally true to it. It
requires each person to think deeply about life's mystery until he or she
reach the final enlightenment. Lesser forms of religion are tolerated in the
recognition that humans cannot all suddenly transcend their human and cultural limitations. Those who see cannot force those who are born blind to see.
Each must come to see by him or herself. We cannot force the pace of the
development of others. We can only stand by to give help when they ask
us.

While recognizing the tortured progressions of our spiritual pilgrimages,
Hinduism does affirm one goal. We are to seek purer forms of worship and
higher revelations until we come to full enlightenment. Then we realize that
we indeed are gods and God. We are all part of the oneness that is reality.

Given this worldview, Western definitions of "conversion" are rejected.
Radhakrishnan notes,

> Hinduism is wholly free from the strange obsession of some faiths that the
> acceptance of a particular religious metaphysic is necessary for salva-
> tion, and nonacceptance thereof is a heinous sin meriting eternal punish-
> ment in hell. Here and there outbursts of sectarian fanaticism are found [in
> Hinduism] . . . but the main note of Hinduism is one of respect and good
> will for other creeds.[4]

Swami Vivekananda, in his final speech at the World Religious Parliament
held in Chicago in 1893, said:

> The Christian is not to become a Hindu or a Buddhist, nor is a Hindu or
> Buddhist to become a Christian. But each must assimilate the spirit of

---

4. Radhakrishnan, *Hindu View of Life,* 28.

the others and yet preserve his individuality and grow according to his own law of growth.[5]

To seek to convert others to a particular faith, even to one of Hinduism's many creedal communities, is seen to deny that each community and person has their own *dharma*, or law of growth. To claim one's own way as the only right way is seen as spiritual arrogance of the highest order.

Conversion as a Way of Life

Given the Hindu worldview that all roads lead to *moksha*, conversion for the individual means entering a course of action—a way of life. Radhakrishnan writes,

> What counts is not creed but conduct. By their fruits ye shall know them and not by their beliefs. . . . Jesus was born a Jew and died a Jew. He did not tell the Jewish people among whom he found himself, "It is wicked to be Jews. Become Christians." He did his best to rid the Jewish religion of its impurities. He would have done the same with Hinduism had he been born a Hindu. The true reformer purifies and enlarges the heritage of mankind and does not belittle, still less deny it.[6]

In contemporary Hindu thought, Gandhi used the term conversion. He was well aware of its religious overtones in Christianity and Islam, but he redefined the word in Hindu terms. In the first place, in line with orthodox Hinduism he defined conversion as a change in behavior. Margaret Chatterjee writes,

> Gandhi was all for a change of heart, in fact the whole technique of *satyagraha* was based on this, and he believed the humblest peasant to be perhaps more capable of it than the intellectual or any other member of what he called "the classes." For Gandhi, a change of heart is seen in changed relationships, for example between employer and employed, between Hindu and Muslim, between caste Hindus and the so-called untouchables. But this was a very different matter from changing one's label, turning one's back on the traditions of one's forefathers and giving intellectual assent to a set of alien concepts which could find no answering chord in the hearts of those whose traditional symbols were of a very different kind.[7]

Gandhi also spoke of converting the other person. Here, however, he used Hindu concepts but filled them with Christian content. For Gandhi,

---

5. Swami Vivekananda, *The Complete Works of Swami Vivekananda*, vol 1 (15th edition; Calcutta: Advita Ashram, 1977), 24.

6. Radhakrishnan, *Hindu View of Life*, 37.

7. Margaret Chatterjee, *Gandhi's Religious Thought* (Notre Dame, Ind.: University of Notre Dame Press, 1983), 49.

the highest road to truth is *satyagraha,* the unswerving search for truth. Orthodox Hinduism exhorts the highest seekers to drop out of society and become *sannyasins.* Gandhi, however, in line with the New Testament which he knew well, called for them to become *satyagrahis,* or those who seek to transform the world around them by staying in it. Because respect for all life is part of *satyagraha,* the *satyagrahis,* or pilgrims on this road, must be nonviolent. If they have to choose between bearing suffering or inflicting it on others, they must do the former. In this nonviolent, positive proclaiming of truth by word and deed, they seek to convert their foes. Chatterjee writes,

> [For Gandhi, the] opponent is to be converted, to undergo a change of heart, when he sees that the *satyagrahis* are willing to stake their all for what they believe to be true.[8]

The basis for this conversion is not a transformation brought about by active proselytization. It is a transformation in behavior stimulated by the encounter with nonviolent action.

> Gandhi believed that, since persons share a common humanity, sooner or later the "opponent" will be won over. This apparent "conquest" by the *satyagrahis* was, however, not a defeat for the other side, but a conquest for them too, in that they had been able to rise above the factors that previously stood in the way of understanding.[9]

CONVERSION AS JOINING A RELIGIOUS COMMUNITY

To convert is to adopt a set of beliefs and practices. In another sense it is to join a religious community. In this sense, to become a Hindu means to enter the Hindu social order. It is to take one's place in the caste system which is the embodiment of Hinduism.

Becoming a Member of a Caste

For the most part, membership in a caste is conferred by birth. To be a true Hindu, one must be born into a Hindu caste. Concomitantly, a person born a Hindu is always, at least potentially, a Hindu. Those who fall away by living in other countries and engaging in behavior not suitable to their caste can be restored to orthodoxy by the rite of *shudhi.* Devala's *smrti,* for example, lays down the rules for the purification of people forcibly converted to other faiths, or of womenfolk defiled and confined for years, and even of people who, for worldly advantage, embrace other faiths.[10]

There is another way to enter the caste system. A tribe or community may enter the caste system through assimilation over a period of time.

8. Ibid., 80.
9. Ibid.
10. Radhakrishnan, *Hindu View of Life,* 29.

Herbert Risley, having observed the process since 1873, wrote in the 1901 Census, "All over India at the present moment tribes are gradually and insensibly being transformed into castes." D. N. Majumdar[11] and Surajit Sinha[12] trace the steps by which outside peoples such as tribals, immigrants, and conquerors gain acceptance and a position in the caste hierarchy. First, they cast off demeaning customs such as sacrificing cows and eating meat and adopt prestigious ones. They then invite Brahmin priests to perform their rituals by offering them generous gifts and grants of land. The Brahmins then "discover" in their scriptures that these people are actually descended from some important Hindu community and provide them with written records of their genealogy. The converts now separate themselves from those in their community who do not want to become Hindus and refuse to intermarry with them. The converts also build temples and celebrate Hindu festivals, adopt Hindu rites for birth, initiation, marriage, and death, and may take up a distinct occupation. In time they are accepted in the Hindu caste system and granted a rank based on their origins and their lifestyles. Once in the caste system, they may strive to raise their status by adopting the practices of the Brahmin elite, such as refusing to remarry their widows and donning the sacred thread of the twice-born.

Betteille[13] points out a third way Hinduism converted local peoples, particularly in South India. Brahmins moved down from the north and persuaded local communities to adopt their rituals and accept them as priests. In this way Hinduism was used to provide theological and ritual foundations for existing social communities.

Conversion by Proselytizing

Despite its emphasis on religious pluralism and tolerance, Hinduism has, throughout history, been actively missionary in its attempt to convert others to its religious beliefs. This was true in the third to fifth centuries when Indian rajas established Hindu kingdoms in Java and Indonesia. It was true in the tenth to twelfth centuries when Hinduism overcame Buddhism in South India through itinerant evangelists who went from kingdom to kingdom preaching the virtues of Hinduism.

During the past two centuries, orthodox Hinduism has been challenged by the conquests and missionary outreach of Islam and Christianity and by the spread of modernity. The result has been a revival of Hindu fundamentalist movements such as the Arya Samaj, R. S. S., and Jan Sang, and reform movements such as Ramakrishna Mission. These are now actively seeking to convert Indian Christians back to Hinduism and to restore them to religious purity through the rite of *shuddhi*. In the West evangelistic movements such

11. D. N. Majumdar, *A Tribe in Transition* (London: Longmans, 1937); *The Fortunes of Primitive Tribes* (Lucknow, India: Universal Publishers, 1944).

12. S. Sinha, "Tribal Cultures of Peninsular India as a Dimension of Little Tradition in the Study of Indian Civilization," *Journal of American Folklore* 71 (1958): 504-18.

13. Andre Betteille, *Caste, Class and Power: Changing Patterns of Stratification in a Tanjore Village* (Berkeley and Los Angeles: University of California Press, 1965).

as the Hare Krishna and gurus such as Maharishi Mahesh Yogi, Prabhupada, and Beyond Ananda are winning followers from the young and disenchanted.[14]

CONVERSION IN BUDDHISM

Buddhism was born in a reaction to the religious tyranny of the Brahmins. Siddhartha, a prince of the warrior caste, rejected the ritualism and extreme asceticism of Hinduism in favor of a moral, well-ordered life.

Buddhism from the first was a missionary religion. After his First Sermon, the Buddha sent his converts into the world with the famous exhortation, "Go forth, O Bhikkus, for the gain of the many, for the welfare of the many, in compassion for the world. Proclaim the Doctrine glorious, preach a life of holiness, perfect and pure." The method of his followers was preaching and discussion.

Buddha's teachings were welcome news to rulers, merchants, and other upper-class people oppressed by the demands of the Hindu priests. Many converted. Buddhist monks traveled constantly, carrying on vigorous propaganda among the common folk to win their support and debating with Brahmins and Jains.

It was the kings and merchants who were largely responsible for the spread of Buddhism throughout India and Southeast Asia. Asoka sent missionaries to Burma, Sri Lanka, and west and central Asia. Later missionaries spread the message to China and Japan.

CONVERSION AND THE DHARMA

Shortly after the death of the Buddha, various schools of thought emerged. By the second century A. D., a split developed between what came to be known as the "Lesser Vehicle" (*Hinayana* or *Theravada*) and the "Greater Vehicle" (*Mahayana*) forms of Buddhism. The fundamental differences between these has to do with differences in *dharma* or beliefs about the path to salvation and the nature of conversion.

Conversion in Theravada Buddhism

The basic beliefs of *Theravada* are that suffering and sorrow are inherent in life; that they can only be eliminated by giving up "desire," "ambition," or "craving" (*tanha*) which are based on the illusion that we are enduring, individual beings; and that we can achieve this by following the Middle Way of right understanding, resolve, speech, conduct, livelihood, effort, recollection, and meditation. Salvation is not "from above," but "from below," and "from within."

In *Theravada*, the path to salvation is personal. A person can help another by example and advice, but no one can save another. Conversion, there-

---

14. Russel Chandler, *Understanding the New Age* (Dallas: Word Publishing, 1988).

fore, is a process of self-discipline in a monastic community. By gradually bringing the senses under control, one can finally annihilate all passions, all longings, all self-centeredness, and live a totally dispassionate life. When this is achieved, one experiences *nirvana*, the steady state of undifferentiated reality. In it there is no flux, no dualism, no self-consciousness. The person who finds it never again loses it, and when he (for this is reserved mainly for men) dies, he enters this eternal state in his "Final Blowing Out." The person who does not find it must be reborn on earth in another life to try again. Few attain release. Fortunately in our era we have had four Buddhas (the last being Sakyamuni) to show us the way, and the fifth is still to come.

Conversion in Mahayana Buddhism

Theravada Buddhism's renunciation of the world and its call for radical discipline limited its appeal to the few, particularly the elite. For the masses caught in the struggles of life, this form of Buddhism was too austere. The Buddhism of self-effort (*jiriki*)—of working out one's own salvation with self-discipline—was beyond the powers of the ordinary people. They were used to worshiping the many gods of India. Consequently, when sculptors began to carve images of the Buddha, the common people took to worshiping these images and the relics of the Buddha with flowers, incense, waving lamps, and deep devotion, just as they do in Hindu temples.

This tension between the atheism of *Theravada* and the theism of popular Buddhism led to a split, and to the emergence of the Greater Vehicle (*Mahayana*). *Theravada* denied that the Buddha was a god. *Mahayana* deified him and added a great many lesser gods. The former denied that the merit of one person can be transferred to another. It held that all persons are lamps unto themselves and must work out their own salvations. The latter taught that a person may give and receive merit from others.

In time this belief in the Buddha as a god led to the belief that people can receive merit from the Buddha and the many *bodhisattvas* (lesser Buddhas who choose to remain on earth to save others rather than to enter *nirvana*). By the third century A.D. the idea of Buddha as the Suffering Savior emerged. It is *Mahayana* that won the Chinese with their belief in spirits and gods, and, through them, the Koreans and Japanese.

Conversion in the Great Vehicle is not to the words but to the person of the Buddha. He is the Ultimate, the One Supreme Reality. To worship him is to win his merit and thereby to attain salvation. Those, who through profound worship and meditation are enlightened and become buddhas, are in turn called to remain on earth so that they can save others by dispensing their merit. In other words, there are stages of conversion leading to buddhahood.

The Pure Land School (Japanese: *Jodo*) of Buddhism emerged in China in the fourth century A.D. The Savior in this school is Amida, a king who joined Buddhism and vowed to establish a Buddha-kingdom—the Pure Land—on earth. Unlike *nirvana,* this is a paradise of material delights. It is open to all who pray the formula, "Namu Amida Butsu" (Adoration to the Buddha Amida), who strive to be worthy of his salvation, and who offer their merit for the salvation of others.

In the twelfth century A.D. Pure Land reached Japan. There works were dropped and only faith in Amida was needed to enter paradise. Amida had earned an inexhaustible store of merit and offered it freely to all who sought his aid. Sinners only need to believe in that store and their own access to it and the Pure Land is theirs. Theravadins said that *nirvana* can only be achieved after many lives of discipline. Teachers of Pure Land taught that anyone could be certain of paradise after death.

One school of thought hard to classify is Zen. While it fits loosely into the Greater Vehicle division, it is the apotheosis of Buddhism. It seeks enlightenment by a direct route, without the use of gods, scripture, rituals, or vows. It is less a religious philosophy and more a method to break the tyranny of reason that keeps us locked into the illusion of reality and the cycle of rebirth. It is to help a person leap from thinking to direct inner experience of the oneness of all things.

Zen uses different bridges to reach *satori*, the Zen name for Enlightenment. One is *mondo,* a rapid question-answer repartee between Master and pupil that aims to speed up the thought processes so that it suddenly transcends human rationality. A second is *koan*, a word or phrase that confuses the intellect and so frees a person from its control.[15]

Conversion in Zen is to set out on the path to *satori*. A person can do this through meditation, art, poetry, and making love. The end of the pilgrimage is to reach the state wherein the pendulum of opposites comes to rest—where light and darkness, good and evil, being and nonbeing are equally valued and become one. To think of *satori* requires the mind, but because it lies beyond the intellect, it cannot be defined. It must be experienced existentially.

Conversion in Tibetan Buddhism

The third major division in Buddhism is referred to as the Vehicle of the Thunderbolt, or as Tantric Buddhism. Early in the history of *Mahayana* female deities entered the pantheon, chiefly as wives of the powerful male gods. The latter were high and aloof. The former were the "force" or "potency" of their husbands and active in the world. Consequently, humans could best approach the gods through the goddesses, and sexual union became the paradigm for religious experience.

In Tibet magical mysticism was added to these ideas. The goal was supernatural power. The means were meditation, hypnosis, ritual sexual unions, and the breaking of all rules such as the taboos on eating of meat, drinking of alcohol, and killing of animals. The deities were the Savioresses (*taras*—often depicted in ferocious poses) and a host of lesser divinities, demonesses, sorceresses, and she-ghouls. Because these cannot be persuaded, they have to

---

15. Christmas Humphreys, *Buddhism: An Introduction and Guide* (London: Penguin Books, 1951), 153.

be compelled through the uses of right formulas (*mantras*) cited in the correct manner, and powerful diagrams (*yentras*) that give magical power to the worshiper and lead him or her to the highest ecstasy. The six-syllable *mantra—Om mani padme hum* ("Ah! The jewel is indeed in the lotus!") is written and repeated thousands of times daily in Tibet.

Conversion in Tibetan Buddhism is both a broad road and a narrow path. The deeper teachings are beyond the capacity of the ordinary people. For them conversion is to venerate the monks and nuns, to worship the many gods, goddesses, spirits, ferocious demons, personified natural forces, and saints. It is to use powerful magical chants, diagrams, and hand positions to control supernatural beings for personal ends. As one lama noted,

> The mind of man . . . is prone to superstition. If left to themselves, ignorant people will invent their own superstitions, and it is better that they find their superstitions prepared for them with a definite object in view. . . . If superstition helps the common people to a better life, why remove it?[16]

For the select few, however, the path to becoming a *bodhisattva,* or small Buddha, is to join a monastery as a lama and to study esoteric techniques under the guidance of a guru.

CONVERSION AND THE SANGHA

Central to conversion in Buddhism is the *sangha,* the communities of monks and nuns who have committed themselves to religious meditation and austerities. It is they who have both preserved and spread the message of the Buddha.

The Sangha

The highest level of conversion in Buddhism is entry into the *sangha.* No other institution of Buddhism has had more far-reaching effect than these monasteries with their inhabitants who took vows of celibacy and separated themselves from their families and societies to give themselves to gaining enlightenment and merit.

The monastic order was founded by Sakyamuni who gathered his disciples around him. In time the followers of the Buddha grew into a vast community, and rules were drawn up to govern this community. These rules, codified as the *Vinaya*, became one of the major divisions of the early Buddhist canon.

Conversion to the *sangha* is often referred to as "leaving home." In many cases, young men and women enter monastic life in order to escape the wheel of rebirth and never-ending suffering. In order to cool the flames of desire into the ashes of nonattachment, they obviously must leave the world

---

16. J.E. Ellam, *The Religion of Tibet: A Study of Lamaism* (London: J. Murray, 1927), 71.

of home and society where attachment is the central motivating force of life. In other cases, particularly in Southeast Asia, parents send their sons to the monasteries for periods as short as a week or two in order to earn merit for the family.

Those who "leave home" do not adopt the withdrawal from the world characteristic of Hindu *saddhus*. Rather, they enter a community of practitioners of meditation and self-control. Because those in the community give up their family names, shave their heads, and deliberately remove themselves from ancestral lineages by not having children, there is a widespread tension between the *sanghas,* and the family and society. Various attempts have been made in Buddhism to resolve this tension, such as short-term monastic stints in Southeast Asia, and the marriage of monks in Japan.[17] In most cases, however, final ordination into monastic life requires a renunciation of the family and society in favor of the *sangha*.

The Laity

The number of persons who "leave home" and become monks and nuns is always small. For most people, conversion to Buddhism is a matter of practicing devotions privately in the home or in the company of other like-minded householders. These practices are often mixed with other beliefs and practices such as ancestor veneration, Taoism, and *tantrism*.

Some, particularly the old who have fewer social responsibilities and greater concern regarding death, retire from normal life and spend their time in devotions, praying, chanting sacred texts, and burning incense before their icons. Others, with more worldly responsibilities, seek to accumulate merit by giving food to monks and nuns, by supporting the monasteries, and by sending their children to join the *sangha* for brief periods or for life.

Many lay persons practice vegetarianism in the belief that all life is sacred and that the killing of animals causes "bad *karma*." Many also regularly perform some variety of meditation to gain spiritual merit, or to promote personal health and longevity.

Finally, to be Buddhist on the lay level is to participate in the Buddhist festivals of the region. These are often mixtures of the beliefs and practices of orthodox Buddhism and local folk religions. For example, in much of China, during the seventh month, the people prepare feasts and make generous offerings to bereaved spirits, or "hungry ghosts." The officiants are monks who tell the story of Mulein who rescued his mother from the torture of the hell in which souls cannot eat. This he did by the grace of the Buddha, who instructed him to make offerings on the fifteenth day of the seventh month to seven generations of ancestors. The ritual is called "ferrying across" because by it the souls of those in limbo or purgatory are ferried across to the other shore of salvation.

---

17. Lewis R. Lancaster, "Buddhism and Family in East Asia," in *Religion and the Family in East Asia,* ed. George A. DeVos and Takai Sofue (Berkeley: University of California Press, 1984), 139-51.

CONCLUSION

Hinduism and Buddhism have religious goals, namely release from the karmic cycles of rebirth. Their paths are different. Hinduism affirms the social order. To be a Hindu is to belong to the Hindu society with its beliefs in purity and its castes that deal with pollution.[18] As a member of society, salvation can be attained by worshiping God or by performing the rituals prescribed by the Brahmins. Those who reject Hindu society can seek salvation as mendicants alone in the forest.

Buddhism offers a middle way. While rejecting society as a means of salvation, it recognizes that most humans are caught up in the struggles of their daily lives. True seekers, however, are invited to join a counter-cultural community, the monastic order. There they encourage one another in meditation and serve society through teaching and conducting rituals. They also give merit they earn to common folk and enable common folk to earn merit by ministering to the monks and nuns.

In both religions, conversion is a process, a series of steps involving changes in belief and practice. In both it is also a social matter, an entry into (or rejection of) a religious social order.

18. Louis Dumont, *Homo Hierarchicus: The Caste System and Its Implications* (Chicago: University of Chicago Press, 1970).

Chapter Two

Conversion in Islam

J. Dudley Woodberry

Traditional Islamic thought has not had a general word for the concept of conversion. What non-Muslims would call "conversion to the Muslim faith" Muslims describe by such words as *islam* (surrender [to God]), *iman* (faith [in God]), and *ihtida'* (following [right] guidance). Conversely, what non-Muslims would call "conversion from the Muslim faith" Muslims call *irtidad* (apostasy).

After describing what is considered to be the formal act of conversion to Islam—confessing the uniqueness of God and the apostleship of Muhammad—we shall look at Muslim understandings of what this activity should involve in individuals and groups. Then we shall consider the actual Islamizing processes by which over one-fifth of the population of the world has been brought into the Muslim community.

The Formal Act of Conversion

There is no rite of conversion like baptism in Islam, although circumcision is often performed and in Java has even been called *"rendering* Muslim" (*njelamakeselam*).[1] What, however, has become the indispensable act of conversion is the confession of faith, "There is no god but God, and

---

1. Pierre Jean de Menasce, "Problemes des Mazdeens dans l'Iran musulman," *Festschrift für Wilhelm Eilers* (Wiesbaden: Otto Harrassowitz, 1967), 225; Richard W. Bulliet, *Conversion to Islam in the Medieval Period* (Cambridge: Harvard University Press, 1979), 144n.1; C. Snouck Hurgronje, *Verspreide Geschriften* 4, pt. 1 (Bonn and Leipzig: Kurt Schroeder, 1924): 205-206; A. J. Wensinck, "Khitan," *Encyclopaedia of Islam* (new ed.), 5:20B.

22

Muhammad is the Apostle of God," called the *shahada* (witness) or *kalima* (word). Traditionally it is pronounced in Arabic in the presence of two witnesses and is preceded by the greater ablution (*ghusl*) in which the entire body is washed. Jewish converts should also confess that Jesus is an apostle of God. The convert is then expected to practice the Five Pillars of Islam— the confession of faith, the ritual prayer, the prescribed alms, fasting during the month of Ramadan, and the pilgrimage to Mecca.

Individual and Family Conversion

The means by which an individual or family can convert to Islam are outlined in a bill passed by the Selangor State Assembly in Malaysia on July 19, 1989. Part VII of the bill on "Conversion to Islam" states that "a person who is not a Muslim may convert to Islam if he has attained the age of majority . . . and is of sound mind" (sect. 67). For it to be a valid conversion persons must utter "in reasonably intelligible Arabic the two clauses of the Affirmation of Faith." At that time they must be aware that they mean "I bear witness" of both clauses, and they must do it of their own free will. One incapable of speech may indicate the meaning by signs (sect. 68). Any natural child of the new convert who has not attained the age of majority automatically becomes converted to Islam at the same time. The age of majority in the form of Shari'a Law practiced in Malaysia is approximately fifteen years for a boy and puberty for a girl.[2]

Group Conversion

An example of a group conversion among Tamils from the "untouchable" caste took place in the village of Kanday, South India, in 1981. Muslims from neighboring areas came for the occasion and embraced those who were to make a profession of their new faith. The ceremony began with a three-point sermon. The first point was theological: They must turn from other gods and idols and worship only God. The second was social: They must forget their old caste; they were Muslims. The last was economic: They should not expect financial miracles or that they would receive Arab oil money.

After the sermon each new convert recited the confession of faith to an existing Muslim. To show their new status they were given Muslim names, and each man was given a Muslim cap (*kulah*). This was followed by the normal noon ritual prayer and then a communal meal where they offered food to their neighbors from their plates using their hands, symbolizing the breaking of caste taboos. Then the women came from their separate ceremony and meal with their saris over their heads. Training by the mullah did not begin until after the conversion event.[3]

---

2. BERITA NECF (Petaling Jaya, Malaysia: National Evangelical Fellowship), 2, no. 3 (August/September 1989):2.

3. Andrew Wingate, "A Study of Conversions from Christianity [*sic*] to Islam in Two Tamil Villages," *Religion and Society* 27, no. 4 (December 1981): 9-11.

Muslim Understandings of Conversion

The earliest passages in the Quran do not appear to be calling the Meccans to convert to a new religion. As the need for a new religious allegiance arose, no single word for conversion was used. Rather a number of words and concepts were used to describe this new allegiance. We shall first look in the Quran at the progression of actions that indicated a new allegiance and then at the various words in the Quran that describe conversion and their interpretation by Muslim theologians.

Actions Expressing Conversion

Initially the Meccans are not called to leave their religious community but to "worship the Lord of this House" (Quran 106:3)—that is, "Allah," the "high god" in the Ka'ba, which was used for worship of the tribal gods. The context shows that he is not distant and unrelated to the Meccans as they probably thought but that he is the source of their prosperity.

Muhammad's followers are first described as those who are to walk uprightly (*tazakka*—Quran 20:76 Egyptian ed./78 Fluegel ed.; 79:18; 80:3). Their most common designation is "people of faith" (*mu'minun*), used prior to the designation *muslimun,* which was not initially a technical term but indicated those who submit to God. These passages do not suggest a radical break from their previous community.

Opposition, nevertheless, developed. Muhammad rejected the "satanic verses" in which he had been tempted to recognize tribal deities and affirmed that "there is no god but God" (37:35/34). He broke with the polytheistic Meccans declaring, "You have your religion and I have my religion" (106:9).

When Muhammad and his band of followers moved to Medina (A.D. 622), he lived among Jews. Apparently he thought that his message was the same as that which they and Christians had received, for the Quran says that it confirms the scriptures they have (2:40-41/38; 3:3/2). When the Jews did not receive him, he broke with them and, seventeen months after arriving in Medina, changed the direction of prayer from Jerusalem to Mecca (Quran 2:142/136). The Quran likewise focuses on Abraham, who, it affirms, was neither a Jew nor a Christian but a monotheist (*hanif*) and a submitter [to God] (*muslim*) (3:67/60). The word *muslim* as opposed to *hanif* did not seem to have initially distinguished Muhammad's followers from Jews and Christians, for it is used of Solomon (Quran 27:44/45) as well as Jesus' disciples (3:52/45). The Muslim community, however, is distinguished from Jews and Christians when it is made an "intermediate community" (Quran 2:143/137), evidently between Jews and Christians. Jews, for example, prayed three times a day on the pattern of Psalm 55:17 (18 in Hebrew), and Christian monks prayed seven times a day on the pattern of Psalm 119:164.[4]

Inclusion in the community involved the internal attitude of repentance (*tawba*) and the external behavior of performing the ritual prayer and giving

---

4. See S. D. Goitein, *Studies in Islamic History and Institutions* (Leiden: Brill, 1968), 84-85.

alms (Quran 9:5,11). The first two outward signs of membership in the community were true for pagans (9:5,11) and Jews (2:43/40). W. Montgomery Watt views these external practices as being the major way that groups jointed the Islamic community, with the result that apostasy involved refusing to pay. He sees the recitation of the confession of faith (*shahada*) as being the more individualistic way of uniting with the community.[5] This distinction between the way groups and individuals joined is helpful but too neat to fit all the historical facts. For example, even though *zakat* (prescribed alms) was required from the tribes, so was the "individualistic" confession concerning God.[6] In any event ritual prayer, almsgiving, and confession of the One God were the early marks of inclusion in Muhammad's community.

The Quran contains the elements of the confession of faith (e.g., 2:255/256; 27:26; 28:88; 7:158/157), although not in the liturgical form it later developed. Use of the *shahada* as the formal act of conversion is found in the earliest biography of Muhammad, the recension of the sira of Ibn Ishaq (85 A.H./A.D.704-150A.H./A.D.767) by Ibn Hisham (d. ca. 218 A.H./A.D. 833). In this account the future caliph 'Umar "became a Muslim" by believing in God and his Apostle (the contents of the *shahada*) and what he had brought from God (the Quran).[7] On the other hand, some even claimed that a man named Iyas, who had heard Muhammad preach but once, evidenced that he was a Muslim by the mere fact that he "praised and glorified God" before he died.[8] Obviously in the early days there were a number of actions that expressed conversion—a concept that only gradually developed in this period.[9]

Hamilton Gibb distinguishes three levels of commitment to the Muslim community at which Islam was received in Muhammad's day. The first was "total conversion" by those who inwardly accepted its spirit and principles. The second was "formal adhesion" by those who accepted the outward duties but not their spirit. The third was "enforced adherence" by those kept in the alliance by force or threat of force.[10] Without pressing the details that may not fit these generalizations, we can see the necessity of discerning what conversion means to different people, which leads us to our next topic.

5. *The Formative Period of Islamic Thought* (Edinburgh: Edinburgh University Press, 1973), 128-129, and "Conditions of Membership of the Islamic Community," *Studia Islamica* 21 (1964): 5-7.

6. Al-Bukhari, *Sahih*, vol. 9, bk. 84, chap. 3, trad. 59; trans. Muhammad Muhsin Khan, *Sahih al-Bukhari* (Beirut: Dar Al Arabia, 1985), 9: 46-47.

7. [Ibn Hisham], *The Life of Muhammad: [Ibn] Ishaq's Sirat Rasul Allah,* trans. and ed. A. Guillaum (London: Oxford University Press, 1955), 227-240; trans. 157-59.

8. Ibid., 286; trans. 197.

9. For this section as a whole see: Watt, "Conversion in Islam at the Time of the Prophet," *Journal of the American Academy of Religion* 47 no. 4 (December 1980): 721-31 and "Conditions for Membership," 5-7.

10. *Studies on the Civilization of Islam*, ed. Stanford J. Shaw and William R. Polk (Boston: Beacon, 1962), 5. For a critique of some of the details see M. Shaban, "Conversion to Early Islam," *Conversion to Islam*, ed. Nehemia Levtzion (New York: Holmes & Meier, 1979), 25-26.

Terms Describing Conversion

The tribal leaders in Mecca described what Muhammad was doing as *saba'a* (to convert, change religion, become a Sabian), using the term which indicates one who thereby becomes an enemy of his people. With their religious observances involving the Ka'ba, pilgrimages, and sacred months—and consequently aiding commerce—any changes were seen as being against Muhammad's own people.[11]

The Quran describes conversion with the clause "men enter (*yadkhuluna*) into the religion (*din*) of God (Allah) in throngs" (110:2). Another general description, which brings out the human and divine elements, used the verb *ghayyara* ("to change"): "God does not change what is in a people until they change what is in themselves" (13:11/12). The other quranic words for conversion are not as general but describe some of its characteristics.

Repentance (especially *Tawba*). Repentance is the first step mentioned in the conversion process discussed above in the Quran 9:5 and 11, where it is linked with ritual prayer and almsgiving. Likewise, in chapter 39:54/55 it is linked with "submitting to God"—*islam*—a basic concept in the Muslim understanding of conversion. In fact, in many cases it is similar in meaning to conversion, involving the same spatial metaphors of turning that are inherent in the English word "conversion" and which underlie many of the biblical references to both concepts. Classical lexicographers sometimes translate *taba*, the most common quranic verb for "repent," as "convert."[12] The two were synonymous when "repentance" referred to those who were turning to the One God from polytheism and disbelief. A difference between the two is that conversion is commonly thought of as a one-time process while repentance must be repeated. The latter is brought out clearly in the saying attributed to Muhammad, "I ask God's pardon and turn to him in repentance more than seventy times a day."[13]

The spatial metaphors (e.g., turning around and returning) are found in words from the roots '*wb, nwb,* and *twb*—the last of which underlies *tawba,* the dominant quranic verbal noun for receptance.[14] This "turning" is certainly from sin—which the context describes as wrongdoing (*zulm*) such as stealing (Quran 5:36/40-39/43; cf. 3:86/80-89/83), evil in ignorance (6:54), and idolatry and sectarianism (30:31/30-32/31). However, the emphasis in the last passage and in most places in the Quran is on turning to God (e.g., 39:54/55). Although the goal of Sufi mystics is union with God, they define

---

11. A. de Biberstein Kazimirski, ed., *Dictionnaire Arabe-Francais* and Ibn Manzur, ed., *Lisan al-'Arab,* s.vv. *sb'*; Shaban, 24.

12. Kazimirski, *Dictionnaire,* s.v. *twb.*

13. *Mishkat al-Masabih,* ed. Al-Baghawi, trans. James Robson, 4 vols. (Lahore: Sh. Muhammad Ashraf, 1965-66), bk. 10, chap. 3; trans. 2:493; Frederick M. Denny, "The Qur'anic Vocabulary of Repentance: Orientations and Attitudes," *Journal of the American Academy of Religion* 47, no. 4, Thematic Issue S (December 1980): 657.

14. For a description of the Arabic roots for repentance and the words derived from them in the Quran, see Denny, "Qur'anic Vocabulary of Repentance," 649-64.

"repentance" (*tawba*) as turning away from sin and abjuring every worldly charm.[15]

Besides the spatial orientation of repentance, there is also an attitudinal one—feelings of remorse and sorrow. Grief (*ghamm*) in the story of Jonah (Dhul Nun) did lead to true repentance—a recognition of his evil and a turning to the One God in praise (Quran 21:87-88). The attitude of remorse, however, is expressed more frequently in the Quran by *nadimin* and *nadama*, although they normally express a regret that has not resulted in a turning to God (e.g., 5:31/34; 10:55/56). Despite the fact that the normal quranic use of these terms falls short of true repentance, Muhammad is reported as saying "*nadam* [remorse] is *tawba* [repentance]."[16] In keeping with this equation, *nadam* gains prominence in later Muslin thought. Islam's most celebrated theologian al-Ghazali (d. 1111) made *nadam* (remorse) one of the necessary ingredients of valid repentance along with conviction of sin and resolution to abstain from it.[17] *Nadam* is used of the broken and contrite heart of the truly penitent in the prayer manuals.[18]

As in the Bible, God in the Quran "repents" (*taba* in the sense of turns) toward those who "repent" (*taba* or turn) toward him (5:39/45). Obviously the meaning is that God turns in mercy and forgiveness. This, however, emphasizes that humans cannot save themselves but need a divine involvement. Another verse states that humans must change themselves first: "God does not modify (*ghayyara*) what is in people until they modify what is in themselves" (13:11/12). This is the reverse of the Calvinistic *ordo salutis* where God by his Spirit takes the initiative in his effectual calling that changes the heart. This would, of course, fit in with orthodox Muslim theology where human nature is initially acceptable, without need of a divine transformation.[19]

There is a quranic passage where God takes the initiative in turning toward people first: "He turned (*taba*) toward them that they might turn (*taba*)" (9:117/118-118/119). Muhammad's biographer explains that the reference is to three Medinan "Helpers" of Muhammad who declined to go on a difficult

---

15. Ignaz Goldziher, "Arabische Synonymik der Askese," *Der Islam* 8 (1918) in Annemarie Schimmel, *Mystical Dimensions of Islam* (Chapel Hill, N.C.: University of North Carolina Press, 1975), 109.

16. *Mishkat*, bk. 10, chap.3; trans. 2:501.

17. Abu Hamid al-Ghazali, *Ihya Ulum id-Din*, trans. Fazal ul-Karim (Lahore: Islamic Book Foundation, 1981), bk. 4, chap. 1; trans. 4:1-67; R. A. Nicholson, "Tawba," *Shorter Encyclopaedia of Islam*, s.v.

18. *Awrad Ahmad al-Tijani*, 40 in Constance E. Padwick, *Muslim Devotions: A Study of Prayer-Manuals in Common Use* (London: S.P.C.K., 1961), 186.

19. See Quran 3:30/39: "Set your face to the religion of the pristine faith (*hanif*)—the states of natural purity (*fitra*) in which he created people"; Al-Bukhari, *Sahih*: "No child is born save in the state of natural purity (*fitra*)" (bk. 60, chap. 230, trad. 298; trans. 6:284); and Badru Kateregga: "Muslims believe that man is fundamentally a good and a dignified creature. He is not a fallen being" (Kateregga and David W. Shenk, *Islam and Christianity* [Nairobi: Uzima Press, 1980], 109).

military expedition and had been punished.[20] Even here, however, the quranic passage shows that, prior to God's turning, their affliction had led them to
the conclusion "that there was no shelter from God['s judgment] except in
him." Therefore they were inclined toward God even earlier. God's initiative
in the Quran is in desire and guidance: "God desires to make clear to you and
to guide you in the institution of those before, and to turn (taba) toward
you" (4:26/31-28/32).

Repentance receives significant attention in the authorized Traditions of
Muhammad.[21] It was the Sufi mystics, however, who paid the most attention
to it since it was for most the first station in the path to union with God.[22] The
Chishtiyyah order advocated repentance for the present, the past, and the
future, by which they indicated a decision not to commit any sin again.[23]

The question may be reasonably asked whether repentance in a Sufi mystical context refers to conversion or to something comparable to what
Christians might call sanctification, since Sufis are interested in a higher
level of spiritual life than the common Muslim. If conversion is normally a
process rather than an event, as will be argued in the final section on the
expansion of Islam, repentance for them may be considered a part of conversion. In what we might consider their *ordo salutis,* "faith" (or "trust in
God") is normally the subsequent station,[24] and should be included in conversion. What will be seen in the expansion of Islam is that a large percentage of Muslims joined the "house of Islam" by initial adhesion, accretion, or
acculturation but internalized their faith through reformation, often stimulated
by Sufis. In fact, Sufis were active both as missionaries outside the Muslim
lands and as revivalists within where they helped Muslims in name become
Muslims in their hearts. Their first call was to repentance.

Faith (Iman). The Quran states that God is forgiving of those who repent
and have faith (20:82/84); so faith is the next act to consider in seeking to
understand conversion. In fact, to have faith is frequently considered as
being converted (e.g., 90:17; 2:221/220).

The meanings of the Arabic root *amn* include "to be secure, trust, and
entrust." Each brings out an aspect of faith. Those who have faith experience
security from God (Quran 6:82). Faith is trusting persons (God and his messenger—24:62) and God's message (7:87/85). And it is entrusting oneself to
God, for having faith involves submitting to him (5:111).

The contexts of the quranic passages indicate what is involved in the act
of faith and what should be the result—both keys to understanding conversion in Islam. Having true faith is not only contrasted with disbelief but also
with having the false faith of fools (2:13/12)—a faith in vanity (29:52),

20. [Ibn Hisham], *Muhammad,* 907-13; trans.β 610-14.

21. E.g., Imam Muslim, *Sahih Muslim,* trans. Abdul Hamid Siddiqi (4 vols.; Lahore: Sh.
Muhammad Ashraf, 1976), vol. 4, bk. 12; trans. 4: 1434-55.

22. Schimmel, *Mystical Dimensions,* 100, 109.

23. Seyyed Hossein Nasr, ed., *Islamic Spirituality: Foundations* (New York: Crossroad,
1987), 299-300.

24. Schimmel, *Mystical Dimensions,* 100, 109.

demons and idols (4:51/54), and associates of God (40:12). It bids to evil (2:93/87). Therefore, the aspect of conversion expressed by having faith involves turning from such false faith and the evil it engenders.

The object of faith is first a person—above all God, but also his earthly messenger (3:179/174), and his heavenly ones (2:285). So important is this type of faith that only those who have faith in God and his messenger are considered people of faith (24:62), and these are to put all their trust in God (67:29), who is to be their Lord (5:83/86) and friend (5:56/61).

Faith in God leads to faith in his words (7:158). Here there is a movement from the personal level toward the verbal, conceptual, and even propositional levels. Previously, people had not known "what the Book was nor faith" (42:52). Now the Muslims have faith in all the Book (3:119/115), which they recognize as the truth (5:84/87). The same verb *amana* is used for faith in a personal God and *believing* a proposition, "There is no god but he" (10:90).[25] The faith in God is also expressed by confident belief in his signs (7:126/123) and the judgment of the Last Day (2:62/59).

The basis of faith in the Quran is knowledge. Previously people did not know what the Book and faith were (42:52), but certain ones have been given knowledge and faith (30:56). Repeatedly, the audience is told to have faith in God's signs (7:156/157). Yet God remains the "Unseen" (2:3/2), so a certain "leap of faith" is required. Some things are signs for people of faith (27:86); so knowledge is partly a result of one's orientation.

Knowledge alone is not enough for faith; a moral choice is necessary. The messenger came with clear signs, but the people would not have faith (10:13/14). No warnings avail such a people (10:101); they are heedless (19:39/40). The reason for this heedlessness is that they are proud (40:27/28).

There is also a divine involvement in faith. When we look at the various facets in the Quran, we can see some of the bases of later disputes among the theologians on free will and predestination. In the Quran, people can only have faith by God's permission (10:100). If God had willed, everyone would have faith (10:99); yet by his word some will not (10:96). God's action seems normally to be a response to the human orientation. God has written faith upon their hearts (58:22). God will guide those who have faith in him (64:11) but will not guide those who do not have faith in his signs (16:104/106). At

---

25. This dual use of *amana* creates a problem in English. Wilfred Cantwell Smith has distinguished between "faith" (as the human side of the relationship between God and humans) and "belief" (as an assent to intellectual expressions of that faith) (*Faith and Belief* [Princeton, N.J.: Princeton University Press, 1979], 17). Furthermore, "faith" in English does not have a verbal form; so "believe" has been used. "Believe," however, has degenerated from assuming the certainty of "reality" that is found in "faith" to meaning in modern usage "imagine" or "guess" (Smith, *Belief and History* [Charlottesville: University Press of Virginia, 1977], 41-67). As a result, Smith argues that "in the Qur'an the concept of 'believe' (as a religious activity) does not occur" (*On Understanding Islam: Selected Studies* [The Hague: Mouton, 1981], 120). Nevertheless, for consistency, "believe" seems appropriate here because its object is a proposition. The certainty of "reality" on the part of the subject, however, is much greater than modern English usage might indicate.

other times his guiding precedes faith (49:17). The blending of the divine with the human comes out in "God has endeared to you faith, decking it fair in your hearts" (49:7).

Subsequent theologians would argue that the content of faith includes an inner commitment and an outward expression by words and deeds. Each has rootage in the Quran. The inner commitment is shown by the contrast of those who only "say with their mouths 'We have faith,' but their hearts do not have faith" (5:41/45). Faith has not yet entered their hearts (49:14). By contrast even those who have been forced to recant can have their hearts at rest in their faith (16:106/108).

The quranic accounts of vocal confession of faith, even by the insincere, show the importance that people must have attached to confession with the tongue (e.g., 5:41/45). The emphasis, however, is on behavior that is in keeping with faith. Repeatedly the Quran enjoins "have faith and do righteous deeds" (e.g. 2:82/76). Many inner qualities and outward actions are listed, including at least seminal forms of what were to become the "pillars" of Islam—confession of faith (10:90; 24:62), ritual prayer (5:6/8), almsgiving (2:264/266), fasting (2:183/179), and pilgrimage (5:95/96). Nevertheless, not all to whom faith is ascribed are called righteous (66:4).

Faith involves people in turning from their religion (5:54/59) and forming a new community, basing marriage and friendship on a shared faith (2:221/220; 3:118/114; 5:51/56). The result of such faith is forgiveness and salvation (20:82/84; 8:29).

The schools of theology and law identified three major elements in the act of faith: conviction with the heart, confession with the tongue, and action with the limbs. Al-Ash'ari (873-935), founder of a centrist school of theology, considered the act of submitting to God and thereby becoming a Muslim (*islam*) to involve more than faith (*iman*). The latter he defined like the fundamentalist Hanbalites as consisting of *words* and *works*.[26] In another work he stated that faith is *tasdiq* in God.[27] In an exhaustive study of *tasdiq* Cantwell Smith interprets it as follows: "to recognize the truth, to appropriate it, to affirm it, to confirm it, to actualize it. And the truth, in each case, is personalist and sincere."[28] This inner conviction of truth and commitment became a hallmark of the school. Its most noted theologian al-Ghazali referred to it not only as the acceptance (*tasdiq*) of the heart but also as the agreement (*'aqd*) of the heart,[29] while the scholar-commentator al-Jurjani (1339-1413) called it belief (*i'tiqad*).[30] Faith was essentially the conviction of the heart,

---

26. Abu 'l-Hasan al-Ash'ari, *Kitab al-Ibana* (2nd ed.; Hyderabad, Deccan: Matba'a Jam'iya Da'ira al-Ma'arif al-Uthmaniya, 1948), 7-8; *Maqalat al-Islamiyyin*, ed. al-Hamid (Cairo, n.d.), 1:327 in L. Gardet, "Iman," *Encyclopaedia of Islam* (new ed.), 3:1170B.

27. *Kitab al-Lum'a*, trans. Richard J. McCarthy, *The Theology of al-Ash'ari* (Beirut: Imprimerie Catholique, 1952), 75; trans. 104 (inadequate here).

28. Smith, *On Understanding Islam*, 135-61, esp. 150.

29. *Kitab Qawa'id al'-Aqa'id*, trans. Nabih Amin Faris, *The Foundations of the Articles of Faith* (Lahore: Sh. Muhammad Ashraf, 1963), 100, 103.

30. *Kitab al-Ta'rifat*, ed. Flügel (Leipzig, 1845), 41 in Gardet, "Iman," 1170B.

ſ

which in classical Arab thought was the seat of reason; hence the intellect (*'aql*) was sometimes substituted for the heart. This conviction required verbal confession, if possible, and its outworking in appropriate behavior. Historically this was originally described as the "action of the limbs" but gradually the action was interpreted more specifically as the performance of the prescribed five pillars.[31]

There is not absolute consistency within the schools, but some bring out various helpful alternate emphases. Many scholars of the moderate Hanafi-Maturidi tradition added to the definition of faith the "knowledge (*ma'rifa*) of the heart" but dropped works as a formal constituent of faith.[32] Ibn Hanbal (780-855), the founder of the fundamentalist school with his name, added to the "words" and "works" of faith the right intention (*niyya*) and attachment to the Practice of Muhammad (*sunna*).[33]

When we turn from the Sunni schools to the Shi'i we do not see a major shift in the understanding of faith. Their earlier views which made "works" an integral part of faith were shared by the rationalistic Mu'tazilites. They also spoke of external (*zahir*) and internal (*batin*) faith—the first referring to verbal affirmation and the latter to the affirmation of the heart, but this perspective was even shared by the Hanbalite Ibn Taymiyya, a model for the later fundamentalist Wahhabis.[34]

The contents of faith are summarized in the confession of faith—the uniqueness of God and the apostleship of Muhammad. The latter part implies belief in all that Muhammad has brought from God. The "necessary" objects of faith, according to the Quran, are: "God, his angels, his books, and his messengers" (2:285) and "the Last Day" (60:6). Muhammad is reported to have said that faith is "that you affirm your faith in God, his angels, his books, his meeting, his messengers and . . . [the] resurrection hereafter."[35]

Submission (Islam). Submission (*islam*) and faith (*iman*) express overlapping acts in the Quran: The disciples of Jesus said, "We have faith: witness our submission" (*islam*—5:111). It also talks of disbelief (*kufr*) after [conversion to] Islam (or submission—9:74/75), indicating that *islam* is a word for conversion.

We shall seek to define this word and note its relationship to faith as its meaning develops through history. In the Quran the verbal form *aslama* has two related meanings—"to submit to God" (inner) and "to profess Islam" (outer). The nominal form *islam* is used both of an inner activity (e.g., God "expands his breast to Islam"—6:125) and of a "religion" (e.g., "Today, I have perfected your religion [*din*] for you. . . . I have approved Islam for your

31. Smith, *On Understanding Islam*, 162-73.

32. *Fiqh Akbar II*, art. 18; trans. in A. J. Wensinck, *The Muslim Creed* (Cambridge: University Press, 1932), 194; Gardet, "Iman," 1171A.

33. "'Aqida I," *Tabaqat al-Hanabila*, ed. Abu 'l-Husain (ed. M. Hamid al-Fiqi; Cairo, 1952) 1:24 in Gardet, "Iman," 1171B.

34. Gardet, "Iman," 1171-72.

35. Muslim, *Sahih*, vol. 1, bk. 1, chap. 2, trad. 4; trans. 1:3.

religion"—5:3/5). When "Islam" is viewed as a religion, as Cantwell Smith has observed, it is used to refer to both ideal Islam and the historical phenomena.[36] We shall focus on the former when we look at the perspectives of the theologians, and we shall look at the latter in the final section of this study when we observe the actual process of Islamization in history.

When we consider the relationship between *iman* and *islam* in the Quran, we see that sometimes *iman* is the more inclusive or fundamental term—for example, 49:14: "The Bedouins have said, 'We have faith.' Say to them, 'You did not have faith,' but say, 'We have converted to Islam (*aslam*).' Faith (*iman*) has not yet entered your hearts." Faith, thus, is the necessary ingredient for *islam* to be effectual. In other passages the two words are roughly equivalent in that they imply each other—for example, 3:52/45: "We have a faith in God; witness our submission."

In the Traditions (*hadith*) of Muhammad more distinctions are made between the two words. *Islam* is submission to God that is evidenced by practicing the prescribed duties in particular. Muhammad is quoted as saying, "*Islam* is built upon the five [pillars]."[37] Ibn Hanbal quotes another tradition that says, "Islam is external; faith belongs to the heart."[38] Islam is thus seen as the concrete expression of inner faith.

The way theologians and jurisprudents defined *islam* and expressed its relationship to *iman*, of course, reflected their definition of the latter. For those like the rationalistic Mu'tazilites who tended to equate faith and works, the same equation was made with faith and *islam*. To ensure the efficaciousness of an act, then, it had to be motivated by good intention (*niyya*). Major sin also resulted in a Muslim becoming a disbeliever (according to the factious Kharijites) or entering an "intermediate state" (according to the Mu'tazilites).

While the moderate Hanafi-Maturidis likewise tended to equate the two, by the eleventh century they defined faith and *islam* as respectively the inner and outer aspects of the same reality, both included in "religion" (*din*).

The centrist Ash'arites and fundamentalist Hanbalites, who together grew to dominate the classical period, held that faith and *islam* implied each other even though they were not the same. *Islam* is the external expression of faith, and faith is the interiorization of Islam.[39]

As has been evident, the meaning of *islam* has evolved through the centuries. It started in Arab poetry and the Quran meaning "submission" by an individual or group—an activity rather than a religious system or institution. The major term for the new community was "people of faith" (*mu'minum*), not "Muslims." Gradually, as Cantwell Smith has demonstrated through a survey of Arabic book titles, *islam* became a more prominent word than *iman* and began to shift in meaning. From referring to sub-

36. Smith, *On Understanding Islam*, 43-44.
37. *Sahih*, vol. 1, bk. 2, chap. 2, trad. 7; trans. 1:17.
38. *Musnad*, 3:134 in Wensinck, *Muslim Creed*, 23.
39. Gardet, "Islam," *Encyclopaedia of Islam* (new ed.), s.v.

mission to God, it shifted to designate an ideal religious system, then the actual, historical religious system, and finally the historic civilization that was produced.[40] In our present study the Quranic materials have shown the meaning of submission and the views of the schools of theology have pointed to its ideal formulation. The final section of the chapter on the Islamization of large parts of the world will refer to the historic reality.

Confession of Faith (Shahada). People formally become Muslims by reciting the *shahada*: "There is no god but God, and Muhammad is the Apostle of God." This section will seek to interpret what this means for many. The confession is introduced by the words "I bear witness" (*ashhadu*). This, therefore, is not merely an assent to beliefs but a declaration of what the confessors, from their perspective, know to be true and on which they are basing their lives and destinies.

The first half, "There is no god but God," implies a commitment to him as Lord unlike the mere intellectual recognition by the devils in James 2:19, who also believed in God's uniqueness but trembled. In Muhammad's Arabia this meant turning from polytheism as it may today among Hindus or African tribal people. For Sufi mystics it means turning from anything that might distract from the worship of, reflection on, or union with God. For all, it implies submission to his will, for he alone is Lord. This first "word" unites Muslims with Jews and Christians, even though many would interpret it as distinguishing them from Christians.

The second half is understood as separating out Muslims as distinct. Cantwell Smith has said, in a study that has lent the basic insights for this interpretation of the *shahada*, that the second affirmation "is a statement not about Muhammad's status so much as about his function."[41] It certainly refers to his function as a conveyer of what God wants to say to humans. Since in Islam God's revelation centers in a Book, the focus is on obedience to what it says in contrast to Christianity where God's revelation centers in a person and the focus is on a relationship with him. To affirm Muhammad's function as an apostle implies accepting and obeying the message in the Quran and by extension the authorized Traditions of Muhammad and Shari'a law derived from them both.

When Smith downplays the application of this affirmation to Muhammad's status, he may be true in the earliest period, but certainly Muhammad's status has been so elevated in the subsequent years that, when Muslims recite the *shahada* now, they mean to affirm his status as well as his function.[42]

The Terms in Context. To discern a Muslim understanding of conversion

---

40. Helmer Ringgren, "Islam, 'aslama and muslim" (Uppsala: Gleerup, Lund, 1949); Smith, *On Understanding Islam*, 41-64.

41. Smith, *On Understanding Islam*, 26-37, specifically 37 here.

42. See Tor Andrae, *Die person Muhammads in Lehre und glaube seiner gemeinde* (Stockholm: P. A. Verstedt og söner, 1918) and Annemarie Schimmel, *And Muhammad Is His Messenger: The Veneration of the Prophet in Islamic Piety* (Chapel Hill, N.C.: University of North Carolina Press, 1985).

we must not only look at these terms in their relationship to each other but also in their relationship to other terms and the broader system of Islamic thought and practice.

Logically, *divine guidance* (*huda*) comes *first*, though like all the other phenomena described by these terms it must continue. The daily prayer of the suppliant is "lead us in the right path" (Quran 1:6). Islamic Law, which applies to every area of life, is called *Shari'a* (the way), and Sufi mystics enter the *Tariqa* (the Path, also used of their Orders).

After divine guidance comes *secondly* the cluster of terms we have discussed under the rubric of *conversion—repentance* (*tawba*), *faith* (*iman*), *submission* (*islam*), and their vocal *confession* (*shahada*). They represent a change of allegiance—a "turning" from sin, self-centeredness, and Satan to God. In the majority Sunni, Islam the concomitant act of turning to God need not be through a "savior" as in Christian faith since God does not require a means of salvation. For many Shi'ites, however, Muhammad's grandson Husein by his "martyrdom" at the hands of the Umayyad rulers provides a substitutionary death.[43]

In the conversion process there is not a terminal point where one may say "I am saved" since God retains the divine prerogative to forgive or not forgive. In fact, many Muslims have not presumed to say "I am a Muslim" without adding "if God wills."[44]

In the conversion process, as we have seen, inner repentance and faith expressed themselves in what increasingly became the outward expression of *islam* which was vocalized in the *shahada*. The *shahada*, however, is also included in the *third* step in what might be called the process of salvation—if we do not read in Christian understandings. This is what Kenneth Cragg has call "*habituation*" through the five "pillars" (*arkan*) of faith— the repetition of the confession of faith, the five daily prayers, regular almsgiving, and the yearly fast, and pilgrimage until the worship of God and Muslim forms of piety become habitual.[45]

This approach is based on a higher view of the innate capabilities of humans than in Christian faith. The Quran and the Traditions portray humans as born in a state of natural purity (*fitra*).[46] Therefore they do not need a divine transformation of their nature—a new birth, regeneration. Shi'ites do speak of a "carnal nature."[47] Their Ayatollah Khomeini said, "Man's calamity is his carnal desires, and this exists in everybody, and it is rooted in

43. See Mahmud Ayyub, *Redemptive Suffering in Islam: A Study of the Devotional Aspects of 'Ashura in Twelver Shi'ism* (The Hague: Mouton, 1978); Peter J. Chelkowski, *Ta'ziyeh: Ritual and Drama in Iran* (New York: New York University Press, 1979).

44. E.g., Ibn Batta, *Kitab al-Sharh wa 'l-Ibana*, trans. Henri Laoust, *La Profession de foi d'ibn Batta* (Damascus: Institut Francais de Damas, 1958), 48-49; trans. 79-82.

45. "God and Salvation," *Studia Missionalia* 29 (1980): 154-66.

46. Quran 30:30/29; al-Bukhari, *Sahih*, bk. 60, chap. 230, trad. 298; trans. 6:284.

47. E.g., Sayyed Hossein Nasr, *Ideals and Realities of Islam* (London: George Allen & Unwin, 1966), 38.

the nature of man."[48] Sufi mystics too have been aware of inner sin and self-centeredness. Neither group, however, has as a result expressed the need for a new birth. Instead Islam's answer has been habituation—the changing of lives as people, largely through their own efforts, regularly obey the will of God.

The *fourth* element is entrance into the visible *community* (*umma*) and the reinforcement and sense of belonging it provides. Reciting of the *shahada* became the formal means of conversion as it gave external evidence of joining the community, as did public ritual prayer. This has been reinforced positively by the direction of prayer and the pilgrimage and negatively by "the law of apostasy" with possible death.

Where Muslims controlled the government this sense of community, habituation, and guidance could all be supported politically. In the final section on the Islamization of large parts of the world we shall see the role Muslim governmental institutions played in conversion through the ambiance they created.

The result of these elements—divine guidance, change of allegiance, habituation, and community reinforced by the government where possible—is a state of welfare (*tawfiq*), success (*fawz*), and well-being (*falah*) in this life and probably Paradise thereafter.

As we have looked at this largely theological analysis of conversion thus far, we see that it involves some knowledge, although in real practice most instruction comes after conversion. It also involves faith, right intention, and prescribed behavior. What we have not seen is the affective dimension—attitudes opposed to or favorable toward Islam. We shall see these in the final section.

CONVERSIONS THROUGHOUT HISTORY

Conversion should not be confused with conquest. Most histories of the Muslim world focus on the latter. Conversion, however, normally took place considerably later than the establishment of Muslim rule and is more difficult to chronicle. Muslim historians paid little attention to it; so we are often left to analyze such symbols as the adoption of Muslim names[49] or the building of neighborhood mosques. We shall not here give a chronological or geographical survey of Islamization.[50] Rather, we shall first propose models to describe its major patterns and then identify some of the factors evident in conversion in varying periods and locations.

---

48. "Islamic Government Does Not Spend for its Own Grandeur," *Kayhan International* (September 4, 1985): 3.

49. See, e.g., Richard W. Bulliet, *Conversion to Islam in the Medieval Period.*

50. The dates of Islamization of each region are listed in J. Jomier, "Diffusion of Islam," *Encyclopaedia of Islam* (new ed.), 4:174-77. A bibliography of conversion in each region is in Nehemia Levtzion, *Conversion to Islam,* 247-65.

GENERAL MODELS

A. D. Nock in his classic study of conversion distinguishes between "conversion," which he applies to prophetic religions that are exclusive and demand commitment, and "adhesion," which he applies to nonprophetic religions that are more pragmatic attempts to meet natural needs.[51] H. J. Fisher and Nehemia Levtzion have shown that the term "adhesion" better describes the Islamization of much of the Middle East and Africa, even though Islam is technically a prophetic religion.[52] There is, therefore, need for some revision of categories.

Four steps are frequently discernible in the process involving conversion, but their order is largely determined by whether they take place in Muslim domains or outside them. Normally, the former is from top (government) to bottom (the people) and the latter from bottom to top. As a rule the first step in the former is military conquest, while the first step in the latter is peaceful witness and influence. Frequently conversion in the former is by groups, while in the latter it is more by individuals or families.

Conversion from Top to Bottom. The major steps in this model are *military conquest*, then *political control*, followed by an *Islamic ambiance* created by the growth of Islamic institutions, and then finally *conversion* of the people. Larry Allan Poston calls this paradigm a "high church model."[53] The final step of conversion should normally be divided into two parts, *accommodation* and *reform*, which are not inevitable nor irreversible. Islam has repeatedly been accommodated to the religious beliefs and practices of the indigenous populations.

Richard Eaton, focusing on the previous belief system, has called the first stage "accretion," where people add new superhuman deities or agencies to their cosmology or identify new ones with existing ones.[54] The "reform" is similar to what Max Weber called "rationalization," the absorption of other beings into the supreme God.[55] The accommodation and reform aspects of conversion correlate with what Clifford Geertz has called the "model *of*" and "model *for*" aspects of religious understanding.[56] In the accommodation phase people's previous beliefs and practices remain a "model *of*" the "real" world but may be called "Islamic." In the reform phase

---

51. Arthur D. Nock, *Conversion* (Oxford: Oxford University Press, 1961), 7-16.

52. H. J. Fisher, "Conversion Reconsidered: Some Historical Aspects of Religious Conversion in Black Africa," *Africa* 43 (1973): 33; Levtzion, *Conversion to Islam*, 21.

53. Larry Allan Poston, "Islamic Da'wah in North America and the Dynamics of Conversion to Islam in Western Societies" (Ph.D. dissertation, Northwestern University, 1988), 100-34.

54. Richard M. Eaton, "Approaches to the Study of Conversion to Islam in India," *Approaches to Islam in Religious Studies*, ed. Richard C. Martin (Tucson: University of Arizona Press, 1985), 111-23.

55. Max Weber, *The Sociology of Religion*, trans. Ephraim Fischoff (Boston: Beacon Press, 1922), 10, 22.

56. Clifford Geertz, "Religion as a Cultural System," *Anthropological Approaches to the Study of Religion*, ed. Michael Banton (London: Tavistock, 1966), 40.

formal Islam is a "model *for*" the "real" world.

Military conquest took place in the early period of Islam as the empire spread across the Middle East and North Africa and subsequently when Muslim people conquered areas like India. An Islamic ambiance was created by the immigration of Muslim populations and the development of Islamic institutions, often with governmental support. These included mosques, religious schools (*madaris*), centers with schools, shrines, and hostels (*zawiya*), Muslim cities, and Sufi mystical orders. Conversions took place in this context, especially if non-Muslim social structures began to crumble.

The reform stage took place with the increased influence of Muslim judges (*qadis*), leaders of mosques (*imams*) and scholars (*'ulama*), who turned people to the formal and legal duties of Islam, and the Sufi mystics, who fostered the internalization of the faith.

Conversion from Bottom to Top. Conversion from the bottom up, which Poston has called the "low church" approach, is common when evangelism is peaceful, outside of Muslim domains, and is more involved with individuals or small groups. Here the sequence of steps tends to be *witness* through word and lifestyle, *conversion*, Muslim *ambiance* or at least a critical mass of Muslims, and finally *political power*. Again the conversion phase must frequently be divided into periods of *accommodation* and *reform*. Force may, however, be used in acquiring the final political power as in parts of West Africa.

The witness phase is seen clearly in the United States where the Islamic Society of North America actively promotes lectures and debates to convert non-Muslims. Even if many are not converted, Muslim missionaries like Khurram Murad have wanted to move to the Muslim ambiance state where everyone will gain a "true understanding of Islam, leading . . . to the acceptance of the values and concepts which Islam teaches."[57]

Fundamentalist reformers in recent years like Hasan al-Banna in Egypt and 'Abul A'la Maududi in Pakistan believed that the Muslims in their areas stagnated at the accommodation stage. They both, therefore, tried to reform society with this same bottom to top approach starting with individuals, creating the System of Islam (*Nizam al-Islami*), and ultimately hoping to change the state.[58] Although in their earlier days al-Banna and his Muslim Brethren society were also open to more militant means, now the Brethren are working through governmental channels.

SIGNIFICANT FACTORS

Various agents and means facilitated conversions, sometimes contributing to the sequences described and sometimes altering them.

Agents of Conversion. The agents of conversion were first *nomads*. The

---

57. "Third Opportunity to Keep Islam in the West," *Islamic Horizons* (November 1986): 10, in Poston, *Islamic Da'wah*, 172-73.

58. Poston, *Islamic Da'wah*, 141-58.

Arabs conquered lands from Iran to Spain, and the Turks pressed into Asia Minor and India. As conquerors and settlers under intelligent leaders they caused the cultural transformation which facilitated Islamization. The major factor determining the date of conversion seems to have been the amount of meaningful contact there was between the nomads and the indigenous population, whether this contact was through local people coming into Arab garrison cities to serve the troops as in Iraq or Arabs settling in small towns as in Khurasan. When, on the contrary, the nomadic Fulbe conquered Futa Jallon in present-day Guinea, they merely displaced the population and subjugated it; so little cultural transformation took place.[59]

Traders were important agents of peaceful expansion in East and West Africa and Central and Southeast Asia. Sometimes they themselves became Muslims because credit, among the Hausa, for example, was hard to get for non-Muslims. Also a universal, rather than a local, religion was better for those who traveled. Their life required that they find people they could trust and hospitality in foreign cities. "Trader" and "Muslim" became almost synonymous in West Africa. In Indonesia the harbor masters were Muslims and made trading alliances. Missionaries often accompanied and followed traders, but there was not a major spread of Islam among the people until the traders made alliances with the tribal chiefs in West Africa and the local rulers in Indonesia.[60]

The other major agents of peaceful conversion were the *saints* and *Sufi mystics*, although the latter also joined in militant expansion in Anatolia, Central Asia, India, and Africa. They founded centers for teaching and social services in conquered territories and were helpful in attracting and integrating the masses. On the frontiers their superior literacy, divination, and magic gave them influence in places like the Sudan. Their syncretism and mysticism helped them reach the masses in Anatolia, Bengal, Java, and Malaya—leading to the religious transmutation of almost the entire population in the last three. They even fostered adhesion after their deaths because many of their graves became objects of pilgrimage.[61]

Means of Conversion. Force was seldom used to bring about conversions. In fact, in India there were fewer conversions in the areas where Muslim rule was strongest. Nevertheless, forced conversions were reported by Christians, Hindus, and pagans in places like Anatolia, India, and Afghanistan respectively.[62]

More important was the desire to *retain or improve one's social, economic, or political status* or to *avoid discrimination*. Following their early con-

---

59. See Levtzion, "Conversion Under Muslim Domination: A Comparative Study," *Religious Change and Cultural Domination*, ed. David Lorenzen (Mexico City: El Colegio de Mexico, 1981), 29-34.

60. Levtzion, *Conversion to Islam*, 15-16, 209.

61. Ibid., 16-18.

62. V. L. Ménage, "Islamization of Anatolia," *Conversion to Islam*, ed. Levtzion, 65-66; T. W. Arnold, *The Preaching of Islam* (Lahore: Sh. Muhammad Ashraf, 1961), 262-65.

quests the Arabs were reluctant to relinquish privileges; so only select groups converted in mass—for example, the Iranian cavalry from the Sasanid army who consequently received the same pension as the Arab warriors. In these territories the upper classes initially retained their social status, property, and jobs as did the Brahmans in India. Thus only the lower classes tended to convert initially because to be second-class to the Arab Muslims was still superior to what they had. In some cases fief holders under the Ottomans in Anatolia and under the Mughals in India converted for the sake of their jobs, property, or finances. Others did so to escape discrimination under Caliphs like al-Mutawakkil (822-861).[63] In 1981 a mass conversion took place in South India among Tamil untouchables who also wanted to avoid discrimination.[64]

Conversion was facilitated by the *breakdown of religious structures*. This happened when the religious system was integrated with the defeated imperial system as was the case with the Greek Orthodox Church in the Byzantine Empire and the Zoroastrian hierarchy in the Sasanid Empire in contrast to the Hindu structure in India where only the political-military class was eliminated. The breakdown also occurred when local religious leaders were cut off from the centers of the faith as the Greek Orthodox for a time were cut off from Constantinople. This breakdown also resulted from ignorance, corruption, and divisions in the churches, coupled with government pressure.[65]

Preaching and *teaching* played their role—by the urban scholars (*'ulama*) in the central cities and by the Sufis on the frontiers as well. The religious schools (*madaris*) they established helped to create the ambiance in which reform could take place. Sometimes, as in West Africa, the scholars formed elite communities that were more influential in reaching the leaders than the masses. Other schools also focused on children—for example, the day schools (*langars*) and boarding schools (*pesantrens*) in Java.

Accommodation to folk beliefs and practices was very influential in animistic areas like Africa and Southeast Asia. Sufis in Africa and "holy men" in Anatolia, for example, engaged in various forms of magic—interpreting dreams, inducing rain, healing, and exorcising spirits.[66] The influence of the Muslims in places like Africa derived from their *superiority* in magic as well as literacy.

Islam was adopted for both political and social reasons. Tribal chiefs in Africa adopted it to *add legitimacy* to their claims or to provide the *cohesive force* to expand their domains to include other tribes. It provided integration

---

63. Levtzion, "Conversion and Muslim Domination," 23-29 and "Comparative Study of Islamization," and P. Hardy, "Modern European and Muslim Explorations of Conversion to Islam in South Asia: A preliminary Survey of the Literature," *Conversion to Islam*, ed. Levtzion, 9-10, 80-81.

64. Abdul Malik Mujahid, *Conversion to Islam: Untouchables' Strategy for Protest in India* (Chambersburg, Pa.: Anima, 1989); Wingate, "Two Tamil Villages."

65. Ménage, "Anatolia," 63-64; Levtzion, *Conversion to Islam*, 11-13.

66. Ménage, "Anatolia," 59-63; H. J. Fisher, "Dreams and Conversions in Black Africa," *Conversion to Islam*, ed. Levtzion, 217-35.

for all types of disorganized peoples as it had for trading networks. This integrating ability was a major reason why the hunter-gatherers and pastoral peoples on the frontiers of the Moghul Empire were able to make the transition into the agrarian-Muslim society as settled agriculturalists. Conversion on a mass scale was best carried out among such previously disorganized people.[67]

Conversion in Islam can be an individual or a group act that involves knowledge, right intention, repentance, faith, and submission to God, witnessed to by verbal confession in God and his Apostle and by righteous deeds; but forgiveness is contingent upon the will of God. It can be the result of the process started by a Muslim government or it can ideally result in the establishment of such a government, but normally it has involved accommodation and reform.

The act is expressed by the people of Kafiristan ("the place of the disbeliever"). When they submitted to Islam, their land was renamed Nooristan ("the place of Light"). Now they join other Muslims in praying, "Our Lord, perfect for us our light, and forgive us" (Quran 66:8).

---

67. Eaton, "Conversion to Islam in India," 111-23.

Chapter Three

Conversion in the Bible

Beverly Roberts Gaventa

Contemporary discussions of Christian conversion often refer to certain biblical motifs, especially those of the "Damascus road experience" and the "born again believer." For that reason alone it is important to consider the ways in which conversion is depicted in both the Hebrew scriptures and the New Testament. But to ask what the Bible says about conversion is also to encounter a number of challenges.

First among these challenges is the diversity of imagery used in the Bible with regard to conversion. Those who expect to find a systematic doctrine of conversion or a manual for conversion will be greatly disappointed. Instead, the Bible offers the prophetic call for Israel's return to God, proclamation of repentance from John the Baptist and Jesus, parables that implicitly demand the conversion of those who hear them. Paul's references to those who "turn to God," Luke's compelling stories of those who join "the Way," and the Johannine call for new birth. To collapse these stories into one story to which all Christian conversions must adhere would be to impoverish the text, reducing it to a limited and confining paradigm.

A second challenge that arises regarding biblical views of conversion stems from the nature of the biblical texts themselves. While conversion plays a minor role in the Hebrew scriptures, the New Testament is naturally concerned with conversion, since virtually all members of the earliest Christian communities entered those communities of faith through conversion. Nevertheless, the New Testament does not directly explain how conversion was understood in the earliest Christian generations. Modern Christians would like to know, for example, what *really* happened to change Paul from ardent persecutor of the church to ardent proclaimer of its gospel.

41

Or, to take another example, we would like to know what piece of history lies behind the story of the Ethiopian eunuch. The texts, however, address their own time and their own concerns, and ours are seldom included.

A third challenge arises from the unclarity surrounding the term "conversion," particularly conversion in the context of the Bible. Over a half-century ago, Arthur Darby Nock wrote what became a classic treatment of conversion in early Christianity. In *Conversion,* Nock argued that what distinguished early Christianity and Judaism alike from the religions of the rest of Greco-Roman antiquity was conversion, by which he meant

> the reorientation of the soul of an individual, his deliberate turning from indifference or from an earlier form of piety to another, a turning which implies a consciousness that a great change is involved, that the old was wrong and the new is right.[1]

The remaining religions of the ancient world expected no such unequivocal, absolute commitment from their followers. One did not convert to the worship of Isis, for example, by turning away from the service of all other deities. Instead, one added the service of Isis to that of other deities already being served. Nock termed this type of religious affiliation "adhesion."

This observation about the nature of early Judaism and early Christianity has endured,[2] and Nock's work remains required reading for anyone who wishes to understand the emergence of Christianity in the ancient world. Despite these important contributions, Nock's discussion of conversion does not provide a nuanced description that might assist us in understanding the varied forms of conversion that we find in the Bible.

Recent years have witnessed a variety of attempts to articulate a typology of conversion. In a previous study of conversion in the New Testament, I argued that conversion takes at least three forms: alternation, pendulum-like conversion, and transformation. An alternation is a conversion that develops naturally out of previously established life patterns. For example, when a Methodist marries a Presbyterian and joins the Presbyterian church, that individual is a convert, but one whose conversion has followed rather than disrupted already established convictions. Pendulum-like conversion is conversion in which the individual's past is rejected in favor of a newly chosen

---

1. A.D. Nock, *Conversion* (London: Oxford University Press, 1933), 7.

2. Ramsay MacMullen, in *Christianizing the Roman Empire* (New Haven: Yale University Press, 1984), argues against Nock's understanding of conversion. MacMullen amasses considerable evidence that many, probably the majority, of converts to Christianity from A.D. 100-400 were not whole-hearted devotees who came to Christianity "body and soul." MacMullen nevertheless acknowledges the distinctiveness of Christianity (like Judaism) in that converts to Christianity were expected to put aside all other forms of worship. The difference between the two studies appears to lie in the questions asked. Nock refers not to the status and attitude of individual converts but to the *expectations* surrounding conversion, while MacMullen looks to the religious experience of the masses, in which Christianity's appeal was often more pragmatic than theological.

religious system. Here we might take as an example a young person grow-ing up in a nominally Christian home in a North American context, who later leaves that setting for the Unification Church. That individual rejects his or her past for what is understood to be a radically different future. Transformation occurs when the past faith of an individual is not rejected, but reinterpreted in the new experience. A possible illustration of this kind of con-version is the experience of Martin Luther, whose reading of scripture caused him radically to reinterpret his past.[3] These are not, of course, mutually exclusive categories. Nor are they exhaustive of the kinds of conversion that occur. They may, nevertheless, be helpful as we examine the biblical texts, particularly as a reminder that not all conversion experiences are the same.

CONVERSION IN THE HEBREW BIBLE

The need to distinguish various kinds of conversion becomes readily apparent when we ask about the nature of conversion in the Hebrew Bible.[4] If the term applies only to those pendulum-like changes in which there is a rejection of the past (e.g., a Protestant converts to Buddhism), there is little that we can call conversion in the Hebrew Bible. That should not be sur-prising, given that the Hebrew Bible largely concerns the religious life of a people united by birth rather than selection. However, when the under-standing of conversion is broadened to include alternation and transforma-tion, more texts enter into the discussion.

While the religious traditions of Israel largely pertained to those who were born into the people of Israel, alongside the Israelites lived a number of other people, people identified in the Bible as strangers or sojourners (*gerim*). Israelites are obligated to treat them with justice and kindness, in memory of their own sojourn in Egypt (Ex 22:21, 23:9; Lev 19:33-34; Dt 10:19). While there are restrictions on the participation of these strangers in the life of Israel (Ex 12:43-45), they might offer sacrifice (Num 14:13-15), and those who had been circumcised could participate in the celebration of Passover (Ex 12:48-49). The texts give us little access to the thinking or convictions of this group, but it is reasonable to assume that they were attracted to the service of Israel's God because they saw such service in their neighbors, and over time it became familiar to them. That is, their behavior grew out of previous life-patterns; as such, it could be classified as an alternation.

A prominent example of alternation would be that of Ruth. In the well-known story of Ruth and Naomi, Ruth is a Moabite woman who is the widow of one of Naomi's sons. When Naomi decides to return to Judah, she asks both her daughters-in-law to stay behind and find husbands among their own

---

3. I discuss this typology in more detail in *From Darkness to Light: Aspects of Conversion in the New Testament* (Philadelphia: Fortress Press, 1986), 8-14. This chapter draws heavily on the work of that book.

4. I am grateful to my colleague, Walter Brueggemann, for his suggestions regarding this section.

people. Oprah does so, but Ruth insists on joining Naomi and her people and her God: "Your people shall be my people, and your God my God" (Ruth 1:16). The story suggests that Ruth acts out of loyalty to Naomi, and her choice of Naomi's God follows from that first loyalty, making Ruth's "conversion" an alternation. Both the favorable outcome of Ruth's decision and the preservation of the story itself testifies to the respect afforded the stranger who chose to serve Israel's God.

In addition to those passages that reflect alternation, a powerful motif in the Hebrew Bible is that of the prophetic call for the return (šûbḥ) of Israel to Yahweh.[5] One of the best examples of this call for the people's return appears in the poetic passage, Jeremiah 3:1-4:4.[6] The passage begins by comparing the people of Israel with a faithless wife who wishes to return to her husband but will not be allowed to do so (3:1). Nevertheless, Israel will be allowed to return:

> "Return, faithless Israel,
>   says the Lord.
> I will not look on you in anger,
> for I am merciful,
>   says the Lord;
> I will not be angry for ever.
> Only acknowledge your guilt,
>   that you rebelled against the Lord your God
> and scattered your favors among strangers under every green tree,
>   and that you have not obeyed my voice,
>   says the Lord" (Jer 3:12-13).

Already in this brief passage one key ingredient in Israel's return emerges. It is necessary that the people repent ("acknowledge your guilt"). This repentance must be sincere, as the final verses of the poem make clear: "Circumcise yourselves to the Lord, remove the foreskin of your hearts" (Jer 4:4a).[7] True repentance involves the return to God, the removal of abominations, and the fidelity to truth, justice, and righteousness (4:1-4). Only then will Yahweh enter into a renewed relationship with Israel.[8] Nevertheless, even the ability of Israel to return to Yahweh is also a gift from Yahweh, as 3:22 indicates: "Return, O faithless sons, I will heal your faithlessness."

Isaiah 55 offers another prominent example of the theme of Israel's return. Here, reflecting Deutero-Isaiah's exilic setting, which calls forth assurances

---

5. On this word, see William L. Holladay, *The Root šûbḥ in the Old Testament* (Leiden: E.J. Brill, 1958).

6. Parts of this passage are thought to have come from a later redaction. See John Bright, *Jeremiah* (Anchor Bible; New York: Doubleday, 1965), 25-27.

7. Cf. Hosea 6:1-6.

8. Walter Brueggemann, *To Pluck Up, To Tear Down* (Grand Rapids, Mich.: Eerdmans, 1988), 46-47.

of hope and comfort, we find both the insistence that Israel return and the promise of God's generosity:

"Ho, every one who thirsts,
    come to the waters;
and he who has no money,
    come, buy and eat!" (Isa 55:1).

The one who returns to the Lord will find mercy and abundant pardon (Isa 55:7),

"For my thoughts are not your thoughts,
    neither are your ways my ways, says the Lord.
For as the heavens are higher than the earth,
    so are my ways higher than your ways
    and my thoughts than your thoughts" (Isa 55:8-9).

The comfort Deutero-Isaiah offers to Israel derives from knowing that God's promises may be trusted for God's power is greater than what human beings can imagine. Israel may trust in God's mercy.[9]

Because of the radical nature of the repentance being urged in these and similar passages, they may be said to invoke the "transformation" of the people. The people of Israel can only return to Yahweh when they reinterpret their past, seeing in it their guilt and God's sustaining power. In that sense, these texts and others like them represent a kind of conversion. Certain elements in them, for example, the reliance on God's power, the insistence on a reformed ethic, and the radical understanding of "turning" have their counterparts in the New Testament as well.

CONVERSION IN THE NEW TESTAMENT

The earlier discussion of types of conversion becomes especially pertinent when examining conversion in the New Testament. For example, while it is conventional to speak of the "conversion" of Paul, many New Testament scholars argue that the term is misleading since Paul does not "leave" Judaism and "join" Christianity. Indeed, Paul continues to speak of himself as a Jew and, in any case, the term Christianity is anachronistic. Instead of referring to Paul as a convert, it is argued, we should speak of his "calling."

What is at stake in this discussion is our understanding of what a conversion involves. If conversion is a change from one religion to another, then it is accurate to say that Paul did not have a conversion. But perhaps the problem is with our definition of conversion, and we have defined the term too narrowly. Using the typology I suggested earlier, we might regard Paul as having experienced a particular type of conversion, namely a transfor-

9. Claus Westermann, *Isaiah 40-66* (Philadelphia: Westminster Press, 1969), 290-91.

mation. As we examine several prominent conversion accounts below, it will be important to ask how they read in relationship to the typologies above.

One further issue needs comment before we turn to the texts themselves, and that is the customary discussion of conversion by means of a word-study. Many discussions of conversion in the New Testament focus primarily on the Greek words we translate as "repent" (*metanoun*) or "convert" (*epistrephein*) and see in those terms a key to early Christian understandings of conversion. The problem with this approach is that these terms are actually used only a limited number of times in the New Testament. More important, they appear in quite conventional ways, that is, in ways that are not different from what we would find in a variety of other religious traditions. What is important, then, is not what these specific words conjure up but in what settings they are found. Who is said to be converted, under what circumstances, and with what results? These sorts of questions shed far more light on conversion in the Bible than do examinations of single words or word-groups.

1. John the Baptist. All of the canonical gospels contain narratives about John the Baptist and his perceived role as forerunner of Jesus. While these accounts vary significantly from one another, common to the accounts in the synoptic gospels is the call of John for repentance. This call for repentance, like the prophetic claims discussed above, is an implicit call for conversion. John does not ask people to change their religious affiliation (alternation), but he does call for a radical change in perspective and behavior (transformation). An examination of the preaching of John will clarify this form of conversion.

In what may be the earliest account of John's activity, that found in Mark 1, we read that he preached "a baptism of repentance for the forgiveness of sins" (Mk 1:4). Mark shows little interest in the content of John's preaching, moving instead to John's role as the one who announces Jesus' coming and baptizes him. Nevertheless, even in this short passage John is clearly identified as one whose role is to call for repentance.

The Matthean and Lukan gospels show more interest in the content of John's preaching,[10] particularly as that preaching becomes polemical:

> You brood of vipers! Who warned you to flee from the wrath to come? Bear fruit that befits repentance, and do not presume to say to yourselves, "We have Abraham as our father"; for I tell you, God is able from these stones to raise up children to Abraham. Even now the axe is laid to the root of the trees; every tree therefore that does not bear good fruit is cut down and thrown into the fire" (Mt 3:7-10; cf. parallel in Lk 3:7-9, with expansion in 3:10-13).

---

10. Given the close parallels between Mt 3:7-9 and Lk 3:7-10, this material probably was preserved in Q, a hypothetical source which contained largely teachings of Jesus and was used by Matthew and Luke, but not by Mark. For a brief introduction to Q, see the article, "Q,"in *Harper's Bible Dictionary* (New York: Harper & Row, 1985), 846.

In common with the prophetic tradition we examined in Jeremiah and Isaiah, John's call for repentance specifies that repentance results in good deeds. Also like the prophetic tradition, John places that call within an eschatological framework; for those who do not heed the call there is judgment.

While our information about John the Baptist is exceedingly slender, the texts do understand him to be a preacher of repentance in thought and deed, a repentance that we might also call transformation. It is likely that there were operating in Hellenistic Judaism numerous such figures who called for repentance and renewal. Because of the connection between John and Jesus, we know John far better than any of the others who may have been on the scene.

2. The Parables of Jesus. One of the ways in which the gospels connect John the Baptist and Jesus is in their preaching of repentance. Jesus's preaching is characterized as a preaching about the kingdom of God, a preaching that culminates in the call for repentance, although the gospels give us little indication what else might have been included in that call for repentance. Instead, what the gospels most often tell us about Jesus's teaching is that he taught in parables. The parables do not, of course, call for conversion or narrate stories about conversion. Within individual parables, however, we find implicit the claim that the awareness of the nearness of the kingdom of God has to do with a changed (transformed) understanding of God and God's relationship with humankind.[11]

A few examples will suffice to illustrate this point. Among the briefest of the parables of Jesus is that found in Matthew 13:44: "The kingdom of heaven is like treasure hidden in a field, which a man found and covered up; then in his joy he goes and sells all that he has and buys that field."[12] The kingdom of heaven is of such importance that it warrants this radical response, in which an individual will risk everything in order to lay claim to the kingdom. Several of the parables of Jesus narrate events in which people's expectations are overturned. Here the audience is challenged, by means of the story, to see God's actions and God's work in a different way. For example, the parable of the Prodigal Son (Lk 15:11-32) shows a father acting in a way that would have been shocking to customs of the day. An even better example is the parable of the Workers in the Vineyard (Mt. 20:1-16), which explicitly states that the owner has the right to act in a way that runs against the expectations of the laborers. None of these parables explicitly narrates a conversion or call for conversion, but they do challenge conventional understandings of who God is and how God acts in the world.

3. Conversion in the Letters of Paul. While countless numbers of Christians and non-Christians alike know Paul best for his conversion from enemy of the church to its ardent apostle, what many identify as the story of Paul's conversion comes from Luke's story in the Acts of the Apostles rather than

---

11. For an introduction to some contemporary work on the parables of Jesus, see "Parables," in *Harper's Bible Dictionary* (New York: Harper & Row, 1985), 747-49.

12. See the parallel in Gospel of Thomas 109.

from Paul's own letters.[13] It is important that we take these two sources, Paul's letters and Acts, separately, for they cast different lights on this aspect of Paul's life. In connection with the letters, we will also ask how Paul refers to, not simply his own conversion, but that of other Christians as well.[14]

What is probably most striking about this question in Paul's letters is how little he has to say. For those who come expecting a story about a miraculous intervention during a journey to Damascus, the disappointment will be keen. In fact, only a few times does Paul refer to what we call his conversion, and in all those cases his comments are brief and allusive. What Paul does say indicates that he understood himself to have been a good and loyal Jew (Phil 3:5-6) who surpassed the devotion even of his peers (Gal 1:14). Despite this sense of achievement, his experience of the risen Lord (1 Cor 9:1-2, 15:8-10) precipitated in Paul a radical change (Phil 3:7), and contained within that change was Paul's call as an apostle (Gal 1:15-16; 1 Cor 9:1-2, 15:8-10).

Paul's comments create the impression that the change he experienced was sudden and unexpected, although he never says that directly. Instead, this impression emerges because of the abrupt shifts that occur when Paul moves from describing his earlier life to speaking of his call (Gal 1:11-17, Phil 3:2-17). More important than the time period in which this change occurred is its character. What Paul describes may be best understood as a "cognitive shift," or what I have termed above a transformation. Both before and after this transformation, Paul understood himself to be a good Jew, one who maintained the important traditions of Israel. The fact that he employs prophetic imagery in connection with his call (cf. Gal 1:15 with Isa 49:1 and Jer 1:5) indicates that he still sees himself within that tradition. What changed, however, were Paul's values and commitments. He experienced a radical change in his understanding of what made his life worthwhile or valuable, as we can see in Philippians 3:8: "Indeed, I count everything as loss . . ." At the center of this change, however, was not Paul's self-understanding but his new understanding of Jesus as the Christ, the Messiah (Phil 3:7-11). It was this recognition that forced Paul to become an apostle and to understand himself to be "in Christ."

It would be a serious misreading of Paul to isolate this transformation, seeing it as a private event distinct from the rest of his understanding of the gospel. Indeed, Paul's few references to his transformation all have as their aim the instruction of believers, not the glorification of Paul's own private experience. He expected believers in the churches he founded to understand that they, as he, had been called from unworthiness to worthiness (1 Cor 1:26-31). Paul concludes his comments about his transformation in Philippians 3 by asking the audience to imitate him (3:17).

---

13. I use the term "conversion" here because of its convenience, with full awareness that many scholars are skeptical about referring to Paul as having had a "conversion." Below I shall attempt to address this issue.

14. There are many scholarly treatments of this topic. For a review of some issues in the debate, see Gaventa, *From Darkness to Light*, 17-21.

In addition to the comments Paul makes about his own transformation, Paul also refers to the conversions of those Christians he addresses. Here again it may be surprising to see how little Paul says about the nature or process of conversion. Nevertheless, the ways in which Paul refers to conversion provide us with an important glimpse into his understanding of the gospel.

When Paul refers to the beginning of faith in Jesus Christ in the life of believers, he generally speaks of God's action of calling (1 Cor 1:2; Gal 1:6), purchasing (1 Cor 6:20, 7:23), granting grace (Rom 3:21-26), liberating (Rom 6:17-18), rather than to a human action of converting or turning. This reflects Paul's conviction that God takes the initiative with believers; God, in fact, is the one who causes believers to turn to God.

Most often, the human response to this action of God is referred to as faith or belief (Rom 13:11), which results in an acknowledgment of God's new creation (Gal 6:15, 2 Cor 5:17) and a radical transformation or renewal which is itself a gift of God (Rom 12:1-2). Despite the fact that Paul understands this transformation to be real and significant, it is never a finished or completed event but is ongoing.[15]

While Paul speaks to the calling and transformation of the individual, he does not address the situation of the individual in isolation from the community of faith. Transformation involves entering a relationship with other believers, a relationship characterized by interdependence. For example, in Romans 15:1-7 Paul exhorts believers to act for the upbuilding of the entire fellowship, and in Galatians 6:1-6 he urges that believers "bear one another's burdens." These ethical exhortations are part and parcel of the individual transformation that Paul envisions as a part of the calling of Christ.[16]

4. Conversion in the Acts of the Apostles. Luke's second volume[17] begins with the risen Lord's promise that the apostles will be witnesses "in Jerusalem and in all Judea and Samaria and to the end of the earth" (Acts 1:8). The events of Pentecost provide the initial fulfillment of this promise, since Peter there acts as a witness and the gathered crowd comes from "every nation under heaven." When, in response to Peter's sermon, the crowd asks what they should do, Peter says, "Repent, and be baptized every one of you in the name of Jesus Christ for the forgiveness of your sins; and you shall receive the gift of the Holy Spirit" (2:38). Perhaps because of the clarity and simplicity of Peter's response, and perhaps because of the large number of people who are reported to have been baptized on that occasion, Acts 2:38 is often regarded as Luke's "theory" of conversion. That is, for Luke, conversion consists

---

15. *Metamorphousthe* in Romans 12:2 translates literally as "[you] be being transformed," indicating that the transformation is ongoing. Notice also that Paul indicates that his own transformation continues (Phil 3:12).

16. On the admonition in Galatians 6:1-6, see Richard B. Hays, "Christology and Ethics in Galatians: The Law of Christ," *CBQ* 49 (1987): 268-90.

17. The overwhelming scholarly consensus is that the gospel of Luke and the Acts of the Apostles were written by the same individual. Here I follow convention in referring to that author as "Luke," without assuming that Luke was either a traveling companion of Paul or a physician.

of repentance, baptism, and the seal of that conversion in the gift of the Holy Spirit. This is an attractive pattern of conversion, because the early chapters of Acts follow it nicely and because Luke elsewhere gives us no "doctrine" of conversion. The problem with reading 2:38 as Luke's theory of conversion emerges, however, when we reach the stories of conversion in Acts 8-10 and find that none of those stories conforms to the pattern of 2:38.

In Acts 8-10 Luke tells three extended stories about the conversions of individuals. He begins with the conversion of the Ethiopian eunuch (Acts 8:26-40), a figure who conjures up mysterious, even exotic, associations for Luke's audience.[18] The eunuch does come from the other end of Luke's world, and his status and prestige, together with his interest in Jerusalem, make him a very positive figure in Luke's story. He represents all those from the ends of the earth who will receive the gospel. Indeed, one of the remarkable features of the story is that the eunuch does not passively receive the gospel but reaches out to grasp it (see 8:34, 37).

The story of the conversion of Saul follows immediately upon that of the eunuch, and the two stories have certain features in common. In each, God or the Spirit directs the action, each occurs in the context of travel, and each involves the mediation of another figure (Philip, Ananias). The stories also differ from one another in important ways, however. Saul is not, as is the eunuch, a willing hearer of the good news. Ananias does not silently respond to the strange instructions he receives (contrast with Philip in 8:27). These dissimilarities underscore Luke's portrayal of Saul as the church's enemy (see Acts 8:1-4 and 9:1-2).[19] Unlike either the Ethiopian or Cornelius, Saul is a Jew, but he is a Jew who has made himself the enemy of the gospel. Luke uses that feature of the story to underscore the power of the gospel even over the enemies of the church.

This story is so significant for Luke that he narrated it not only in Chapter 9 but again in Chapter 22 and in Chapter 26. In the second account, which introduces Paul's defense speeches in Jerusalem, Paul describes himself as a Jew who has remained loyal to the "God of our fathers," but who has been called by that God as a witness to all people. In the third account, in Chapter 26, Paul again defends himself, this time by arguing that his persecutors are simply acting on an inner-Jewish conflict. This account also emphasizes that Paul's conversion was a call to witness (26:16-18). What we have in the three accounts is Luke's telling of the story in three different ways, each of which he shapes to fit the larger narrative context.

Luke follows the initial story of Saul's conversion with brief accounts of the healing of Aeneas (9:32-35) and the raising of Dorcas (9:36-43), concluding each with the notice that many believed in the Lord. Luke then turns to the most elaborate of all his conversion stories, that of Cornelius and Peter.

Again in this story there are threads that repeat themselves from the sto-

---

18. See Gaventa, *From Darkness to Light*, 98-107.
19. Ibid., 54-67.

ries of the Ethiopian and of Saul. The double visions of Ananias and Saul (9:10-12) recur in the double visions of Peter and Cornelius (10:1-6, 9-16). Here also a representative of the church protests the task set before him (10:14-16). The inclusion of Cornelius, who is plainly identified as a gentile, makes explicit the inclusion at which the conversion of the Ethiopian eunuch only hinted. And Peter is forced to acknowledge, "Truly I perceive that God shows no partiality, but in every nation any one who fears him and does what is right is acceptable to him" (10:34-35). In this important account, both Cornelius and Peter are converted, since Peter must change his own perspective in order to see what God is doing in and through Cornelius.

While these stories do not contain a systematic treatment of conversion, they do reveal something about Luke's view of conversion. Clearly Luke does not present any of these stories as the typical or ideal account of conversion. Each of these individual converts stands for some larger group or some element in Luke's narrative. No single conversion, not even that dramatic account of the conversions at Pentecost, establishes a pattern that later believers follow or that later sermons employ as a pattern.

What this leads us to see is that, for Luke, conversion is not an end in itself. Instead, conversions are stories about beginnings: Pentecost begins the community of believers at Jerusalem; the story of Saul begins his mission among the gentiles; the story of Cornelius begins the church's acceptance of gentiles; Luke tells about conversions as part of the development of the church, not in order to glorify individual converts or their experiences.

While Luke tells the stories of individual converts, he does not tell them as individualistic events. That is, they do not take place apart from the larger community of faith. When Luke tells of the conversion of large numbers of people, he follows those accounts with reports of the fellowship among believers (2:43-47). The Ethiopian, Saul, and Cornelius all experience the mediation of an individual who represents the church as a whole. Even Saul, isolated as he seems to be by his blindness, is brought into the community first by Ananias and later by Barnabas.

Conversion is, for Luke, a gift that comes from God, who initiates all of the conversions. While it is customary to speak of the mission *of* the church, in Luke's story it is God who has a mission *for* the church. God directs events in the stories of the conversions of individuals, and God likewise creates the occasions that lead to the conversions of the masses. Conversion, for Luke, is not an act of the church nor an act of the convert, but an act of God.

5. The Motif of New Birth. While some forms of contemporary Christianity often speak of converts as "born again," the motif of new life appears in the New Testament only in the gospel and epistles of John and in 1 Peter.[20] The

---

20. See also Titus 3:5. The synoptic tradition preserves in Mark 10:15, Matthew 18:3, and Luke 18:17 a saying that may be related to John 3:3. On the connection between the two, see R.E. Brown, *The Gospel According to John I-XII* (Garden City, N.Y.: Doubleday, 1966), 143-44.

motif is important in these texts, however, because in each instance it bears some key elements in the author's understanding of Christian faith.

Before turning to the texts themselves, it is important to note that concepts of new birth and new life do not originate with these New Testaments texts. References to being or becoming God's children occur in postexilic Judaism as well as in pagan writers. For example, the Jewish writer Philo refers to the life of the soul after death (*paliggenesia*, in *On the Cherubim*, 114), and the Talmud describes a proselyte to Judaism as a"child just born" (b. Yebam. 22a).[21] It appears that imagery of birth and renewal was (and is) a conventional way of referring to conversion. The significant question to ask regarding its use in the New Testament is how the imagery is understood there.

The best known reference to new birth occurs, of course, in the story of Jesus' conversation with Nicodemus in John 3. Having been approached by Nicodemus at night, Jesus says, "Truly, truly, I say to you, unless one is born anew (*gennēthe anōthen*) he cannot see the kingdom of God" (3:13). The difficulty with this translation is that the Greek word *anōthen*, here translated as "anew," has two meanings, and the passage turns on the double entendre created by these two meanings. *anōthen* means both "from above" (cf. James 1:17, 3:15) and "again" (cf. Gal. 4:9). While Nicodemus's response interprets Jesus' statement to mean that one must literally be born again, it is clear that the Johannine Jesus means that one is to be born "from above" (cf. 3:31, 19:11).[22]

Birth "from above," when seen within the larger context of the Johannine gospel, means several things. First, birth from above implies discontinuity in the life of the one who receives this birth. The individual receives not merely an "improved" life but one that has a new origin, an origin in the Spirit. John's gospel elsewhere distinguishes between "this world" and that which is above (8:23-24) and between light/sight and darkness (8:12, 9:39). All of these distinctions enhance the sense that a radical discontinuity enters the life of the individual who is born "from above." Second, the one who is born spiritually enters into a relationship with Jesus. John later describes at some length the close nature of the relationship between Jesus and those who believe in him (e.g., 15:1-7, 15:18-19, 17:6-10). To be born "from above" is to belong to Jesus. Third, the one who is born *anōthen* is the recipient of a new spirit. As the newborn baby receives breath (*pneuma*), so the newly born believer receives spirit (*pneuma*) (as do the disciples following the resurrection of Jesus [20:22]).

When this motif is placed within the context of the gospel as a whole, it is clear that the new birth is corporate in nature rather than private or individualistic. In Jesus' statement to Nicodemus, "You must be born again," the "you" in the Greek is plural rather than singular, suggesting that it is not Nicodemus alone who must receive the new birth, but all must be so born.

---

21. For further discussion of this motif outside the Bible, see Gaventa, *From Darkness to Light*, 133-35, and the literature cited there.

22. See Gaventa, *From Darkness to Light*, 133-35, and the literature cited there.

Even in John 3:5 the reference to baptism by water suggests that one is born into the community of the baptized. In the later discourses of Jesus and in the Johannine epistles, emphasis is placed on the fellowship of those who believe in Jesus, who belong both to him and to one another (John 17; 1 John 4:7-11).

New birth also involves a new life, that is to say, there is an ethical component in this new birth. Following Jesus' conversation with Nicodemus, the discourse ends with the distinction between those whose deeds are evil and those who belong to the light, whose deeds are light (3:19-21). Those who belong to Jesus act in such a way as to produce the good (15:1-12).

While the use of the language of new birth in 1 Peter (1:3-5, 1:14, 1:23, 2:2) differs in some ways from what is found in the Johannine literature, there are important common elements as well. One of the important tasks of 1 Peter is to create a social boundary around the community. Recent scholarship indicates that this letter addresses a group of believers who face the attractive possibility of conforming themselves to the ways of the larger gentile world, and in response the author emphasizes the distinctiveness of this new community (a chosen race [2:9], a household of God [4:17]).[23]

In this context new birth refers not only to the time of one's conversion but also refers to the move a believer makes into the boundaries of the new community. Theologically speaking, new birth in 1 Peter refers to soteriology, to the promise that salvation belongs *in the future* to those who have been reborn (1:5, 1:13, 2:2-3). As in the Johannine use of the image, also in 1 Peter new birth has ethical implications. The writer calls on the community to be holy in its conduct (1:14-15) and to act out of love (1:22-23). For the writer of 1 Peter, to be born anew means that one enters into a new community which is grounded in God's action and which is able to live confidently even in a social setting that is constantly threatening.

CONCLUSION

At the outset of this discussion, I suggested that there are several different types of conversion that appear within the pages of the Bible: alternation, pendulum-like conversion, and transformation. It will be helpful now to review the ways in which each of these kinds of conversion occur in the Bible.

Alternation, the conversion that may be described as a change that continues an earlier behavior pattern, appears only infrequently in the Bible. It is best illustrated in the behavior of Ruth in the Hebrew Bible. In the New Testament, a good example of alternation would be the Ethiopian eunuch, who already worships the God of Israel and who is eager for what Philip has to say to him. Cornelius offers yet another example of conversion, since Cornelius is portrayed, even before his conversion, as a devout believer

---

23. David L. Balch, *Let Wives Be Submissive: The Domestic Code in 1 Peter* (Chico, Calif.: Scholars Press, 1981); John H. Elliott, *A Home for the Homeless: A Sociological Exegesis of 1 Peter, Its Situation and Strategy* (Philadelphia: Fortress Press, 1981).

whose conversion is a natural consequence of his own piety.

The Hebrew Bible gives us little that might be called pendulum-like conversion, in which the past is rejected for a new present and future. In the New Testament, this form of conversion may be seen in Luke's story of the conversion of Saul in Acts 9. There the contrast between the persecutor who storms off to Damascus and the preacher who emerges at the end of the account and dominates the story, and Saul's past is utterly lost in his new identity as witness. While less dramatically explained, the motif of new birth in John's gospel and in 1 Peter also assumes a radical discontinuity between past and present.

Both in the Hebrew Bible and in the New Testament the dominant understanding of conversion is that of transformation. The prophetic call for Israel to return to Yahweh is a call for Israel to be transformed by repentance and by the very power of God; the same may be said of John the Baptist's preaching and also of Jesus' teaching through parables. The old ways of being are to be reshaped by God's healing power. In a similar way, Paul's comments about his own conversion reflect the awareness that the revelation he received (Gal 1:11) caused him not to reject but to reinterpret both his past and his future.

Chapter 4

Conversion in Judaism

Arthur F. Glasser

INTRODUCTION

When the Israelites left Egypt under the leadership of Moses, the record states that "a mixed multitude also went up with them" (Ex 12:38). This mixed multitude consisted of those who seized the opportunity to leave Egypt by joining the Israelites but without having rootage in the religious traditions of the larger community. Nor did they share in any real commitment to the God who made the Exodus possible. They subsequently became the occasion for dissension and sin within Israel (e.g., Num 11:4).

Actually, even among the Israelites themselves there were two types of people, religiously speaking. There were the committed and the nominal. Whereas at the time of the Exodus deliverance all the Israelite households actively participated in killing a passover lamb, marking their doorposts and lintel with its blood, and thereby escaping the judgment of God (Ex 12:1-51), no one would presume to claim that at that time all were in vital relationship and spiritual communion with the living God. This dual pattern becomes apparent again and again when we review Israel's subsequent history.

Although Israel was an elect nation, only a portion of the people really believed in God. A case in point: the reaction of the people to the reports of the twelve men Moses sent to spy out the land of Canaan. Within the twelve there were ten whose report was so negative and so totally accepted by the people that God said to Moses: "How long will this people despise me? And how long will they not believe in me?" (Num 14:11). In contrast, he found in Caleb "a different spirit" and commended him for his wholehearted obedience (14:24). Admittedly, one would not want to superimpose such New Testament categories as "saved" or "lost" on these particular Israelites, but it would be unwarranted to assume that no essential difference existed among them at that moment in their history. We must keep in mind that God made a separation within Israel when he denied entrance to the land to the great majority (Num 14:26-35).

Furthermore, we find in the New Testament this same division between those who follow the Lord and those who do not. In his day Jesus Christ pointedly taught that one can only discern the true from the nominal "by their fruits" (Mt 7:16-20). The true will reflect God-centeredness, ethical consistency, and social concern. Even so, in the final analysis only the Lord knows those who are truly his (Num 16:5; 2 Ti 2:19). Suffice it to say that the problem of nominality has plagued the church throughout her long history, and particularly in our day.

"CONVERSION": THE HEBREW PROPHETS AS EVANGELISTS

When God made a covenant with Abraham and his posterity via Isaac and Jacob and later supplemented it with a covenant at Sinai with the Israelites whom he had just delivered from the Egyptian oppression, the dominant intent of his action was to constitute them as a people (nation) and to pledge that his covenant with them would be eternal (Ex 19:5,6). He would never abrogate it. In response the Israelites freely accepted his terms and pledged to do all in their power to keep them (Ex 19:8). Even so, both God and they soon realized that they would fail to obey his law (e.g., Ex 32—the incident of the Golden Calf). The people then began to realize for the first time that the Sinaitic legislation made gracious provision via priesthood and sacrifice for the nation and for individuals within it to repair their corporate or personal violations of the covenant and to reaffirm its continuity as the basis of God's dealings with them. Although individual Israelites might completely repudiate the covenant and give no allegiance to Yahweh, the divine intent was that it be everlasting (Gen 17:7,13,19). To seal this fact God pledged that the people of Israel would never cease to exist (Jer 31:35-37). They are still with us today!

Furthermore, God also provided a means whereby the people of Israel might be helped to resist the temptation to nominality and covenant violation. Beginning with Moses (Dt 34:10) he brought forth an order of prophets to address the nation while the Hebrew canon was in process of development. The prophets were men and women whom he called and equipped to make known his true nature and character and to exercise a ministry of spiritual renewal among the people. In a very real sense they were the evangelists/revivalists of Israel. They exposed the sinfulness of nominality and all violations of the covenant. They warned of divine retribution, won people to repentance, and guided the penitent in the ways of righteousness. They constantly proclaimed that the highest good was the experiential knowledge of

God, and they exhorted the Israelites to turn to him for relationship and fellowship. God was not impossible to please.

But there first had to be repentance, then faith, expressed by an ongoing pattern of obedience. Sin had to be acknowledged and sorrow for it expressed. Only then would God in grace receive them. When the Hebrew canon was closing, the prophetic order waned and finally ceased altogether (c. 400 B.C.?). In the centuries that followed, God continued this prophetic ministry and spoke to the people by his Spirit through their reflection on his written Word.

During this long period the key thrust of the prophetic ministry whether vocal or written focused on the word *šûbh*: "to turn, return."[1] Since the prophets sought to call the Israelites to vital faith and trust in God, their ministry was solidly based on what he had initially promised to the Patriarchs, achieved by the Exodus deliverance, and communicated in the Sinaitic covenant. As far as the prophets were concerned, it was this total Torah—the record of the divine redemptive activity on Israel's behalf—that "converted" or "revived" the soul (Ps 19:7).

The tragedy, of course, was the sinfulness and waywardness of the Israelites. Whereas on occasion they might honor God with their lips, their hearts were invariably far from him (Is 29:13; Ez 33:31). Indeed, more often than not, their waywardness led to outright idolatry (Jer 50:38; Hos 4:17). The prophetic corrective was particularly revealed on that occasion when Elijah challenged the worship of Baal, exposed the double-mindedness of the people, and affirmed that God would bless their land with rain, if only they turned their hearts back to him (1 Kgs 18:20-45).

Indeed, this preaching of the need for "turning" is widespread throughout the historic period covered by the Hebrew Bible. God repeatedly called upon his people to "rend their hearts," to "turn again," to "be converted." No Jewish person today who is at all familiar with the Bible can possibly take offense at such language as long as the word "convert" does not imply the total rejection of one's cultural heritage to embrace an entirely new religious allegiance.

The wistful appeal God made through Malachi is normative: "Return to me, and I will return to you" (3:7). In this context the Israelites were being urged to reaffirm the religious heritage of their people and "seek" the Lord personally (Ps 27:8). Malachi was calling them to turn to the one who could bring to fullness their nominal faith in God. It is apparent from even a cursory review of the Hebrew Bible that as a result of the ministry of the prophets, spiritual Israel was always clearly differentiated from political Israel. Zephaniah spoke of this distinction when he appealed:

---

1. For a detailed study of the covenantal use of *šûbh* consult *The Root šûbh in the Old Testament* by William L. Holladay (Leiden: E.J. Brill, 1958). Its key meaning, "a change of loyalty on the part of Israel or God, each for the other" (p.2). Also "having moved in a particular direction , to move thereupon in the opposite direction, the implication being (unless there is evidence to the contrary) that one will arrive again at the initial point of departure" (p.53).

Seek the Lord, all you humble of the land, who do his commands; seek righteousness, seek humility; perhaps you may be hidden on the day of the wrath of the Lord. . . . I will remove from your midst your proudly exultant ones. . . . I will leave in the midst of you a people humble and lowly. They shall seek refuge in the name of the Lord (2:3; 3:11,12).

The "humble of the land" to whom Zephaniah addressed his message are occasionally referred to as the believing "remnant" within Israel. When the word "remnant" first appeared in the Hebrew Bible, it did not have this theological significance, rather, it only had the meaning of "survivors." Despite the most severe judgments that Yahweh allowed to fall on his people because of their sins, there would always be those who survived, thus enabling the purpose he had for Israel to move forward (Is 43:3,4). Then, one finds a few passages that introduce the concept of a believing people within the nation, virtually an *ecclesiola in ecclesia* (Is 6:13; 10:20-23; 28:5; Mi 5:7). It is this thought that Paul seizes in his exploration on the ongoing role of Israel in God's redemptive purpose for Israel herself and the gentile nations (Rom 11). His whole argument turns on the distinction made earlier in this epistle between nominal Israelites and the believing company of Abraham's true descendants in the nation:

He is not a real Jew who is one outwardly, nor is true circumcision something external and physical. He is a Jew who is one inwardly, and real circumcision is a matter of the heart, spiritual and not literal. His praise is not from men but from God (Rom 2:28,29).

POSTEXILIC JUDAISM: THE SECOND TEMPLE

We now turn to the subject of Judaism and its relation to conversion. At the outset it is necessary to review the manner in which Jewish scholars define "Judaism." In his writings, *Judaisms and Their Messiahs at the Turn of the Christian Era*, Jacob Neusner frequently confronts us with the various Judaisms that emerged and flourished during the period of the Second Temple (from Cyrus the Persian through the Greek period and until its destruction in A.D. 70 by the Romans).[2] In general terms, Judaism represents the dynamic reconceptualization of the religion of ancient Israel into forms that were regarded as congenial to the varied diasporal experience of the Jewish people.

Nebuchadnezzar's earlier destruction of the Temple and Jerusalem, his reduction of the cities of Judah to rubble, and his deportation of the leadership segment of the people to Babylon provoked a massive spiritual crisis among those who survived. All knew that Israel's sins against God, particularly its idolatry, had brought this calamity to their nation (2 Ch 36:5-21;

2. Jacob Neusner, *Judaisms and Their Messiahs at the Turn of the Christian Era* (Cambridge: Cambridge University Press, 1987), ix-xiv.

Amos 5:25-27). The prophets who had predicted this judgment had been terribly vindicated.

But what were the exiles in Babylon to do? Jeremiah was explicit. He encouraged them to make Babylon a more decent place through their presence and prayers. Furthermore, provision should be made for the ongoing of the race during its seventy-year removal from the land they had so grievously abused (29:4-14). At its end God, through a surprisingly benevolent Cyrus, urged them to return to Judah and reestablish its theocratic essence by rebuilding the Temple and reinstituting its worship.

Strangely, not all were willing to rise to this exciting though demanding challenge. Those who chose to remain in the midst of Babylonian, Persian, and Grecian civilizations as a diasporal people were obliged to develop religious forms of Judaism that were devoid of priests and sacrifices as they scattered throughout the Middle East and the Mediterranean basin. But whether the Jewish people lived in the land of Israel or in the surrounding nations, they all constantly faced the terrible possibility of becoming assimilated by the pagan peoples surrounding their minority communities. Inevitably, they turned inward and structured their religious and cultural life to prevent this.

Those who returned to the land and rebuilt the Temple were in the vanguard of efforts to model a pattern of life that reflected continuity with the past and salutary benefit from the failure of their fathers to take the demands of the covenant to heart. It was the early reform of Ezra (Ezr 7:6-10; Neh 8:1-10:39) that convinced them of the primacy of the Pentateuch. They made it the divinely appointed basis for a distinct style of life and thought that has shaped Orthodox Judaism ever since. Its object was to make every aspect of daily life immune to gentile influence. This precipitated the development of an oral tradition of additional rules whereby obedience to the Law would be fully secured. National pride was promoted, non-Jews were regarded with contempt, and all Jewish communities tended to draw ever more tightly within themselves. The term "Jew" gained precise definition: "Every Jewish child is a Jew by birth." The yoke of the Law was accepted by one and all. All sought to affirm their Jewishness by obeying and fulfilling the Sinaitic law and the burdensome "Oral Law," since this was regarded as the only way to "win the divine favor." Inevitably, human limitations prevented even the most zealous from achieving this goal (Ecc 7:20). In fact, all the people knew themselves to be liable to divine punishment and hence facing deprivation of "the bliss of God's presence" (Is 59:2). What were they to do? They could only presume that God's "compassion for human weakness" had provided in the Law the means whereby the penitents could "find their way back to the divine source—the way of repentance." This heightened their preoccupation with legal rectitude.[3]

---

3. The forms of Judaism that emerged among diasporal Jews all tended to downplay the Temple, its priests, and the sacrificial system. This emphasis was later to characterize the unified Judaism that was developed following the destruction of the Second Temple (A.D. 70).

But not all allowed themselves to be trapped in this demanding legalism. Not a few began to drift into nominality and became indifferent to the Law. This precipitated the emergence of an inner group, the "Hasidim." They saw themselves as the preservers of the Law, both in its written form (the Pentateuch) and in its oral form: the growing "tradition" of supplementary legislation to guarantee obedience to God. Inevitably, there were Jews who rejected this fiction that an oral law was also given by God to Moses at Sinai. They appealed to Exodus 24:4 with its statement that Moses recorded "*all* the words of the law." It is not without reason that Neusner concludes that during this period several competing systems of Judaism emerged. All were agreed, however, that Judaism involved a belief in ethical monotheism that made Law observance mandatory, but on the matter of religious authority their differences not only eventuated in separate parties but in bitter quarrels.

One tragedy of this infighting was a diminished emphasis on the centrality of God. Whereas in the religion of ancient Israel the idea of God was "eminently personal, supramundane but not extramundane, exalted but not remote," these Judaisms tended to exile God from the world. The proper name Yahweh ceased to be commonly used. It was largely confined to the Temple liturgy. God was so exalted in lonely majesty that something most important was sacrificed: the immediacy of relationship with him: the intimacy of communion between individuals and the God of Abraham.

In the third century before the Christian era the Pentateuch was translated into Greek. Years later the rest of the Hebrew Bible was also translated. This became necessary because many diasporal Jews, particularly in Egypt, became so Greek-oriented in language and culture that they no longer could read the scriptures in Hebrew. This translation, the Septuagint, reflects this tendency to depersonalize God. Many of the anthropomorphic expressions in the original text were recast to make God so absolutely transcendent that the impression was conveyed that intimate knowledge of him arising from one's personal experience with him was no longer possible. He had practically become unknowable.[4] Obviously, this made the earlier appeals of the prophets to "turn" to the living God in repentance and faith both remote and somewhat less relevant.

Before we close this section, mention should be made of a significant institution that diasporal Jews created in order to keep Jewish tradition and

---

It is significant that the exposition of the word "repentance" in *The Universal Jewish Encyclopedia* places stress not on the Levitical code of "confession and the bringing of animal sacrifice" which is regarded as "rather mechanical," but on the manner in which the prophets "spiritualized" it. "Sacrifice is unnecessary," "repentance and good deeds are at least as efficacious." "Judaism indeed recognizes the need of divine grace, but it also declares that man can and must attempt his own moral regeneration: the doctrine of return (*teshubah*) is an affirmation of human freedom" (Vol. 9, pp. 134, 135).

4. Charles T. Fritsch generated no small debate among Jewish scholars when his doctoral dissertation was published: *The Anti-Anthropomorphisms of the Greek Pentateuch* (Princeton, N.J.: Princeton University Press, 1943).

religious practice alive: the local synagogue. Its function was to educate and edify all classes within the community in Jewish religion and morality. These local synagogues soon became not only centers for religious instruction; they also served to stimulate intellectual, social, and cultural life. Indeed, few would challenge the claim that the creation of the synagogue precipitated nothing less than "one of the greatest revolutions in the history of religion and society."[5] It became the prototype of Christian churches and Muslim mosques. The synagogue greatly shaped the Jewish sense of call to the academic tradition. One's life should be devoted to study, particularly of the Torah. One could not devote too much time to disciplined reflection on the ethical concerns it stimulated. As a result Jewish people today tend to downplay the charismatic, what they call "mystical" or experiential religion. With the passage of time this preoccupation with the cognitive tended to minimize the call to be primarily concerned about one's need for personal encounter with God himself.

JUDAISM ENCOUNTERS JESUS OF NAZARETH

We have already intimated that the postexilic period witnessed the proliferation of religious parties (Judaisms) that sought to cope with the implications of the destruction of Solomon's Temple. Following the restoration of the Temple and its cultic life under the inspiration of the prophets Haggai and Zechariah, a slow but inevitable gravitation to Jerusalem took place on the part of the wealthy and aristocratic. Among them there emerged an ultra-conservative priestly party known as the Sadducees. Although not particularly strict regarding religious observance, they were adamant in their contention that "we are to esteem those observances to be obligatory which are in the written word, but are not to observe what are derived from the tradition of our forefathers."[6] Since they tended to play the political game with Rome, they were naturally suspect by the common people.[7] When their negotiations with Rome resulted in the Temple area being decreed out of bounds to gentiles, and when they transformed the Temple Court of the gentiles into a place where animals were kept and money changers served, Jesus protested (Mk 11:15-18) and re-affirmed God's intention that the Temple be a house of prayer for all nations (Is 56:6,7). This public disruption of the Sadducees' lucrative exploitation of those who came to Jerusalem to worship was deeply resented. Jesus was too forthright in his denunciation of their vested interests to be regarded with any measure of favor.

---

5. *A History of the Jewish People*, edited by H.H. Ban-Sasson. Part III: "The Period of the Second Temple" by Menahem Stern, pp. 185-303. (Cambridge: Harvard University Press, 1976), 285.

6. *The Life and Works of Flavius Josephus* translated by William Whiston (Philadelphia: The John C. Winston Company, no date). "Antiquities of the Jews"—Book XIII, Ch. X, Par. 6, p. 397.

7. Ibid. Flavius Josephus: "The Sadducees are able to persuade none but the rich, and have not the populace obsequious to them" (p. 397).

But it was the Pharisee party that particularly provoked Jesus' wrath.[8] Although he found elements of their ministry to be commendable (Mt 23:2,3), and although we find several outstanding Pharisees in the gospels, it was the Pharisees' preoccupation with the "Oral Torah"—the traditions handed down by men—that aroused Jesus' antipathy. "For the sake of your tradition, you have made void the Word of God" (Mt 15:6).

On the other hand, what offended these fiercely pious Pharisees was the unique authority Jesus constantly assumed and exercised. It far exceeded that of Israel's earlier prophets. He felt free to abrogate the Law, assumed the right to forgive sin, proclaimed the universal efficacy of his atonement, and claimed the ability to reveal God to whomsoever he chose. It was inevitable that the religious leaders of Israel—scribes, Pharisees, priests, and Sadducees—should mount the challenge: "By what authority are you doing these things, and who gave you this authority?" (Mt 21:23). Jesus was also an offense to other parties: the Herodians, whose narrow nationalism was threatened by Jesus' universal concern; the Zealots who were offended by Jesus' pointed rejection of the revolutionary option; and the Essenes whose separatistic tendencies clashed with Jesus' call to kingdom proclamation and involvement. Indeed, the total religious establishment of Israel became increasingly hostile to him.

Here and there throughout the surrounding gentile world, diasporal Judaism retained its appeal to certain segments of the people. It represented moral strength, the intellectual vigor of a consistent monotheism, the attractiveness of a disciplined way of life, and the martyr tradition of a persecuted minority. This meant that the question of who these Jewish people were was constantly raised by their gentile neighbors. Eventually, a pattern of informal religious encounter gradually developed and in time resulted in a lay form of missionary activity. One significant factor that prompted this witness was the exposure of diasporal Jews to the universal concerns of their great Hebrew prophets. The stress they had placed on the divine election of Israel made world witness an inescapable obligation. How could any devout Jew not be moved by the universal concern of God for the nations? "Turn to me and be saved, all the ends of the earth. For I am God, and there is no other" (Is 45:22)? Faced with similar appeals, many diasporal Jews could only reason: "If there is but one God, there can only be one true religion. If we Jewish people alone know and worship this God, then should we not be his instruments as a light to the nations that his salvation may reach to the end of the earth" (Is 49:6)?[9] Actually, not all agreed to this. In general, however, one gains the impression that proselytes were welcomed, but not always sought. Naturally, those who persevered in their efforts to convert to Judaism

8. "The Pharisees have delivered to the people a great many observances by succession from their fathers, which are not written in the laws of Moses; and for that reason it is that the Sadducees reject them. . . . but the Pharisees have the multitude on their side" (p. 397).

9. George F. Moore, *Judaism in the First Centuries of the Christian Era* (Cambridge: Harvard University Press, 1927). This particular theme is developed in Vol. I, Ch. 1, "Nationality and Universality," pp. 219-234, particularly pp. 228,229.

had to be circumcised and accept a rigorous regimen of submission to the Law.

It is rather significant that Jesus did not condemn per se this missionary outreach. He only denounced the efforts of the Pharisees to transform into their own unloving image the gentiles who responded (Mt 23:15). But it is easy to see that in the Jewish mind the idea of conversion was something to which gentiles could submit. It was not something for the Jewish people themselves.

This brings up a significant point that is easily overlooked. The Pharisees in Jesus' day did not exceed 6,000, and the Sadducees were even fewer in number. But it is estimated that at that time the total Jewish population in the land exceeded two million. What then of this bulk of the people, the *Am-ha-aretz*, the "great throng who heard him gladly" (Mk 12:37)? They were hardly caught up in the minutia of legal observance or the casuistry involved in rabbinical circumventions of the written Law. They were the humble, morally earnest Jews who inhabited the towns and villages of the land. They had responded to the prophetic ministry of John the Baptist and had become the followers of Jesus. With them Jesus had no controversies. They had been faithful in their worship at the local synagogue and in the Temple. Indeed, their religion was largely that of preexilic Israel.

Suffice it to say, it was the message and ministry of Jesus and his followers that restored the prophetic stream to Israel. Since God in the earliest tradition was strictly personal, he can only be met in personal encounter. This concern of the prophets came to culmination in Jesus and characterized from that time onward the renewal movement he launched in Israel and which streamed out into the gentile world after Pentecost.

To summarize: According to the ministry of Jesus people need to enter into fellowship with the living God, to come into vital contact with the One who is life, so that his implanted "newness of life" in them might begin the necessary total process of renewal: intellectual, emotional, and spiritual. In sharpest contrast, the narrow focus of Judaism on the Law meant nothing less than significant departure from all that is subsumed under the prophetic call to turn, to return, to be converted. Jesus described his own ministry in these terms: "I came that they may have life, and have it abundantly" (Jn 10:10). When he spoke of "the good news of the kingdom," he invariably called it the kingdom of God, for it involved people deliberately coming under the reign of God. Inevitably, this demanded not only a new frame of reference (a "creation"—2 Cor 5:17) but also a new birth if one is to see, much more enter that kingdom. It is tragic that when Jesus sought to explain this primary truth to a Pharisee named Nicodemus, this hungry-hearted "teacher of Israel" found it utterly incomprehensible (Jn 3:1-21). His inability to understand the reality or essentiality of conversion was then and has become virtually the hallmark of Judaism ever since.

CRISIS: THE MESSIANIC MOVEMENT VS. RABBINIC JUDAISM

The first two centuries of what the Jewish people designate as the Common Era witnessed two dramatic and far-reaching religious changes among the

Jewish peoples. The first change was brought about by the advent of Jesus Christ and the prophetic movement he launched within Jewry and to which he gave the task of making disciples of all nations, the Jews included. The second change was precipitated by the savage Roman suppression of the Jewish revolt in the land of Israel, particularly the reduction of Jerusalem to rubble and the destruction of the Temple. This tragedy forced the surviving rabbis to cope with the theological and existential implications of such an unmitigated disaster. They had to restructure Pharisaism, the one form of Judaism that survived, and enable the Jewish people to rationalize and transcend the loss of their priesthood and cultus. They also had to render them impervious to the growing movement of Nazarenes in their midst.[10]

Actually, the Messianic movement that suddenly burst on the Jewish scene in Jerusalem (Pentecost, A.D. 33) was initially regarded as just another sect in Jewry. Its followers studied the Hebrew Bible, observed the Law, worshiped in the Temple, and participated in the religious and social life of the synagogue (Acts 2:46; 3:1; 5:13; 10:14). But there were significant differences.

The Nazarenes not only proclaimed that Jesus was "Lord and Christ" by virtue of his death and resurrection (2:32-36). They also sought to persuade their fellow Jews to call upon him "to be saved" (2:21; 4:12). Indeed, Peter proclaimed in no uncertain terms that when Jews turn to Jesus Christ in repentance and faith, they are doing nothing less than reaffirming their personal allegiance to the Abrahamic-Sinaitic Covenant that God had made with ancient Israel. To reject him was to repudiate their essential relationship to God via this covenant (3:12-26). Their submission to baptism and their possession of the Holy Spirit gave them a deep sense of conviction that they were nothing less than the vanguard of something new that God was doing on behalf of Israel and the nations of the world. Understandably, they did not deliberately withdraw from association with their fellow Jews. The probability is that at first they aroused curiosity more than hostility, for the breach between non-Messianic synagogues and the Jesus-oriented house congregations did not appear very wide—that is, until Stephen's martyrdom.

It was Stephen's outspoken confession of Jesus as the Christ whom the Israelites had rejected that brought him into open conflict with the Jewish authorities and eventually to a formal hearing before the Sanhedrin. He was charged with "speaking against Moses and God . . . against the Temple and the Law" (6:8-15). His response was a radical reinterpretation of the historic and sacred encounters of God with Israel outside the land and apart from the Temple. When it became apparent that Stephen was moving in the direction of challenging Jewry's cherished particularism and advocating a uni-

---

10. Phillip Sigal in the first of his two-volume series, *The Emergence of Contemporary Judaism*, has produced a remarkable chapter (No. 7) on the rise and separation of Christianity (pp. 377-507). It is refreshing to read an account that is so fair and balanced in its treatment of both sides of this tragic schism (Pittsburgh: The Pickwick Press, 1980). The second volume, *Appendix D*, particularly reflects Sigal's fairness: "The Impact of Christianity at Yavneh" (pp. 297-305).

versal faith that superseded Temple worship, the council rose up in wrath and destroyed him (7:51-56).

We should not minimize this tragic event. It represented the official action of the highest court in Jewry. By it the Jewish leaders revealed once again their implacable hatred of the Jesus whom they had earlier condemned to death (Mk 14:55-64). From this time onward the Sanhedrin began increasingly to authorize the persecution of all followers of this growing movement. To them it posed a mortal threat to the ongoing validity of all Jewish institutions. Missiologically speaking, in those early years the disciples of Jesus confined their witness to the large number of receptive Jews in the land who earlier had been responsive to the renewal ministry of John the Baptist and to the prophetic ministry of Jesus. The movement grew, despite the fact that within the land of Israel during those years prior to the beginnings of the first revolt against Rome (A.D. 66), Jewish believers in Jesus were repeatedly and increasingly persecuted, sometimes officially but more often by mob action. This involved flogging in the synagogues and executions as Jesus had predicted (Mk 13:9; Acts 4:5-20, 5:17-42; 8:1-3; 22:3-5; 23:12; etc.). But the movement kept growing.

The resultant growth in numbers and maturity made its apostolic leaders increasingly open to the larger task of evangelizing the gentile world. Through the outreach of Peter, Paul, and Barnabas it became abundantly clear that gentiles could also enter into personal relationship with God through the gospel and gain equal spiritual status with believing Jews (10:39-48; 11:19-24; 13:1-14:28; 15:1-11).

But when the national revolt against Rome increasingly involved all Jews in the land, the followers of Jesus began to draw back and refuse to participate. They fled from Jerusalem when Roman armies began to encircle the city. They did this in obedience to Jesus' earlier instruction (Lk 21:20-24). Inevitably, they were regarded by the enraged populace as lacking in real concern for their own people. This marked the beginnings of an irreparable breach between rabbinic Judaism and Messianic Christianity that remains to this day.

In the years following the destruction of the second Temple, the followers of Jesus interpreted this catastrophic event as the judgment of God on the nation for rejecting its Messiah. Numerous biblical texts were used with telling force to buttress this viewpoint (e.g., Dn 9:26 is a prediction that shortly after God's "Anointed One" is "cut off," the city of Jerusalem and the Temple will be destroyed). Naturally, this further infuriated the followers of rabbinic Judaism.

It takes little imagination to realize the terrible spiritual crisis that came to the Jewish people at this time. Paralysis and confusion bordering on despair followed the loss of the Temple, the priesthood, the sacrificial system, and the Sanhedrin. Under the influence of Rabban Johanan ben Zakkai and with the tacit approval of the emperor, a small coastal town called Javneh became the center where he and his fellow rabbis engaged in heroic efforts to rebuild Jewish life. The Sanhedrin was reconstituted, an academy for the study of

Torah was formed, and a campaign was undertaken to define a strict and noncompromising uniformity in Jewish law (Halakhah—literally, "the way to walk,") and custom. A pattern was developed at that time that was to be followed faithfully for many centuries. This involved reducing to writing the traditions of the past and supplementing them with new strictures to render Judaism congenial to a scattered people. This resulted in the Mishnah (literally, "teachings"), a codification of the meaning, intent, and authority of the Torah in the light of the development of centuries of "oral tradition." It was finally completed by the Tannaim (rabbis up to A.D. 250). In turn the Mishna became the foundation of two great expository works: the Jerusalem or Palestinian Talmud and the Babylonian Talmud. The Talmud or Gemara as it came to be known was developed by the *Amoraim* (rabbis from A.D. 250-450). In addition, ceremonies were developed for use in celebrating the ancient festivals of Israel now that the earlier, mandatory pilgrimages to the Temple were no longer possible.

Community prayers were developed and made obligatory, especially the malediction that had to be recited daily, calling down judgment on those Jews who believed in Jesus Christ. This was inserted in the synagogue liturgy around A.D. 90 and came to be known as *Birkat Haminim* ("Benediction against the heretics"). This implied that these Judeo-Christians "shall have no hope" in their belief that the Messiah has already appeared on earth.[11] One can readily imagine the sense of total ostracism from his own people that the Messianic Jew would experience when he sought to worship in the local synagogue. This curse remains part of synagogue worship today.

PARTING OF THE WAYS: FURTHER DETAILS

The Hebrew Bible makes abundantly clear the major reason for the destruction of the Solominic Temple and the Babylonian Captivity that followed. The destruction of the Second Temple and the uprooting of the people from Jerusalem was not as easy to fathom. Of course, Jewish Messianic believers were quick to point out that this judgment came to their people for rejecting Jesus as their Messiah (Mt 21:33-46; 22:7; 23:34-39).

But the rabbis bitterly resented this facile explanation and chose rather to blame the disaster on the infighting that had constantly taken place between the various contending religious parties in Israel ("hatred without cause").[12] Hence, they were determined to so reconceptualize and unify Judaism that from henceforth all Jewry would reflect not only ethnic unity but unity in culture and religion.

---

11. The 12th Benediction reads as follows: "For persecutors let there be no hope, and the dominion of arrogance do thou speedily root out in our days; and let Christians and minim perish in a moment, let them be blotted out of the book of the living and let them not be written with the righteous." W.D. Davies, *The Setting of the Sermon on the Mount* (Cambridge: Cambridge University Press, 1964), 275. See also Jakob Jocz: *The Jewish People and Jesus Christ* (London: S.P.C.K., 1949), 51-57, 174-190.

12. Talmud: Babylonian Shabbat 32b.

And yet, while they were seeking to develop an interim Judaism in antic-ipation of a future rebuilding of the Temple and return to the land, they also had to cope with the Messianic movement growing in their midst with its intolerable penchant for incorporating gentiles as well. Jakob Jocz contends that the fixed tradition which they fashioned to solidify Judaism also "exists by virtue of its negation of the Christian faith." Only thereby did the rabbis feel that they could preserve the Jews as a separate and distinct people.[13]

Cyrus Gordon, a distinguished Jewish scholar, has described some of these changes in a notable essay: *Jewish Reaction to Christian Borrowings.*[14] He begins by calling attention to the eschatological predictions of two of Israel's most honored prophets—Jeremiah and Ezekiel. Both predicted that a radical religious renewal would come to Israel through God initiating a "new covenant" with his people (Jer 31:31-34; 32:39-41 and Ez 36:26,27; 37:24-28). Inevitably, Jewish Christians seized on this (Lk 22:20; He. 8:8-12; 10:16,17) to the consternation of the rabbis. Here was no small problem. Jeremiah and Ezekiel antedated the coming of Jesus by centuries and now, because of their predictions of a new covenant, these Jewish believers in Jesus were calling the writings of their apostles "The New Covenant." This meant that the rabbis had to convince the Jewish people that the only valid covenant was the "old" one made with ancient Israel. And this was only the first of many major problems provoked by the emergence of the Messianic movement. In this connection Gordon argues: "Jewish elements stressed by Christianity tended to be played down by Judaism by way of reaction. Accordingly, Christianity has determined to a great extent what Judaism has become."[15]

For instance, local Messianic congregations accorded the Ten Commandments a highly honored place in their liturgy, following the long-held example of the synagogues. Admittedly, the rabbis could not remove the Decalogue from the Law of Moses, so they merely removed it from the syn-agogue prayer book. Today only in Reform Judaism has it reappeared.

When the Christian churches began to emphasize religious art, the syna-gogues called an end to their earlier art forms. When Christians embraced the Hebrew custom of baptism, the synagogues retreated, and today only the Orthodox retain a vestigial ritual baptism. Whereas formerly the Jewish people knelt in prayer (Is 45:23; Dn 6:11), now only the cantor kneels on the Day of Atonement. Whereas it used to be widely held that Judaism has no place for religious communities such as monasteries and nunneries, separated from the mainstream of secular life, with the discovery of the ancient Qumran, Christians are now free to speak of their indebtedness to the Jews for this phe-nomenon. Before ever there was a Benedictine regula, Qumran's Hebrew

---

13. Jakob Jocz, *The Jewish People and Jesus Christ After Auschwitz* (Grand Rapids, Mich.: Baker Book House, 1981), 124.

14. Cyrus H. Gordon's essay, "Jewish Reaction to Christian Borrowings" (pp. 685-690) in the Festschrift in honor of David H. Freedman, *The Word of the Lord Shall Go Forth* (Winona Lake, Ind.: Eisenbrauns, 1983).

15. Ibid., 685.

Manual of Discipline had long been in existence. Before Christians thought of heaven, hell, and the Messianic Age, the Hebrew Scriptures mentioned these things, even though today Jewish people claim no interest in such "unworldly" concerns.

If Jesus took a relaxed approach to the Sabbath, Judaism stressed it. When he downplayed what goes into a person's mouth in contrast to the defiling things that come out of people's hearts (Mk 7:15-23), Judaism went far beyond the Sinaitic regulations on food and developed the strict dietary laws known as *Kashrut*. Because Jesus modified for his people the burden of the Sinaitic Law and taught that one entered by faith into relationship with God, the rabbis stressed obedience to the 613 commandments embodied in their understanding of Torah.

However, this does not mean that there was no place for conversion to God in rabbinic thought. In this connection Phillip Sigal is vigorous in his contention that Christianity is not alone in its desire that all people be converted to God. He reminds us that the *Alienu* prayer that closes every statutory service in the Jewish community is an affirmation of the reality and importance of conversion. However, it does not apply to Jews! This prayer looks forward to the time when all non-Jews will confess Judaic monotheism by taking upon themselves the yoke of God's sovereignty and the yoke of the *Halakhah*. Sigal states: "In essence the *Alienu* looks forward to the eschatological attainment of the hope that all will confess and comply with Deuteronomy 6:4-9."[16] For this reason when Christians emphasize repentance and faith as essential to conversion now, this is not at all relevant to the Jewish people. They are already within the covenant people of God. All they have to do is to study and obey the Torah.

But how were the rabbis to downplay the "New" Testament? Christians stressed that "the Law was given through Moses; grace and truth came through Jesus Christ" (Jn 1:17). This was flatly denied: "The Torah is unchangeable. No other Moses will come to bring another Torah, for there is no other Torah left in Heaven" (Midrash Dt. R. 8:6). But was it enough to state this so categorically? Apparently not, for Sanhedrin 10:1 adds: "Among those who have no part in the world to come is he who reads the outside books." The phrase "outside books" refers to Jewish-Christian writings; in other words, the New Testament. Centuries later the Maimonidian Creed (twelfth century) committed Jews to the immutability of the Law: "I believe with perfect faith that this Law [i.e., the Law of Moses] will not be changed, and that there will never be any other Law from the Creator, blessed be his Name."[17]

The reason behind this exclusion of the New Testament is its witness to

---

16. Phillip Sigal, *Emergence of Contemporary Judaism*, Vol. II, Appendix C: "Dual Covenant Theology" (pp. 287-291), p. 288.

17. Article 9 in the Creed of Maimonides was directed against the claim of Messianic believers that the New Testament was given by God as inspired and authoritative as the Law that was given to Moses. *The Authorized Daily Prayer Book of the United Hebrew Congregations* (London: Eyre and Spottiswoode, 1962).

Jesus Christ coupled with the ways in which his advent changed forever the law in terms of its function, as well as the gentiles in their relation to him. The rabbis had to discredit his person and claims and make illegitimate his approach to the Law and the gentiles.

We must keep in mind that the Messianic congregations in those early years had no intention of separating from the synagogue. They were forced out of the Jewish communities in such a way that coexistence became impossible. The most effective weapon used against them was the ban (Lk 6:22, Jn 9:22; 12:42; 16:2). The Tosefta Hullin expressed this as follows:

> One does not sell to them [the Minim] or receive from them or take from them or give to them. One does not teach their sons a trade, and does not obtain healing from them (2:20f).

This ban arose out of the disassociation of Messianic Jews from the Jewish political liberation movement, from A.D. 66 to 135. At first, under the peace movement launched by Yohanan ben Zakkai, they were tolerated. However, during the incumbency of his successor, the more volatile Gamaliel who had instigated the *Birkat Haminim* in the synagogue liturgy, the ban was increasingly used and further drove an irrevocable wedge between Messianic Jews and rabbinic Jews. Understandably, the parting of the ways became total and final by the end of the Javneh period (A.D. 135). By the fourth century when the church gained political power, its uncritical allegiance to the state meant that it often became either a tacit supporter or an active accomplice in the state's anti-Semitic activities.

Over the centuries rabbinic Judaism has clung to its impressive integration of religion (ethical monotheism), race (ethnic roots), and culture (personal, family, and community life). It was able to do this rather successfully until the eighteenth century. The ancient prophetic concern that all individuals within its corpus need personal relationship with God has been replaced by the conviction that, because they are his chosen people they have been endowed by him to lead a reasonable and righteous life. The Jewish people are particularly taught to be self-reliant and to take full responsibility for their lives. They sense no need for a Savior coming to their aid from outside. And this is confirmed to them in a thousand ways when they observe that gentile Christians—who claim such a Savior—do not live very impressive lives.

Actually, the issue of Jesus the Jew is easily dismissed. Of course, he was an extraordinary person. Why not? He was a Jew! True, he claimed to be the Messiah, possessed impressive healing powers, and was dominated by a sense of universal mission. But he was executed by the Romans as an insurrectionist. And his so-called resurrection never happened. What his followers did was to exaggerate his claims, develop a gentile world religion in his name, and perpetuate an unending pattern of anti-Semitism by blaming the Jewish nation for his death.

JUDAISM: FROM THE ENLIGHTENMENT TO THE PRESENT

Such ideas persisted without significant change until a significant change in intellectual climate came to Western Europe in the eighteenth century. At that time such concepts as the equality of all people and their inalienable right to life, liberty, and the pursuit of happiness began to fill the minds. This changing mood, the Enlightenment, was the result of two conflicting ideologies partially converging: the conviction that both private and public virtue were possible without religion and widespread reaction against the excesses of state churches in Europe.

It was the Enlightenment that brought about the emancipation of the Jewish people. They slowly began to leave the stultifying rigidities of their ghetto enclaves, entered the gentile world, and found to their growing surprise that they could obtain the full rights of citizenship. This meant that they could begin to participate in the economic, social, political, and cultural life of their respective countries. Naturally, long troubled years had to be consumed in their struggles to take full advantage of their social emancipation. For one thing, their very success in the public arena made gentiles envious of their achievements, and the Jewish people began to encounter different, more virulent, not church-related forms of anti-Semitism. In fact, they began to realize that not all gentiles were Christians any more than all Jews were positively related to the synagogue.

Reform movements began to surface in Judaism. The Jews who were able to secure secular education became aware of the ways in which the Talmud had denigrated Jesus the Jew from Nazareth. Some even began to study the gospels critically. Inevitably the ethical teachings of Jesus came under careful scrutiny and were found to be impressive. At the same time Orthodox Judaism was subjected to critical review. Eventually, the focus of reflection was directed to the tragic events of the first century: the destruction of the Second Temple and the emergence of Messianic congregations followed by the ostracism from the Jewish community of all followers of Jesus.

Although there was deepest agreement among educated Jews that the claims Christians made of Jesus were sheer madness, they could not deny that his followers throughout the world had gained innumerable adherents and had brought about the social transformation of nations. It seemed as though everyone knew about the God of Abraham, Isaac, and Jacob. This provoked the natural desire to reclaim Jesus as their own, but freed from the myths that Christians had built up around him. It is not without reason that Samuel Sandmal begins his book, *We Jews and Jesus* (1965), with the ringing statement: "In the past one hundred and fifty years there has taken place what amounts to a reversal of eighteen centuries of Jewish and Christian attitudes toward each other."[18]

---

18. Samuel Sandmel, *We Jews and Jesus*. His opening sentence (p. 13) is quoted in Donald A. Hagner's impressive volume: *The Jewish Reclamation of Jesus* (Grand Rapids, Mich.: Academic Books, Zondervan, 1984), 60.

From the Enlightenment until the present within Protestantism there has emerged a growing evangelical movement, committed to historic biblical Christianity and determined to share the good news of Jesus Christ with all peoples of the world, and with the Jewish people. Their proclamation of the gospel followed by issuing the call to conversion sounded strange to most Jewish people, although here and there individual Jews who had drifted from the synagogue gave them a hearing because of their sheer hunger for contact with the living God. Some came to faith and frequently became active in lay mission organizations engaged in Jewish evangelism.

At first it was most difficult for any Jews to believe that anything other than monetary or social advantage bribes could persuade Jews to "convert," which was regarded as leaving one's Jewish identity and assuming a radically different religious orientation. Such a conversion appeared as nothing less than the betrayal of one's Jewish roots, family, and heritage, totally rejecting historic Israel and repudiating the Abrahamic-Sinaitic covenant. Unfortunately, during the early centuries of Roman Catholic triumphalism, no Jew could be baptized into that church without publicly breaking all ties with the Jewish people. This tended to confirm to Jews that Judaism and Jewry were one and the same. To leave rabbinic Judaism and embrace the faith of Jesus meant that one was ceasing to be a Jew and entering an entirely different religious system. Even so, in the latter part of the eighteenth and throughout the nineteenth centuries Jewish people started coming to faith in Jesus Christ in increasing numbers. One Jewish scholar puts the figure as high as 200,000.[19] The tragedy is that not a few Protestant traditions were also unable to separate religion from culture, race, and nationality. Judaism was uncritically assumed as the national religion to which all Jews belong.

But in recent decades it is being recognized that when a Jewish person accepts the Messiahship of Jesus and commits his/her life to him, this is nothing less than an affirmation of the ongoing significance of the ancient prophetic faith of Israel and its fulfillment in Jesus Christ. A case in point would be the religious experience of Cardinal Aaron Jean-Marie Lustiger, currently the Archbishop of Paris. In 1982 he was interviewed by two Israeli journalists (Y. Ben Porat and D. Judkowski) for publication in *Yediot Haharonot*, an Israeli daily.[20]

This interview aroused great interest in Israel and throughout the world, because Lustiger is a Jew who is adamant in his claim to be a Jew, even though he has come to Christian faith. Furthermore, most of his family was destroyed in the Holocaust. As to his Jewishness:

I cannot repudiate my Jewish condition without losing my own dignity and the respect I owe to my parents and to all those to whom I belong. . . . In

---

19. Israel Cohen states that 204,542 Jews were baptized throughout the world during the nineteenth century. *Jewish Life in Modern Times* (New York: Dodd, Mead and Company, 1919), Chapter III "Drift and Apostasy," 268-283, especially 273-274.

20. Cardinal Jean-Marie Lustiger, *Dare to Believe* (New York: Crossroad, 1986), 33-66.

becoming a Christian I did not intend to cease being the Jew I was then. I was not running away from the Jewish condition. I have that from my parents and I can never lose it. I have it from God and he will never let me lose it.[21]

As to his conversion to Jesus Christ:

It was Christ who gave me the key to my searchings, Christ as Messiah and image of the Jewish people. . . . I reread the gospels. . . . My parents absolutely refused to accept that I was convinced; they thought it was disgusting. I said to them, "I am not leaving you. I'm not going over to the enemy. I am becoming what I am. I am not ceasing to be a Jew; on the contrary, I am discovering another way of being a Jew."[22]

As to Judaism:

The contents of Judaism were not different from what I was discovering in Christianity. . . . It found its fulfillment in welcoming the person of Jesus, the Messiah of Israel; it was in recognizing him, and only in recognizing him, that Judaism found its meaning. . . . The person of Jesus, once he was recognized as Messiah, brought into focus a whole range of Jewish expectations which were seen to have a special spiritual content and which were experienced, at that moment, as fulfilled in the Christian experience.[23]

Perspectives such as these are being widely promoted in our day, largely by other Jewish people who have come to faith in Jesus Christ. Some serve in lay mission groups such as Jews for Jesus. Within recent decades other Jews have formed what are called Messianic Jewish congregations. These function as Christian synagogues and seek to bridge the Jewish community and the largely gentile Christian movement. Today, in North America there are probably 40,000 Jewish followers of Jesus. About 80 percent of them are identified with Christian churches, but the remainder feel the need to be a visible loving witness within the Jewish community via their one hundred or so Messianic Jewish congregations in North America.

All these Jewish people have responded to the prophetic concern of scripture to "seek the Lord while he may be found, call upon him while he is near" (Is 55:6). They have found in Jesus their Messiah and the fulfillment of the promises of the ancient prophets of Israel. Furthermore, they refuse to grant to any the presumption to declare that they are no longer Jews.

Tragically, they are bitterly resented by the synagogue and misunderstood by many in the churches. But they appeal to the scriptures, Old and New,

---

21. Ibid., 37,38.
22. Ibid., p. 41.
23. Ibid., p. 37,46.

to substantiate the thesis that when the Messianic movement began to receive gentiles as well as Jews, it was early decided that no effort should be made to Judaize gentile believers or to gentilize Jewish believers. Race and culture are not to be repudiated when Jesus Christ, the Savior of the world, is embraced.

One tragic fact remains. Despite all that has been stated above and implied concerning the growing openness of many within the Jewish community to the gospel of Jesus Christ within mainline Protestantism, a contrary movement is gaining momentum. This is known as the "Two Covenant Theory" and was, strangely enough, popularized by the Jewish existentialist, Franz Rosenzweig (1886-1919), who openly stated he was "anti-Christian."[24] He grew up in Germany at a time when the influence of Christianity was at its zenith, and many upper-class Jews were going over to Christianity. He was impressed with the positive worldwide achievements of the Christian movement, yet intensely loyal to the synagogue. How could he bring an end to mission to the Jews? His solution was to call attention to John 14:6 and the claim of Jesus to be the only way to the Father. In effect he endorsed the Great Commission and said that the gospel should be preached to all peoples, that they might "come to the Father." But he added: "The situation is quite different for one who does not have to reach the Father because he is already with him. And this is true of the people of Israel." He then added the disclaimer: "Although not of individual Jews."[25]

So then—the argument goes—there are two covenants, one with gentiles through Christ and the other with Jews through their membership in Israel, the covenant people of God. Gentiles need the mediation of Christ, whereas Jews by blood and race are automatically related to the Father and have access to him because they are uniquely of "the seed of Abraham" (Heb 2:16). This means that God has two ways of saving people: by linkage to a privileged race or by the Old Testament pattern of Aaronic priesthood and blood sacrifice which came to fullness and universal relevance through Jesus Christ.

Many mainline denominations have uncritically accepted this theory and are calling a halt to all evangelistic work among the Jewish people. This is tragic, for the semi-plausible arguments used to support it are incapable of biblical defense. Fortunately, at the 1989 gathering of the Lausanne Consultation for World Evangelism (Lausanne) II many evangelicals felt that the lordship of Jesus Christ was at stake on the issue of Jewish evangelism. As a result, they drafted and adopted the following affirmation:

---

24. Maurice G. Bowler summarized the theological issues raised by Franz Rosenzweig in his article, "Do Jews Need Jesus?" *Christianity Today* 18, no. 2 (26 October 1973): 12-14. This is a distillation of his unpublished master's thesis: "The Reconciliation of Church and Synagogue in Franz Rosenzweig" (1973).

25. Quoted by Maurice G. Bowler in "Rosenzweig on Judaism and Christianity" (Mishkan 11/2, 1989) from Nahum Glatzer, *Franz Rosenzweig: His Life and Thought* (New York: Schocken, 1961), 341.

It is sometimes held that in virtue of God's covenant with Abraham, Jewish people do not need to acknowledge Jesus as their Messiah. We affirm that they need him as much as anyone else, that it would be a form of anti-Semitism, as well as being disloyal to Christ, to depart from the New Testament pattern of taking the gospel to "the Jew first. . . ." We therefore reject the thesis that Jews have their own covenant which renders faith in Jesus unnecessary.[26]

And so, the struggle of almost four thousand years continues. It began with Israel's prophets, was heightened by Jesus and the apostles, and has been continued by faithful Christian witnesses down through the centuries. The great theme throughout this period was succinctly stated by Jesus Christ: "Salvation is of the Jews" (Jn 4:22). By this he meant that within the stream of Israel God has provided the good news of salvation for Jew and gentile alike. The redemptive work of Christ on the cross was retroactive for all peoples, past, present, and future (Rom 3:19-26). But there has never been a time when it did not have to be appropriated personally, by repentance and faith.

---

26. *The Manila Manifesto*, Sect. A., Par. 3 in *The Whole Gospel for the Whole World*, ed. Alan Nichols (Ventura, Calif.: Regal, 1989), 114.

Appendix: On Outsiders Entering the Community of Israel

A. During the centuries from Moses to the destruction of the First Temple, the Israelites did not alone occupy the land. The Old Testament mentions three distinct types of non-Israelites: natives (*'ezrachim*), foreigners (*nokhrim*), and sojourners (*gerim*). Most common were the *gerim*, people without nationality, who placed themselves under the legal protection of the enfranchised Israelis. They were not fully entitled to become part of the "congregation" or "assembly" of Israel but were permitted involvement in much of the religious life of the people (Dt 5:14; 16:11, 14; etc.). In 31:12 it is explicitly stated that the *gerim* are to be present for the solemn reading of the law; in other words, they were exposed to the demands of the law.[1]

Because of this, we conclude that as long as the Israelites remained in the land, their openness to non-Israelites was genuine. The problem of children of mixed marriages was resolved by appealing to the invariable pattern of biblical genealogies: Only the names of men are listed, except in cases where the mother was notable in Jewish history. David was definitely Jewish, although two gentile women (Rahab and Ruth) were among his ancestors. This stress on paternity is reinforced by appealing to the case in Leviticus 24:10-12 in which "the son of an Israelitish woman, whose father was an Egyptian" is not identified as an Israelite.

B. A period of radical change took place in Israelite history and religion following the destruction of the First Temple. It changed the individual status of Jews. Not only were the Jewish people undergoing the transformation from a nation whose identity was only related to the land, to one that included the diasporal communities beyond its borders. What now legitimized their Jewish identity was physical descent.

Those born within the land or in diasporal communities of Jewish parents were Jews by birth. It became increasingly accepted that no response to any prophetic call to turn to YHWH was needed to make them more surely Jews. This was most unfortunate. Even a cursory review of the ministry of the Hebrew prophets indicates a distinct differentiation between spiritual Israel and political Israel (Zep 2:3; 3:11, 12).

Be this as it may, when the *gerim* in the midst of whom they dwelt increasingly began to attach themselves in varying relationships to this strange people and their singularly different faith, problems arose.[2] The *gerim* were now regarded as potential proselytes, drawn to the Jewish congregation by its law. The informality of the past was replaced by rigid conditions. Admittedly, not many became proselytes (i.e., formally converted to Judaism).

---

1. See article on the *ger*: *Theological Dictionary of the Old Testament*, Vol II (Grand Rapids, Mich.: Eerdmans, 1975), by D. Kellerman, pp. 439-449.

2. Lawrence H. Schiffmann, "Jewish Sectarianism in Second Temple Times," in *Great Schisms in Jewish History*, ed. Raphael Jospe and Stanley M. Wagner (New York: Ktav Publishing House, 1981), 1-46.

The majority of those attracted were content to develop only a loose attachment to the Jewish people and came to be known as "God-fearers," but not real Jews. In general, however, one gains the impression that proselytes were welcomed, but not always sought. Naturally, those who persevered in their efforts to convert to Judaism had to be circumcised and accept a rigorous regimen of submission to the Law.

It is thought that during this crisis the leaders in Judaism interpreted Deuteronomy 7:3, 4 to the effect that the Jewish status of a child depends upon that of its mother.[3] Actually this text contains the divine prohibition against Israelites making marriage arrangements with the Canaanites, lest they weaken the allegiance of Israel to YHWH. In Ezra's day many Israelites, including priests and Levites—the leaders of "the holy race"—intermarried with non-Jewish neighbors and became involved in their "abominations" (9:1, 2). The rabbis recognized that since mothers tend to shape the spiritual development of children more than fathers, and since a child's maternity is more easily traced than its paternity, the decision was taken that only those whose mothers were Jews were certified as Jews by descent.[4]

Understandably, those Jews who lived outside the land in diasporal situations became increasingly concerned with rectitude in these matters. Not only did genealogies become important but increasing concern developed among them to formalize and normalize the procedures whereby converts would be admitted to the community.

This concern came to focus on the issue of circumcision. All male children of Jewish parents, despite the blood ties that destined them for admission to Jewry, had to be circumcised. All were agreed: This alone separated them unto God and his service, and made them members of the covenant. Circumcision likewise was essential to the transformation of even the most zealous converts into what their conversion experience could not make them: real Jews. It is not surprising that the rabbis referred to circumcision as "being born again."[5] This stress on circumcision was fundamental to all the various Judaisms during the time of Jesus. Only by ritual circumcision could one enter the redeemed community. Joachim Jeremias comments:

> The whole community of Judaism . . . was dominated by the fundamental idea of the maintenance of racial purity. Not only did the priests, as the consecrated leaders of the people, watch anxiously over the legitimacy of priestly families . . . but the entire population itself . . . was classified according to purity of descent . . . the nation was considered God-given and its purity was God's will . . . pagans converted to Judaism could not of course become part of the pure seed . . . but they were indeed received into the larger community of the people.[6]

3. Roland de Corneille: *Christians and Jews* (New York: Harper & Row, 1966), p.4.
4. Daniel Juster: *Jewish Roots* (Gaithersburg, MD: Davar Publishing Company, 1986), 191-95.
5. See Oscar Cullmann: *Baptism in the New Testament* (London: SCM Press, 1950), 57, 60, 61.

We conclude this section by stating that throughout the entire length of the Second Temple period, Judaism was a diverse phenomenon and "tolerated sectarianism and schism," despite the intense desire of the Jewish people to remain racially pure.[7]

C. In the period following the destruction of the Second Temple and the removal of all Jews from the land, a hardening gradually took place in the basic requirements for conversion to Rabbinic Judaism and admission to the Jewish community. One rabbinic tradition became normative: the thesis that all proselytes should follow the same sequence that Israel passed through prior to entering into covenant relationship with God at Sinai. This began with circumcision based on the myth that all male Israelites were circumcised just prior to the Exodus deliverance, then followed eating the passover lamb (sacrifice), and immersion in the Red Sea (baptism). After this, the candidate was ready to receive the yoke of the law (Ex 20:6) and enter the community of Israel.

What became important in this sequence was the thesis that all converts were literally changing their heredity by becoming Jews. In turn they would pass on to their children something not inherited but acquired when the Torah was accepted. They were not identified with the entire historic experience of the Jews, were called to a life of holiness, and through bringing a sacrifice were expressing their readiness to draw near to the divine presence and become full members of the people of Israel.[8] This has been the pattern followed ever since by the Orthodox Rabbinate. Conservative, Reform, and Reconstructionist branches of Judaism are regarded as having diluted this procedure, hence their converts are not fully acceptable by this body.

6. Joachim Jeremias, *Jerusalem in the Time of Jesus* (Philadelphia: Fortress Press, 1975).

7. Lawrence H. Schiffmann: *Who is a Jew? Rabbinic and Halakhic Perspectives on the Jewish Christian Schism.* (Hoboken, N.J.: Ktav Publishing House, 1985), ix-xii.

8. Ibid., 39.

Chapter Five

Conversion Process in the New Religions

James T. Richardson

INTRODUCTION: HISTORICAL AND STRUCTURAL FOUNDATIONS OF PROSELYTIZATION

America is a conversionistic nation and has been since its inception as a country with formalized separation of church and state. No religious tradition has a monopoly in America and none is formally sanctioned by the state. This forces religious groups that desire permanence to compete in an open religious market.[1] This competition for members, resources, and legitimacy has resulted in many religious traditions being somewhat evangelical. They have had to convert members or die (or at least not grow very much or very rapidly). Even newer religions from the Hindu tradition have become more oriented toward conversion within the context of American society.[2]

This structural fact of free market competition between religions within the American context does not, of course, explain why certain religions grow more rapidly than others and why certain religious ideas and practices seem to "catch on" in certain time periods and locations. Also, the simple fact of competition does not itself explain why some people respond to conversion appeals, while others ignore them. Much more psychological, socio-

---

1. Peter Berger, *The Sacred Canopy* (New York: Doubleday, 1967).
2. Thomas Pilarzyk, "Conversion and Alteration Processes in the Youth Culture," in David Bromley and James T. Richardson, eds., *The Brainwashing/Deprogramming Controversy* (New York: Edwin Mellen Press, 1983).

logical, and historical information is needed before one can even begin to understand the varying effectiveness of conversion processes of various religious groups in America.

America has always had its share of "new religions." Some of yesterday's new religions are today's accepted denominations. Some die out, while others develop a "market niche" for themselves.[3] But new religions take the place of those that fail, as the religious ferment of American society continues, even in (or perhaps because of) this most secular of times. This chapter attempts to explain the process whereby certain groups are able to gain converts and remain a part of the religious landscape in America.

CONVERSION PROCESSES

The conversion processes of new religions have been examined in considerable depth in the literature concerning recruitment to new religions.[4] However, that conversion literature, immense though it is, focuses typically on the individual convert, and much of the literature takes a decidedly psychological bent. We will attend here mainly to the *structural arrangements* set up by the groups and organizations to recruit new members and to re-socialize them to new norms and values. Some of this material can be gleaned from a close examination of the conversion literature, because often some discussion of the organizational efforts to recruit is included in such research reports. Also, some of the literature on new religions contains rather thorough discussions of the recruitment/resocialization mechanisms developed by the groups.

Before proceeding however, one point needs to be made. There is little evidence that these groups have some mysterious or magical techniques to attract and hold new members. There are no "Manchurian Candidate" types of processes being used; what takes place is remarkably normal and ordinary.[5] The greatest evidence for this statement is the extremely high attrition rates of the groups.[6] The groups are usually experimenting to develop techniques

---

3. Berger, *Sacred Canopy*.

4. James T. Richardson, ed., *Conversion Careers: In and Out of the New Religions* (Beverly Hills, Calif.: Sage, 1978); "The Active vs. Passive Convert: Paradigm for Conflict in Conversion/Recruitment Research, *Journal for the Scientific Study of Religion* 24, vol. 2 (1985): 163-79.

5. See discussions in Bromley and Richardson, eds., *The Brainwashing/Deprogramming Controversy* and Brock Kilbourne and James T. Richardson, "Psychotherapy and New Religions in a Pluralistic Society," *American Psychologist* 39, vol. 3 (1984): 237-51.

6. M. Galanter et al., "The Moonies: A Psychological Study of Conversion and Membership in a Contemporary Religious Sect," *American Journal of Psychiatry* 136 (1979): 165-69; James T. Richardson, Jan van der Lans, and Frans Derks, "Leaving and Labeling: Voluntary and Coerced Disaffiliation from New Religious Movements," in K. Long and G. Lang, eds., *Social Movements, Conflict and Change*, vol. 8 (Greenwich, Conn.: JAI Press, 1986); Trudy Solomon, "Integrating the 'Moonie' Experience," in T. Robbins and D. Anthony, eds., *In God We Trust* (New Brunswick, N.J.: Transaction Books, 1982): Eileen Barker, "Who'd Be a Moonie? B. Wilson, ed., *The Social Impact of New Religious Movements* (New York: Rose

that work and more often than not have difficulty recruiting and retaining participants. With that caveat, we will now examine several ways in which new religions have tried to recruit and resocialize their members.

The Unification Church

The Unification Church (UC), popularly known as the "Moonies," is one of the best known of the newer religions. This is in part the result of deliberate tactics on the part of the UC to use the media to communicate their message to as many as possible. They have also achieved notoriety through some of their activities, such as group marriage ceremonies involving hundreds of young members, and through the much-discussed trial of Reverend Moon on tax evasion charges. A major share of the notoriety, however, derives directly from the allegations of brainwashing that have been made against the UC by ex-members and other detractors.

The term brainwashing is, of course, not a scientific term with a readily understandable meaning in the scientific community. However, the term is used in popular parlance and often therapists and other professionals use the term to refer to techniques used by groups such as the UC to recruit new members.[7] As we will see, however, the techniques of the UC may be intense in some instances, but they are neither new nor especially potent.

Recruitment methods are well-described in Lofland;[8] Galanter et al.;[9] Bromley and Shupe;[10] and Barker.[11] Lofland, in fact, offered a systematic discussion of UC recruitment methods, using the early efforts of the UC as examples for this theorizing. Thus, he presented at the same time a great deal of specific information about the recruitment methods of the UC and some important theorizing about the conversion process. His earlier well-known conversion model, which was based on his study of the UC, was presented in 1965,[12] and has been the most popular such model in the conversion literature.

Lofland[13] started his analysis by contrasting *embodied* and *disembodied*

---

of Sharon Press, 1981); Fred Bird and B. Reimer, "Participation Rates in the New Religious Movements," *Journal for the Scientific Study of Religion* 21 (1982): 1-14.

7. See John Clark, "Problems in Referral of Cult Members," *Journal of the National Association of Private Psychiatric Hospitals* 9, vol. 4 (1978): 19-21; Richard Delgado, "Religious Totalism as Slavery," *New York University Review of Law and Social Change* 9 (1979):51-8; Margaret Singer, "Coming Out of the Cults," *Psychology Today* 12 (1979): 72-82.

8. John Lofland, *Doomsday Cult*, enlarged ed. (New York: Irvington, 1977); "Becoming a World Saver Revisited," in Richardson, *Conversion Careers.*

9. Galanter et al., "The Moonies."

10. David Bromley and Anson Shupe Jr., *"Moonies" in America* (Oxford: Basil Blackwell, 1979).

11. Barker, "Who'd Be a Moonie?"

12. John Lofland and Rodney Stark, "Becoming a World-Saver: A Theory of Conversion to a Deviant Perspective," *American Sociological Review* 30 (1965): 862-74.

13. Lofland, *Doomsday Cult.*

access and *covert* vs. *overt methods*. Embodied access refers to face-to-face methods, whereas disembodied access are methods that do not involve face-to-face contact (use of media, printed brochures, newspaper ads, handbills, posters, etc.). Overt and covert carry the usual meaning of the terms. Lofland also distinguished between recruitment in secular as opposed to religious locations, focusing on different target populations (leaders vs. ordinary people, young vs. old, etc.). Thus he offered an analytical structure for describing the proselytizing done by the UC and other groups.

Lofland's book on the Unification Church (he called them the "Divine Precepts") described the haphazard way in which various methods of recruitment were tried, usually with little success. The UC initially shifted back and forth between overt and covert methods and used both embodied and disembodied access to attract converts. We are told about paltry efforts to get people to listen to the message of Reverend Moon and of gatherings where the main center of attraction was a tape recorder playing tapes of Moon speaking in broken English about his views. These efforts were directed at anyone who would listen and those attracted by these unsystematic efforts were usually people on the fringes of society—social misfits of sorts.

In the 1977 edition[14] of his book, and in another publication,[15] Lofland included a lengthy epilogue section updating developments in the UC organization. He claimed that the members became more duplicitous, and he reported much more systematic proselytizing tactics being developed, with a focus on the affective or emotional level. He also described large media events planned by the UC during the early 1970s and other ways in which they sought attention (these efforts are also described in Bromley and Shupe.[16]) We will use Lofland's analysis of the social psychological processes of conversion/recruitment to illustrate the development of perhaps the most sophisticated set of recruitment procedures of any newer religion. Barker's work presents a more detailed and full discussion of the methods of the UC in England and America, and her treatment should be used to supplement this brief discussion.

Lofland[17] states that UC's recruitment methods changed dramatically around 1972, becoming much less haphazard and more focused on the emotional. The earlier methods were presented in the classic paper, Lofland and Stark.[18] He presented five "quasi-temporal phases" in his 1978 treatment: picking-up, hooking, encapsulating, loving, and committing.

Picking-up refers to the way in which casual, face-to-face contact between UC recruiters and members of the public was used to interest potential recruits. UC members systematically approached young men and women in areas frequented by such people. They would often do this somewhat covertly, using a "front organization" and general talk about changing soci-

14. Ibid.
15. Lofland, "Becoming a World Saver Revisited.
16. Bromley and Shupe, *"Moonies" in America.*
17. Lofland, "Becoming a World Saver Revisited."
18. Lofland and Stark, "Becoming a World Saver."

ety or improving the world. Out of this initial contact would come an invitation to a lecture or a dinner to meet and discuss important issues with people similar to the potential convert. Note the emphasis on public, secular places of recruitment, its somewhat covert flavor, and the focus on a target population of rather well-to-do, educated, and alienated youth.

Hooking took place after the initial successful contact with a potential convert. It involved promotional techniques such as lectures or dinners with UC members and other potential converts, with a heavy emphasis on the emotional level. Recruits were assigned a "buddy" who was always with the recruit. The buddy and other UC members would attempt to find out what the recruit was interested in as a way of "hooking" them into conversions, and also as a way of showing interest. This technique was something like a "rush" at a sorority in college. At the dinners or other meetings there was usually a lecture or talk presenting some of the general principles of Unification theology, sometimes in such an obscure fashion as to make it difficult to know the group was the UC. Thus, while there was some effort to appeal to the cognitive or intellectual side of the potential recruit, the emphasis was on the emotional level. People visiting the dinner or lecture would be made to feel that everyone there cared for them and that the entire atmosphere of the group was one of love and caring. Most people rejected this appeal,[19] but it worked with some to the extent that they were willing to move on to the next stage—*encapsulating*.

During lectures and dinners with potential converts an invitation was usually offered to participate in a weekend workshop at one of the organization's rural facilities. The most well-known of the Unification rural retreats was Camp K, operated in Northern California in a beautiful setting with redwoods and other natural beauty. Barker visited there and offers a good description of what happened. Also, Galanter et al.[20] did his research in this location.

At these weekend retreats recruits were encapsulated totally within the UC recruitment experience. This encapsulation allowed the promotion of affective ties as well as the continued presentation of Unification theology. Some have claimed that even during the weekend experience they were not told that the group was the UC, but most apparently knew and participated anyway. Lofland notes that the encapsulation process involves a total absorption of attention, with every waking hour programed with group activities, thus offering a completely collective focus. There is an exclusive input to recruits, as use of television and radio are discouraged and all the members (who make up about half those present) are continually talking about the topics the UC desire to discuss. *Fatigue* plays a role, according to Lofland, because of the intensity of the experience. All this leads to a better situation for gaining acceptance of the principles of the theology.

The encapsulating process involved a further sifting process; those han-

---

19. See Galanter et al., "The Moonies" and Barker, "Who'd Be a Moonie?"
20. Ibid.

dling the weekend experience well were often invited to participate in longer sessions of from one to three weeks at the rural retreat centers. A small proportion of those initially contacted agreed to go into this last phase. For those who went, there was an increasing dose of UC theology. The focus of efforts was to develop the affective ties and more exposure to UC ideas.

Lofland included as a separate analytical element the idea of *loving*. The entire situation at the retreat was designed to make the person feel loved. The term "love bombing" has been used by the UC and the term has gained usage in scholarly literature as well. Recruits were welcomed into what was a loving commune, and encouraged to stay and participate in the group on a permanent basis.

Commitment was developed by getting recruits to participate in UC activities such as street witnessing (picking up), selling flowers, or other money-raising activities. They were encouraged to practice their new-found beliefs, and they were discouraged from maintaining ties with outsiders. The process was a gradual one, and throughout it encapsulation was maintained.

The process described by Lofland seems thorough, as if the UC was sparing no effort to gain new recruits. The organization was dependent on new recruits to do a number of important group functions (such as fund-raising), and thus they had to have a relatively large number of people flowing through the organization, if only to maintain certain key activities.

There is little doubt that the elaborate process described could be effective. However, the reader should not be misled into thinking that the process was effective with everyone or even a large proportion who went through it. This was far from the case, as the studies of Galanter and Barker show. Galanter et al.[21] notes that less than 10 percent of those participating in a several-week-long retreat actually stayed in the organization when the retreat was over. Barker makes similar claims and adds that of those who did stay, over half were no longer members two years later. Thus it appears that, similar to other new religions, the UC were relatively ineffectual in their recruitment efforts. The overall size of the Unification Church in America evidences this, with scholars such as Lofland, and Bromley and Shupe estimating that there are only a few thousand full-time members in the country.

HARE KRISHNA

Rochford's[22] book on the Hare Krishna contains a thorough treatment of the evolution of recruitment practices of the Krishna. His careful work reveals that during the time of most rapid growth of the Krishna in America about half of the converts were obtained by initial contact in public places; the rest were obtained by friendship ties with devotees or others. Rochford also points out some interesting differences by sex, with females being more

21. Galanter et al., "The Moonies."

22. Burke Rochford, *Hare Krishna in America*, (New Brunswick, N.J.: Rutgers University Press, 1985). See also Pilarzyk, "Conversion and Alteration."

prone to have joined through personal ties and males being more prone to have been contacted at a public location. It is important to note that a sizable proportion of new members was obtained through interpersonal networks, which is, of course, the "normal" way traditional religious organizations gain most new members. Some important differences were found by locale in the way recruitment was carried on at the various Krishna locations. This Rochford sees as an important indication that, even in such a strongly ideological movement as the Krishna, local conditions could dictate that conversion processes would occur in different ways.

Because of its importance to the movement, the public conversion practices of the Krishna will be examined in more detail. Recruitment of new members was originally a major aim of the sacred Krishna practice of *sankirtana*. This involved going into public places to chant (dressed in saffron robes and with shaved heads), distributing literature, recruiting new members, and soliciting funds for the support of the organization. Groups of devotees would go out to street corners and shopping centers where some would chant and march around while others "worked the crowd" by asking for donations, handing out literature, and talking to people about participating. This practice is very public and overt, and it tended to focus on target populations of young people in certain parts of the country. Rochford points out that originally the target group in New York was older, more ordinary citizens; however, it was quickly discovered that they were uninterested and the target group shifted to younger people.

Thus, during the Krishna's salad days of the early 1970s most converts were gained through this public kind of effort. People would be contacted directly through *sankirtana*, or they would take the literature and read it, which quickened the interest of some, especially if they were what is called in the literature on conversion-"seekers." Anyone expressing interest in participating was immediately drawn into temple activities that included a heavy regime of meditation, chanting, change of diet to vegetarianism, acceptance of celibacy, and no use of stimulants. A great deal of self-selection took place, of course, as some found that the requirements of membership were too rigorous, while others responded favorably (see Gregory Johnson[23] for a good analysis of the importance of getting involved in temple life to eventual conversion into the group). For the really dedicated, communal living in a temple center was possible, and this was the major thrust of recruitment. Full-time committed members were sought and for a time relatively large numbers of them were obtained.

However, the halcyon days did not last, as Rochford amply describes. Pressure developed to take advantage of the fact that *sankirtana* was able to collect considerable money, and there was a discernible shift away from

23. See Gregory Johnson, "The Hare Krishna in San Francisco," in C. Glock and B. Bellah, eds., *The New Religious Consciousness* (Berkeley: University of California Press, 1976); Pilarzyk, "Conversion and Alteration Processes"; and Rochford, *Hare Krishna in America*.

using the sacred practice to recruit and spread literature toward a focus on fundraising. This shift is quite similar to that noted with another well-known group, the Children of God.[24] The place of activity shifted from street corners where there were many young people to airports and other places where the general public gathered. This shift led to several major changes in the Hare Krishna. The number of converts dropped off and has been declining since then; and a very negative public reaction developed against the Krishna because of their public solicitation methods. The methods themselves became more duplicitous and covert, with many allegations being made of various kinds of petty fraud, such as short-changing people when they agreed to pay for a book. Also, some Krishna members began concealing their true identity by wearing ordinary clothing and wigs, or even Santa Claus suits. Thus, the practice of *sankirtana* was dramatically changed in function.

Since public street recruitment is not being practiced as frequently, where do the Krishna now get converts? The first response is that they are not gaining as many new members and their overall membership is declining. There are a number of reasons for this decline which are detailed in Rochford's book. Out of necessity the Krishna, like many other newer religions, are accepting more part-time, less committed members (Barker says this about the UC, as well).[25] The Krishna are developing into something of a denomination, albeit a small one, with a congregational lifestyle, which means that ordinary people in the neighborhood may participate on a part-time basis, as do most church-goers in America. Also, and very importantly, the Hare Krishna organization is attracting new participants out of the Indian communities in areas where there are Krishna temples. Some Indians have attained leadership positions in Hare Krishna temples, and Hare Krishna temples have become centers of Indian community life in some areas. Thus we see a remarkable change taking place in this organization's recruiting, with a marked decline in the public recruiting and conversion of well-to-do white youth that targeted the Krishna for much animosity from the public.

A JESUS MOVEMENT ORGANIZATION

Harder, Richardson, and Simmonds[26] and Richardson, Stewart, and Simmonds[27] presented a detailed analysis of one of the major Jesus Movement organizations that were so much in the news in the 1970s. Part of their analysis focused on the elaborate recruitment and resocialization processes devel-

---

24. Rex Davis and James T. Richardson, "The Organization and Functioning of the Children of God," *Sociological Analysis* 37, vol. 4 (1976): 321-40; James T. Richardson and Rex Davis, "Experiential Fundamentalism: Revisions of Orthodoxy in the Jesus Movement," *Journal of the American Academy of Religion* 51, vol. 3 (1983): 397-425.

25. Eileen Barker, *The Making of a Moonie* (Oxford: Basil Blackwell, 1984).

26. Mary W. Harder, James T. Richardson, and R. B. Simmonds, "The Jesus People," *Psychology Today* 6 (1972): 45.

27. James T. Richardson, Mary Stewart, and Robert Simmonds, *Organized Miracles* (New Brunswick, N.J.: Transaction Press, 1979).

oped by Christ Communal Organization (a pseudonym). Christ Communal Organization (CCO), like many other new religions developing out of the turmoil of the late 1960s and early 1970s, gained its members from street witnessing, which is a public form of proselytizing among the disaffected youth so available at that time in our society. Members of the first communes operated by CCO went out into areas where large numbers of young people collected and overtly and openly sought to convince the youth that they should accept the new beliefs and lifestyles. New communes were deliberately established close to major areas of congregating youth or close to highways where there were many hitchhikers. Sometimes members even moved into drug-oriented communes in an effort to convince users to give up drugs and "try Jesus."

The group offered friendship, a place to sleep, food and other necessities to hundreds of young people. Many accepted the offer and moved into the commune, whereby they were agreeing to adopt the ascetic and spartan lifestyle of the other members. This meant no drugs, no alcohol, no sex outside marriage, and hard work. The latter was especially the case because the CCO chose not to solicit for money on the street and not to beg for sustenance, but instead worked for funds at all kinds of tasks. The full history of this work-oriented development is recounted in Richardson et al.,[28] but for our purposes here suffice it to say that the work regime taught useful skills, kept the converts very busy, earned money for the organization, and served as a kind of "work therapy" for those with personal difficulties. It was important to the resocialization process for the members, most of whom had used drugs regularly and were engaged in other sorts of deviant lifestyles.

As the group matured, other organizational arrangements were made to develop commitment in new members. A nationwide headquarters was established which had as its major function the further training of new converts, so that they could in turn go out and win more converts. This headquarters, called "The Land," was in a beautiful rural setting several miles outside of Eugene, Oregon. Although the group bought The Land without any facilities, within a few years they had built a number of buildings, including classrooms, dormitories, and various enterprises where the young people were taught useful skills such as animal husbandry, auto mechanics, and other needed tasks. Two separate schools were established that operated for several years. One was called Lamb's School, for newer members, and the other was called Team's School, for more long-term members who were preparing to go out as evangelism teams.

Lamb's School usually lasted for three months, with daily teaching of Bible and related courses, and half of the day was devoted to teaching useful skills needed in the organization. After graduating from Lamb's School, members usually worked somewhere in the organization, which at that time was nationwide with communities in about thirty states. Many of the mem-

---

28. Ibid.

bers were placed on future evangelism teams and brought back to The Land within a year for further training. After three months of additional training which focused on evangelism methods and a deeper understanding of group theology, the teams would be sent out to start the process anew—bringing in new members.

The organization also developed many other methods of recruitment and evolved rapidly, becoming much more differentiated. Figure 1 shows some of the ways in which the evangelism methods developed and demonstrates the elaborate and sophisticated nature of CCO's efforts to win converts. As with other newer religions, even more changes were to

Figure 1: Evolution* and Differentiation of Evangelism and Resocialization Methods

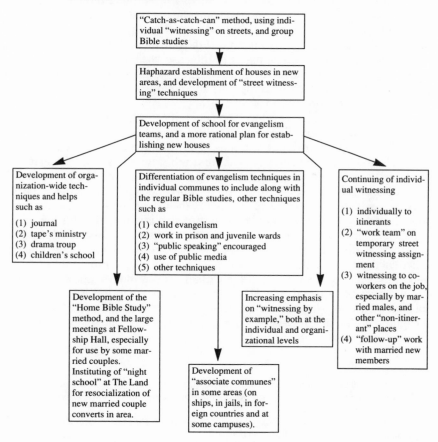

* The establishment of an exact pattern of evolution of evangelism methods is impossible, and unnecessary for our purposes. This figure should be treated as more a presentation of the differentiation itself, rather than a statement about exactly when the differentiation occurred, although some chronology is represented in movement from top to bottom of the figure.

occur, particularly after the demise of the large target population of itinerant youth and the establishment of so many family units within CCO as members married and started families. Toward the end of its illustrious history as an autonomous organization, CCO became much more congregationally oriented, and came to resemble a regular denomination in many ways (see Lofland and Richardson for more analysis of these later developments[29]).

In Richardson and Stewart[30] the CCO conversion methods are compared to those presented in Lofland and Stark,[31] which is the most cited conversion model in the literature. The methods used by the CCO seemed a good test of the Lofland and Stark approach. The major finding of this application was that affective ties might work differently in CCO than they did in the UC group Lofland studied. Lofland had indicated in the earlier model that in order to convert someone the person had to have loosened ties with outsiders and developed affective ties with insiders. That sounds quite logical but only operates if the outsiders have negative views of the group, such as was apparently the case with the UC. In the CCO group a number of parents had quite positive views of the CCO, and thus positive affective ties between parents and potential converts might actually contribute to conversion.

The comparison also revealed the necessity to offer new perspectives to the ones Lofland and Stark indicated. They said that potential converts could interpret problems and solutions in one of three perspectives—political, religious, and psychiatric. Taking a religious view (which derived from early socialization) contributed to the probability of conversion, according to Lofland. Richardson and Stewart added a "physiological perspective" which was defined as "including the use of elements or activities to affect the body and mind in ways to furnish some meaning for the person."[32] The prior use of drugs and sex by many converts illustrate this perspective, as did the use of exercise, dieting, health foods, vitamins, and other such activities that directly impact the body. The critique of Lofland and Stark's model also revealed some other needed modifications, including the possible special role played by early socialization into a fundamentalist culture. However, this latter point, which made use of Toch's[33] intriguing notion of "oversocialization," seemed applicable mainly to Jesus Movement groups such as CCO.

---

29. John Lofland and James T. Richardson, "Religious Movement Organizations: Elemental Forms and Dynamics," in L. Krisberg, ed., *Social Movements Conflicts and Change*, vol. 7 (Greenwich, Conn.: JAI Press, 1984).

30. James T. Richardson and Mary Stewart, "Conversion Process Models and the Jesus Movement," in Richardson, *Conversion Careers*.

31. Lofland and Stark, "Becoming a World-Saver."

32. Richardson and Stewart, "Conversion Process Models," 28-29.

33. Hans Tock, *The Social Psychology of Social Movements* (Minneapolis: Bobbs Merrill, 1965), 128-29.

CONCLUSIONS

We have used three major new religious groups that developed in the 1960s and 1970s to show some typical ways in which newer religions tried to gain converts. Virtually all new religions, even those of Eastern origins, were proselytizing organizations. They were forced to proselytize or die an early death as an organization. The three chosen were representative of some of the larger more sophisticated groups. Many other groups were much more haphazard in their recruitment efforts and were usually less effective in gaining members.

A typical conversion process for the groups described can be discerned. Each group initially spent considerable time and resources with public forms of street witnessing and gained most converts through this approach. As they became established, and less transient, more recruitment was done through friendship and kinship networks. Mainly because of the social and demographic changes that resulted in fewer street people being available, the groups diversified their recruitment methods, or they began to see a drop-off in membership numbers, because of the usually high turnover of most such groups. As families developed within the organizations a "domestication effect"[34] was felt, leading to a tendency toward congregational (as opposed to communal) lifestyle and more recruitment among friendship networks. Thus the groups that have managed to survive are becoming more "normal" as time passes in many ways, including their conversion/recruitment methods.

---

34. Richardson, "Active vs. Passive Convert."

Part II

Theological Perspectives on Conversion

With the demonstration of diverse meanings and procedures of conversion in Part I, one may wonder if there is any systematic way to approach this aspect of the great world religions.

In this section Christian scholars review conversion as a part of theological systems of Western Europe and North America. The chapters begin with the study of biblical evidence by Gaiser. In the midst of diversity he finds a basic emphasis on transformation, which was the conclusion of Gaventa in chapter three. In chapter six, the context that surrounds conversion is highlighted in discussions of God's involvement in the world as creator, redeemer, convicting and guiding Spirit. Along with an examination of these divine themes in scripture, Gaiser examines biblical anthropology, the human response to God's initiative through Christ for salvation.

In Roman Catholicism the models for conversion were found in individual turning of the heart. The experience of St. Augustine became a classic in his *Confessions*. In chapter seven, Hudson shows the tension between this model and later scholastic preoccupation with metaphysical analysis. The unifying theme for Catholic understanding of conversion is the church as the mystical body of Christ.

How is this biblical evidence organized into comprehensive systems of thought about God and his creation? This is the task of systematic theology. In chapter eight, McKim provides an overview of the major or minor place of conversion in mainline Protestantism. He begins with the Reformed emphasis upon conversion as part of the broader plan of God in vocation, or the calling of the elect to receive salvation. He then notes the nuances of conversion in Lutheran, Reformed, and Arminian dogmatics. Each of these involves some model for redemption and seeks to answer questions generated by their diversity.

A unifying, ecumenical evangelism is presented in chapter nine. Reid speaks from a lifetime of ministry about the conviction of sin and new life

91

through salvation that comes through the conversion experience. This is essential in evangelism. Historical defintions that divide Christians are not essential. He provides a meliorist position in which the sharpness of theological divisions and the precision of dogmatic formulations are mellowed. This is an example of how conversion themes might be communicated to congregations. It represents the application of conversion to the local church.

Chapter Six

A Biblical Theology
of Conversion

Frederick J. Gaiser

CONVERSION IN THE BIBLE

The Biblical Vocabulary

Readers of English versions of the Bible will run across terms like "conversion" or "convert(s)" or "to convert" only rarely.[1] Passages in which they occur would provide insufficient data to support even a definition of the term, much less a book on the phenomenon. Yet definitions abound, and the phenomenon—the unconditional turning of the human toward God—is seen as fundamental to biblical religion.[2]

Biblical studies of conversion (which this chapter does not mean to reproduce, but which it presupposes) regularly examine several Hebrew and Greek terms.[3] The primary Old Testament root is *šûb* (to turn back, return).

---

1. In the KJV/RSV tradition, "conversion" occurs only once (Acts 15:3); other forms of the root occur a handful of times.
2. "The whole proclamation of Jesus ... is a proclamation of unconditional turning to God," J. Behm, *metanoeō*, in *Theological Dictionary of the New Testament* (hereafter cited as *TDNT*), ed. G. Kittel, trans. and ed. G. Bromiley (Grand Rapids, Mich.: Eerdmans, 1967), IV.1002.
3. Cf. the chapter in this volume by Beverly Gaventa. Among the several biblical studies previously available, see especially: J. Behm and E. Würthwein, *metanoeō, TDNT* IV.975-1008; G. Bertram, *strephō, TDNT* VII.714-29; G. Bromiley and H. N. Malony, "Conversion," in *The International Standard Bible Encyclopedia*, ed. G. Bromiley (Grand Rapids, Mich.: Eerdmans, 1979), I.768-770; J. Fichtner et al., "Bekehrung," in *Die Religion in Geschichte und*

The Greek New Testament uses principally the terms *epistrephō* (to turn, turn around, turn back), *metamelomai* (to change one's mind, regret, repent), and *metanoeō* (to change one's mind, repent, be converted). Although an examination of the biblical theology of conversion must pay careful attention to the very large number of passages which employ these terms, it cannot be limited to a study of one or several words. The phenomenon of radical change, of transformation, of turning in repentance and faith away from one focus of life to another (or back to a former one) cuts across biblical theology from beginning to end. Understanding conversion requires understanding what the Bible thinks about the nature and work of both God and humanity.

Conversion as Transformation

Whether in the Old Testament ("Behold, I am doing a new thing," Is 43:19) or the New ("The old has passed away, behold, the new has come," 2 Cor 5:17), God's transformation of all things—the heavens and the earth, humans and all creatures—is at the heart of biblical theology. This transforming work of God provides the framework within which biblical conversion can properly be understood. Reading isolated conversion stories might make conversion seem to be an occasional, sometimes bizarre phenomenon; indeed, the Bible does report dramatic and intense religious experiences, experiences open to profitable study by students of comparative religion, psychologists, and others. The biblical theologian will be deeply interested in the results of such study. Yet, the Bible has remarkably little interest in psychological analysis (if only because it represents a time when such differentiated fields of study had not been developed); it is interested in what God is doing in the world. It seeks to name experience—both the ordinary and the bizarre—theologically and to relate it to the creating and saving work of God in the old and new covenants.

In the Old Testament the psalms present most forcefully the transforming experience. Virtually without exception, the psalmists of lament, though beginning in distress and terror, experience a turn, a transformation, a movement from disorientation to reorientation.[4] The one who cries, "How long, O Lord? Wilt thou forget me for ever?" (Ps 13:1), is heard to exclaim, "I will sing to the Lord, because he has dealt bountifully with me" (v. 6).[5] This

---

Gegenwart, 3rd ed. (Tübingen: J. C. B. Mohr [Paul Siebeck], 1957), I.976-84 (hereafter cited as *RGG*); K. G. Kuhn, *proselytos, TDNT* VI.727-44; F. Laubach, J. Goetzmann, and U. Becker, "Conversion, Penitence, Repentance, Proselyte," in *The New International Dictionary of the New Testament*, ed. C. Brown (Exeter: Paternoster Press, 1975), I.353-362; J. A. Soggin, *šûḇ*, in *Theologisches Handbuch zum Alten Testament*, ed. E. Jenni and C. Westermann (Munich: Chr. Kaiser; Zurich: Theologischer Verlag, 1976), II.884-891. For a more extended study, see W. L. Holladay, *The Root šûḇh in the Old Testament* (Leiden: E. J. Brill, 1958).

4. This language is employed by W. Brueggemann, *The Message of the Psalms* (Minneapolis: Augsburg, 1984). Cf. also his other related writings: "The Formfulness of Grief," *Interpretation* 31 (1977): 263-275; "From Hurt to Joy, from Death to Life," *Interpretation* 28 (1974): 3-19.

5. For an example of the many studies of this phenomenon in the psalms, see C. Westermann, *Praise and Lament in the Psalms* (Atlanta: John Knox, 1981).

movement (a true conversion experience) is not mechanical or guaranteed, not gained through bargaining or manipulation, not predictable or always the same. It is a personal experience of the restoration to life wrought by God's redemption.

Studies show that this structure of transformation permeates the entire Old Testament.[6] Nor is it left behind in the movement to the New Testament— the title of which is a Christian confession that the decisive transformation or conversion of the world has taken place. Jesus' parables expound the decisive move from old to new. The Johannine literature represents the work of Christ as bringing "new birth," as a passing from death to life and from darkness to light. The concept of a radical transformation effected by the revelation of God in Christ is the foundation of Pauline theology. From the beginning of the biblical literature to the end it provides the theological norm and center by which the traditional accounts of conversion are measured and understood.

THE THEOLOGICAL CONTEXT OF BIBLICAL CONVERSION

God's Involvement in the World

An investigation of the biblical theology of conversion must, of course, begin with God. But, as the great Old Testament theologian Gerhard von Rad noted in another context, this is "simply the beginning of the whole question: What kind of a Yahweh is he?"[7]

By using God's personal name, Yahweh, von Rad's comment ushers us into a key concept: When the Bible speaks of God it does not have in mind a general or vague notion of a beneficent higher power; it speaks of a personal God, actively involved in the everyday affairs of the world and especially in the history of Israel and the life, death, and resurrection of Jesus Christ. This essential idea becomes most fully expressed in the New Testament's witness to incarnation: The Word, who is God, has become flesh (Jn 1:1-14). But the Yahweh of the Old Testament is already seen to have a radical inclination toward incarnation.

Both the beauty and offense of this particularity are evident in the Bible's talk of conversion. The language used is common and ordinary: to turn, turn around, return, change one's mind. Though the words can and will become technical shorthand to refer to a profoundly religious reality, their source is not cultic worship or the religious realm; it is everyday experience in all its variety. In biblical grammar, as in human life, there are many kinds of turning: One can turn to something new or return to the old, turn back or turn away, turn or be turned, turn often or once-for-all, turn oneself or something (or someone) else, or simply turn (without an object). The rich variety and

---

6. Cf. Brueggemann, "From Hurt to Joy"; F. Gaiser, *Songs in the Story* (Ph.D. dissertation, University of Heidelberg, 1984).

7. Gerhard von Rad, *Old Testament Theology* (New York: Harper & Brothers, 1965), II.415.

humble origins of this language stand as a caution against all attempts to systematize too exactly or define too narrowly the idea of conversion, at least as understood in the Bible—to refer it, for example, to one kind of emotional experience or only to a unique and unrepeatable act, to identify those phenomena which must accompany it, or to find the approved order in which these must occur.[8] Constructive syntheses are not without value and are part of the theological task, but the biblical witness will groan against the strain of being forced into too precise a mold.

The fundamental biblical observation that God is active in human affairs will also raise an early warning against a dogmatic insistence that conversion is either solely the work of God or primarily the work of the human person. Arguments over the relation between divine sovereignty and human response have forever fueled the fires of theological controversy, especially in the matter of conversion. They will need to be examined again in the present study.

Yet, from the outset it is important to recognize that the biblical record will not always be as clear on this issue as many present observers would prefer. This is neither a failure on the part of biblical writers to think consistently (though, of course, there are real differences in emphases by different writers in different situations) nor an assertion from biblical theology that the question of agency is of no interest; rather, the fluidity of biblical language in this matter (who is the actor in human conversion?) is permitted because of the central biblical confession that God is actively involved in human events. Without succumbing to a simplistic determinism and without denying the possibility of unmediated divine intervention, the Bible's incarnational perspective insists that God's work in the world need not be neatly distinguished from the work of his creatures. For the authors of scripture, Yahweh's demand ("Return, O faithless children," Jer 3:14) is in no way incompatible with Israel's cry ("Turn us again, O God," Ps 80:3 [KJV]).

God as Creator

While celebrating God's work through human beings, biblical theology is clear about the source of creative action. God is the creator; human power, though real, is derivative. This assertion, first presented canonically in the creation narratives, is basic to a biblical understanding of conversion.

Conversion is, among other things, a creative event. It is a matter of life and death (Ez 18:32; Acts 11:18). In conversion, a person or nation turns (or is turned) from evil (Acts 8:22) and death (2 Cor 7:9f) to life (Ez 33:14-15) and to the good (Acts 26:20)—in short, to God (2 Chr 30:6). Therefore, like all matters of life and death, conversion is, first and foremost God's business. This conclusion will be determined, not by counting and comparing subjects of the biblical verbs to turn, but by understanding that in biblical theology

---

8. For a brief introduction to what has been involved in these issues, see C. B. Johnson and H. N. Malony, *Christian Conversion: Biblical and Psychological Perspectives* (Grand Rapids, Mich.: Zondervan, 1982), 103-110.

all life belongs to God and only God can give life.[9]

In the primeval act of creation (Gn 2:7) and in the eschatological act of redemption (Jn 3:16), life is the gift of God. Given in birth and in new birth, life is daily sustained by the Spirit of God (Ps 104:27-30). Death is separation from God (Ps 6:5), while abundant life is found precisely and only in relationship with God (Jn 10:10). By connecting conversion and life (Acts 11:18), the Bible connects conversion and creation (Acts 14:15). Although conversion experiences will differ, conversion is God's creative work

God as Redeemer

Conversion is a creative work of God, but it is, of course, not identical to creation "in the beginning." It is a new creation or re-creation—which assumes there is some need for this. The human God created has strayed; conversion has become necessary. Thus, conversion is also a redemptive act.

In the Bible, God is known both as creator and as redeemer.[10] God redeems or rescues his people from danger; God redeems or liberates his people from sin; God redeems the world from evil. Both Old and New Testaments relate conversion to forgiveness and redemption (Is 55:7; Lk 24:47). Return and repentance become possible because of the mercy and compassion of the Redeemer; they are enabled by divine grace.

The preaching of Jesus, reminiscent of that of John the Baptist, makes this clear: "Repent, for the kingdom of heaven is at hand" (Mt 4:17; cf. 3:2). This might be understood as threat, and indeed it contains that element; when God appears, the frailty and danger of the human condition become evident. But the coming of God's kingdom was not fundamentally a threatening reality for Israel; it was their consummate hope. The announcement of the kingdom was the announcement of the new age, the gracious transformation of all things. Jesus' hearers were enabled and invited to participate personally, through repentance or conversion, in a cosmic transformation.

The Bible as a whole sees God's redeeming work elliptically; i.e., redemption revolves around two foci: the exodus from Egypt and the death and resurrection of Jesus. These are the central events of the Old and New Testaments, respectively, the touchstones to which everything else is referred.

Conversion is no exception. The hortatory preaching of Deuteronomy promises return to the land (the goal of the Exodus) for those who return to Yahweh (4:30; 30:2-3). Second Isaiah's call to Israel to return (44:22) includes the return to God and the return to the land in a new exodus. Peter's Pentecost

---

9. For the sake of clarity, theology often distinguishes between conversion and regeneration, emphasizing the sole work of God in regeneration (the creation of new life) and the work of both God and human in conversion (e.g., Johnson and Malony, *Christian Conversion,* 75f). Nevertheless, as the biblical texts make clear, the connection between the two is close and essential. Conversion needs to be seen, among other things, in the context of God's gift of life.

10. Whether or not these two activities can always be clearly distinguished is a matter of debate among biblical theologians. Isaiah 40-55, for example, uses some of the strongest biblical creation language to describe God's redemption of Israel from Babylonian exile. Cf. C. Stuhlmueller, *Creative Redemption in Deutero-Isaiah* (Rome: Biblical Institute, 1970).

sermon, calling for the conversion of Israel (Acts 2:38) focuses entirely on the death and resurrection of Jesus.

This historical focus is essential to a proper understanding of biblical conversion. Conversion, though personal, is never private; it is never unrelated to God's public work of redemption, the work of the gospel. The psalmist relates the conversion of sinners to the public teaching of God's ways (Ps 51:13). Again, a personal experience of redemption (Ps 66:16) is balanced poetically and theologically by God's corporate deliverance of Israel (Ps 66:5). Paul's conversion—profoundly personal—becomes publicly accountable as an instance of dying and rising in Christ (Phil 3:2-11).

For the biblical writers, relating individual conversion to historic redemption did not diminish the personal intensity of the experience; on the contrary; it deepened its significance by making every conversion a sign of the exodus or a sign of death and resurrection. Biblical conversion is, no doubt, a religious experience, similar to such experiences seen elsewhere, but it is made unique by its connection to the demonstrable historical work of God for the world to which scripture bears witness.

This historical reference gives biblical conversion a sacramental character. This is already implied by the Old Testament's relating the spiritual return to Yahweh of the nation or individual to the return to the land; spiritual renewal is related to history and to the stuff of the world. When Naaman, the Syrian leper, is converted to the worship of Yahweh (2 Kgs 5:15), he requests that he be given two mules' burdens of Israelite earth to take back with him to Syria (v. 17). This is not merely a sign of primitive henotheism; it is a recognition that Yahweh's promises are inextricably tied up with the land: They are particular and tangible. It is a sacramental request to partake in the promise.

In the New Testament conversion and baptism are frequently related (Mk 1: 4; Acts 2:38). Many Christian commentators speak of baptism as an obligation of the convert,[11] and the New Testament no doubt does recognize baptism as an obligation. But, as Pauline theology makes clear,[12] baptism is, first and foremost, gift; it is God's work, uniting the believer with the death and resurrection of Christ. In this light, the call to baptism is an invitation rather than an obligation—a summons to participate in God's eschatological redemption of the world. Biblical conversion entails nothing less.

Similarly, the eucharist, offering as it does forgiveness of sins and new life (Jn 6:50) and proclaiming "the Lord's death until he comes" (1 Cor 11:26), is for Christians a kind of conversion experience. In communion, the Christian partakes anew in the redemptive victory over death won by God once-for-all

---

11. For example, William Barclay, *Turning to God* (London: Epworth, 1963), 50.

12. Although Paul rarely employs the technical vocabulary related to conversion, conversion in the broader sense—God's radical transformation of the world—is central to his theology. Cf. B. R. Gaventa, *From Darkness to Light: Aspects of Conversion in the New Testament* (Philadelphia: Fortress, 1986), 17-51. G. Friedrich argues in RGG I.979 that for Paul conversion and justification are the same.

through Christ and given once-for-all to him or her in baptism.

It is this reference to the public redemptive work of God in history that makes conversion accountable to something other than internal experience. The Bible knows it is possible to turn away from God (toward other gods) just as it is possible to turn away from other gods toward the God of Israel and of Christ (Nm 14:43). Presumably the psychological experience is the same in either case. What is different is the historical referent—the name and work of the God to whom one turns. Thus, though conversion is a work of the Spirit, it is possible and necessary "to test the spirits to see whether they are of God" (1 Jn 4:1). The test is not an appeal to personal experience, not even a personal experience of God as proclaimed in the apostolic faith, but the historical confession "that Jesus Christ has come in the flesh" (v. 2).

The Spirit of God

The biblical accounts of conversion, especially in Acts, are sometimes explicitly viewed as the work of the Spirit of God.[13] For Acts, the entire apostolic ministry is carried out as a sign of the fulfillment of Joel's prophecy: "I will pour out my spirit on all flesh" (Jl 2:28; cf. Acts 2:17-21). Conversions effected by the preaching of the apostles were manifestations of the Spirit's presence.

Although elsewhere in scripture, terminological connections between conversion and Spirit are not frequent, Acts' theological assertion that conversion is the Spirit's work is hardly anomalous. The transformation of all things which lies at the center of Paul's message (and which we already related to conversion) is regularly ascribed to the Spirit (e.g., Rom 8:9-11; Gal 4:6-7). The transforming power of the Spirit is known to the Old Testament as well (Is 61:1f).

There is considerable variety among the biblical references to the Spirit of God. On the one hand, the Spirit is the intangible power of life itself, related linguistically[14] and phenomenologically to breath and wind; it is this Spirit which gives life to humans (Gn 2:7) and to everything that lives and breathes (Eccl 3:19; Ps 104:29-30). On the other hand, the Spirit is the intensified personal presence of God, bringing particular charismatic gifts for leadership and ministry (1 Sm 10:6).

Both ideas are essential for understanding a biblical theology of conversion. On the one hand, as has been seen, conversion is a creative act, renewing the breath of life, restoring what once was; on the other, it is a transforming act, making the impossible possible, producing what has never been.

Since the Spirit, like the wind, "blows where it wills" (Jn 3:8), there is always something mysterious and unpredictable about biblical conversion. Since the Spirit is as real, but as invisible, as breath, conversion will be a matter of intense and internal experience. Since the Bible makes clear that God's

---

13. See the review in Johnson and Malony, *Christian Conversion*, 87-101.
14. In both Hebrew and Greek, the word for spirit is also the word for breath.

breath of life blows in all people, all people will have common religious experiences (whether or not they are believers in the biblical God). But since, according to the New Testament, the Spirit of God comes to all through the historical work of Jesus Christ, Christian conversion will be unique. It will be more than personal experience; it will be a sign of the gospel, both for the one converted and for the world. It will point to Christ.

The Unity of God

Scripture's fundamental theological confession is the Old Testament *shema*: "Hear, O Israel: The Lord our God is one Lord" (Dt 6:4). "There is no god beside me," says Yahweh; "I kill and I make alive; I wound and I heal; and there is none that can deliver out of my hand" (Dt 32:39). Thus, biblical conversion is a change of focus or a change of lords. The nation or the individual is called to turn away from that which is not God to the one who alone is God. Particularly poignant is the divine lament over those who "keep on praying to a god that cannot save" (Is 45:20), which serves as prelude to the call for the conversion of the nations: "Turn to me and be saved, all the ends of the earth! For I am God, and there is no other" (45:22).

God's unity is the source of God's jealousy (Ex 20:5)—a difficult divine attribute which means both judgment and salvation for God's people. Since Yahweh alone is God, he will stand for no idolatry, no false worship. To turn away from God is to die (Jos 24:20). In the Old Testament's anthropomorphic language, such judgment can sound petulant or capricious, as though God will simply eradicate those who annoy him. Ezekiel reminds us, however, that God has "no pleasure in the death of any one" (Ez 18:32). Death comes because apart from God there is death. Death results from sin because evil acts have evil consequences (Ps 7:14-16).[15] Therefore, Yahweh's call to turn from evil, to repent, to be converted is precisely a call to life: "So turn, and live" (Ez 18:32). Yahweh's anger or wrath is in the service of Yahweh's compassion; it exists in order to call people back to him and to life (Mal 3:7).

The Bible recognizes, of course, that such a call is an appeal to faith. Jesus came preaching, "Repent, and believe in the gospel" (Mk 1:15). Especially Paul draws the connection between conversion and faith. The believer is "in Christ," thus becoming a new person. For Paul, human transformation (or conversion) comes through faith in Jesus Christ. This produces not only a new person, but a new community, in which all are one in Christ Jesus (Gal 3:23-28). Thus, in faith, human beings are converted, becoming children of God and participating in the divine unity.

Divine Repentance

Surprisingly perhaps, God can also be the subject of the technical verbs used in the Bible to describe what we have called conversion (to turn, to

---

15. Cf. Klaus Koch, "Is There a Doctrine of Retribution in the Old Testament?" in *Theodicy in the Old Testament*, ed. J. L. Crenshaw (Philadelphia: Fortress; London: SPCK, 1983), 57-87.

repent, to change). "God repented of the evil which he had said he would do to them" (Jon 3:10).[16] Apparently the Bible's high view of God ("I am the first and I am the last," Is 44:6; cf. Heb 13:8, "Jesus Christ is the same yesterday and today and for ever") does not exclude the possibility of divine response, of genuine interaction between God and God's creatures. It would be wrong to argue that the Bible presents a God who requires conversion; but a study of conversion would be incomplete without recognizing that the God of the Bible is genuinely interactive. Change in God which is seen as capricious or as a fundamental shift in God's nature gives rise to terror (Ps 77:10; Lam 5:22); yet an important part of God's compassion is his willingness to change, even to "repent" (cf. Hos 6:4-6 and 8:8-9).

The significance of this for human conversion is seen, for example, in Psalm 90. The psalmist's realistic appraisal of the human condition gives little reason for hope or optimism.

> The years of our life are threescore and ten,
> or even by reason of strength fourscore;
> yet their span is but toil and trouble;
> they are soon gone, and we fly away. (Ps 90:10)

But over against this notion of a frail and changing humanity, to what does the psalm appeal? Not to a changeless deity but to a personal Yahweh who can and will "turn": "Return, O Lord! How long? Have pity on they servants!" (v. 13). God's turning and compassion are equated. Hope comes to the human whom God turns (*šûbh*) to dust (v. 3) through God's own turning (*šûbh*) toward the human. According to the psalm this divine return gives significance to human work (v. 16-17); more broadly in biblical theology it is what makes human conversion possible.

THE HUMAN: THE NEED AND POSSIBILITY OF CONVERSION

The Human as Creature

The Bible holds the human in high regard. People are after all God's creation, "little less than the angels," crowned "with glory and honor" (Ps 8:5). Humans, male and female, are created in the image of God (Gn 1:27), an essential aspect of which is addressability and responsibility: the human person is one whom God can address as "you" and an "I" who is responsible before God.[17] The creation narrative assumes the human can respond to the divine imperative (Gn 2:16-17)—a view which will require further investigation in a study of biblical conversion.

---

16. For a recent study of divine repentance, cf. T. Fretheim, "The Repentance of God: A Key to Evaluating Old Testament God-talk," *Horizons in Biblical Theology* 10 (1988): 47-70.

17. So K. Barth, *Church Dogmatics* (Edinburgh: T. & T. Clark, 1958), III/1.182f, who sees this as the essential component of the image of God in humans. For a review of the history of interpretation of Genesis 1:26-27, see C. Westermann, *Genesis 1-11* (Minneapolis: Augsburg, 1984), 147-55.

The Need for Conversion

Yet, the human did not respond—at least not positively. The human the Bible knows in real history (rather than in the primeval garden) is "fallen." Humanity no longer lives in Eden, in direct intimate contact with God, but in a world of anxiety and distress, alienated from God and from one another. Humanity is in need of conversion.

The Human as Sinner

Biblical literature presents the human condition in more than one way. The significance of conversion will depend upon how one views the problem. The traditional perspective, most often employed in discussions of conversion, is the Adamic.[18] Here the fallen human situation is humanity's fault, totally the result of sin. Humans, created good, used their first freedom to rebel against God, ushering in the disastrous personal, social, and cosmic consequences of such rebellion.

Sin, as rebellion, is described as a turning away from God (Ps 78:40-41). The result of this human self-alienation is an alienation or turning away of God (Dt 23:14). The appropriate solution is the call for humans to return or repent—to convert (Jer 25:5-6; Ez 33:11). Humanity's return is followed by God's return and restoration (Dt 30:2-3).

Conversion in the Adamic perspective takes on the mirror-image characteristics of the problem. Sin is an individual act of rebellion; conversion is an individual act of return. Sin comes in the instant, with permanent consequences; conversion is a decisive and one-time act. Sin is death; conversion is life. Sin comes through Adam; conversion comes through turning to Christ in whom the consequences of Adam's sin are reversed (Rom 5:12-21). Since all evil consequences arise from human sin, theology's primary concern will be the conversion of the individual—which will thereby have beneficial social, political, and cosmic results.

The Human as Victim

Although the Adamic view is dominant in scripture and in Christian tradition, it is not the only biblical perspective. In the "ritual" vision of the world, evil is present already in the origin of things; it is the chaos with which God struggles in the creative act.[19]

Now humans are not so much individually responsible for their own condition; they are victims of forces beyond themselves from which they need liberation. Called by God to respond, they are unable "because of their bro-

---

18. To discuss the human condition, I will use the terminology and two of the four categories employed by Paul Ricoeur, *The Symbolism of Evil* (Boston: Beacon, 1967). As used here, "Adamic" does not refer to a male Adam, but to *'adam,* the Hebrew word for humankind. Cf. pp. 232-78.

19. Cf. Ricoeur, *The Symbolism of Evil,* 175-210. In his recent book *Creation and the Persistence of Evil* (San Francisco: Harper & Row, 1988), Jon Levenson has shown the strong lasting influence of this cosmogonic perspective on biblical literature.

ken spirit and their cruel bondage" (Ex 6:9). Heroic conversion is not the solution so much as release.

Nevertheless, the language and/or phenomenon of conversion and transformation come into play in this view also. Here the return of God is implored (Ps 6:4), while the turning away of the enemies (Ps 6:10) and the restoration (*šûbḫ*) of God's people (Ps 18:24) are celebrated. Yet this perspective also presents an internal transformation of the victim. That may come through the experience of deliverance by which the person comes to know or know again the saving power of God (Ps 6:8-10), or it may come through a (re)birth of faith which enables the victim to know God's presence even in the midst of tribulation (Ps 73:15f; Jb 42:1-6; 2 Cor 12:9-10). Such conversion provides a new way of seeing reality, as though a veil were lifted (2 Cor 3:15-16). The experience of liberation is possible even in the midst of fire and water (Is 43:2). The believer is released from the power of Satan and comes under the lordship of God (Eph 2:1f). The battle against evil powers will result in human liberation (rather than vice versa, as in the Adamic view).

The Possibility of Conversion

In the biblical world, conversion is possible, first and foremost, because of the power and compassion of God. Nevertheless, in biblical language and experience, it makes sense to call upon the sinner to turn or to return to God. The human, even outside of Eden, remains responsible and addressable.

The Bible does not, of course, portray the fallen human with the same freedom as that given in creation. Alienation is complete, and the result is death (Col 1:21; Rom 6:23). This radical understanding of sin requires affirming divine sovereignty and initiative in conversion. The human, as sinner, cannot return to God (Jn 6:44). Only God can open eyes (Acts 26:18) and hearts (Acts 16:14) toward conversion. Reconciliation and life come only from God. At the same time, in biblical theology sinners and unbelievers can be said to retain the image of God[20]—a matter of considerable importance for the subject of conversion if responsibility and addressability are included under the divine image. Even though the image for a fallen humanity will be fully restored only in Christ (Col 1:15f), the image given in creation remains after the fall to be passed on to all humankind (Gn 5:3). The human creature retains a dignity conferred by God and, even without knowing redemption, a measure of accountability for his or her actions (Is 47:5-7; Rom 2:15). So, just as God spoke "to them" (Gn 1:28) when he first blessed humans—the addressability implied in the words "to them" is lacking in the blessing of the animals (Gn 1:22)—God continues to speak to humans (generally through other humans), positing in them responsibility and calling them to turn. Conversion remains also a

---

20. The issue of the loss or retention of the divine image in the fall has been much debated in Christian theology. For a recent review, cf. P. E. Hughes, *The True Image: The Origin and Destiny of Man in Christ* (Grand Rapids, Mich.: Eerdmans, 1989).

human event, and human experience is honored, even under a biblical theology which carefully retains for God the initiative in matters of creation and redemption.

The Subject of Conversion

Individual and Community In current usage, conversion is generally reserved for an internal experience of individual persons. Yet historical biblical studies point out that the earliest calls to return generally came to God's people as a whole (e.g., Jer 31:6). While it might be rightly argued that this reflects to some degree an earlier stage of human development prior to the emergence of the individual or the interest in psychology in the modern sense, it would be incorrect to assume there were no early accounts of individual turnings (cf. the lament psalms) or later accounts of appeals to a whole people (cf. the preaching of John the Baptist). The distinction between communal and individual conversion cannot be plotted exactly on a time line.

Accounts of individual conversions, especially in the book of Acts, report unique and dramatic events, fundamentally and forever altering the theological and ethical perspective of individual human beings. Such a possibility can be offered a person as gift, precisely when the larger community is lost in meaninglessness and disarray (Ez 18:1-32).

Nevertheless, the Bible recognizes that the human is created for community (Gn 2:18) and finds meaning in community (Eccl 4:9-12). Thus, the direction taken by the community will profoundly affect the life of the individual; the call to the community to turn to God promises life to each one within that community—whether or not that one will be able to claim an individual religious experience. The return to God which makes one well is also the return to the community of believers (Lk 17:19).

Male and Female From one end of scripture to another, both men and women are called upon to turn and follow God. In his letters, Paul greets both men and women who have been converted to Christ (e.g., Rom 16). Acts reports the conversion of Lydia (16:11-15) alongside the stories of conversions of men. The gospel knows no distinction between male and female (Gal 3:18).

Nevertheless, if conversion is described primarily as the dramatic return to God of the rebelling sinner, some biblical theologies would wonder if this applies equally to women. Feminist interpretations have sometimes identified woman's primary sin as self-denial rather than self-assertion. Rather than pride, sin takes the form of refusal to be the self intended by God.[21]

With this in mind, it is instructive to compare the conversion stories of Ruth and the prodigal son. The prodigal's story (Lk 15:11-32) is the more familiar; indeed, it often becomes the stereotypical model of Christian conversion:

---

21. For a summary of this position, see Wanda W. Berry, "Images of Sin and Salvation in Feminist Theology," *Anglican Theological Review* 60, no. 1 (1978): 25-54.

The rebellious son demands his own rights, turns away from the security of father and family, and sinks into a life of dissolution until in despair he humbly returns to the waiting father. The feminist critique sees it as a quintessentially male story.

Ruth's conversion to the worship of Yahweh comes about differently, however (Ruth 1:6-22). It comes through her loyalty to her mother-in-law Naomi (an Israelite) and, through Naomi, to Naomi's God. In an interesting twist of language, to return (*šûb*) in this story is at first precisely not to convert, but rather to remain untouched in Moab (1:8, 11, 12, 15, 16). Conversion comes for Ruth in traveling with, in sharing Naomi's return (1:10, 22) which does then become Ruth's return as well (1:22). Ruth's is a story of loyalty rather than rebellion, but it is no less a story of conversion.[22]

It would be a serious mistake to try to absolutize these gender distinctions—there are female rebels and male loyalists. Nevertheless, the feminist contribution here, which tends to see the human (especially perhaps the woman) as victim in the cosmogonic drama rather than only as rebel in the Adamic tradition, expands a biblical understanding of conversion.

The Old and the New

Despite the reality of sin and death, there remains in biblical thought an addressable human whose conversion is possible. Similarly, there is both continuity and discontinuity between the converted person—the new—and the person prior to conversion—the old.

The biblical record celebrates the radicality of God's new creation (Is 43:19; 46:6-8) while at the same time calling to mind the significance of the old (Is 46:8-11). Discussions of conversion or transformation emphasize the new—speaking of the convert as a new creature (2 Cor 5:17) with a new name (Acts 13:9), contrasting the old life of the flesh with the new life of the spirit (Rom 7:4-6). Nevertheless, memory of the old life remains beyond conversion (Gal 1:13-14); the significance of the works of the flesh, even though now "counted as loss," endures (Phil 3:4-6). The new person was recognized by God already in the old person (Gal 1:15).

The account of Paul's experience on the Damascus road is instructive in this regard (Acts 9:1-19). Is this event properly called a conversion or a call? In fact, it shares elements of both kinds of biblical stories—the conversion, with its greater emphasis on discontinuity (a new person, a new religion), and the call, with its greater place for continuity (a new task within the same religious community).[23]

In biblical theology, the converted person retains through creation a continuity with the preconversion self and with all humankind, even as through redemption there is an experience of discontinuity, an entry into a new reality.

---

22. Later tradition builds on and strengthens the conversion theme. In the Targum, Ruth's monologue of commitment (1:16-17) becomes a catechetical dialogue in which Ruth responds positively to Naomi's instructions and questions about Judaism. Cf. E. Levine, *The Aramaic Version of Ruth* (Rome: Biblical Institute, 1973), 22.

23. For a review of this debate in biblical studies, see Gaventa, *From Darkness to Light*, 1-46.

THE PARADOX OF AGENCY

Who is the active agent in conversion? The question has already emerged several times in our discussion. Biblical theology insists that only God has the power to give life, to instill faith, to produce repentance; yet the reality of human experience in conversion is not denied. God's work among humans does not negate human agency.

A central feature of biblical theology which helps us understand this paradox is the creative power of the divine word. The word through which God creates the heavens and the earth is the same word which calls people to turn or repent, which proclaims to them the gospel. Thus, this divine call, which (mediated or unmediated) is a regular feature of biblical conversion accounts, sets up not merely one choice among many. It sets life or death before the person and, because it is the creative power of God, it makes life possible.

This is clear in the story of the conversion of Nineveh (Jon 3:1-10). Jonah's proclamation of divine judgment produces wholesale repentance (including even the cattle!), and Nineveh is spared. The story assumes that human conversion is essential for life, yet the narrator is careful not to undermine divine sovereignty (Jon 3:9). Nineveh's new life is made possible, not by its own repentance or its own decision, but by the divine compassion which spoke the word to empower repentance. Without that creative word there would have been no repentance—indeed, no story. The word of God accomplishes its purpose (Is 55:10-11). Still, human agency is not dismissed. The conversation between God and Nineveh set in motion by Jonah's words is real, as are the alternative futures which the story allows: repentance and life or rejection and destruction. But both alternatives are made possible by the word of God.[24]

Thus, the Bible can speak of a genuine mutuality between God and humanity in conversion ("Return to me and I will return to you," Mal 3:7) without compromising the divine initiative.[25] It can call people to choose God (Jos 24:14-15) because it has made clear that God has chosen them (Jos 24:1-13).

THE ESCHATOLOGICAL VISION

In the present era, the Bible lives with the mystery and offense that "many are called, but few are chosen" (Mt 22:14). Faith, though intended for all, is found among some and not others. God calls all to conversion but not all will be converted.

---

24. On history as a divine/human conversation, see H. W. Wolff, "The Understanding of History in the Old Testament Prophets," in *Essays on Old Testament Hermeneutics*, ed. C. Westermann (Atlanta: John Knox, 1979), 336-55.

25. Holladay, *The Root šûbh* defines a covenantal usage of the verb to turn; it expresses "a change of loyalty on the part of Israel or God, each for the other" (116).

Nevertheless, the Bible looks forward to a time when all will know, "from the rising of the sun and from the west, that there is none besides me" (Is 45:6), when "every knee should bow, in heaven and on earth and under the earth, and every tongue confess that Jesus Christ is Lord, to the glory of God the Father" (Phil 2:10-11). In the final revelation of God's glory, all nations shall come to its brightness (Is 60:1-3). The New Testament proclaims the coming of this light in Christ; thus, through conversion, followers of Jesus enter already the age to come. They live in hope for the conversion of all people (2 Pt 3:9), for the consummation of this age and the transformation of creation itself (Rom 8:19-25). Conversion holds out a cosmic promise, a participation in the work of God beyond the self.

Conversion is a call to return, promising a restoration of the original intimate relationship between God and humanity experienced in creation. Nevertheless, it is not a nostalgic call to the old or a return to the past but an entry into something completely new. Biblical conversion promises nothing less than singing at last, with the mountains and the hills, a new song to the Lord (Is 55:12-13).

Chapter Seven

The Catholic View of Conversion

Deal W. Hudson

Conversion represents the turning of the human heart and mind toward a new vision of the world and the beginning of a new life. As such, its range of relevant themes, historical figures, and significant issues is almost unlimited. However, at the very least the most important questions are these: What causes this turning? What effects should result? How does God intervene in the direction of a human life? Do we turn to God freely? No doubt such questions take us onto ground where the veil of mystery cannot be removed. Since a mystery is nonetheless knowable by a suprahuman intellect, this invocation does not silence speculation but serves as a reminder of what inevitably will *not* be said.

Taken in itself, conversion does not belong to the church alone; it represents the capacity for self-examination and change, the malleability of human character and identity. Conversion, thus, involves moral and spiritual risk. It is unpredictable. Vatican II theologian Yves Congar conceded that a conversion, as "a change in the principle or principles which control the synthesis or direction of our life," may be for good or ill.[1]

Conversion is an inherited idea, coming from both the prophetic tradition of Judaism and, as Arthur Nock has shown,[2] from the philosophical schools of Greece and Rome. Converts have not necessarily been religious, Christian, or Catholic; they have embraced psychological, moral, political, or intellectual ends, rather than a supernatural one. The Catholic Church is in a

---

1. Yves M.-J. Congar, "The Idea of Conversion," *Thought* (Spring 1958): 5.
2. A.D. Nock, *Conversion: The Old and the New in Religion from Alexander the Great to Augustine of Hippo* (New York: Oxford University Press, 1933).

unique historical situation to acknowledge this diverse legacy, and does.

Very little about a conversion can be taken for granted or systematically decided upon in advance. Caution is necessary. In the case of Catholic conversion, its causes and motives, excepting the grace of God, are irreducibly individual. G.K. Chesterton, himself an influential convert, wrote: "The church is a house with a hundred gates; and no two men enter at exactly the same angle."[3] As can be seen from St. Augustine's *Confessions*, a conversion can be multifaced and multilayered; it can encompass the lessons of personal experience and friendship, the tides of political and social history, the inspiration of art and philosophy, and the enactment of institutional rite and ritual. The dominating text of Catholic conversion, the *Confessions*, bears witness that there is nothing, no matter how private or public, which cannot fall under the providential gaze of God in leading men and women to salvation.

In defending this divine initiative, he set the foundation of Catholic conversion squarely on St. Paul's proclamation of all-encompassing grace. Augustine insisted that grace could not be explained, as Pelagius insinuated, by crediting human merit against the account of divine justice. God's grace was all-in-all. Robert O'Connell suggested the real scope of a Catholic account of conversion in this comment on Augustine: "The very heart of our universe, he knew, beats with a maternal care that was, like all maternal care, profoundly unaccountable."[4] The life of Augustine, the Catholic convert *par excellence*, culminated with the discovery that the church, the body of Christ, embodied this same motherhood.

The following sections on conversion—1) classical themes, 2) contemporary emphases, 3) the church and the sacraments, and 4) converts—can only hope to introduce a concept of this scope and richness.

CLASSICAL THEMES

Most commentators recognize that classical theology did not focus its discussion of conversion on the church, cosmology, salvation history, or the providential knowledge of God, but on the act of justification. Yet it should be remembered that Augustine, standing at the culmination of the Patristic age and anticipating the Medieval, narrated his experience of conversion within a much broader context, at once personal, intellectual, historical, and sacramental. No account of the Catholic "view" of conversion can be adequate if it does not acknowledge this plenitude of factors.

This is not to say that the story of a conversion cannot be told simply or conveyed in dogmatic terms. At the climax of the *Confessions* Augustine hears a voice telling him to pick up the New Testament sitting next to him and read—*Tolle, lege; Tolle, lege.* In that moment a single line from a Pauline epis-

---

3. G.K. Chesterton, *The Catholic Church and Conversion* (New York: Macmillan, 1950), 30.

4. Robert J. O'Connell, *Imagination and Metaphysics in St. Augustine* (Milwaukee: Marquette University Press, 1986), 24.

tle elicits a complete self-consciousness change in the life of St. Augustine. "For instantly, as the sentence ended, there was infused in my heart something like the light of full certainty and all the gloom of doubt vanished away."[5] For some this moment of insight may represent *the* conversion, conveying as it does a reminder of the Apostle's own episode on the Damascus road.

Still, such simplification misses much of the point, not only of the *Confessions* itself, but also of traditional and contemporary Catholic teaching about conversion. Conversion cannot be isolated and reduced to a self-conscious moment. Otherwise, the human personality in the foreground is being allowed to overwhelm the divine background. Allowing a single moment, no matter how dramatic, to represent conversion diminishes both the subjective psychological process of the convert and the myriad avenues of God's grace.

At the same time conversion cannot be limited to its dogmatic criteria, a reduction which is a central concern in the current literature. Before reviewing some of the traditional doctrinal teaching concerning conversions to the Catholic Church, it is important to clarify this issue in the present debate. Some contemporary Catholic writers tend to regard the discussions of conversion following the *Confessions* as a backward step. Walter Conn, for example, lauds Augustine's "eloquent articulation of the profound *experience* of interior transformation" and laments that "the dominant Scholastic mode of theology effectively lost the experience of conversion in the metaphysical analysis of faith, grace, and justification."[6]

Conn's complaint sets the tone for a number of other Catholic writers, who, reflecting the recent theological usage of the developmental theory, want to situate conversion within a psychological and social experience. Whether or not the "experience of conversion" was actually lost in medieval scholasticism cannot be debated here, but certainly it is necessary to ask how those doctrinal discussions have shaped the Catholic view of conversion. Neither can we debate whether Conn or others are guilty of overtaxing the psychological foreground of the convert to the detriment of the rest. Congar warned against the growing tendency of psychological explanations of conversion to restrict attention to a narrow "phenomenal" aspect. "For a conversion coming from God is not merely a psychological fact, it is a spiritual fact; it is not only an end, a refuge after a storm; it opens, rather a source for others, entering into the inexhaustible history of charity and the return of creation to God by means of light, love, and suffering."[7]

Between the time of Augustine and the Council of Trent (1542-1563), the discussions of conversion, couched in the traditional categories of justification, grace, and faith, all have a similar aim—upholding the primacy of

---

5. St. Augustine, *Confessions* and *Enchiridion*, trans. and ed. Albert C. Outler (Philadelphia: Westminister, 1955), 156.

6. Walter Conn, *Christian Conversion: A Developmental Interpretation of Autonomy and Surrender* (Mahwah, N.J.: Paulist, 1986), 6.

7. Congar, "The Idea of Conversion," 11.

God's action in the history of redemption and preserving the reality of human freedom in response. The Augustinian debate over the challenge of Pelagianism and semi-Pelagianism actually set the basic lines of these discussions in terms which are familiar to both Protestant and Catholic: What is God's part and what is man's part in the turning of a soul toward God? The answer remains consistently clear throughout the Catholic tradition: A saving conversion is impossible without the initiative of God. This was established among the official documents of the church as early as the Council of Carthage (418), and reaffirmed by the Council of Orange (529), which condemned the proposition "that by the force of nature we can right think or choose anything that is good . . . without the Holy Spirit's illumination," and affirmed that "God loves us as being such as we are about to become by his gift, not as we are by our own merit."[8]

The issue had been brought to a fine point by the semi-Pelagians who agreed with Augustine's emphasis on the divine initiative of grace but had also argued that in order to understand the "cooperation" of grace with nature in the act of conversion there must be some free human act, called the *inituim fidei*, which was the commencement of faith. In this view a person actively and freely disposes himself toward the reception of grace, coming to merit, *de congruo*, the first reception of grace. The answer of the Council of Orange, repeated by both Thomas Aquinas and the Council of Trent, was emphatic: Not even the disposition toward grace can be brought about by the unaided effort of the human will. But the question of this cooperation between grace and human freedom has remained the focus of debate, particularly with Protestants. "All the controversies and the heresies that have arisen concerning justification derive from the difficulties posed by this mystery of co-operation in the working out of man's Subjective Redemption."[9]

One will look in vain in Aquinas and the other medievals for extended treatises on "conversion," although the idea was used and discussed in various contexts. The reasons for this are both historical and theological. The drama of Augustine's life, in a way similar to Martin Luther's, occurred against the backdrop of an alien culture. In the largely unified culture of medieval Europe, at least until the time of Aquinas himself, salvation was usually a result of birth and baptism; adult conversion appeared of greater consequence to those peoples on the fringe—heretics, Jews, and Muslims.

One of Thomas Aquinas's two great *Summas*, the *Summa Contra Gentiles*, was written (1258-1263) to train Dominican missionaries for the evangelization of Muslims in Spain. Although the theological focus of both *Summas* rests on the order of divine grace and the act of justification, Aquinas neither ignores the idea of conversion itself nor its affective complexity. That conversion was at the center of his theological reflection can be seen by looking

8. Henry Bettenson, ed., *Documents of the Christian Church* (New York: Oxford University Press, 1963), 61.

9. Ludwig Ott, *Fundamentals of Catholic Theology*, trans. Patrick Lynch (St. Louis: B. Herder, 1958), 219.

at the tripartite design of the *Summa Theologiae*. Part 1a discusses God and creation, part 2a the principles of morality and the virtues, and part 3a Christ and the sacraments. Without exaggeration it can be said that the whole work is primarily intended as a description of how the creation, particularly its free human creatures, is converted, or "turned back" toward the Creator,

Within this Neo-Platonic framework of divine *exitus*, God's "exit" in creation, and human *reditus*, the return to God in redemption, conversion is such an obvious concern to Aquinas that it becomes almost unnoticeable.[10] Aquinas's separate treatises on Providence, Angels, Divine Government, Happiness, Gifts and Beatitudes, Law, Grace, Faith, Hope, Love, Christ, and the Sacraments each have a particular importance in describing the economy of salvation, reflecting in a systematic way the plenitude of factors witnessed to in the *Confessions*. Attempting to fix a moment of conversion in Aquinas would be as futile as selecting a comparable moment in Dante's *Commedia*.

It is typical of Aquinas's theological imagination that one of the most important texts on conversion would be found in the treatise on angels (1a. 50-64). Here he posed the question: "Does an angel need grace in order to turn [*converteretur*] to God?" (1a. 62, 2). Even Augustine could not have provided a more anti-Pelagian answer: The angels, though the most perfect creatures in the hierarchy of created beings, share with the human creatures the need for grace in order to turn to God. Angels need grace since the aim of their conversion, God, surpasses their "natural" power of volition, making the intervention of a supernatural principle necessary. "Grace" is the operation of such a power, and "conversion" the motion of the will toward God which results.

Since there exist several differing kinds of grace, Aquinas distinguishes three kinds of conversions: 1) a perfect delight in God requiring "consummate grace," 2) a turning that *merits* perfect happiness produced by "habitual grace," and 3) the turning that consists in disposing oneself to receive grace, which also presupposes action by God. Thus, in reverse order, he presents what have been described as the three phases in conversion: preparation, merit, and glory. Once again, Aquinas suggested that a conversion is nothing less than the entirety of the redemptive return to God.

The fullest treatment of human conversion by Aquinas is found in the treatise on grace (1a2ae. 106-114).[11] It is complicated by the fact that human salvation, unlike that of the angels, involves time and history. The different orders of angels chose their salvation or damnation at the first instant of their creation (1a. 63, 5). All of the divisions and subdivisions Aquinas designated within the order of grace are intended to do justice to

---

10. See Thomas Gilby, "Structure of the *Summa*" and "The Dialectic of Love in the *Summa*," Appendices 1 & 10 in St. Thomas Aquinas, *Summa Theologiae*, vol. 1, trans. Thomas Gilby (New York: McGraw-Hill, 1964).

11. Translations are taken from St. Thomas Aquinas, *Summa Theologiae*, vol. 30, trans. Cornelius Ernst (New York: McGraw-Hill, 1972).

the temporal and social aspects of human conversion.

This is the rationale behind the primary distinction between *gratiam gratum facientem* ("grace which makes pleasing," often called sanctifying grace) and *gratiam gratis datam* ("freely bestowed grace"). The idea of a "freely bestowed" grace confirms the social matrix of conversion: "The cooperation of one man with another so that he might be brought back to God," through teaching or other means of persuasion (1a2ae. 111, 4). The grace which "makes pleasing," or sanctifies, attests the necessity of a new interior *habitus* in the convert, of what Kierkegaard called "subjectivity." Likewise, the next distinction between operative and cooperative grace is critical because it preserves both ways in which God can move us: either cooperatively by through our willing or as the result of a divine operation alone. Operative grace, it could be said, occurs "in spite of" us.

The temporal component of conversion is further accentuated by Aquinas's differentiation of prevenient and subsequent grace. The five effects of subsequent grace span both earthly and heavenly life, beginning with the healing of the soul and ending with the attainment of glory. The healing of the soul is called a prevenient grace in respect to the second effect, the willing of the good. The second effect is called subsequent in respect to the first, and so on (1a2ae. 111, 4). Once again what matters is not solely a metaphysical distinction but a recognition of how God accomplishes the conversion of creatures who exist in history, in society, and in freedom.

The decisive act in the process of conversion is justification, itself defined as a movement from the state of sin to the state of justice (1a2ae. 113, 5). Justification includes the establishment of a right order with God and "rightness of order in man's own interior disposition" (1a2ae. 113, 1). Aquinas categorizes the former as operative grace and the latter cooperative: "God does not justify us without us, since while we are being justified, we consent to God's justice by movement of free choice" (1a2ae. 111,2). In addition to the act of faith (1a2ae. 113, 4), there are four requirements for justification: the infusion of grace, free choice directed towards God, free choice directed at sin, and the forgiveness of sin (1a2ae. 113, 8).

In this way, operative grace does not remain external to the converted; it becomes cooperative: "Someone is said to cooperate with another, not only as a secondary agent with a principal agent, but also when he helps one to reach an end already defined in advance. Now by operative grace man is helped by God in order that he might will the good" (1a2ae. 111, 3.ad 3) As Bernard Lonergan said of this passage: "Here the metaphysical category of instrumentality is given a psychological content."[12] In pointing to this usually unnoticed dimension in Aquinas, Lonergan highlighted the psychological, not simply metaphysical, dependence resulting from the instrumentality of grace. The same dependence can be inferred from Aquinas's analysis of the cooperative acts, such as the conversion of the heart [*convertentis*

---

12. Bernard Lonergan, *Grace and Freedom: Operative Grace in the Thought of St. Thomas Aquinas* (New York: Herder and Herder, 1971), 124.

cor], servile fear, and filial fear, which prepare for the repentence (3a. 85, 5).

The basic tenets of Aquinas's theology of grace and freedom are easily recognized in the famous "Decree Concerning Justification" from the sixth session of the Council of Trent (1547). But it would be a mistake to forget that Trent repeats affirmations dating back to the Councils of Orange and Carthage, Augustine's refutation of the Pelagians, and St. Paul's epistles. The decree on justification, meant as an answer to the challenge of the Reformers, begins by stressing the fallenness of man under sin and the redemption made possible by Christ's death. It defines justification as a *"translatio"* from "that state in which a man is born (under original sin), to the state of grace" (ch. IV).[13] For this "translation" to take subjective effect, the Council recognized the reality of a prevenient, operative grace which disposed a person towards a full cooperative friendship with God. These steps of preparation begin with faith and "when, understanding themselves to be sinners, they, by turning themselves (*se convertendo*) from the fear of divine justice, by which they are salutarily aroused, to consider the mercy of God, are raised to hope . . . and they begin to love . . . are moved against sin by a certain hatred and detestation, that is, by repentence that must be performed before baptism" (ch. VI).

The Council also warned against the Reformers' "ungodly confidence" in salvation (ch. IX), which was not to be considered a mode of self-consciousness—faith in one's faith. "No one can know with the certainty of faith, which cannot be subject to error, that he has obtained the grace of God" (ch. IX). The Council was determined to check the growing tendency among Protestants to view the criterion of justification as the scrutiny of a psychological state, a Christian version of Descartes' "clearness and distinctness." Surely the Council's defense of infant baptism and its conferral of justifying grace, without any self-awareness on the part of a child, makes the Catholic position clear. About this Yves Congar remarked, "It is a rather curious note that Protestantism, which originally insisted upon pure grace and the passivity of man, has come around on the one hand to questioning and even to challenging infant baptism, and on the other hand to emphasizing the role of experience in conversion."[14]

Clearly, the leaders of the Reformation and the leaders of the Counter-Reformation—St. Ignatius of Loyola, St. John of the Cross, St. Teresa of Avila, St. Philip Neri—reintroduced a type of inward scrutiny which had not been seen since Augustine. Yet, given this resemblance, there remain between these Catholic spiritual masters distinctive attitudes toward conversion. For example, the author of the *Spiritual Exercises*, St. Ignatius of Loyola sounds rather militant, fierce, even world-denying, when compared with the affectionate and accepting counsel of St. Philip Neri, the founder of the Oratory.

Among the writings of the Reformers, however, there is a repeated theme

---

13. Translations are taken from *Canons and Decrees of the Council of Trent*, ed. and trans. H.J. Schroeder (St. Louis: B. Herder, 1941).

14. Congar, "The Idea of Conversion," 12.

that Catholic theologians have rejected almost unanimously. This is an insistence on grace that annuls the free cooperation of the human will with divine grace. The Council of Trent opposed this teaching, just as it would be opposed in its seventeenth-century Jansenist form, for its portrayal of a purely passive will in relation to grace. This extreme pessimism was not deemed necessary to recover the subjective reaches of the self before God, as the work and example of St. Teresa would demonstrate.

CONTEMPORARY EMPHASES

Among contemporary Catholic theologians Bernard Lonergan has placed the most importance on the theology of conversion. Lonergan proposed that the renewal of theology itself could result from a systematic reflection upon conversion; the phenomenon of conversion should become the starting point of an empirical approach to theology. Since conversion is one of the fundamental facts of a religious life, Lonergan argued, "It follows that reflection on conversion can supply theology with its foundation and, indeed, with a foundation that is concrete, dynamic, personal, communal, and historical."[15]

Method in Theology, which implemented this approach, treats conversions of three kinds—intellectual, moral, and religious conversions—as distinctive modes of" self-transcendence." A conversion of any kind radically changes or transposes an individual's "horizon," the field of vision that provides a person's context of meaning. In continuing to stress the Thomistic connections between operative and cooperative grace, as he did in *Grace and Freedom*, Lonergan described the religious climax of conversion and a creation of a Christian horizon as a "sublation" of all three modes in one life. And being sensitive to the complexity of conversion, Lonergan maintained that these modes have no necessary order or sequence: "There is no fixed rule of antecedence and consequence, no necessity of simultaneity, no prescribed magnitudes of change."[16]

One of the most recent comprehensive views of conversion, Walter Conn's *Christian Conversion* starts from Lonergan's interpretation of conversion. By placing the three modes within the developmental schemes of Lawrence Kohlberg, James Fowler, and others, Conn succeeds in opening up theology to the kind of empirical grounding that Lonergan originally urged.

Karl Rahner also tried to put conversion more to the front in Catholic theology. He was concerned that the administration of the sacraments in the average parish often "masked" the experience of conversion behind baptism, confirmation, and first communion.[17] It is a mistake, he thought, to forget the conversion that takes place apart from or prior to sacramental

---

15. Bernard Lonergan, "Theology in its New Context," in *Conversion: Perspectives On Personal and Social Transformation*, ed. Walter Conn (New York: Alba House, 1978), 14.
16. Lonergan, "Theology in its New Context," 13.
17. Karl Rahner, "Conversion," in Conn, *Conversion*, 206.

practice. In an increasingly secular world, Catholics ought to give up their suspicion of the "conversion phenomena."

Just as Rahner encourages the church to embrace the tradition of conversion, he also discouraged any potential ruptures in the Christian ecumenical community that might result. True ecumenism does not bar the reception of a convert to Catholicism from other Christian community, as some argue, but discourages the targeting of a particular Christian group for proselytizing. In the spirit of the Vatican II "Decree on Ecumenism" (1964) and "On Dialogue with Unbelievers" (1968), Rahner urged that evangelism should aim at the "re-Christianization of contemporary atheists," in which he included "nominal" Christians, rather than practicing members of other Christian communions.[18]

For Christians who wish to change their community, the Catholic Church has the responsibility of shaping their subsequent attitude toward the former church. It should not be negative: "One should be able to notice that these converts were once Protestants. They should not regard their heritage merely as something past, but as charging them with a mission to their new church."[19]

However, Rahner did mention one caveat to incoming Protestants: If they are to become Catholics, they should not treat the choice of the church as if it were one of the many items on the spiritual menu. The Catholic and the genuine convert "are convinced," Rahner wrote, "that the truth of Christ is not 'divided,' that on the contrary where there exists a declaration by the Catholic church which makes absolute claim to the obedience of faith on the part of Catholics and insofar as it does so, and where *this* is in real contradiction to the declaration of another confession, the Catholic Church alone thus undivided possesses and declares the truth of Christ."[20]

Perhaps the most influential interpretation of conversion in Catholic parishes has been the growing emphasis on its social effects. The social teaching of the popes has led strongly in this direction, not merely since Vatican II, but as long ago as the encyclical *Rerum novarum* ("On the Condition of the Working Classes," 1891) of Leo XIII. Recently, the works of South American "liberation" theology have made the social, political, and economic dimensions of conversion *the* central theme. In *A Theology of Liberation* Gustavo Gutiérrez exploded any residual connections between liberal individualism and conversion: "To be converted is to commit oneself to the process of the liberation of the poor and oppressed, to commit oneself lucidly, realistically, and concretely."[21] Conversion, for Gutiérrez and other liberation theologians, is not authentically Christian if it does not affect the social structures that deny people access to basic human rights, including eco-

18. Ibid., 210.
19. Karl Rahner, *Theological Investigations*, vol. 3, trans. Karl-H. and Boniface Kruger (New York: Crossroad, 1982), 382.
20. Ibid., 379.
21. Gustavo Gutiérrez, "A Spirituality of Liberation," in Conn, *Conversion*, 309.

nomic and political rights: Conversion is "conversion to the neighbor."

Similar language is found in the 1983 Pastoral Letter of the French Bishops "Winning the Peace" and in the 1986 Pastoral Letter of the U. S. Bishops "Economic Justice for All: Catholic Social Teaching and the U. S. Economy." The American bishops begin and end their letter with an urgent appeal for the church to recognize the social responsibility of a converted life: "This letter calls us to conversion and common action, to new forms of stewardship, service, and citizenship," and later, "The transformation of social structures begins with and is always accompanied by a conversion of the heart."[22] Although their teaching parallels the work of the liberation theologians it owes a greater debt to the tradition of the great social encyclicals (*Rerum Novarum*, 1891; *Quadregesimo Anno*, 1931; *Mater et Magistra*, 1961; *Pacem in Terris*, 1963; *Populorum Progressio*, 1967; *Laborem Exercens*, 1981; *Sollicitudo Rei Socialis*, 1988).

THE CHURCH AND THE SACRAMENTS

Central to the Catholic understanding of conversion will always be the reality of the church and its sacraments. The theological debates over grace and freedom, the act of justification, the social fruits of conversion all converge in the fact of the church as the "Mystical Body of Christ." The church contains within itself the entire mystery of redemption. There could be no turning toward God if it were not for the sacrifice made by Christ that created the church. In *Heart of the World* Hans Urs von Balthasar looked at the church from the perspective of its founder: "But see: we live, you and I, for I have died once and whoever eats of my death will live eternally, and I will awaken him on the Last Day—and each day is the last. I have died once, and only once does my Body, my church, pass over from death to life. This is the one turning. Each of your members must make it a reality in union with me, each in his own place, in his own century, but in the unity of the one change, in the transubstantiation of this world into the other (they are the same). There is but one turning wherein earth becomes heaven, and this turning point is the church."[23]

As embodying the historical continuity of God's effort at redeeming his creation, the church must be accepted by the Catholic convert in a dual aspect. This is a favorite theme of Henri de Lubac, another important theologian of the Vatican II era, who elaborated the significance of viewing the Catholic Church under either its "visible" or "invisible" aspect. The meaning of this duality, he thought, is contained within the metaphor of the church as the bride of Christ: "The wretched being on whom the Word took pity and whom he came to save from prostitution at his Incarnation; on the

---

22. "Economic Justice for All: Catholic Social Teaching and the U.S. Economy," *Origins* 16 (27 November 1986): sections 1.27 and 5.328.

23. Hans Urs von Balthasar, *Heart of the World*, trans. Erasmmo S. Leiva (San Francisco: Ignatius Press, 1979), 200.

other hand, the New Jerusalem, the bride of the Lamb coming out of heaven from God."[24] The convert to Catholicism enters into an ecclesial reality that reflects both the shabbiness of the "wretched being" and the glory of the "New Jerusalem." The convert embraces, at once, a historical institution and the Mystical Body—one which claims to contain all the redemptive activity of God in history. Therefore, when the convert stands before God in the church, he or she does not stand alone and isolated; entering the church leaves little room for individualism. "No one is a Christian for himself alone."[25]

Similarly, the sacraments are administered not only as the means of grace but as instruments of unity in the church. The sacraments place the whole of the conversion process in its communal and historical context. What may begin for a person in the study of old books, with a passionate concern for injustice, or in the crucible of personal guilt must be opened to the presence and radical dependence upon the whole body of other baptized Christians—past, present, and future.

Few modern theologians have related the converting dimension of the sacraments better than Bernard Häring. The seven sacraments are called "sacraments of the basic and ongoing conversion . . . a conversion to a life in the fullness of faith, hope, love, justice, and peace, of adoration and truth."[26] Taking a sacramental view of conversion involves the church itself in the call to conversion: "A humble church which, in creative fidelity and liberty, takes all the risks involved in an ongoing renewal is a great sign, a sacrament of conversion for all persons and communities."[27] Traditionally, the sacrament of baptism represents the turning point of conversion, particularly for adults. Baptism confers the grace of justification in the remission of sin and in the beginning of the process of inward sanctification. The baptism of children is valid, since the faith lacked by the child is replaced by the faith of the church.[28] Confirmation is the sacrament that continues what baptism began. By the laying on of hands, the baptized person is given the sanctifying grace for growth in beatitude. The sacrament of penance is thought of by Häring not as a reconversion, as some described it, but as a "means of ongoing purification."[29]

Yet the center of the Mass remains the celebration of the eucharist, which in the words of Vatican II is "the true center of the whole Christian life" and "the summit of . . . the action by which God sanctifies the world in Christ."[30]

---

24. Henri de Lubac, *Catholicism: A Study of Dogma in Relation to the Corporate Destiny of Mankind*, trans. Lancelot E. Sheppard (New York: Mentor-Omega Book, 1964), 40-41.

25. Ibid., 131.

26. Bernard Häring, *Free and Faithful in Christ: Moral Theology for Clergy and Laity*, vol. 1 (New York: Seabury, 1978), 430.

27. Ibid., 429

28. Ott, *Fundamentals*, 359.

29. Häring, *Free and Faithful*, 433.

30. *Vatican II: The Concilliar and Post-Concilliar Documents*, ed. Austin Flannery (Northport, N.Y.: Costello, 1975), 106-7.

The communion signified in the eucharist is participation in the very life of God, and through the partaking of the Christ's body and blood points to the inexplicable mystery at the heart of Christian conversion.

The Catholic Church has always rejected the tendency of some Protestants to narrow the meaning of the eucharist to the forgiveness of sins. Eucharist not only cleanses but restores; it bestows both remission of sins and the strengthening of sanctifying grace. What baptism and the other sacraments have begun, Häring writes, "the eucharist brings to completion, if we understand our life as ongoing conversion and purification in order to reach full union with Christ."[31]

The changes made by Vatican II in the reception of converts include all of these contemporary concerns but, even more, seek to educate the catechumens into the sacramental life and liturgy of the parish (see the "Decree on the Church's Missionary Activity," art. 2, 1965). The R.C.I.A. program (Rite of Christian Initiation for Adults) used in the American church begins meeting weekly in September and culminates at Easter with confirmation at the Saturday vigil and first communion on Easter morning.

CONVERTS

Although the theological issues raised earlier are probably only dimly present to the mind of the potential convert or, even to the practicing Catholic, the actual stories of conversion have always played a more immediate role. The *lives* of saints and converts continue to have tremendous influence upon both potential converts as well as the Catholic faithful. These stories illustrate what Hilaire Belloc calls "the action of *expanded experience*" through which a convert passes to enter the church.[32]

This is born out in the testimony of two of the most influential converts of this century—Jacques and Raissa Maritain (1882-1972; 1883-1960). In her first volume of memoirs, Raissa told the dramatic story of their conversion, which saved them from the consequences of a suicide pact, she the daughter of Russian Jews, he the son of a Protestant father and a mother both Protestant and staunchly anti-Catholic. Although they both came to be known later as leading members of a modern Thomist revival in France and the United States, it was not the rational light of Aquinas which started them on the road to Rome. In the chapter "The Call of the Saints," Raissa described what their friend Leon Bloy had done to provoke their spiritual hunger: "He placed before us the fact of sanctity."[33]

This was a fact displayed in Bloy himself and in the books he advised them to read, such as those of Anna Catherine Emmerich, and proved decisive in bringing about the Maritains' baptism. The discovery of Aquinas

31. Häring, *Free and Faithful*, 436.

32. Chesterton, *The Catholic Church and Conversion*, 7.

33. Raissa Maritain, *We Have Been Friends Together and Adventures in Grace: The Memoirs of Raissa Maritain*, trans. Julie Kernan (Garden City, N.Y.: Image Books, 1961), 120.

over a year later would form the core of another conversion which, in the words of Jacques, would "liberate reason" from the deadening influence of the modernism taught to him by his Sorbonne professors. In 1923 the Maritains began a "Thomist Circle" outside Paris at their home at Meudon, which became until 1938 a mecca for artists and intellectuals all over continental Europe, the United States, and Great Britain, resulting in many prominent converts.

Many more influential conversions to Catholicism took place against the backdrop of modernism. The conversion of John Henry Newman (1801-1890) and the Oxford Movement, portrayed in his *Apologia pro Vita Sua*, shaped an entire half-century of Christianity in England. Newman's departure from the Church of England, conversion to Catholicism in 1985, ordination, and establishment of an Oratory would result within his lifetime in the conversion of over three hundred clergy and Oxford graduates, and over 1400 Anglican priests by the late 1950s.[34]

Apart from Newman, one of the powerful modern accounts of conversion is that of the Danish poet and essayist Johannes Jorgensen (1866-1956). In his memoir, *An Autobiography*, said to be comparable to Augustine and Rousseau, Jorgensen carefully detailed his release from the nineteenth-century credos of vitalism, aestheticism, and existentialism: "At last, at last, I had had enough of making up religion on my own account."[35] At the beginning of the next century two more eloquent voices continued in a similar vein— G.K. Chesterton (1874-1936) and Hilaire Belloc (1870-1953)—finding in the Catholic Church a bastion against the encroaching secularity of the modern world. This attitude is summed up in Chesterton's famous dictum: "The Catholic Church is the only thing which saves a man from the degrading slavery of being a child of his age."

Many of the well-known converts of the second half of the twentieth century would harden Chesterton's attitude, most notably the journalist Malcolm Muggeridge and the historian Paul Johnson. But others, like Jacques and Raissa Maritain, would have a more nuanced and hopeful attitude. For example, few converts in the United States have been more widely read and beloved than Thomas Merton (1915-1968). Readers of Merton's account of his conversion in *The Seven Storey Mountain*, of his struggles to break the bonds of sensuality, aestheticism, and Communism, found his testimony reflected their own struggle to live for God in the twentieth century.

One of Merton's several turning points was the discovery of an idea that enabled him for the first time to think about God. The book was *The Spirit of Medieval Philosophy* by the Thomistic philosopher Etienne Gilson; the idea was God's *aseity*, the power of a being to exist in virtue in itself alone. In rediscovering the ancient way of conceiving divine existence, Merton was

---

34. John A. O'Brien, *Giants of the Earth: Conversions Which Changed the World* (Garden City, N.Y.: Hanover House, 1957), 137-38.

35. Johannes Jorgensen, *An Autobiography*, vol. 2 (New York: Longmans, Green, 1929), 41.

freed from his intellectual naturalism and his resistance to the Catholic Church began to break down.[36] Merton was baptized a Catholic in 1938 and ordained a priest in 1949. Although his philosophical and theological reflections were always rooted in the Fathers and Doctors of the Church, Merton's work on contemplation, spirituality, art, and ecumenism reflects the growing concern of the American Catholics with the issues of *aggiornamento*. Few scenes portray Merton's wonderful and unique character better than his entertaining the aged Jacques Maritain at the Hermitage, during Maritain's last visit to the U.S., with the music of Bob Dylan.[37]

Similar combinations of the old orthodoxy and an engagement with contemporary causes can be seen in the lives of three women converts: Edith Stein (1891-1942), Dorothy Day (1897-1980), and Simone Weil (1909-1943). The experience of Edith Stein, who was recently beatified, illustrates how the testimony of converts has often started a chain reaction. Born to a German Jewish family, Stein went to the University of Freiburg where she became assistant to the phenomenologist Edmund Husserl. Her uncompromising search for truth eventually took her beyond philosophical studies to a life-shattering reading of the autobiography of St. Teresa of Avila, the founder of the Carmelite order. St. Teresa herself had been moved toward conversion by reading Augustine's *Confessions*. Stein took Carmelite vows in 1935 and was eventually martyred in the concentration camp at Auschwitz, but prior to her death continued to write philosophical and religious works combining Carmelite spirituality, the phenomenological method, and Thomism.

Simone Weil was also a philosopher of Jewish parentage whose attraction to the Catholic Church, though she was never baptized, was through its ascetic and contemplative tradition. Weil combined a life of contemplative prayer, teaching, philosophical-spiritual writing, and social engagement. She participated in the Spanish Civil War, worked as a laborer in a French auto factory, and joined the French resistance movement during World War II. Weil's refusal to eat more than the daily ration of food allowed in occupied France helped bring about her early death from pleurisy. Simone Weil and Edith Stein are recognized as two of the major philosophers of this century and are ranked close to the top among all women philosophers.

Dorothy Day is probably best known for her association with the Catholic Worker Movement. However, prior to her conversion, Day, by her own admission, lived anything but a sanctified life, living rather tempestuously with a common-law husband and giving birth to a daughter. But it was through her problems with her lover, her desire for her daughter's baptism, her long-standing love for the impoverished and suffering, and her study of numerous Catholic books, such as St. Teresa, St. John of the Cross, *The Imitation of Christ*, and Sigrid Undset's great novel *Kristin Lavransdatter*, that Dorothy

---

36. Thomas Merton, *The Seven Storey Mountain* (Garden City, N.Y.: Image Books, 1970), 211-12.

37. John Howard Griffin and Yves R. Simon, *Jacques Maritain: Homage in Words and Pictures*, with a Foreword by Anthony O. Simon (Albany, N.Y.: Magi Books, 1974), 35.

Day ended her "long loneliness" and entered the church in 1927. Although remaining a theological conservative after her conversion, Dorothy Day's Catholicism only increased her ardor on behalf of pacificism and social-economic justice. Her work with Peter Maurin on *The Catholic Worker* has had a permanent effect on the political face of American Catholicism.

Books by and about converts continue to appear with steady regularity. The editor of *The New Catholics* goes so far as to say that "there is a new Oxford movement in America today."[38] In fact, this volume includes testimonies not only from several prominent ex-Anglicans, including the author of *A Severe Mercy*, Sheldon Vanauken, but also from ex-Evangelicals and ex-radicals of various stripes. Another recent book that deserves notice, particularly for its urbanity, warmth, and unassuming tone, is the actor Alec Guinness's *Blessings in Disguise*. Just as Dorothy Day felt the urge to convert through love for her daughter, it was concern for his son's health which induced Guinness to promise God that he would not stand in the way of his son's conversion. Following his son's recovery and confirmation, Guinness entered a Trappist monastery to examine himself and to explore his growing interest in Catholicism. Thoughts of conversion were interrupted by the filming of *The Swan* in California, where he attended a Mass with his co-star Grace Kelly and was almost dissuaged by the arrogance of the priest. But after returning to England, Guinness asked to be received into the Catholic Church (1956). Remembering this moment thirty years later, he would employ a phrase from another convert to write: "Like countless converts before and after me, I felt I had come home—'and known the place for the first time.'"[39]

(The author would like to express thanks to Stephen Hemphill for his help in the preparation of this chapter.)

---

38. Dan O'Neill, *The New Catholics: Contemporary Converts Tell Their Stories* (New York: Crossroad, 1987), xi.
39. Alec Guinness, *Blessings in Disguise* (New York: Knopf, 1986), 42.

Chapter Eight

The Mainline Protestant Understanding of Conversion

Donald K. McKim

In Christian systematic theology, conversion traditionally refers to the changing or turning of one's life by responding in faith to the Christian gospel. As a theological expression, conversion has been defined in numerous ways. Theologians consider it in relation to their understandings of many other theological terms and issues. The term conversion has played a central role in numerous theological disputes through the centuries. A number of images have been used to define conversion. These illuminate various theological systems as a whole since they capture some of the basic directions and emphases present throughout a whole theology. While some of these images are more directly drawn from biblical pictures, others relate more closely to the language and thought forms of a particular theology itself. As systematic theologians have crafted their theologies, "conversion" has played at times a major and at times a minor role. Each theology which wrestles with the concept of conversion is drawn into a series of theological issues that it resolves in various ways.

LOCUS OF CONVERSION

In classical Christian theology, conversion is located within the broader theological issue of sanctification. Sanctification refers to the renewal of the whole person in the image of God so the person is "enabled more and more to die to sin and live to righteousness."[1] This is the dimension of theology that deals with the Christian life and the growth of the Christian person in faith and obedience to God in Jesus Christ. It is the sustaining and developing work of the Holy Spirit within Christian believers.

Conversion has been seen as the first step of faith or the first exercise of God's grace in the lives of those called by God, justified by faith and who are now beginning to live the Christian life. The biblical terms *shuv* (Heb.) and *epistrephein, strephein* and *metanoia* (Gr.) mean "to turn," "to turn again," "to return," and "repentance." When applied theologically to life, they denote the radical change in life direction and lifestyle that results when one turns away from sin and turns toward the living God. In the New Testament, "conversion" and its related terms center on the person and message of Jesus Christ.

Conversion in Christian theology relates to one's personal or "subjective" response to God's decisive intervention in life in Jesus Christ. As an element in the process of sanctification, conversion is the initial action whereby a person in response to the gospel of Christ, by faith is enabled by God to die to the power of sin and by the work of the Holy Spirit will be enabled to live in a righteous relationship with God. It is the initial action of the Christian life. The locus of "conversion" within systematic theology, then, is a part of the doctrine of sanctification, made possible by the person and work of Jesus Christ (soteriology).

FOCUS OF CONVERSION

Christian conversion is focused on Jesus Christ. God's work in Christ makes conversion possible. Those who are "converted" are "turned around" and released from the bondage of sin and by the grace of God are enabled to live a new life of joyful obedience to God in Jesus Christ through the power of the Holy Spirit. The entire Trinity is involved in the work of conversion. But the focus of the "new life" is on obedience to God's will as God is known in Jesus Christ. Thus conversion is focused in soteriology and involves a complete reorientation of the human being and a restoration of the image of God (Eph 4:23-24) in Jesus Christ who is himself, "the image of the invisible God" (Col 1:15).

While conversion is focused in Christ, it is more generally focused on soteriology and thus stands in integral relation to God's work of salvation as a whole. This involves some understandings of the relationship of conversion to other theological terms that are also part of soteriology. Some of the classical Protestant theologians have used terms such as calling, regeneration, conversion, and faith synonymously.[2] Others, however, especially in the period

---

1. See *The Constitution of the Presbyterian Church (U.S.A.): Part I: The Book of Confessions* (New York and Atlanta: Office of the General Assembly, 1983), 7.035; hereafter cited as *Book of Confessions*.

2. See Heinrich Heppe, *Reformed Dogmatics*, rev. and ed. Ernst Bizer, trans. G.T. Thomson (Grand Rapids, Mich.: Baker, 1978), 526. Cf. Peter Toon, *Born Again: A Biblical and Theological Study of Regeneration* (Grand Rapids, Mich.: Baker, 1987).

of Protestant orthodoxy in the seventeenth century, made careful distinctions among these various words. This was primarily because they wished to convey a precise description of the whole "order of salvation" (*ordo salutis*) from the perspective of the mind of God. This meant they needed to say exactly what term described each step in the process. Consequently the theological terms involved with soteriology or how salvation occurs were given more exact definitions.

Those in the Reformed theological tradition in the period of Protestant orthodoxy distinguished conversion from other terms in this manner. Consistent with their stress on election and predestination, the Reformed saw conversion as part of the broader plan of God in vocation, or the "calling" of the elect to receive salvation. This calling (from the perspective of God), involves the elect individual's "union with Christ" (*unio cum Christo*) and (from the individual's point of view) is the beginning of the appropriation of salvation, of fellowship with God in Christ, and ultimately of participating in God's glory.[3] This calling is by an act of the Holy Spirit and results in the person becoming a new creation by God's grace (2 Cor 5:17).

The direct effect of the calling of the elect is the "regeneration of human nature." This involves the gift of new, divine life to those who are spiritually dead in sin. Regeneration is the transformation of the sinful nature and the creation of a "new heart" within a person by the Holy Spirit.[4] Regeneration is what happens within the person as the concrete realization of justification which is what happens to or for a person. Justification is the declaration of righteousness on the basis of the work of Christ. Regeneration is the renewal of human nature and the reception of a new heart, mind, and spirit so that there is effectually a "new birth." The new birth or restoration of the image of God in Christ in regeneration occurs through the divine gift of faith that is granted by the Holy Spirit. The Reformed emphasis has been on the complete passivity of the individual and the reception of faith as God's gift of grace. The direct effect of regeneration is faith.[5]

Conversion, then, in Reformed theology is the first action of faith wherein God through the renewal of the human mind and will begins the process of sanctification. Here, according to the Reformed theologian Bucanus, at

---

3. See Heppe, *Reformed Dogmatics*, 511. See the chapter on "Effectual Calling" in the Westminster Confession of Faith," *Book of Confessions*, 6.064-6.067.

4. Charles Hodge spoke of regeneration as an "instantaneous change from spiritual death to spiritual life," a "spiritual resurrection," the "beginning of new life." See *Systematic Theology*, 3 vols. (New York: Scribner's, 1871), 3:5. His son, A.A. Hodge, said that in regeneration "the Holy Spirit implants a new principle of spiritual life in the soul," *Outlines of Theology* (New York: Robert Carter and Brothers, 1879), 521.

5. Heppe, *Reformed Dogmatics*, 526. As Donald Bloesch has written: "Regeneration and conversion signify the coming to faith. Indeed, no one can be born again unless [one] believes, and if [one] believes, [one] is indisputably born again. . . . The new birth is not fulfilled apart from the decision of faith. This means that faith itself is a manifestation of the work of the Spirit within," *Essentials of Evangelical Theology: Life, Ministry, and Hope*, 2 vols. (San Francisco: Harper & Row, 1979), 2:8.

the time at which the conversion actually takes place the will is not like a log, but when healed by the H. Spirit it also is in an active state; i.e., the will in conversion is not idle or motionless or insensible (like a statue), but follows the Spirit who draws it. God brings it about at the same moment, that by grace we will and really will, that is, He moves and bends our will and secures that we really will: yet in such wise that the whole effectiveness of the action is and remains with God's Spirit.[6]

The emphasis here is on conversion as the act of God which enables the new human will to will that which is in accord with the will of God and not, as in the former state of sin, that which is according to the sinful will of fallen human nature. Faith is the expression of conversion. Conversion is made clear through one's new obedience to the will of God. Concurrently, conversion entails repentance and the renunciation of sin, again effected by the power of God. Conversion then, as the starting point for sanctification, includes both faith and repentance, the "aversion from bad and turning towards good" (Wollebius), by the power of God's Holy Spirit.[7]

THEOLOGICAL DISPUTES

The Reformed understanding of conversion is expounded to see how it stands in relation to other positions. At numerous points there have been theological conflicts among varying views. These disputes have related not only to conversion itself but also the theological issues surrounding conversion.

One of these disputes has concerned the issue of "free will" (*liber arbitrium*). In the Reformed view, the effects of human sin are seen as so pervasive that the human will is enslaved to the power of sin. Since the will is corrupted, it is not able to reach out to God on its own to receive the gospel message of salvation. Theologically, this meant the human will "does not cooperate with God, but remains passive in its attitude toward God's action."[8] Thus in conversion, God "acts in a divine way and with such grace, power, and effectiveness that in the issue [God] removes wickedness from the will and inserts righteousness and so makes the [person] free instead of slave, willing in place of unwilling, obedient instead of resistant."[9] As Keckermann

---

6. Gulielmus Bucanus, *Institutiones Theologicae* (Geneva, 1609), XVIII, 10, cited in Heppe, *Reformed Dogmatics*, 521.

7. See Heppe, *Reformed Dogmatics* 572. Bloesch distinguishes: "While the new birth happens only once, conversion is a broader term which applies to the whole of the Christian life. Conversion is both an event and a process in that what has been begun must be carried forward and completed," *Essentials*, 2:15.

8. Ludovicus Crocius, *Syntagma Sacrae Theologiae* (Bremen, 1636), 918, cited in Heppe, *Reformed Dogmatics*, 520.

9. Crocius, p. 918, cited in Heppe, *Reformed Dogmatics*, 520. The Westminster Confession says that in conversion God's grace enables a person "freely to will and do that which is spiritually good," *Book of Confessions* 6.062. Toon notes that "the passivity of the human subject . . . is conveyed by the Latin expression *conversio habitualis seu passiva*, and the activity of the subject . . . by *conversio actualis seu activa*," p. 123.

put it: "In the conversion of a [person] there is no concurrence of the power of free *arbitrium*. Conversion must be solely the work of God who liberates the human will and by the Holy Spirit gives a new heart and will to believers."

"Freedom of the will" was prominent in the debates between Augustine and the Pelagians, Luther and Erasmus, Calvin and his opponents, and the "Calvinists" and "Arminians" at the Synod of Dort (1618-1619).[10] Against the Reformed view is the position that even in the state of sin, human nature still has the capacity and ability to choose good over evil and to respond to the Christian gospel. Various positions have emerged with regard to how to understand the work of the Holy Spirit and the essential liberty of humanity to choose the good and the gospel. But against the Reformed stress on the depravity and sinfulness of the human will has been the insistence of some that sin does not impair the abilities to cooperate with God through the Holy Spirit or for humans to be able to respond to the gospel by virtue of their free, human choice. It is thus apparent that how conversion is viewed is closely related to one's anthropology or Christian doctrine of humanity.[11]

A related theological issue surrounding conversion is whether or not persons can make any "preparation for conversion" (*praeparatio ad conversionem*). This theological dispute took particular shape within English and New England Puritanism. New England Puritans, building on the teachings of various English Calvinist Puritans and Continental theologians, asked questions about the preparatory process one might follow to predispose one's self to receive God's saving grace and be converted. The tensions this created were heightened when this concern for understanding how the heart might be prepared for God's grace is seen in light of the larger, Calvinist framework of election and predestination where conversion was solely the work of God and not in any way aided by human participation.[12]

Some Puritans tried to resolve this tension by following William Perkins (1558-1602), a leading Puritan, and divide the work of preparation for con-

10. See John Calvin, *Institutes of the Christian Religion*, trans. Ford Lewis Bettles, ed. John T. McNeill, Library of Christian Classics (Philadelphia: Westminster, 1960), 2.3.6f. Cf. Alan P.F. Sell, *The Great Debate: Calvinism, Arminianism, and Salvation* (Grand Rapids, Mich.: Baker, 1983). Jonathan Edwards (1703-1758) wrote a major treatise on the *Freedom of the Will* (1754).

11. For a survey of the various positions see Millard Erickson, *Christian Theology* (Grand Rapids, Mich.: Baker, 1987), chs. 43-46. The issue of "free will" has implications for understanding the relationship of conversion and regeneration. As Erickson points out, Calvinists and Arminians have differed over the order here. Against the Calvinist view that sinful people cannot respond to God in conversion unless they are first regenerated by God, Arminians have insisted "that conversion is prior. It is a prerequisite to new birth. One repents and believes, and therefore God saves and transforms," p. 932.

12. See Norman Pettit, *The Heart Prepared: Grace and Conversion in Puritan Spiritual Life* (New Haven, Conn.: Yale University Press, 1966); Patricia Caldwell, *The Puritan Conversion Narrative: The Beginnings of American Expression* (Cambridge: Cambridge University Press, 1983); and John Morgan, *Godly Learning: Puritan Attitudes towards Reason, Learning, and Education, 1560-1640* (Cambridge: Cambridge University Press, 1986), ch. 2.

version into two parts. Perkins spoke of the "beginnings of preparation" which come from seeing one's life in light of God's law. This included the accusations of conscience, fears and terrors of hell, and the compunction of the heart to see the corruption of one's whole life. The second part of preparations for conversion was the "beginnings of composition" which are "all those inward motions and inclinations of God's Spirit that follow after." Here, one's will or desire for conversion and regeneration is "the effect of regeneration begun." Those who will not ultimately be converted may come to the point of the "beginnings of preparation" since these are the "fruits of the Law." But only those whom God ultimately converts will have the "beginnings of composition" which are the fruits of God's Spirit already at work in beginning to bring one to conversion. By holding together a view of radical sinfulness with a concern for human affections and actions, Perkins combined the Calvinist emphases on conversion as the work of God and humanity's theological passivity with an ability to appeal to his readers and listeners (when preaching) to look to God for the promises of everlasting life. One might prepare one's self, even through perplexities and doubtings.[13]

The two theological disputes just mentioned have important implications for further dimensions of Christian theology but especially for the preaching of the gospel. The way the Christian message, "repent and believe" is understood and proclaimed will be significantly affected by one's understandings of *how* repentance and *how* faith occur. How one understands the work of God in relation to human work in conversion will be a factor, too. If one can make "preparations" for conversion, a certain type of preaching and introspection may result. If these preparations are not a valid activity and if one remains in a purely passive position while God does the work of converting, another type of preaching and activity (or inactivity!) may result. If "preparations" are possible, does this also imply that conversion may take place gradually, over a period of time rather than in a single instant? Whether one understands "conversion" as occurring instantaneously or more slowly will also shape and structure the way the gospel of Jesus Christ is proclaimed. Thus, the issues raised by the theological disputes of the past continue to have important ramifications for the life of the church in its preaching and teaching today.

THEOLOGICAL POSITIONS

The theological disputes just mentioned point to sharp differences on the issue of conversion among some major theological positions. The Reformed

---

13. William Perkins, *Works*, 3 vols. (Cambridge, England: John Legatt, 1616-1618), 1:638-451; 2:13. Cf. Pettit, *The Heart Prepared*, 64-65. For Jonathan Edwards' approach see John H. Gerstner, *Steps to Salvation: The Evangelistic Message of Jonathan Edwards* (Philadelphia: Westminster, 1960). Perkins' bifurcation here is typical of his Ramism. See Donald K. McKim, *Ramism in William Perkins' Theology* (Bern: Peter Lang, 1987).

view, based and developed out of Calvin's theology, stresses that by the work of the Holy Spirit regeneration precedes faith and repentance is the fruit of faith.[14]

Calvin noted, "The whole of conversion to God is understood under the term 'repentance,' and faith is not the least part of conversion." This is because "the Hebrew word for 'repentance' is derived from conversion or return; the Greek word, from change of mind or of intention. And the thing itself corresponds closely to the etymology of both words." For Calvin, the meaning of these terms is that, "departing from ourselves, we turn to God, and having taken off our former mind, we put on a new." Thus Calvin defines repentance as "the true turning of our life to God, a turning that arises from a pure and earnest fear of him; and consists in the mortification of our flesh and of the old man, and in the vivification of the Spirit" (3.3.5).

This "turning to God" requires "a transformation, not only in outward works, but in the soul itself" (3.3.6). "Mortification of the flesh" consists of self-denial, denying the sinful nature. "Vivification of the Spirit" is the work of the Holy Spirit in imbuing souls with holiness and "both new thoughts and feelings, that they can be rightly considered new."[15] The work of the Spirit does not bring believers into "perfection," since they are still sinners throughout their present lives. But, while sin is present in the Christian life, it has lost its power to dominate the life and it is sin that is forgiven by God (3.3.10-11). So repentance and thus conversion for Calvin are lifelong processes.[16]

In contrast, it has been noted that in Luther's view "the sequence is always repentance and faith, never faith and repentance." For him, *poenitentia* means "the knowledge of sin, which is followed by the knowledge of grace, and in which moreover the movement of life, which is the real center of interest for the Lutheran spirit, seems to be settled and strictly speaking can only be repeated over and over again."[17] Melanchthon's *Apology* to the

---

14. See Calvin, *Institutes*, 3.3.ff. Earlier, Calvin noted that God both begins the work of conversion and completes the work "by confirming us to perseverance." The human will is "effaced; not in so far as it is will," but "it is created anew," being "changed from an evil to a good will." Calvin affirms that "this is wholly God's doing," 2.3.6. Further references to the *Institutes* will be made in the text.

15. Calvin, *Institutes*, 3.3.8. Calvin says: "In a word, I interpret repentance as regeneration, whose sole end is to restore in us the image of God that had been disfigured and all but obliterated through Adam's transgression." Here his use of these terms is more fluid than his successors.

16. Calvin, *Institutes* 3.3.9. Calvin writes that in order for believers to reach the goal of growing in the image of God, "God assigns to them a race of repentance, which they are to run throughout their lives" (cf. his phrase, "continual repentance," 3.3.20). Repentance produces "fruits" or results such as piety toward God, charity toward others, and "in the whole of life, holiness and purity" (3.3.16).

17. E.F.K. Müller, *Symbolik* (Erlangen, 1896), 314, in Wilhelm Niesel, *The Gospel and the Churches: A Comparison of Catholicism, Orthodoxy, and Protestantism*, trans. David Lewis (Philadelphia: Westminster, 1962), 207. Luther's own "conversion experience" has been much debated by Luther scholars. For a study of his primary understandings see Marilyn J. Harran, *Luther on Conversion: The Early Years* (Ithaca, N.Y.: Cornell University Press, 1983).

Augsburg Confession indicates the parts of repentance are "contrition and faith." But, in the Lutheran view, it is the recognition of humanity's utter sinfulness by the law of God that causes one's repentance and conversion. In faith, this is completed. The Christian life, for Luther, was a continuing repentance. In the first of his 95 Theses, he wrote that "when our Lord and Master, Jesus Christ, said, 'Repent,' he called for the entire life of believers to be one of penitence."[18]

The Arminian position, adopted by John Wesley and others, stressed the freedom of human response to the gospel and the view that conversion precedes regeneration. When one repents and believes, God saves and transforms that person. Thus God regenerates on the basis of a person's repentance and belief. The "subjective aspect" of regeneration is stressed. In this view, conversion is what humans have to do; regeneration is what God alone can do.[19] Repentance is turning away from sin; conversion is turning toward God. Conversion is followed by the "assurance of salvation" whereby for believers, as Wesley said, "the same Spirit bearing witness with yours and with our spirits 'that we are the children of God.'"[20]

THEOLOGICAL IMAGES

One way to understand Christian conversion in systematic theology is to study theological images for conversion that capture the essence of a theological position. These are tags or models representing a perception of what conversion is and how it functions. To this point, no discussion of the social dimensions of Christian conversion has been prominent. While all theological views of conversion have social implications to a greater or lesser degree, some models stress the social over the corporate as the major way to understand conversion and see how it affects human society today.[21]

New Birth. A common image for conversion is "new birth," a picture drawn specifically from the encounter of Jesus with Nicodemus (Jn 3:3, 7). In particular, American Fundamentalism and various Evangelical traditions have been drawn to this image as part of the gospel calls for repentance and

---

18. *Martin Luther: Selections from His Writings*, ed. John Dillenberger (Garden City, N.Y.: Doubleday, 1961), 490. Cf. the statement in the Smalcald Articles that "in Christians this repentance continues until death, because, through the entire life it contends with sin remaining in the flesh."

19. See Niesel, *The Gospel and the Churches*, 336, from Nass, "Large Catechism," 1868.

20. John Wesley, "Marks of the New Birth," in Timothy L. Smith, *Whitefield and Wesley on the New Birth* (Grand Rapids, Mich.: Zondervan, 1986), 115. Cf. "The Witness of the Spirit," Discourse II on Rom. 8:16, Sermon XI in *The Works of the Rev. John Wesley, A.M.*, 14 vols., 3rd ed. (London, 1829-1831), 5.123f., cited in Niesel, *The Gospel and the Churches*, 337. This testimony of the Spirit is distinguished from the work of the Spirit in regeneration. It is God's positive seal and pledge of grace promised.

21. A helpful volume on various viewpoints is *Conversion: Perspectives on Personal and Social Transformation*, ed. Walter E. Conn (New York: Alba House, 1978). Cf. Cedric B. Johnson and H. Newton Malony, *Christian Conversion: Biblical and Psychological Perspectives* (Grand Rapids, Mich.: Zondervan, 1982).

personal decisions of faith in Jesus Christ. The image of the new birth stresses the complete spiritual revolution that occurs in a person's life when one is converted. As Billy Graham has written: "Yes, [humanity] can be changed, radically and permanently, from the inside out. There is the possibility of a completely new [person]."[22] Graham defines conversion as "turning" and writes of the "two elements in conversion—repentance and faith." Of repentance, he says that "all you have to do is to be willing. God will help you." Of faith, Graham writes that "in order to be converted, you must make a choice." The "radical spiritual and moral change" is "brought about by God himself," says Graham. Persons do not have within themselves "the seed of the new life; this must come from God himself."[23] Graham and others have stressed the instantaneous nature of conversion and many who are drawn to the new birth image can point to a specific experience and time in which they were "born again."[24]

Transition. An alternative image to the abrupt picture of the "new birth" is conversion as transition. A representative of this view is Horace Bushnell (1802-1876), a pioneer of liberal theology in New England and one whose thought paved the way for the reception of Liberal theology in America in the late nineteenth-century. One of the leading concepts in Bushnell's thought was the "immanence of God in human personality." What was needed, according to Bushnell, was "Christian nurture" so a child would "grow up a Christian, and never know himself as being otherwise."[25] If God is immanent within human personality, response to the Christian message should be natural as physical growth. One could grow into the Christian faith through a series of natural life transitions. No dramatic experience or "turning" is necessary.

Education. Liberal theology in the late nineteenth and early twentieth centuries in Europe reacted against the experiential emphases of Pietism in stressing religious conversion and in America against the popularity of religious revivalism. If, as Liberalism maintained, salvation is achieved through the unfolding of capacities for the good that are inborn, the dramas of instantaneous conversions are not needed. George Coe (1863-1951) stressed "salvation by education" in hearkening back to Bushnell's view and combining it with the emphases of American educational reforms at the turn of the

---

22. Billy Graham, *World Aflame* (Garden City, N.Y.: Doubleday, 1965), 140. Cf. his *How to Be Born Again* (Waco, Tex.: Word, 1977). Cf. Toon's discussion of John 3, pp. 26-29 and his analysis of Graham's views, pp. 177-182.

23. See Graham, *World Aflame*, 150, 152, 142. Cf. Graham's, *Peace with God* (Garden City, N.Y.: Doubleday, 1956), ch. 11: "The New Birth," where he says that "being born again is altogether a work of the Holy Spirit. There is nothing that you can do to obtain this new birth....The new birth is wholly foreign to our will. In other words, the new birth is a divine work—we are born of God," p. 136.

24. In his theologically informed discussion, Bloesch writes that "the new birth is both an event and an experience, but it is primarily and essentially the former and only secondarily the latter. What is regenerative is the event of the new birth, even though it cannot happen apart from an upwelling of joy and an outpouring of love," *Essentials*, 2:10.

25. This is how Bushnell began his book, *Christian Nurture* (1847).

twentieth century. He argued that "religion and education have moved toward a consciousness of a common goal and a common inner principle." The goal of Christians is to "raise the commonplace to a sublime level by making it the abode of God." This can happen through education which is "not two— religious and secular—but one." Christianity is to be "as pervasive as the atmosphere, as natural as conscience or as love." For "only then shall we show the mature and rounded spiritual life that is demanded by the relation of the church to the modern world."[26]

Renewal. The theology of Karl Barth (1886-1968) and the "Neo-Orthodoxy" movement rejected the main theological tenets of Liberalism and attempted to recover biblical and Reformation theological insights. In Barth's *Church Dogmatics*, his views of Christian conversion are found in his volumes on reconciliation. For Barth, Christians are those "who waken up. As they awake they look up, and rise, thus making the counter-movement to the downward drag of their sinfully slothful being." Christians are "those who waken up, however, because they are awakened. They do not waken of themselves and get up. They are roused, and thus caused to get up and set in this counter-movement." This rousing and "rising up" takes place in conversion. According to scripture, "waking and rising from sleep is turning around and going in the opposite direction." Conversion, and therefore life in this movement, writes Barth, "means renewal." It recognizes that God is for us and we are for God.

Conversion will express itself in a concern for other people and relationships with them. Conversion as renewal will affect the whole of a person— heart, thinking, will, disposition, actions, and abstentions. It is not an "end in itself, as it has often been interpreted and represented in a far too egocentric Christianity." Conversion is renewal "in the totality of our being" and leads one to accept public responsibility. For "it is the great God of heaven and earth who is for us, and we are for this God." Conversion is not just for one period of one's life since "it is neither exhausted in a once-for-all act, nor is it accomplished in a series of such acts." It "becomes and is the content and character of the whole act" of one's life. Conversion has its basis and origin in Jesus Christ.[27]

New Being. The theology of Paul Tillich (1886-1965) was indebted to several philosophical movements, including existentialism. For Tillich, salvation is found in "the reunion with the ground of being," from which humanity has been estranged.[28] Humans are estranged from the ground of their Being (God) to "beings" such as themselves. This is idolatry and unbelief. As

26. See *American Protestant Thought in the Liberal Era*, ed. William R. Hutchison (Lanham, Md.: University Press of America, 1985), ch. 11, from George A. Coe, *The Religion of a Mature Mind* (Chicago: Revell, 1902).

27. See Karl Barth, *Church Dogmatics*, trans. G.F. Bromiley (Edinburgh: T. & T. Clark, 1958), IV/2, 553-84.

28. Paul Tillich, *Systematic Theology*, 3 vols. (Chicago: University of Chicago Press, 1951, 1957, 1963), 1:147. For Tillich, "the religious word for what is called the ground of being is God," 1:146.

Tillich puts it, "The disruption of the essential unity with God is the inmost character of sin."[29] In traditional Christian terms, "salvation" or "healing" occurs when the estrangement of sin has been overcome and humanity is reunited and reconciled with God.

Salvation comes through the revelation of the biblical picture of "Jesus as the Christ." In this biblical symbol, the power of the "New Being" to transform reality was uniquely present. Through this symbol, humans are brought into "a creative and transforming participation" in revelation and are converted into new persons. Participation in the New Being is regeneration (in Pauline theology, being "in Christ"). In justification, humans recognize by faith that they are "accepted" by God.[30] Continuing transformation and participation in the New Being through the Spirit is sanctification. Thus conversion for Tillich is the human transformation into the New Being.

New Identity. One form of process theology would describe conversion as bringing a new identity through faith. Marjorie Suchocki discusses how a positive response to the gospel adds Christ to a person's past so one's past is felt in a new way. In process thought, God "prehends" or feels the person who responds to the proclamation and "re-enacts" that person within God's "consequent nature." The person is integrated into God so one "moves into that constellation within the depths of divine harmony made actual by Christ," the person's reality "participates in Christ in God." This integration of God's feelings of the person in union with Christ results in "a new possibility being given" to the person for the next moment of one's finite existence. Thus a "Christly repentance, a Christly joy, or a Christly comfort and triumph may be the immediate possibilities for reflecting the divine harmony" which are given to the person. Who the person is, in each instant, is a function of the person's future and past, now integrated in the unity of the present. When a person's immediate possibility for the future or aim is made available to the person in and through Christ in God, then the person's actualization of that aim is one's reception of Christ for that person. So, "through the aim," Christ enters into the person's identity and transforms it each moment.[31] A new identity through faith is the result of this "conversion."

Liberation. Conversion as "liberation" can describe the views of various forms of liberation theology. A prominent theme in liberation theology is the kingdom of God. This kingdom is "not presented simply as something to

---

29. Tillich, *Systematic Theology*, 2:48. See John Macquarrie, *Principles of Christian Theology* (New York: Scribner's, 1966), 238, for his discussion of sin. Macquarrie's thought is also heavily influenced by existentialism. Macquarrie writes of sin: "Ontologically expressed, this is the 'forgetting of Being' of which Heidegger speaks; theologically expressed, it is idolatry."

30. Tillich, *Systematic Theology*, 2:178. Cf. Tillich's, *The Courage to Be* (New Haven, Conn.: Yale University Press, 1952) and his sermons in *The New Being* (New York: Scribner's, 1955).

31. See Marjorie Hewitt Suchocki, *God, Christ, Church: A Practical Guide to Process Theology* (New York: Crossroad, 1982), 130-31. Suchocki writes that "the church is the community of all those whose identities have been so formed through faith," p. 133.

be hoped for in the future; it is already being made concrete in Jesus' actions." The kingdom is "a gift of God offered gratuitously to all." But the way of entry into the kingdom is "through the process of conversion." The conversion Jesus demands "does not mean just a change of convictions (theory) but above all a change of attitude (practice) toward all one's previous personal, social, and religious relationships."[32] For liberation theologians, "to place oneself in the perspective of the kingdom means to participate in the struggle for the liberation of those oppressed by others."[33] Throughout the world, liberation theologians are involved in many ways with struggles for liberation. These encompass liberation from social, political, economic, and spiritual oppression.[34] As James Cone has summarized it for a black theology of liberation: "The event of the kingdom today is the liberation struggle in the black community. It is where persons are suffering and dying for want of human dignity. It is thus incumbent upon all to see the event for what it is— God's kingdom. This is what conversion means."[35] Conversion in liberation theology, as João Batista Libânio has said, "is fundamentally an announcement (faith) and a transforming action (liberation) with the fulfillment of the kingdom in mind."[36]

Reorientation. Contemporary feminist theologians have focused attention on the need for conversion from sexism and patriarchal domination as fundamental evils. There are varieties of Christian feminist thought.[37] But as Rosemary Radford Ruether has written:

> Conversion from sexism is truly experienced as a breakthrough, as an incursion of power and grace beyond the capacities of the present roles, an incursion of power that puts one in touch with oneself as a self. Metanoia for women involves a turning around in which they literally discover themselves as persons, as centers of being upon which they can stand and build their own identity.[38]

Conversion is a reorientation of all life. As Ruether writes, "The grace of conversion from patriarchal domination opens up a new vision of humanity for

---

32. Leonardo Boff and Clodovis Boff, *Introducing Liberation Theology*, trans. Paul Burns (Maryknoll, N.Y.: Orbis, 1987), 54.

33. Gustavo Gutiérrez, *A Theology of Liberation*, trans. and ed. Caridad Inda and John Eagleson (Maryknoll, N.Y.: Orbis, 1973), 203.

34. See Deane William Ferm, *Third World Liberation Theologies* (Maryknoll, N.Y.: Orbis, 1986) and Phillip Berryman, *Liberation Theology* (New York: Pantheon Books, 1987) for surveys.

35. James Cone, *A Black Theology of Liberation*, 2nd ed. (Maryknoll, N.Y.: Orbis, 1986), 125.

36. Cited in Guillermo Cook, *The Expectation of the Poor* (Maryknoll, N.Y.: Orbis, 1985), 137, from *Evangelização e Libertação* (1976), 9, 91.

37. For a brief survey see Donald K. McKim, "Hearkening to the Voices: What Women Theologians Are Saying," *The Reformed Journal*, 35, no. 1 (January 1985): 7-10.

38. Rosemary Radford Ruether, *Sexism and God-Talk: Toward a Feminist Theology* (Boston: Beacon, 1983), 186.

women and men, one that invites us to recast and re-create all our relationships."[39] Feminist theologians hold differing views about the place of Christology in relation to this type of conversion. Further implications for ministry and community are variously spelled out as well.[40]

The images just mentioned constitute some, but certainly not all, the theological options for understanding conversion today. They are each oriented toward a particular theological position and each is but one component of a theological structure as a whole.[41]

THEOLOGICAL ISSUES

The various disputes about conversion, the theological positions and the images used in systematic theology to capture the essence of conversion display the many dimensions and implications of the term. This material (and much more) raises theological issues perennially present in theological discussions of Christian conversion. These grow out of past disputes and are implicit as well in theological positions today. Among these are:

1. The relation of the divine and human in conversion. How is the work of God in conversion understood in relation to the human response to the gospel, to repentance, faith, and the ongoing work of the Holy Spirit?

2. The understanding of conversion as a moment or a process. Must conversion occur instantaneously through a significant religious experience or may it be understood as a process that can take place over a long period of time?

3. The shape of sanctification. How is conversion as a theological term distinguished from and related to other terms such as calling, regeneration, union with Christ, adoption, etc.?

4. The nature of the church. What is the relation of the individual believer to the corporate body of Christ? Is conversion primarily social or individual in nature? Is ecclesiology grounded in a collection of "converted individuals" or in another aspect of God's work?

5. The nature of Christian conversion. Given the different terminologies relating to conversion in scripture, the diversity of conversion experiences through the history of the church, and contemporary contentions over the most appropriate images to capture the crux of conversion, are there common elements and unifying themes that constitute an "essence" of Christian conversion?[42]

---

39. Ibid., 193.

40. See Ruether's ch. 5: "Christology: Can a Male Savior Save Women?" and ch. 8: "Ministry and Community for a People Liberated from Sexism." On Christology, see also Patricia Wilson-Kastner, *Faith, Feminism and the Christ* (Philadelphia: Fortress, 1983).

41. For a similar approach to various contemporary views of scripture as a basis for their theological thought, see Donald K. McKim, *What Christians Believe About the Bible* (Nashville: Thomas Nelson, 1985).

42. For varieties of conversion descriptions see *Conversions: The Christian Experience*, eds. Hugh T. Kerr and John M. Mulder (Grand Rapids, Mich., Eerdmans, 1983).

Answers to these questions will come from the variety of traditions and systematic viewpoints on the current scene. Each will emphasize different aspects and appeal to differing sources of authority. But each will, as well, wrestle with those ongoing mysteries that will always surround Christian conversion.

Chapter Nine

The Evangelical Protestant Understanding of Conversion

David H. C. Read

The umbrella word "Protestant" covers today a great variety of theological and ecclesiological points of view. For some it means little more than non-Roman Catholic. For others it refers to the mainstream denominations who are the heirs of the Reformation. In recent years it has almost been replaced by the word "Evangelical" which itself has undergone confusing shifts in meaning.

It might therefore be helpful when addressing the topic of conversion to try to unravel the uses of the word "evangelical," and to distinguish between what it has recently come to mean (with the underlying theology of conversion) and the traditional use of the word in Reformed theology.

Every now and then words that have been quietly circulating for centuries among theologians of the inner circles of the church surface with a splash in the secular press and soon become current in the talk of the town. They move almost overnight from ecclesiastical ghettos to the cocktail circuit.

There was "existential"—a word used when I was at seminary only by those who wanted to prove that they had read Kierkegaard but which is now thrown around in everyday discussion and TV talk-shows. "Charisma" is a word that has taken only a few years to move from the recesses of Pauline theology to the advertising world of Madison Avenue. Even "eschatological"—a word young preachers in my day were supposed to know all about but never to use publicly—looks like becoming a fierce new weapon in popular debate.

Then a more familiar word from our church vocabulary was suddenly
on everybody's lips. Some will remember the year 1976 was baptized by
the press as the "Year of the Evangelical." Politicians and columnists awoke
to the fact that there is a vast body of people in this country, spanning many
religious denominations, whose convictions and outlook could be described
by this word. Their existence had been largely ignored by the commentators
and policy-makers since they had seldom been politically organized. There
was some consternation and confusion as people went around asking: Who
are these evangelicals we now hear so much about? Even church members
have been bewildered by expressions such as "born-again Christians" and
comments like: "It's the evangelical churches that are growing right across
the country while others are declining." So it's time to ask: "Just what is an
evangelical and what is an evangelical church?"

The word itself simply means one who believes and proclaims the evangel, or the gospel. Thus it is really just another name for "Christian." But over
the years this adjective has come to be used to describe a certain emphasis in
Christian doctrine and a certain temper of Christian behavior. It is often
used to refer to the more personal and emotional kind of belief over against
the stress on the institution and its disciplines. Evangelical movements, such
as that of John Wesley within the established Church of England, sought to
confront those who were satisfied with the normal religious routines with the
need of a personal decision, an experience of conversion or rebirth in Christ.

Over the years within Protestantism the evangelical was thought of as
one who valued the Bible more than the church, preaching more than the
sacraments, and personal devotion more than social action. In some communions the evangelical was contrasted to the Catholic who emphasized
the tradition, the continuity, and the ritual of the Christian faith. In others the
evangelical was opposed to the liberal, or modernist, who was eager to adjust
the faith to modern thought, and was less concerned with the contents of
the Bible than the challenge of social evils. In other parts of the world "evangelical" took on different meanings. In Germany, for instance, to this day
"*Evangelisch*" simply means the Lutheran Church.

My guess is that, for many today the word "evangelical" has no very precise meaning but vaguely refers to the kind of Christians who speak freely
about their relationship to the Lord, support evangelistic campaigns, talk
about conversion and re-birth, are unafraid to open their mouths in prayer,
and are inclined to settle all questions with a text from scripture. "By grace
you have been *saved* through faith." That is a favorite text that conveys the
central emphasis of Reformation theology, but it contains a word which has
now become the property of a certain kind of evangelist—"saved."

I suspect that, for many, an evangelical is one who is comfortable with the
word "saved," while others who call themselves Christians are uneasy with
it. "Being saved," "Salvation," "Are you saved?"—I can remember how, as
a boy raised in the decorous rituals of the Church of Scotland, I was alarmed
and disturbed when I first met a group of "evangelicals" who freely used
these words.

It is worth noting that this kind of evangelical has developed an accepted vocabulary by which "orthodoxy" is tested, and that it includes words and phrases which are not to be found in the creeds and confessions of the Reformed Church—or even in the New Testament. I am thinking, for instance, of *"personal* Savior," "getting saved," and "unsaved." We shall see how this vocabulary reflects how the understanding of conversion in such circles differs from historic Reformed theology.

If I were preaching on the word "evangelical," I would say that it means being grasped by the truth that lies in these words: "by grace through faith." Forget all the subtleties and shades of meaning, all the pride and the prejudice that have surrounded the word "evangelical" and listen to what is indeed the heart of the matter—the truth by which a Christian lives and dies. It is a truth that shines through some of the great pages of the prophets and the psalmists and that broke with power upon the world when Jesus lived and died and came back from the dead. It is a truth that overthrows popular ideas of what religion really is. It is a truth that continually has been obscured throughout Christian history down to the present age. But it is a truth that breaks in upon anyone of us again and again with transforming power. The evangel is the news of how we can be delivered from the fears and frustrations, the sense of isolation from God and other people, and the sense of guilt that often paralyzes the soul. "By grace are you saved through faith"—that is the evangel.

That makes me glad to be an evangelical, and happy that mine could be known as an evangelical church. There is no special type of Christian who should be so labeled—except all who have discovered that this gospel is true. An evangelical can be young or old, conservative or liberal, Catholic or Protestant, simple or sophisticated, black or white, emotional or down-to-earth, exuberant or reserved. All that matters is that we put our trust in the God who meets us in Jesus Christ and live daily by his grace alone.

Sounds simple? In a way it is—and yet being an evangelical is by no means easy. We are always tempted to seek another way to express our religion. "For by grace you have been saved through faith; and this is not your own doing, it is the gift of God—not of your selves, lest any man should boast." There it is. This is the truth that makes an evangelical.

The first world that hits us is the word "saved." An evangelical is one who admits the need to be saved. If that word bothers you then use another—rescued, delivered, liberated. You cannot be an evangelical if you feel that there is nothing much the matter with you that a little personal discipline or a visit to a psychiatrist cannot clear up, or if you believe that you've always been in a happy relationship with your God, or that the human race needs nothing more than better education and some social engineering to banish your troubles. The evangelical, like our Lord, takes evil seriously. Jesus, you remember, described his purpose in coming to our world as "to seek and to save that which is lost," and when he wanted to describe our situation he told stories about a lost coin, and a lost sheep, and a lost son.

The evangelical then shares with all religious people the belief that we need to be set right with God and with our neighbors, that there is something wrong with us and with all humanity that cries out for divine help. Many have the idea that Christianity is simply one among many religions that offers a way of salvation, a set of religious exercises that will help to overcome the evil in us and in the world. But the gospel, the evangel, is, in fact, something totally different from a religious program to bring us nearer to God. It is the announcement of how God has come near to us. It is the rejection of any notion that we can work our passage and accumulate merit before God and humanity by any religious exercises whatever. "For by grace you have been saved through faith; and this is not your own doing, it is the gift of God—not because of works, lest any man should boast." It is God who does the converting.

This is not what is sometimes referred to as "Pauline doctrine"—a theological brew that has little to do with the teaching of Jesus of Nazareth. It is exactly what Jesus said—only he said it in pictures, rather than propositions. Think of a parable of Jesus. Here are two men, religious men, at prayer. They both recognize their need to be saved, to be liberated, to be justified (which means "made just, made right with God"). But the one is an evangelical who knows what this text of ours means although he had never heard it; and the other isn't. He has the deep-rooted conviction which dies hard in any of us that the way to be saved, the way to be justified, the way to God, is to prove that we're doing what he wants, that we're working our passage. "God, I thank thee," he prays, "that I am not like other men, extortioners, unjust, adulterers—or even like this tax-collector" he adds as he gives way to the temptation of religious people to contrast their behavior with that of notorious sinners. Then he lists a couple of his religious virtues: "I fast twice a week, I give tithes of all that I get."

So is this the way to be saved? We enter our claim. "God," we say, "you must help me out of my troubles. I've done my best to live a decent life, to fulfill my religious duties and to be thoughtful about the needs of others. At least I've done a lot better than old so-and-so at the office, or that aunt of mine who is pretty mean in spite of her religion. I never get roaring drunk, and, on the whole, I stay away from pornography and that sort of thing. My pledge to my church may not be a big item in my budget, but at least I pay it up, and you know all the other things I support. So I think I have the right to a little special treatment from you, and at least a modest niche in your heaven when the time comes."

I put it like this because we have always been tempted to locate this Pharisee with his claims on God somewhere other than in ourselves. He's the proud, self-satisfied religious leader with whom Jesus had such trouble. He's the legalistic Christian who fought against St. Paul's gospel of grace. He's the medieval churchman with his system of sacraments and penances, indulgences, and works of merit. He's the hypocrite who thinks he is in good standing with God because he does all the outward exercises of religion. In fact, he is the insistent voice within us all that wants to justify ourselves before God and our neighbors. He is the sense of grievances we sometimes feel when we are not rewarded for our virtues. And he is by no means confined to those who are members of a church. Have you never heard this: "I reckon I'm a better Christian than most of those who go to church"?

Let's have a look at the other man—the true evangelical. "The tax collector, standing far off, would not ever lift up his eyes to heaven, but beat his breast, saying, 'God be merciful to me a sinner.'"

What makes an evangelical is just this casting aside of all our pretensions, all our claims, and living by the mercy of God. The Bible, and many evangelical preachers of a former age, may seem to exaggerate our need, to inculcate a kind of groveling attitude before God. (Just last week I heard a speaker declare that she hated to sing the words in "Amazing Grace" that speak of saving "a wretch like me." I was tempted to point out that John Newton actually wrote "a worm like me"!) It's just as hypocritical to pretend to be worse sinners than we really think we are as to claim virtues we do not possess. But the point of this language is to shake off the last trace of any self-assertion before God, any claim on his favor by virtue of our good deeds. The foundation prayer of a true evangelical must be, "God, be merciful to me a sinner." There is a similar prayer that some have been using as a kind of Christian mantra. It consists of repeating, morning and evening, the words: "Lord Jesus Christ, Son of God, be merciful to me, a sinner."

But what makes an evangelical in the strongest sense of the word is not just this humility before God. It is the conviction that he has come to meet us with his amazing grace. The evangelical is one who knows that the gap between us and God has been spanned, not by our pushing out the frail bridge of our good deeds and religious duties done, but by God himself who crosses that gap to meet us in Jesus Christ. This is what we mean by grace—the rescuing, restoring, forgiving, re-creating presence of God. For us this is no mere theory. It is personified in Jesus Christ. He crossed the gap to share our helplessness, to meet our needs, and to bear our sins. And it is he who offers to turn us around and give us what he calls the abundant life that God has designed for all of us. It is he who responds to the least flicker of acceptance in our hearts and minds and covers our weakness with his strength.

"By grace are you saved through faith." Faith is simply the trust we have in someone worthy of our trust. It's not forcing ourselves to believe what our minds reject. It is like human friendship. We don't approach our best friend with an attitude of fear, or of self-justification. Friendship, in Paul's language, "is not of works." It is sheer grace and trust. A chorus I used to sing as a boy goes: "The perfect friend is one who knows the worst about you and loves you just the same." You don't make a tally of each other's virtues and vices. You simply accept each other. That chorus goes on: "There's only one that loves like this, and Jesus is his name." What that means is that only the God we meet in Jesus really knows the worst about us and that he does truly offer us his friendship. If his grace is the great divine hand thrust down to where we sit, then faith is the trusting hand of ours allowing itself to be gripped.

If that has happened, if this is the way you want to walk, you are an evangelical. And if this is the heart of the worship and work of a church, then it is an evangelical church.

The historic Protestant (which was really Reformed Catholic) faith places the emphasis in the work of conversion from beginning to end on the initiative of the Spirit of God. Grace comes first as is symbolized by the retention of the practice of infant baptism. And the Spirit, like the wind, "blows where it wills." It is clear from the New Testament that conversions that are recorded do not follow some standard pattern. Salvation is not pictured as being always a sudden once-for-all human decision. Conversion is a process. Being born again is something that keeps happening as the new life keeps pouring and transforming the believer. And salvation is not depicted in terms of a highly emotional experience but as a growing discovery of the "unsearchable riches of Christ." It was not a feeling that "his heart was strangely warmed," but a financial decision on the part of Zacchaeus which led to Jesus' remark: "This day has salvation come to this house." John Wesley's conversion cannot be precisely dated and linked to his Aldersgate experience. Scholars have found it impossible to discover what John Calvin meant by his one reference to his conversion. And I have noticed that even the most rigid exponents of "getting saved" as a datable totally determinative experience will sometimes be led to admit that, in their own case, a Christian upbringing had something to do with their conversion.

Conservative scholars have been noting that some of the modern "evangelical" movements give much more emphasis to the human element in religious experience than the divine and thereby have departed from the Reformed understanding of conversion. The stress is apt to be on techniques for inducing "decisions." (It is good to note that Billy Graham does not claim that those who publicly respond to his message are "converts": They are "inquirers" who are directed to counselors from the churches.) Televangelists will publicly dictate to viewers the exact form of words to use to "get saved." In spite of the "mass-movement" nature of evangelistic campaigns, the message is directed to the individual as if conversion has nothing to do with the holy, catholic church, nor the communion of saints. In the New Testament we read not only of Zacchaeus that "salvation is come *to this* house," but converts are described in the Book of Acts as being "added to the church." The Reformers never spoke as though conversion was a purely personal experience to be followed up by baptism and joining the "church of your choice."

There are other aspects of the "neo-evangelical" understanding of conversion that are difficult to reconcile with historic Protestantism. Within the reformed family of churches, the attitude to revivals and "awakenings" has varied from enthusiastic support to theological disapproval, particularly in the Presbyterian tradition. At the present time agreement on a definition of conversion tends to be found in a "neo-evangelical" movement that cuts across denominational barriers and rouses little theological dissent. Among the shibboleths that unite this movement are some which have little to do with traditional Protestantism as understood by the Reformers. Notable among these is the moralistic definition of the "world" from which the convert is saved.

Some years ago I heard a TV program in which a speaker complained that Protestantism had lost its roots. When asked to name a few he answered: "opposition to alcoholic drinks, tobacco, gambling, and total separation of church and state." I reflected that no one of the Reformers would have recognized any of these as "Protestant principles." We might add that a legalism based on a doctrine of biblical inerrancy would have horrified both Luther and Calvin.

The tragedy of the present situation is that the historic churches that today represent Protestantism have tended to react against the militant neo-evangelicals by rejecting evangelism, or extending its meaning to cover everything an active church does, while the neo-fundamentalist movement successfully and devotedly presents a version of the gospel that is neither truly biblical nor acceptable to the "cultured despisers" of the faith. The historic denominations who claim the name "Protestant" still have the nominal allegiance of probably the greatest number of professing Christians in our land, yet they have not been marked by spiritual zeal, joy in the gospel, or eagerness to promote conversion. The attempt to win "members" by watering down the supernatural dimension of the gospel and secularizing both Word and Sacrament, has obviously failed. (It is worth noting that when a prominent personality publicly becomes a convert to Christ it is not a reductionist but an orthodox faith and church that is embraced.)

The understanding of conversion to which I look forward will not be Protestant in the sense that it will be hostile to the Roman or Orthodox communions and seek converts from either. It will be truly ecumenical in the light of the Lord's prayer "that they all may be one. . . . that the world may believe." It will mean a constant rediscovery of the gospel of grace, and an openness to the reforms which the Spirit will prompt in those who keep turning again to become as "little children."

Part III

Conversion in the Social/Behaviorial Sciences

The goal of conversion is love of God and neighbor with heart, soul, and mind (Lk 10: 27-28). In chapter ten, Warren Brown and Carla Caetano examine these relationships in such combinations as epilepsy and mystical experience. They suggest models for the conversion experience that include identification of the way a person thinks. This includes a searching of memory to understand how the particular experience of conversion fits into the larger schema of life, purpose, identity.

Closely related to the studies of neurocognition by Brown and Caetano are the analyses of perception, cognition, emotion, and behavior by Lewis Rambo. In chapter eleven he distinguishes four psychological approaches to the study of conversion: psychoanalytic, behaviorist, humanist or transpersonal, social and holistic. Although he favors the transpersonal approach, Rambo brings contributions from all approaches into a heuristic stage model of conversion.

At times, psychological studies of conversion have been so introspective that love of God seems to be everything and love for neighbor is forgotten. An opposite omission is sometimes found in sociological studies of conversion, for, as William Bainbridge notes in chapter twelve, social science has no tool to research the supernatural in and of itself. He details the frustrations of emerging social-scientific theories that seek to explain conversion. The "strain" theory would emphasize a need for deprived people to satisfy conventional social desires through conversion. The "social influence" theory would concentrate on the attachments that a person already has with members of a religious group. To strengthen the attachment, the person joins the group by embracing, or at least verbalizing assent to group norms.

In chapter thirteen Alan Tippett brings his experience as a missionary anthropologist to a discussion of how conversion occurs in other cultures. His prime thesis is that conversion is a process which must be intricately related to the worldview and structure of the culture in which it occurs if conversion is to result in lasting life-change. He presents a model that includes points of encounter and incorporation coupled with period of awareness and decision. This model provides a framework for understanding culture in all societies, Western and non-Western.

Chapter Ten

Conversion, Cognition, and Neuropsychology

Warren S. Brown and Carla Caetano

The science of human *cognition* is the study of thinking. In cognitive science one attempts to describe systems and mechanisms which are fundamental to mental activity. These descriptions often borrow concepts from the world of computer science and information processing, e.g., "resource allocation," "limited capacity processor," "automatic vs. controlled processing," "propositional networks," "pattern recognition," and "schema." *Neuropsychology* describes the same processes of thought and behavior but with regard to the activity of specific brain areas or systems. As one would expect, there is a rough correspondence between the cognitive mechanisms discussed in cognitive psychology and the brain systems described by neuropsychology. What follows is a discussion of the cognitive and neuropsychological systems which may participate to a significant degree in Christian (or other religious) conversion.

Any discussion of the role of cognitive or neuropsychological systems in conversion confronts one with a philosophical and scientific mine field to be traversed with exceeding care. First, there is the problem of the paucity of scientific data in this area. At present, information about the participation of neurocognitive systems in religious conversion must be inferred from introspective accounts of the conversion experiences of normal individuals or from descriptions of the abnormal and exaggerated religious behavior of some psychotic or brain-damaged persons.

More dangerous, however, is the philosophical problem of reductionism. There is a tendency in discussions of the neurocognitive basis of human mental function to fall into a fundamental fallacy of thought aptly termed by Donald MacKay "nothing-buttery."[1] The fallacy is to suppose that if a mental process (Christian conversion in this case) can be shown to have describable neurocognitive consequences it is therefore "nothing but" a neurocognitive event. MacKay argues that this kind of thinking would be like supposing that a computer which is solving a mathematical equation is "nothing but" the physics of the flow of electrons within the various microchips. MacKay points out that from the point of view of physics the meaning of the mathematical calculation is ignored.[2] The laws of physics, when applied to the electrical events occurring within an operating computer, cannot adequately represent the meaning of the calculation being carried out. Similarly, a neurocognitive view of conversion would have no concepts for representing, and therefore must ignore, both a meaning and a reality which faith confirms.

In this discussion of cognitive and neuropsychological views of conversion we adopt a specific perspective on conversion which, because of the inherent limitations of these fields of inquiry, ignores much of the meaning and important dimensions of the reality of Christian conversion. By way of the computer metaphor, we discuss the nature of the systems and structures of the computer likely to be operative, but not the content or meaning of the programs which the computer is running.

Our discussion does suppose, however, some degree of embodiment of "spirit" within fleshly systems.[3] That is, for the period of our earthly existence, we are embodied beings such that our eternal selves (thinking, memories, emotions, actions) are expressed within the spatial and temporal limits of neurobiological systems. Thus, events which have eternal spiritual significance take place within the "limits" of an incredibly powerful neurobiological information processing system whose characteristics are, at best, poorly understood by modern cognitive and neurological science.

BIBLICAL LANGUAGE ON CONVERSION

An adequate discussion of neurocognitive correlates of conversion must reflect, at least to some degree, the quality of biblical descriptions (though likely not their richness). Biblical descriptions of conversion emphasize changes in belief, worldview, affect, and behavior.

Belief: The scriptures teach that in conversion we must both "confess with our lips" and "believe in our hearts."[4] Conversion, thus, has a propositional aspect, i.e., expressible in new statements of truth and belief. These new

---

1. Donald MacKay, *Human Science and Human Dignity* (Downers Grove, Ill.: InterVarsity Press, 1979), 27f.
2. Ibid.
3. Donald MacKay, "Brain Science and Human Responsibility," in M.A. Jeeves, ed., *Behavioral Sciences: A Christian Perspective* (Leicester, England: InterVarsity Press, 1984), 47.
4. Romans 10:9.

statements made by the converted individual have the force of conviction. We "believe in our hearts" that these new ideas and statements are true.

Worldview: Biblical descriptions of conversion go beyond mere statements of belief, however sincere these may be. Something fundamental in the "nature" of the person is changed. "He is a new creation, the old has passed away, behold, the new has come."[5] There has occurred some discernible discontinuity in the person. This process is described as being "set free from sin,"[6] "walk(ing) not according to the flesh, but according to the Spirit,"[7] and "walk(ing) in newness of life."[8] Despite many individual differences in the specifics of the descriptions of the conversion experiences, a common confession is that life is "seen" in some fundamentally different way. Converts often express this change retrospectively in the words of the man born blind whom Jesus healed, "Once I was blind, but now I see."[9]

Emotion: The shift in conversion to a new life perspective is often accompanied by emotion. There is a feeling of the profound significance of the decision. Joy, ecstasy, a sense of well-being, or the excitement of discovery are frequently reported affective experiences.

Behavior: This change of "nature" is evidenced in a change in behavior described biblically as the "fruits of the spirit."[10] Fundamental changes in attitudes lead in some cases to sudden-and-dramatic, but more typically progressive-but-noticeable, changes in one's behavior.

Thus, a biblical description of conversion would include: 1) changes in sincerely made verbal expressions of belief; 2) changes in the broader, largely ineffable, life-perspectives on the basis of which attitudes are formed and behaviors expressed; 3) some degree of positive affective experience, particularly in the case of more sudden and dramatic conversions, and 4) some consequent changes in observable behavior.

EPILEPSY, MYSTICAL EXPERIENCE, AND CONVERSION

There are two fundamentally different neurocognitive models of religious conversion we must consider. First is the view that conversions are the result of abnormal experiences which have their origin in a malfunctioning brain. Second is the possibility the religious conversion is an extension of normal mental activity, differing from other mental activity only in its content and perceived significance.[11]

---

5. 2 Corinthians 5:17.
6. Romans 6:22; 8:2.
7. Romans 8:4.
8. Romans 6:4.
9. John 9:25.
10. Galatians 5:22-23.
11. A third possibility would be that conversion is an entirely supernatural event, occurring entirely outside of neurocognitive systems. The mind-brain-spirit monistic point of view (i.e., embodiment) from which this chapter is developed would have no relevant terminology to discuss this option, although it represents an option worth serious consideration.

Seizures: A prominent neuropsychiatric model for dramatic religious conversions is a pathological model which posits that the mystical religious experiences associated with conversion are the result of abnormal brain activity.[12] The aura preceding some types of epileptic seizures, as well as the post-seizure confusional state, are often perceived by the individual as a significant mystical experience.[13] That is, patients might describe hearing divine voices or seeing visions of God. They might have a blissful, celestial feeling of God's presence, or a feeling of being cosmically united with the entire universe.

In an often quoted passage from Dostoyevsky's *The Idiot,* Prince Myshkin describes the experience of the aura preceding his epileptic seizures:

> In his attacks of epilepsy there was a pause just before the fit itself . . . when suddenly in the midst of sadness, spiritual darkness, and a feeling of oppression, there were instants when it seemed his brain was on fire, and in an extraordinary surge all his vital forces would be intensified. The sense of life, the consciousness of self were multiplied tenfold in these moments, which lasted no longer than a flash of light; all torment, all doubt, all anxieties were relieved at once, resolved in a kind of lofty calm, full of serene, harmonious joy and hope, full of understanding and the knowledge of the ultimate cause of things.[14]

Dostoyevsky, himself an epileptic, presents his analysis of these experiences in the thoughts of Myshkin:

> Thinking about this moment afterward, when he was again in health, he often told himself that all these gleams and flashes of superior self-awareness and, hence, of "a higher state of being" were nothing other than sickness . . . and, if so, were not the highest state of being at all but on the contrary had to be reckoned as the lowest. And yet he came finally to an extremely paradoxical conclusion. "What if it is sickness?" he asked himself. "What does it matter if it is abnormal in intensity, if the result, if the moment of awareness, remembered and analyzed afterward in health, turns out to be the height of harmony and beauty, and gives an unheard-of and till then undreamed-of feeling of wholeness, of proportion, of reconciliation, and an ecstatic and prayerlike union in the highest synthesis of life?" . . . If in that second—that is, in the last lucid moment before the fit—he had time to say to himself clearly and consciously: "Yes, one

---

12. For a review of the clinical literature on epilepsy and religious conversion, including some modern case studies, see K. Dewhurst and S.W. Beard, "Sudden Religious Conversions in Temporal Lobe Epilepsy," *British Journal of Psychiatry* 117 (1970): 497-507.

13. S. Snyder, *Biological Aspects of Mental Disorder* (New York: Oxford University Press, 1980), 175.

14. F. Dostoyevsky, *The Idiot,* trans. Henry and Olga Carlisle (New York: Signet Classics, 1969), 245.

Callslip Request   4/30/2012 7:26:24 AM

Request date:4/28/2012 12:08 AM
Request ID: 34468
Call Number:291.42 M257
Item Barcode:

Author:
Title: Handbook of religious conversion
Enumeration:c.1

Patron Name:Michael Lee
Patron Barcode:

Pickup Location:

Request number:

Route to:
I-Share Library:

Pick-up Location:

might give one's whole life for this moment!" then that moment by itself would certainly be worth the whole of life.[15]

The undeniable existence of a relationship between seizures and mystical religious experiences in some epileptic patients has led to the speculation that the experience of St. Paul on the Damascus road may have been just such an event.[16] Certainly there are some features in common. In a similar way, other individuals throughout religious history have been given a post hoc "diagnosis" of epilepsy primarily on the basis of the quality of the paranormal religious/mystical experiences which they have described or have been reported in historical documents.[17]

Temporal Lobe Epilepsy (also called "psychomotor epilepsy" or "complex partial epilepsy") is particularly marked among the seizures disorders for the frequency of seizure-related mystical religious experiences.[18] Because of the brain system in which the seizure activity begins, the aura of these individuals is characterized by dramatic mood changes (euphoria, anxiety, fear), dreamy states, feelings of familiarity or strangeness, hallucinations, delusions, and a "crescendo" feeling of rising emotion. A feeling of deep significance is often an integral part of the seizure. It is therefore not surprising that the content associated with such strong sensations and emotions might have a religious flavor, especially since the seizure experiences are typically perceived as alien to the person and unrelated to situational context.

The Epileptic Personality: Recent research has also suggested that persons with long-standing temporal lobe epilepsy often manifest abnormally pervasive religious concerns which are not limited to seizure periods per se. Thus it has been suggested that there is a personality style which is characteristic of patients who have suffered from temporal lobe seizures for many years.[19] These patients are described as being overly emotional, obsessional, viscous (i.e., repetitive and abnormally persistent, overly detailed), humorless, and somewhat paranoid. Particularly interesting for this discussion is the characterization of these patients as having heightened philosophical interest, a sense of personal destiny, and increased religiosity. The religiosity of these patients is described by Bear and Fedio[20] as "holding deep religious beliefs, often idiosyncratic," undergoing "multiple conversions," and experiencing "mystical states."

Based on an assessment of the prevalence of this personality profile

---

15. Ibid., 245-46.

16. D. Landsborough, "St. Paul and Temporal Lobe Epilepsy," *Journal of Neurology, Neurosurgery and Psychiatry* 50, no. 6 (1987): 659-64.

17. Dewhurst and Beard, "Sudden Religious Conversions."

18. S. Snyder, *Biological Aspects.*

19. D.M. Bear and P. Fedio, "Quantitative Analysis for Interictal Behavior in Temporal Lobe Epilepsy," *Archives of Neurology* 34 (1977): 454-67.

20. D.M. Bear, "The Temporal Lobe: An Approach to the Study of Organic Behavior Changes." In M.S. Gazzaniga, ed., *Handbook of Behavioral Neurology: Volume II Neuropsychology* (New York: Plenum Press, 1979), 81.

among seizure patients, Bear and Fedio[21] theorizes that the seizure events are creating a "hyperconnectivity" between cortical brain areas involved in conscious thought and limbic brain areas which mediate emotional experience. Because of this unusual limbic-cortical connectivity, all thought and experience is given greater significance, importance, and meaning for the individual. Although Bear and Fedio's description of the characteristic personality of seizure patients is supported by many reports in the clinical literature (see Table 1, Bear and Fedio), others have failed to find this personality profile to be particular to epilepsy patients.[22] Nevertheless, the epilepsy literature and Bear's concept of thought-emotion hyperconnectivity provides a suggestive model for one possible source of religious conversions and general religiosity, at least in some individuals.

Paranormal Experiences in Normals: Based on the clinical literature regarding religious experiences in seizure patients, Persinger[23] has speculated that individuals within the "normal," ostensibly nonseizure, population who have experienced significant mystical or paranormal religious states might in fact have had what he describes as "microseizures," i.e., slight abnormal electrical discharges of the limbic, emotional brain sufficient to sustain a mystical experience. Based on this hypothesis Persinger developed an inventory to measure the prevalence in normal individuals of temporal-lobe-seizure-like experiences, the Personal Philosophy Inventory.[24] This inventory included a cluster of items which assessed the frequency of less intense equivalents of the experiences of individuals with temporal lobe epilepsy or experienced during electrical stimulation of the temporal lobe (termed Complex Partial Epileptic Signs, or CPES).[25] CPES includes items regarding feelings of the intense personal significance of events, unusual visual, auditory, or olfactory perceptual experiences, and the experience of deja vu or jamais vu.

In a population of normal college students Persinger and Makarec found a high correlation between scores on the CPES questionnaire and the frequency of reports of "paranormal (mystical, with religious overtones) experiences and a 'sense of presence.'"[26] Individuals with such paranormal experiences and high CPES scores were also found to have a relatively high

21. Ibid.

22. D. Mungas, "Interictal Behavioral Abnormality in Temporal Lobe Epilepsy: A Specific Syndrome or Nonspecific Pathology," *Archives of General Psychiatry* 39 (1982): 108-111.
D. Tucker, R. Novelly, and P. Walker, "Hyperreligiosity in Temporal Lobe Epilepsy: Redefining the Relationship," *Journal of Nervous and Mental Disease* 175 (1987): 181-84.

23. M.A. Persinger, "Religious and Mystical Experiences as Artifacts of Temporal Lobe Dysfunction," *Perceptual and Motor Skills* 57 (1983): 1255-62.

24. M.A. Persinger, "People Who Report Religious Experiences May Also Display Enhanced Temporal Lobe Signs," *Perceptual and Motor Skills* 58 (1984): 163-97.

25. M.A. Persinger, and K. Makarec, "Temporal Lobe Epileptic Signs and Correlative Behaviors Displayed by the Normal Population," *Journal of General Psychology* 114 (1987): 179-95.

26. Ibid.

incidence of abnormal temporal lobe brain wave activity.[27] Persinger suggests that there exists a continuum of functional hyperconnectivity between limbic and cortical areas in "nonseizure" patients which predisposes some normal individuals to mystical and religious experiences.

Drug Related Experiences: Mystical/religious experiences associated with hallucinogenic drugs would have much in common neuropsychologically with temporal lobe seizure. The two phenomena occur because of abnormal activity in the same neural systems, i.e., the limbic structures of the brain. Both categories of experience should thus be seen as abnormal activity in the neurocognitive systems involved in signaling the significance of events and controlling emotional tone. Temporal lobe seizures and mind or mood altering drugs provide hallucinogenic additions to ongoing experience, or amplification of ordinary experience with extraordinary quantities of emotional valence.

Comment: Religious experiences associated with brain seizures (or drugs), although undeniably a contributor to the conversions of some individuals, have a number of weaknesses as a general neuropsychological model of religious conversion. Most importantly, the accounts of mystical/religious experiences in the clinical epilepsy literature are not characteristic of *typical* Christian (or other) religious conversions. Seldom do individuals describe their religious conversion in terms confusable with seizures, i.e., as based on paranormal experiences having a sudden onset and perceived as discontinuous with one's ongoing stream of consciousness. At least in the case of the majority of modern Christian conversions, a more typical description would be a conscious, deliberate decision based on either the consideration of normal life experiences which seem to have given life new perspective, or the affective impact of an experience not, however, considered outside the range of normal. "Feeling of presence," when they occur, are much more typically experienced as the aftermath of, not the precursor to, a conversion experience. Even the more emotional ecstatic conversions do not have the flavor of discontinuity with immediately preceding events which is typical of the seizure experience.

The proposition that religious experiences in the normal population are related to "microseizures" seems to rest on a tautology, i.e., unobserved "microseizures" are hypothesized on the grounds that individuals with paranormal religious experiences score high on the CPES, which itself includes questions regarding significant paranormal experiences. There is little evidence to directly support the notion that the CPES is diagnostic of subclinical temporal lobe seizure events among apparently normal individuals. The Personal Philosophy Inventory and CPES are more likely to be simply different ways of asking individuals about unusual religious experiences. The hypothesis might be extracted from the suspicion of containing a tautology

---

27. K. Makarec and M.A. Persinger, "Temporal Lobe Signs: Electroencephalographic Validity and Enhanced Scores in Special Populations," *Perceptual and Motor Skills* 60 (1985): 831-43.

by replication of the existence of abnormal temporal lobe brain wave activity in individuals scoring high on the CPES and reporting paranormal experiences. We would consider the brain wave measure of Makarac and Persinger[28] unconvincing.

Certainly, other than the as yet undocumented possibility of "microseizures," the incidence of religious conversion in the general population would be considerably higher than the incidence of abnormal brain waves or outright seizures. Thus, on purely numerical grounds, conversion related to abnormal brain activity is not broadly inclusive and would explain only a small percentage of religious conversions.

From a theological point of view nothing is accomplished by establishing that a particular conversion may have been related to abnormal brain activity; that is, the epistemological problem of the *truth* of the content of the experience is not solved. Imagine, for example, that you have the strong impression that someone is standing behind you but also know that you are having a seizure. It is still necessary to confirm or disconfirm the possibility that someone is there by turning and looking. The fact of the seizure does not bear on the fact that someone may well be standing behind you. In the case of St. Paul, if the Damascus road experience happened to involve a seizure it would have little relevance to the theological question of the truth of what he preached, taught, and wrote. If it is posited that God can communicate through normal human experience, he could just as well communicate via abnormal or paranormal experiences associated with seizure activity of the brain. This point is echoed by Dostoyevsky in Myshin's question, "What if it is sickness?"

A COGNITIVE DESCRIPTION OF CONVERSION

The second option for a neurocognitive model of conversion is that conversion represents an extension of the normal operation of human cognitive systems. Thus, conversion would be described in terms of the normal activity of cognitive mechanisms, unique only in its religious content. Currently, two major concepts by which cognitive psychology describes and understands mental life are "propositional network" and "schema." Much research has been done regarding the existence and development of propositions and schemata within the mind of an individual, as well as work on schema and proposition change with experience.[29] However, to our knowledge, no research has yet been done in relation to propositions and schemas in religious belief and conversion. Thus what follows is speculative in its application to religious conversion.

Propositional Networks: A proposition is a small unit of knowledge and a propositional network can be understood as an interlinking of small units

---

28. Ibid.

29. J.R. Anderson, *Cognitive Psychology and Its Implications* (New York, W.H. Freeman, 1980), 114-33.

of knowledge into a meaningful "idea syntax." Units of knowledge (or "nodes") in these networks are linked in ways which embody our understanding of relations in the world; e.g., subject, object, and agent, antecedent and consequent, time and space relations, etc. For example, the propositional network surrounding the concept "driver's license" might have strong links to "wallet" or "purse," "picture," and "car"; with more distant linkages to "identification," "speeding-ticket," etc. For a young person, not yet of driving age, "driver's license" might have concepts of "freedom" or "popularity" associated with it. Perception and thinking in this analysis involves successive "activation" of these memory nodes, with activation (or thought) tending to move along relational linkages to surrounding nodes; i.e., "spread of activation."[30]

One might reasonably speculate that a religious conversion would alter propositional networks around important ideas and concepts related to faith. Conversion would thus involve new units of knowledge and/or new relational linkages between concept nodes. The impact of Christian conversion on the thinking of the individual might, for example, involve new linkages around concepts like "God," "Jesus," "cross," "blood," "grace," "church," "self," "community," "love," etc. Thus, according to this associational theory of mental activity, the conversion experience would be represented in the mental life of the individual by new concept nodes and by changes in the ordering and patterning of propositions.

Probing Thought via Associative Priming: It is possible to study the characteristics of an individual's propositional networks by tests of "associative priming."[31] In this procedure, subjects are asked to make rapid word/nonword discriminations in a situation in which test items are very immediately preceded by "priming" words. If the "priming" and "test" words are closely linked in the individual's propositional network, recognition of the test word as an acceptable English word is more rapid. Associative priming provides a model for the flow of thought via "spreading activation," i.e, one thought prompts another along associational network linkages.[32] Thus, it should be possible (in theory) to observe conversion-related changes in a person's propositional networks and consequent patterns of association. To our knowledge, research on changes in propositional networks with religious conversion has not been reported.

Schemata: A "schema" is another way information is represented within our mental systems.[33] A schema is a template-like representation of a highly complex system of knowledge. It is a summary of the general properties of a knowledge category by which new experiences may be understood.

---

30. Ibid, 146-55.

31. D.E. Meyer and R.W. Schvaneveldt, "Facilitation in Recognizing Pairs of Words: Evidence of a Dependence Between Retrieval Operations," *Journal of Experimental Psychology* 90 (1971): 227-34.

32. Anderson, *Cognitive Psychology*, 146-57.

33. Ibid, 124-32. Also see J.W. Alba and L. Hasher, "Is Memory Schematic?" *Psychological Bulletin* 93 (1983): 203-31.

Schemata provide a means by which the highly ramified interrelationships of smaller units of information can be immediately recognized on the basis of whether or not the current complex of information fits one mental schematic pattern or another. We have schemata for rather simple concepts like "cup" or "dog" (i.e., a schema which covers all the variations of "cup-ness" or "dog-ness"), as well as for more complex concepts like "friendly" and "democratic." One's concept of the personality of a particular friend or one's self-concept are both complex and highly ramified systems of information which can be conceived of as schematic. Schemata also exist for expected sequences of social behavior, often referred to as "scripts."[34]

Schemata, of course, are modifiable through experience. Greater breadth of experience may cause us to switch the schema by which we understand a particular situation, event, or idea. For example, the concept "church," while a proposition linked to various other ideas within the propositional networks discussed above, is itself a concept represented by a complex set of attributes (i.e. a schema) variously satisfied by the different specific instances of "church" one has encountered. However, an entirely new and unusual "church" experience may cause one either to significantly modify one's "church" schema, (perhaps including new aspects or weighting more or less importantly various existing aspects of the pattern), or to completely switch the schematic pattern by which one understands and interacts with "church." In Christian conversion, among other changes which occur, the "self" schema would likely undergo considerable alteration, perhaps including aspects of sinfulness and forgiveness, as well as notions of spirituality and immortality.

Schema-fitting: The process of schema-fitting (i.e., searching one's memory for an appropriate schema by which to understand information at hand) must be considered a nonoptional mental task. Schema-fitting can engender a sense of satisfaction and reinforcement when satisfactorily completed and a sense of anxiety and frustration when a schema cannot be found which adequately fits all the aspects of a particular experience. For example, we frequently have the experience of uncertainty in the first few sentences of a telephone call from a person we do not immediately recognize. "To whom am I talking?" "Is this a social call, a business call, or just more telemarketing?" There is an "ah-ha" experience when we have satisfied ourselves that we have been able to match our current experience with a well-fitting schema and thus recognized the situation at hand. We experience relief from our previous sense of anxiety.

The point of the above illustration is that adequate schema-matching is not a passive or optional process, but is fundamental to perception and understanding. By adopting the correct schema we not only recognize a situation but obtain thereby a basis upon which we can anticipate what is likely to happen and be prepared to respond appropriately. Finding that our current

---

34. R.C. Schank and R. Abelson, *Scripts, Plans, Goals and Understanding* (Hillsdale, N.J.: Erlbaum, 1977).

schema doesn't fit leaves us with a feeling of uneasiness. Cognitive dissonance occurs when one cannot fit all or most of the data at hand into a familiar pattern. A sense of satisfaction, if not joy, accompanies finding a new and better-fit schema.

One could conceive of Christian conversion as involving the adoption of a better-fit life-schema, with all of the accompanying sense of satisfaction, release from anxiety, and joy. Life holds less cognitive dissonance; more of life experience seems to "fit." There is therefore the feeling of having made an important discovery and a sense of release, closure, satisfaction, excitement, and even joy.

COMMENTARY

To some degree both the pathological and normal cognitive models must be accepted as accurate representations of neurocognitive processes in conversion, but in different individuals and in different specific experiences. At least in the more extreme cases where one has a clinically diagnosed seizure disorder there is a small but significant probability that abnormal brain activity will be associated with experiences which are perceived as mystical and religious, in some cases leading to a religious conversion. However, we would question the applicability of this model beyond the clinically diagnosed epileptic, or even to all experiences of any particular seizure patient. The normal cognitive model, although not yet seriously researched, represents more fertile soil for developing a more comprehensive model and deserves further consideration and study.

The normal/abnormal distinction suggests the necessity for the development of tools which would adequately distinguish normal, healthy religious experiences from those related to abnormal brain activity. Such a tool would be helpful in the study of the psychology of religious experience, in the practice of clinical psychology and psychotherapy with religious individuals, and in neurology where patient accounts of religious life are nearly always treated as symptoms. The Religious Status Interview developed by Malony[35] may prove helpful in this regard.

Until such time as a valid measure of normal vs. seizure-related religious experience is available, several criteria might be suggested for distinguishing these phenomena. First, seizure experiences tend to be experienced as out-of-context, i.e., as unusual and not related to environmental or mental events immediately preceding. They are paroxysmal and disconnected. A normal conversion experience would be more consistent with preceding historical, environmental, and mental events. Second, seizure events tend to be repetitive occurrences which have a stereotypical quality in each occurrence. A more normal conversion tends to be a unique event, not regularly repeated or stereotypical in quality. Finally, in temporal lobe seizures, affect and vague

35. H.N. Malony, "The Clinical Assessment of Optimal Religious Functioning," *Review of Religious Research* 30 (1988): 3-17.

feelings of awe and significance are often primary, with content of the experience somewhat secondary. In conversions of a non-seizure nature, affect is more likely to be experienced as a secondary byproduct of a new view or perspective or a new understanding.

It should perhaps be reiterated in closing that any discussion of neurocognitive events in religious experience and conversion are only descriptive of the human embodiment of the experience and have no bearing on the theological truth of the experience.

Chapter Eleven

The Psychology of Conversion

Lewis R. Rambo

Conversion has been an important topic in psychology since the inception of the discipline in the late nineteenth century. William James, Edwin Starbuck, G. Stanley Hall, and other early figures were fascinated by the phenomenon of religious change.[1] Because the most prevalent and obvious form of conversion at the time was the apparently sudden conversion which occurred at revival meetings, these early studies focused primarily on conversion as a dramatic, radical change, usually involving adolescents or young adults.

Though instantaneous conversions do occur, most conversions are gradual. Religious change is usually a process involving a complex interweave of personal, social, cultural, and religious forces.

In the last two decades it is not so much psychologists as other human scientists, especially sociologists and to some degree anthropologists, who have examined conversion, investigating the new religious movements and the processes of religious change instigated by missionaries in Third World settings.

The existing psychological literature on conversion falls into one of two broad categories. The first is experimental and microscopic in its concerns, exploring, for example the role of depression, suggestibility, or some other

---

1. For an excellent survey of this early history, see Robert O. Ferm, *The Psychology of Christian Conversion* (Westwood, N.J.: Revell, 1959), 19-50. See also Lars I. Granberg, "Some Issues in the Psychology of Christian Conversion," *The Reformed Review* 15 (1962): 1-36.

such variable in the conversion process.[2] The other major type is more theoretical and global in its quest to understand the human predicament and uses a broader, case-study, clinical method.[3]

While these studies are suggestive, their limited scope makes clear the need for a broader theory of conversion, a theory that takes into account the extension of the boundaries of psychology into sociology, and anthropology and the other human sciences.[4]

This chapter will provide an overview of psychological approaches that have been used in the study of religious change.[5] Its main purpose, however, is to suggest that conversion is a process of religious change that takes place in a dynamic set of force fields involving people, institutions, events, ideas, and experiences. The study of conversion must take into account, in addition to the personal dimension, the social, cultural, and religious matrices with which personal life is embedded. For conversion to be understood in its variety and complexity, the relevance of anthropology, sociology, psychology, and religious studies must be acknowledged and explored. Finally, this chapter will suggest an approach to the psychology of conversion which allows us to view the individual within the matrices of social, cultural, and religious forces.

This project will look specifically at Christian conversion in the United States and Western Europe. Even within the Christian tradition, however, there is an extraordinary range of possibility for the nature of religious change.[6] Conversion is what a particular group says it is. No one type of

---

2. For excellent examples of the experimental approach, see John P. Kildahl, "The Personalities of Sudden Religious Converts," *Pastoral Psychology* 16 (September 1965): 37-44, and Charles M. Spellman, Glen D. Baskett, and Donn Byrne, "Manifest Anxiety as a Contributing Factor in Religious Conversion," *Journal of Consulting and Clinical Psychology* 36 (1971): 245-47. For a fine discussion of methodological problems in experimental studies of religion, see Richard L. Gorsuch, "Measurement: The Boon and Bane of Investigating Religion," *American Psychologist* 39 (March 1984): 228-36.

3. For an elegant and controversial example, see Sidney Tarachow, "St. Paul and Early Christianity: A Psychoanalytic and Historical Study," vol. 4, *Psychoanalysis and the Social Sciences* (New York: International Universities Press, 1955), 223-81.

4. Two fine examples of holistic approaches to Christian conversion are Cedric B. Johnson and H. Newton Malony, *Christian Conversion: Biblical and Psychological Perspectives* (Grand Rapids, Mich.: Zondervan, 1982) and Hans Kasdorf, *Christian Conversion in Context* (Scottsdale, Pa.: Herald Press, 1980).

5. For a fine survey of some of the persistent issues in the psychological study of conversion, see James R. Scroggs and William G. T. Douglas, "Issues in the Psychology of Religious Conversion," *Journal of Religion and Health* 6 (1967): 204-16. The issues they outline are still central.

6. A wide range of theological options exist within the Christian tradition. As a generalization, it could be said that "conservative" Christians tend to affirm and appreciate the sudden, dramatic conversion while "liberal" Christians tend to understand and foster gradual religious change. I feel that each side should be more open to the variety and validity of forms of religious change. The theological debates about conversion are paralleled in the human sciences. The literature is full of definitional battles. It is my opinion that most of the debates arise when a scholar takes his own research data and forces all other conversions into the

conversion can be seen as normative from a psychological point of view. Some Christians insist that conversion is precisely defined in both content and process. Certain things are to be rejected and certain things are to be embraced. Certain beliefs, behaviors, and experiences are normative and required before a particular church can accept a person's conversion as valid. There is a rich diversity of types of conversion within the various denominations and parachurch organizations. I assume that there is no fundamental difference empirically between the conversion processes to Christianity and conversion to Islam or Buddhism. This paper focuses on Christian conversion but will include a variety of Christian forms.[7]

Psychological understanding is merely a human attempt to comprehend what is ultimately, to the person of faith, an encounter between a majestic and mysterious God and a person who is a being with vast potential, perversity, and extraordinary complexity. Scientific psychology is a human discipline which can only attempt to use theories to understand a phenomenon that is beyond the scope of human comprehension.

The field of psychology is a cluster of orientations. Diverse though it is, psychology focuses on the person and his or her patterns of perception, cognition, emotion, and behavior. As a science and a technique, psychology seeks to understand, predict, and control persons.[8] The psychological study of conversion can be analyzed in terms of four different approaches. The first and probably largest has been the psychoanalytic study of conversion. Inspired by Freud's brief essay, "A Religious Experience" (1928), many psychoanalysts have sought to untangle the web of factors which make conversion interesting to the clinician.[9] The psychoanalyst focuses on internal emotional elements, especially as they are shaped by the individual's ambivalent yearnings for and hostilities toward his or her mother and father.[10]

The second approach is the behaviorist. The behaviorist approach empha-

---

mold advocated by his particular research subjects. Several resolutions to the conflict have been suggested. See John Lofland and Norman Skonovd, "Conversion Motifs," *Journal for the Scientific Study of Religion* 20 (1981): 372-85; and Mircea Eliade, ed., *The Encyclopedia of Religion* (New York: Macmillan, 1987), s.v. "Conversion," by Lewis R. Rambo.

7. As an example of the diversity of views of conversion within the evangelical framework, compare Billy Graham, *How to Be Born Again* (Waco, Tex.: Word, 1977) and Jim Wallis, *The Call to Conversion* (San Francisco: Harper & Row, 1981). For a splendid description of fundamentalist conversion, see Nancy Tatom Ammerman, *Bible Believers* (New Brunswick, N.J.: Rutgers University Press, 1987). For a good overview of views of conversion, see Walter E. Conn, ed., *Conversion* (New York: Alba House, 1978). For an introduction to Roman Catholic views of conversion, see Robert Duggan, ed., *Conversion and the Catechumenate* (New York: Paulist, 1984).

8. For an interesting discussion of what psychology is, see Joseph D. Matarazzo, "There is Only One Psychology, No Specialties, but Many Applications," *American Psychologist* 42 (October 1987): 893-903.

9. Sigmund Freud, *Collected Papers*, Volume 5, trans. and ed. by James Strachey (New York: Basic Books, 1959), 243-46.

10. A classic essay on the psychoanalytic interpretation of conversion is Leon Salzman, "The Psychology of Religious and Ideological Conversion," *Psychiatry* 16 (1953): 177-87.

sizes the impact of the immediate environment on conversion. The behaviorist William Sargant, a British psychiatrist, popularized a Pavlovian understanding of conversion in his famous book *The Battle for the Mind*.[11]

The third approach is represented by the humanistic and transpersonal psychologists. William James' *The Varieties of Religious Experience* launched this orientation. The humanistic/transpersonal perspective stresses the way conversion allows a person self-realization or fulfillment. Unlike the psychoanalytic and behavioristic approaches, this third group generally holds a more affirmative attitude toward religion and the conversion experience.

The fourth approach I call the social/holistic, is more difficult to specify because the scholars in this category rarely study conversion per se and therefore cannot easily be grouped in a school of thought delineated in terms of conversion. This is an eclectic, holistic approach which attempts to synthesize the other three approaches. Robert Ziller, Theodore Sarbin, and Nathan Adler are representative of the social/holistic approach.[12]

The views of this fourth group are most compatible with those presented here. Each theoretical perspective offers insights into the conversion process. The psychoanalytic point of view elucidates the emotional factors in conversion, the behavioristic the environmental factors, the humanistic/transpersonal tradition the growth-producing or positive sources and consequences of conversion, and the eclectic/holistic point of view the cognitive and social elements of conversion. By itself each is limited and, in some cases, interprets conversion as a manifestation of psychopathology.[13] Yet together these four points of view provide an overall understanding of the diversity and complexity of conversion phenomena.

A heuristic stage model of conversion may serve as a framework to integrate the research of these four psychological approaches, providing a fuller understanding of the multilayered processes involved in conversion. A stage model is appropriate for conversion understood as a process. A "stage" is a phase or period during a sequence of interactions. Each stage is characterized by a cluster of themes, patterns, and subprocesses. Lofland and Stark envision their stage model as a sequence of elements that were multiple, interactive, and cumulative over time. In contrast, the stage model proposed here is not unidirectional. The stages do not always follow each other sequen-

---

11. William Sargant, *Battle for the Mind* (London: Heinemann, 1957).

12. See Robert C. Ziller, "A Helical Theory of Personal Change," *Journal for the Theory of Social Behavior* 1 (1970): 33-73. This essay is, I believe, a seminal piece. Ziller proposes a model in which self concepts, roles, behavior, values, and attitudes are related to one another on a hierarchical spiral. The ordering is based on the notion of ease of change—beginning with attitudes (which he defines as self reports to questions) as the easiest to change, to self which is the most difficult. Ziller's essay is an attempt to orchestrate the diverse subfields of psychology and social psychology in such a way as to relate the different features of human change. My own thinking has been greatly influenced by Ziller's approach.

13. It is my opinion that one of the valuable contributions of psychoanalysis is its vigilance for pathology. Given the proclivity of religiously oriented psychologists to be sufficiently uncritical of conversion, this is a valuable counterpoint.

tially, and stages can reciprocally interact.[14] A "model" is an intellectual construction designed to organize complex data and processes. Although the model has been developed through research and its usefulness thus demonstrated, one should see it not as universal and invariant but as one attempt to organize the complex data and vast literature on conversion.[15] The following stage model consists of seven stages: context, crisis, quest, encounter, interaction, commitment, and consequences.

CONTEXT

The context is the total social, cultural, religious, and personal environment. It is useful to distinguish between the macrocontext and the microcontext.

Macrocontext. The macrocontext is the cultural and social milieu of the larger environment. For instance, in the United States and Great Britain the macrocontext combines industrialization, extensive mass communication, high mobility rates, and the shrinking of Christianity's influence and power. Such a situation allows people within the culture an enormous, sometimes overwhelming, range of options.[16] This pluralism can create perplexity and alienation; consequently, people may eagerly choose a new religious option to lessen anxiety, find meaning, and gain a sense of belonging.

Microcontext. This is the more immediate world of the family, ethnic

---

14. In fact, Gerlach and Hine suggest that the stage model begins with the encounter. The advocate reframes the potential convert's interpretative framework, and thereby generating a crisis and facilitating a quest. See Luther Gerlach and Virginia H. Hine, *People, Power, Change: Movements of Social Transformation* (Indianapolis: Bobbs-Merrill, 1969).

15. My stage model is a modification of the work of Tippett and Lofland and Stark. See Alan R. Tippett, "Conversion as a Dynamic Process in Christian Mission," *Missiology* 5 (April 1977): 203-21. See also John Lofland and Rodney Stark, "Becoming a World-Saver: A Theory of Conversion to a Deviant Perspective," *American Sociological Review* 30 (December 1965): 862-75. The Lofland and Stark essay has generated much debate in the field of sociology of religion. Numerous assessments of the Lofland and Stark stage model have appeared. See John Segger and Phillip Kunz, "Conversion: Evaluation of a Step-Like Process for Problem-Solving," *Review of Religious Research* 13 (Spring 1972): 178-184; David A. Snow and Cynthia L. Phillips, "The Lofland-Stark Conversion Model: A Critical Reassessment," *Social Problems* 27 (April 1980): 430-47; William B. Bankston, H. Hugh Floyd Jr., and Craig J. Forsyth, "Toward a General Model of the Process of Radical Conversion: An Interactionist Perspective on the Transformation of Self-Identity," *Qualitative Sociology* 4 (Winter 1981): 279-97. Lofland himself has suggested that stage models be heuristic tools and not rigid formulas. He believes that stage models should be developed for specific cases and/or situations. See John Lofland, "'Becoming a World-Saver' Revisited," *American Behavioral Scientist* 20 (July/August 1977): 805-18. As an example of such a stage model based on one particular type of conversion, see James V. Downton Jr., "An Evolutionary Theory of Spiritual Conversion and Commitment: The Case of Divine Light Mission," *Journal for the Scientific Study of Religion* 19 (1980): 381-96.

16. For an excellent analysis of the pluralistic, secular milieu, see the books and articles by Peter L. Berger. See especially *The Heretical Imperative* (Garden City, N.Y.: Doubleday, 1979).

group, religious community, and local neighborhood. These groupings play an important role in the creation of a sense of identity and belonging. Microcontextual groups interact with the macrocontext in various ways: Some approve and facilitate the larger context, while others reject or seek to alter the macrocontext. The microcontext can counteract the influence of the macrocontext, intentionally or unintentionally. For instance, isolation from the wider world can intensify the impact of a religious group.

Psychologists typically do not address the context of religious conversion because their emphasis is on the individual. Until recently they tended to focus on issues that ignored or downplayed cultural and social variables. However, we cannot talk about a person's psyche adequately without contextualizing. The person growing up in a small, remote town lives in a very different world than the person in an urban environment with its supermarket of social, moral, and religious options. The Buddhist in India will have a different set of symbols, rituals, and myths with which to express and experience religious life than the Christian in the United States. The context not only provides the social/cultural matrix which shapes a person's myths, rituals, symbols, and beliefs, it also has a powerful impact in terms of access, mobility, and opportunity for even coming into contact with religious change. The increased mobility of our modern world, for example, makes it easier for the advocate to move into new areas to propagate religious ideology. Increased mobility enables the potential convert to move more readily from old patterns of social relationships, which may feel constricting, into new options.

Psychiatrist Robert Jay Lifton recognizes the role of the larger matrix in the creation of psychological reality. Lifton argues that in the modern world, because of the erosion of cultural tradition, the high rates of mobility, instantaneous communication networks, and increasing secularization, the self is no longer clearly defined and has become fragile. He develops the concept of the "Protean" personality to describe a self that is malleable according to the socio-cultural situation. Because our cultural context fosters a great deal of change, he suggests, the people within this context experience fluctuation of identity and self-definition.[17]

The fragility of the self Lifton describes can be a powerful motivation for conversion to conservative religion, whether fundamentalist Christian, orthodox Jewish, or fundamentalist Muslim. Conversion to a religion which offers clear answers and belief systems can provide relief from the overwhelming multiplicity of options, the cacophony of voices pulling in different directions. It can provide a coherent center from which to conduct life in a world where the center has been lost. Such a provision of focus can be viewed negatively, as a constriction of options, or positively, as a creative center of gravity which can enrich and expand one's life.

Another theorist who examines contextual factors is Philip Cushman. Citing elements of modern life such as child-rearing practices, increased mobility and social change, and the erosion of a unified culture, he con-

---

17. Robert Jay Lifton, "Protean Man," *Partisan Review* 35 (Winter 1968): 13-27.

structs a view of the self as narcissistic, empty, and hungry for confirmation.[18] The drive to find nurture and to fill the inner void renders people vulnerable to charismatic leaders, dogmatic belief systems, and rigidly controlled lifestyles. Though Lifton developed his ideas of the Protean personality in the 1960s and Cushman in the 1980s, both writers, by recognizing the importance of contextual factors, provide similar approaches to the psychology of conversion. It is imperative that psychologists undertake more systematic research and theorizing by making explicit the links between personality and the larger cultural/social environment.

Stephen Sales' study in the early 1970s is the only one I know of that seeks to study empirically the relationship between the larger environment and motivations for conversion. He studied the economic flucuations in Seattle and the rates of church attendance in various types of churches there. He found that conversion rates to authoritarian churches increased when there were economic problems.[19]

CRISIS

Most students of conversion agree that a crisis or disorientation precedes conversion. The crisis may be religious, political, psychological, or cultural, or it may be a life situation that opens people to new options. During the crisis, myths, rituals, symbols, goals, and standards cease to function well for the individual or culture. Such a crisis creates great disorientation in the individual's life.

Others view the crisis as an opportunity for revitalization, when myths, rituals, and symbols are rediscovered, people transformed, and energies mobilized to create new possibilities.[20]

The literature which explores this area of the conversion process is primarily psychoanalytic in approach and takes the view that crisis implies a debility, a break-down. From this perspective the motivation to convert is a deficiency motivation, generated from fear, loneliness, or desperation. The conversion itself is seen as an adaptive mechanism which attempts to resolve psychological conflict.

Research by humanistic/transpersonal psychologists offers an alternative

---

18. Philip Cushman, "The Self Besieged: Recruitment-Indoctrination Processes in Restrictive Groups," *Journal for the Theory of Social Behavior* 16 (March 1986): 1-32.

19. Stephen M. Sales, "Economic Threat as a Determinant of Conversion Rates in Authoritarian and Nonauthoritarian Churches," *Journal of Personality and Social Psychology* 23 (1972): 420-28.

20. The extraordinary work of Anthony F. C. Wallace should be of interest to psychologist. See "Revitalization Movements," *American Anthropologist* 58 (April 1956): 264-81; "Mazeway Resynthesis: A Biocultural Theory of Religious Inspiration," *Transactions of the New York Academy of Sciences* 18 (May 1956): 626-38; and, "Mazeway Disintegration: The Individual's Perception of Socio-Cultural Disorganization," *Human Organization* 16 (Summer 1957): 23-27. See also Barbara W. Lex, "Neurological Bases of Revitalization Movements," *Zygon* 13 (December 1978): 276-312.

view. Fulfillment motivation can operate just as strongly as deficiency motivation. Some people are spiritual questors, always growing, learning, developing, maturing. Rather than passive victims of aggressive advocates, these people are actively searching for new options, stimulation, ideas, depths of involvement.

The psychoanalysts, because their subjects are drawn from their clinical case load, and are primarily people who are "emotionally ill," regard the primary motivation for conversion as a search for emotional resolution. The humanists, because they tend to examine psychologically "healthy" people, view conversion as a quest for intellectual, spiritual, and emotional transformation and growth.

One of the few comparative studies which attempts to move beyond this dichotomy by examining a more diverse sample of converts was conducted by Chana Ullman. Ullman studied ten converts to Jewish orthodoxy, ten Roman Catholic converts, ten Hare Krishnas, and ten adherents of Bahai, comparing and contrasting factors such as the degree of trauma or family conflict in their lives during childhood and adolescence, their degree of interest in religious and existential questions, and their degree of involvement with religious groups. Though Ullman at first theorized that the main motivation for conversion was the need for cognitive meaning, she eventually found that the main issues were emotional, involving problematic relationships with father, unhappy childhoods, and a past history of disrupted, distorted personal relationships.[21]

Joel Allison conducted a comparative study of twenty male Protestant seminary students. He compared seven who had intense religious conversions, seven who had mild conversions, and six who had no conversion experience at all. He found that almost without exception those who converted had absent, weak, or alcoholic fathers. Those who did not convert came from intact families. He theorized that conversion for the first group was adaptive and growth-producing: They were able to move away from dependence upon and enmeshment with the mother by identifying with strong father figures, namely God and Jesus. Allison's is one of the few psychoanalytically oriented studies to view the adaptive element of conversion as constructive.[22]

Studies like Ullman's and Allison's point to the need for further comprehensive, comparative research in adult populations to provide a more accurate empirical picture of religious change.

---

21. Chana Ullman, "Cognitive and Emotional Antecedents of Religious Conversion," *Journal of Personality and Social Psychology* 43 (1982): 183-92.

22. Joel Allison, "Religious Conversion: Regression and Progression in an Adolescent Experience," *Journal for the Scientific Study of Religion* 8 (1969): 23-38; "Adaptive Regression and Intense Religious Experience," *Journal of Nervous and Mental Disease* 145 (1968): 452-63; and, "Recent Empirical Studies in Religious Conversion Experiences," *Pastoral Psychology* 17 (September 1966): 21-34.

QUEST

Quest is a process in which people seek to maximize meaning and purpose in life. Under abnormal or crisis situations this active searching intensifies; people look for resources for growth and development in order to "fill the void." In some religious traditions people say that in the quest spiritual forces are working. Social scientists have recently begun to see people as active agents in the creation of meaning and in their selection of religious options.

The classical psychology of religion literature has portrayed the convert as passive. This passivity can be transpersonal, external, or internal. Either God intervenes to bring about the conversion, or the person is enticed by a converting agent who is able to exploit the potential convert's vulnerabilities and draw him or her into a religious movement. The convert is portrayed as responding to unconscious needs so powerful he or she cannot control them.

Recent thought in the sociology of religion suggests that the image of the passive convert is inadequate. James Richardson and Roger Strauss, for example, argue that the convert is actively searching for new experiences, new depths of spiritual understanding, and transformation. Both passive and active modes exist. A person's mode of response falls along a continuum that ranges from complete passivity on one end to intentional, consciously self-directed activity on the other. Psychologists need to conduct studies which explore the full range of response mode. How exactly do people search for health, development, and expansion?[23]

Walter Conn has studied the research and theories of the developmental psychologists Lawrence Kohlberg, Erik Erikson, Jean Piaget, Robert Kegan, and James Fowler. He believes their work may offer a key to a person's inherent motivation for self-transcendence and conversion. Conn feels that developmental research and theory portrays persons moving through a series of developmental stages in which he or she strives to mature cognitively, affectively, and morally offers evidence of a primary human yearning for transcendence. Conn suggests this innate drive to go beyond one's present level of development can be the motivating factor in conversion rather than a defensive coping mechanism resulting from an absent father or unnurturing mother. Conn sees conversion, not as an aberrant process, but one integrated into healthy questing and growth. There are limitations to develop-

---

23. James T. Richardson, "The Active vs. Passive Convert: Paradigm Conflict in Conversion/Recruitment Research," *Journal for the Scientific Study of Religion* 24 (1985): 163-79. See also Roger A. Straus, "Religious Conversion as a Personal and Collective Accomplishment," *Sociological Analysis* 40 (1979): 158-65. The major, and perhaps most popular, argument for the passive view of the convert is the work of Flo Conway and Jim Siegelman, *Snapping: America's Epidemic of Sudden Personality Change* (Philadelphia: Lippincott, 1978). For a fascinating assessment of the complex arguments concerning the issues surrounding the "brainwashing" model of conversion, see Thomas Robbins, "Constructing Cultist 'Mind Control,'" *Sociological Analysis* 45 (1984): 241-56.

mental theory. The question arises whether the developmental stages are as universal and invariant as claimed. Conn's work nevertheless offers a theologically and philosophically sophisticated approach to a normative theory of conversion.[24]

Whether a person is active or passive in the conversion process and whether a person's drive to convert is compensatory or constructive are only some of the variables psychologists examine when studying motivation. There are many theories of motivation. Some theories attempt to identify one overriding motivational factor, such as conflict resolution or relief of guilt. People are motivated, however, by a wide variety of factors, and these factors can change over time. Seymour Epstein offers a model which attempts to integrate the many possibilities. Epstein believes there are four basic motivations: the need to acquire pleasure and avoid pain; to possess a conceptual system; to enhance self-esteem; and to establish and maintain relationships. The strength of each of these motivations, Epstein suggests, will vary among people as well as within an individual at different times and in different circumstances. A religious movement which offers warm fellowship, for instance, will appeal to someone searching for relationships. Persons with a deep need to understand themselves and the world better may be motivated to convert because a religious movement provides a coherent, compelling conceptual system.[25]

I would add to Epstein's model a motivation rarely discussed in the literature of the psychology of conversion: power. James Beckford suggests that the focus on religion's function as a generator of meaning and identity, prominent in the late sixties and early seventies, overlooked the role of power in religious experience, ideology, and institutions. Beckford catalogues different kinds of power which have been recognized as playing a role in religion, like the power to heal, the power to be successful, the power to gain control over one's life, and the power over death.[26]

The motivations that operate in the quest stage extend through the encounter and interaction stages as attractions to a new religious orientation. Ultimately, they operate through the commitment stage, as reasons to solidify commitment. Motivations to convert are multiple, complex, interactive, and cumulative. A recognition of this diversity is an important

24. Walter Conn, *Christian Conversion: A Developmental Interpretation of Autonomy and Surrender* (New York: Paulist, 1986). For excellent brief introductions to Conn's thought, see "Adult Conversions," *Pastoral Psychology* 34 (Summer 1986): 225-36; and, "Pastoral Counseling for Self-Transcendence: The Integration of Psychology and Theology," *Pastoral Psychology* 36 (Fall 1987): 29-48.

25. Seymour Epstein, "The Implications of Cognitive-Experiential Self-Theory for Research in Social Psychology and Personality," *Journal for the Theory of Social Behavior* 15 (October 1985): 283-310. See also Seymour Epstein and Edward J. O'Brien, "The Person-Situation Debate in Historical and Current Perspective," *Psychological Bulletin* 98 (1985): 513-37.

26. James A. Beckford, "The Restoration of 'Power' to the Sociology of Religion," *Sociological Analysis* 44 (1983): 11-33.

step toward a fuller psychological understanding of the conversion process.[27]

ENCOUNTER

The encounter stage involves the contact between the potential convert and the advocate and takes place in a particular setting. Many factors influence the outcome of the encounter. At the least, most social scientists believe that congruence or compatibility of ideology, age, sex, education, and similar attributes play an important role.[28] The encounter stage includes not only the affective, intellectual, and cognitive needs of potential converts but also the needs of the advocate (missionary).

In the past, scholars of conversion have focused their studies almost exclusively on the convert.[29] An essential and dynamic interplay exists, however, between the advocate and the potential convert. Both sides strategize, maneuver, and engage in mutual interaction during the encounter stage. The advocate is assessing the potential audience, trying to create persuasive tactics to bring converts into the religious community. The convert also behaves to enhance his or her own perceived best interests. The ways advocate and convert reciprocally meet each other's needs is an important topic requiring further research.[30]

---

27. One way to examine the issue of motivation is to take into account the extensive discussion of intrinsic and extrinsic religiousness. For a fine general survey of this approach, see Michael J. Donahue, "Intrinsic and Extrinsic Religiousness: Review and Meta-Analysis," *Journal of Personality and Social Psychology* 48 (1985): 400-19.

28. One of the most extensive, detailed studies of the multiple factors involved in conversion is Flavil Ray Yeakley Jr., "Persuasion in Religious Conversion" (Ph.D. diss., University of Illinois at Urbana-Champaign, 1975). He discovered that most converts to the Church of Christ were those who manifested many continuities with those who were the agents of conversion and with the congregation's membership profile. See also *Why Churches Grow* (Arvada, Col.: Christian Communications, 1979).

29. An important exception is the work of Leon Festinger, Henry W. Riecken, and Stanley Shacter, *When Prophecy Fails: A Social and Psychological Study of a Modern Group that Predicted the Destruction of the World* (New York: Harper & Row, 1956). Using the theoretical notion of cognitive dissonance, Festinger and his colleagues argued that a major motivation for missionary activity was to find new converts as a means by which to resolve the cognitive dissonance produced by the fact that the world did not come to an end when predicted. As far as I know, this idea has not been systematically studied in Christian contexts. I suspect that cognitive dissonance theory may be a useful concept that should be tested. Intuitively one has the sense that some Christians seek to convert others as a way to find validation for their own fragile beliefs. Two examples of the application of cognitive dissonance theory to Christian beliefs are: Uri Wernik, "Frustrated Beliefs and Early Christianity," *Numen* 22 (August 1975): 96-130; and, Hugh Jackson, "The Resurrection Belief of the Earliest Church: A Response to the Failure of Prophecy," *Journal of Religion* 55 (October 1975): 415-25.

30. See David A. Snow, Louis A. Zurcher Jr., and Sheldon Ekland-Olson, "Social Networks and Social Movements: A Microstructural Approach to Differential Recruitment," *American Sociological Review* 45 (October 1980): 787-801; and, E. Burke Rochford Jr., "Recruitment Strategies, Ideology, and Organization in the Hare Krishna Movement," *Social Problems* 29

Missionary strategy, like response style, exists along a continuum. Some groups are self-conscious and aggressive about their recruitment strategies. Others are less so. Some groups do not reach out to incorporate new members at all. Some do so in a limited manner. Whatever the strategy, the encounter occurs within a dynamic force field in which both advocate and convert are generally active agents.

Susan Harding, an anthropologist, has examined the vital and persuasive role of language in conversion and thus recognized the centrality of the advocate's method in the conversion process. She examines how rhetoric is used by fundamentalist Christian advocates to insinuate themselves into the psychology of the potential convert. As the advocate tells the story of the Bible and about various Christian beliefs, he or she personalizes it in a way which draws the potential convert into the new rhetorical and interpretative framework. For instance, the metaphors of the death, burial, and resurrection of Jesus Christ may be related to the convert's recent divorce and the need to "resurrect" to a new life. In this way the convert's life history is incorporated into the ideology and narrative being presented so that the group's story becomes the convert's story in a powerful, personal way.[31]

Another anthropologist, Peter Stromberg, stresses the importance of this integration between theological system and personal life. He calls the point at which the religious story becomes personalized the "impression point." When the convert connects the sermon or story to his or her own life an integration is achieved. The theological system makes sense on a personal, human level. Religious symbolism is seen to parallel the convert's life experience. At this point the symbolic system becomes plausible, meaningful, and attractive, and the convert is able to identify with and adopt the system as his or her own, to enter into this new story.[32]

The work of Harding and Stromberg represents excellent examples of interdisciplinary approaches to conversion. Again, though their observations are discussed in relation to the encounter stage, the interactions they describe continue to weave back and forth through and influence the interaction and commitment stages as well.

Another classic topic of discussion which can benefit from a cross-dis-

---

(April 1982): 399-410. For an interesting account of the potential convert's creative assessment and exploitation of new options see Jack Goody, "Religion, Social Change, and the Sociology of Conversion," in Jack Goody, ed., *Changing Social Structure in Ghana* (London: International African Institute, 1975): 91-106. It is not just social scientists who are aware of various methods of evangelization. Many groups are very conscious of what they are doing. For an example of a conservative, Protestant approach, see Em Griffin, *The Mind Changers: The Art of Christian Persuasion* (Wheaton, Ill.: Tyndale House, 1976). For an example of Mormon missionary strategy, see Ernest Eberhard, "How to Share the Gospel: A Step-by-Step Approach for You and Your Neighbors," *Ensign* 4 (June 1974): 6-11.

31. Susan F. Harding, "Convicted by the Holy Spirit: The Rhetoric of Fundamentalist Baptist Conversion," *American Ethnologist* 14 (1987): 167-81.

32. Peter G. Stromberg, "The Impression Point: Synthesis of Symbol and Self," *Ethos: Journal of the Society for Psychological Anthropology* 13 (Spring 1985): 56-74.

ciplinary perspective is the role of charisma in the conversion process. In the encounter stage particularly, the charisma, or personal attraction, of the religious leader or advocate can have a powerful effect on the convert. Charisma, however, like conversion, is an interactional phenomenon in which the needs, expectations, and hopes of both leader and follower are involved. Just as followers need leaders, leaders need followers. The charismatic leader offers the follower such things as a role model, guidelines for living, and affirmation of the follower's value as a person. The new convert fulfills the leader's need for adoration, affirmation, and obedience. Questions about whether the effect of the charismatic leader is to victimize or empower the follower and whether the leadership is used for evil or good purposes are complicated and must be viewed within the interactional model suggested. Responsibility for charismatic power resides not in the leader alone; the acquiescence of the follower must be explored as well.[33]

Emotional bonding between the convert and advocate is a consistent and important finding in the study of conversion. While connection with the charismatic leader is dramatic and important for some converts, the more typical connection is between advocates and converts already within the friendship and kinship networks or relationships fostered by the advocate for the sake of proselytizing. Many scholars have found that the major "pathway" for conversion is via friendship and kinship networks.[34] Benjamin Weininger treats the establishment of an interpersonal connection in the conversion process as a powerful experience. In fact, for some potential converts the experience of finding someone who loves and cares for them enables them to transcend immobilizing conflicts and utilize their energy to thereby relearn and construct a more productive life.[35] Establishing a bond between the advocate and potential convert makes transition to deeper involvement possible.

INTERACTION

If people continue with the group after the encounter, the interaction intensifies. In this stage the potential convert learns more about the teachings, lifestyle, and expectations of the group. The group provides various opportunities, both formal and informal, for people to be more fully incorporated into the group. The intensity and duration of this phase varies. Important variables which operate in this stage include the degree of control the group exerts over communication and social interaction,[36] the nature of the per-

33. For a further discussion of these issues, see Lewis R. Rambo, "Charisma and Conversion," *Pastoral Psychology* 31 (Winter 1982): 96-108.

34. Rodney Stark and William Sims Bainbridge, "Networks of Faith: Interpersonal Bonds and Recruitment to Cults and Sects," *American Journal of Sociology* 85 (May 1980): 1376-95.

35. Benjamin Weininger, "The Interpersonal Factor in the Religious Experience," *Psychoanalysis* 3 (Summer 1955): 27-44.

36. An important process that is rarely discussed by psychologists is the encapsulation process. See Arthur L. Greil and David R. Rudy, "Social Cocoons: Encapsulation and Identity Transformation Organizations," *Sociological Inquiry* 54 (Summer 1984): 260-78.

suasion process, the formation of personal relationships, and the degree to which the convert must reject the old way of life to embrace the new or may be allowed to integrate the two worlds.

Theodore Sarbin and Nathan Adler have delineated common elements found among people who had undergone significant change or transformation. They identified five recurring thematic patterns. The first is the importance of the relationship between the convert and a teacher, mentor, or guide who provides a model for the new way of life. In almost all systems of change there is a guide to the journey. The second is the centrality of ritual as a way for the convert to participate in the new religious system. Through ritual, the convert goes beyond, or even bypasses, cognitive understanding, to achieve direct experience of new beliefs and practices. Social psychologists have thus demonstrated that behavior changes can produce and consolidate changes in belief systems, reversing the common assumption that changes in beliefs precede changes in behavior.[37]

A third common pattern of change identified by Sarbin and Adler is proprioceptive stimuli, or bodily experience. Whether the convert fasts, meditates, or experiences some form of sensory deprivation, in all systems of significant change the involvement of the body is a necessary factor.[38] A fourth thematic pattern is metaphors of death and rebirth. Like Harding, Sarbin and Adler recognize that the way a person conceives change is important to the way a person changes. Metaphors of death and rebirth are congruent with the Christian imagery of the death and resurrection of Christ, which may reinforce the convert's repudiation of the past and embrace of a new beginning.[39] Finally, Sarbin and Adler describe the "trigger," or catalyst, as the moment or turning point when the external religious story becomes relevant and compelling to the person and begins to be internalized.

Though Sarbin and Adler are describing personal change in general rather than religious conversion per se, their model for change can contribute to further understanding of the conversion process.

The description and interpretation of the process of conversion can be rather bland in comparison to the actual experience of conversion. Terms such as "identification" and "internalization" cannot capture the poignant, powerful, and extraordinary experiences some people have in conversion. Murphey's psychoanalytic interpretation of Puritan conversion comes close

---

37. Theodore R. Sarbin and Nathan Adler, "Self-Reconstitution Processes: A Preliminary Report," *The Psychoanalytic Review* 57 (Winter 1970): 599-616.

38. For a fascinating study of this issue, see Stephen R. Wilson, "Becoming a Yogi: Resocialization and Deconditioning as Conversion Processes," *Sociological Analysis* 45 (1984): 301-14.

39. A crucial area for future research would be the examination of the role of metaphors in the shaping of consciousness and experience. See Ralph Metzner, "Ten Classical Metaphors of Self-Transformation," *Journal of Transpersonal Psychology* 12 (1980): 47-62 and *Opening to Inner Light: The Transformation of Human Nature and Consciousness* (Los Angeles: Jeremy P. Tarcher, 1986). See also George Lakoff and Mark Johnson, *Metaphors We Live By* (Chicago: University of Chicago Press, 1980).

to portraying the drama and intensity of some Christian conversions. In Murphey's view conversion entails the transformation of the person's entire emotional world. God who was once hated and reviled is now loved and adored. The self that was once worshiped is now rejected and surrendered to God. The convert's emotional economy is transformed by establishing new patterns of life.[40]

COMMITMENT

The convert is often required to make explicit and public his or her involvement with and participation in a new religious option. Crucial elements of the commitment stage include biographical reconstruction, testimony, rituals, pain induction, decision making, and surrender. The juncture of commitment is sometimes presented as a clear-cut fork in the road or reversal of direction. Some Christian groups require public rituals, such as baptism, to indicate the person's new membership. Potential converts often feel they are confronted with a choice between the way of life and the way of death.

Carrying forward the factor discussed in the encounter stage of adopting the story of a new group as a convert's own, in the commitment stage the new story is more fully appropriated, so that a convert undergoes an experience of biographical reconstruction. Although all of ordinary human life can be seen as a subtle process of reorganizing one's biography, in religious conversion there is often a requirement, implicit or explicit, to interpret life with new metaphors, new images, new stories.[41]

In groups that require the convert to give a public testimony as a ritual of commitment, we see the process of biographical reconstruction encapsulated in dramatic form. Testimony is more than a simple telling of a life story or the experience which led to conversion. It is a creative process which explicitly links the convert's personal story to the group's story. To give testimony in this way, the convert must be alert to the cues of the group and tell his or her story in a way that makes clear that the convert is indeed a person who fits this group. Following testimony, the convert will employ the story, along with other interpretive strategies, as a new way of interpreting experience.[42]

---

40. Murray G. Murphey, "The Psychodynamics of Puritan Conversion," *American Quarterly* 31 (Summer 1979): 135-47.

41. See James A. Beckford, "Accounting for Conversion," *British Journal of Sociology* 29 (June 1978): 249-62; Brian Taylor, "Conversion and Cognition," *Social Compass* 23 (1976): 5-22; Brian Taylor, "Recollection and Membership: Converts' Talk and the Ratiocination of Commonality," *Sociology* 12 (May 1978): 316-24; David A. Snow and Richard Machalek, "The Sociology of Conversion," *Annual Review of Sociology* 10 (1984): 167-90; Mordechai Rotenberg, "The 'Midrash' and Biographic Rehabilitation," *Journal for the Scientific Study of Religion* 25 (1986): 41-55.

42. Another way of explaining the process of biographical reconstruction is attribution theory. See Bernard Spilka, Phillip Shaver, and Lee A. Kirkpatrick, "A General Attribution Theory for the Psychology of Religion," *Journal for the Scientific Study of Religion* 24 (1985): 1-20 and Wayne Proudfoot and Phillip Shaver, "Attribution Theory and the Psychology of Religion," *Journal for the Scientific Study of Religion* 14 (1975): 317-30.

As Sarbin, Adler, and Ziller have recognized, the rituals which may be a part of the commitment stage are powerful methods by which new learning takes place. Baptism, for example, is an explicit, experiential process by which a person declares the old life dead and the new life born.[43] In some religious traditions, requirements to modify one's clothing, diet, or other patterns of behavior can serve this same function of reinforcing the rejection of old patterns and behaviors and the incorporating of new behaviors into a person's life.

A fascinating insight into the process of commitment is provided by Alan Morinis. Morinis examines ordeals of initiation in which groups require the mutilation of the body (such as circumcision, scarification, beatings, amputation of fingers, or removal of teeth) to deliberately induce pain. He theorizes that the inducement of pain serves two purposes: to heighten self-awareness, and to demonstrate that to become a part of the group the individual must sacrifice something of the self. Although no Christian group I know of requires physical mutilation of the body as a part of the conversion process, pain and trauma are often intensely present in conversion. The stories of religious converts are steeped in agonized descriptions of struggles with sin and alienation from God. I think it is possible that the emphasis in conservative Christianity on sinfulness, perversity, and depravity before turning to God is one way to create the same effect as mutilation rituals.[44]

The decision making which is an integral part of the commitment stage is often the occasion for an intense, painful confrontation with the self. It is no accident that making a decision for Christ is a major theme in evangelical theology. At the same time that a potential convert may be attracted to Jesus Christ and the new religious community, he or she may still be enmeshed in the old way of life. The vacillation between the two worlds can be very confusing and painful.[45] The decision to cross the line into a new life, on the other hand, can be the occasion for tremendous relief and joy. This feeling of new freedom can itself be a powerful psychological experience which confirms the theology being embraced.[46]

---

43. See the excellent article by Lucy Bregman, "Baptism as Death and Birth: A Psychological Interpretation of its Imagery," *Journal of Ritual Studies* 1 (Summer 1987): 27-42.

44. Alan Morinis, "The Ritual Experience: Pain and the Transformation of Consciousness in Ordeals of Initiation," *Ethos: Journal of the Society for Psychological Anthropology* 13 (Summer 1985): 150-74. Compare with E. O. Boyanowsky, "The Psychology of Identity Change: A Theoretical Framework for Review and Analysis of the Self-Role Transformation Process," *Canadian Psychological Review* 18 (April 1977): 115-27.

45. No one portrays the struggle better than Paul W. Pruyser's *Between Belief and Unbelief* (New York: Harper & Row, 1974).

46. See the excellent discussion of decision making and choice in Eileen Barker, "The Conversion of Conversion: A Sociological Anti-Reductionistic Perspective," in *Reductionism in Academic Disciplines*, ed. Arthur Peacock (London: Society for Research into Higher Education, 1985), 58-75. Also see C. David Gartrell and Zane K. Shannon, "Contacts, Cognitions, and Conversion: A Rational Choice Approach," *Review of Religious Research* 27 (September 1985): 32-48.

Many converts report that surrender to God and/or Jesus Christ is a crucial turning point in their conversion process. Unfortunately the topic is rarely given much attention in psychology, or in sociology or anthropology for that matter. Harry Tiebout, in his studies of Alcoholic Anonymous, points in a promising direction. People will often struggle with an issue or a problem for a long period of time, and that their anguish depletes them. In A.A. the person finally faces the reality that he or she is an alcoholic and is totally helpless to change that reality. Paradoxically, upon a genuine acknowledgement of that helplessness, the person is empowered to begin the process of dealing with alcoholism. I believe a similar process is sometimes at work in Christian conversions. When a person confronts his or her predicament as a lost sinner, the surrender to that knowledge and a surrender to Jesus Christ as a deliverer is the very point at which energy becomes available for a new life. Tiebout's psychoanalytic interpretation centers on the concept of energy. Much energy is spent to maintain the struggle. With surrender, energy is released to be used in other aspects of the person's life.[47] Marc Galanter proposes a similar process that he calls the "relief effect" which takes place when a person identifies with a group.[48]

As noted in relation to the encounter stage, initial participation in a religious group is often facilitated by the establishment of emotional bonds between the potential convert and the advocate. It appears that whether a person decides to make a long-term commitment a group is determined, to some extent, by the degree of connection the person feels with the new group as opposed to outside connections. As far as I can determine, no research has been done on Christian groups in this area, but Marc Galanter and his colleagues' study of the Unification Church ("Moonies") is suggestive. They found that after participating in a recruitment workshop most of the potential converts acquired virtually the same level of Unification Church beliefs. In other words, all of those who completed the workshop had been persuaded to affirm the belief system. The major factor for those who remained in the group was not their level of belief, but whether or not the person had stronger relationships with people in the group than he or she had with people outside of the movement.[49]

CONSEQUENCES

The nature of the consequences is determined, in part, by the nature, intensity, and duration of the conversion. How many aspects of life are affected by the conversion? How extensive are these changes? To what

---

47. Harry M. Tiebout, "The Act of Surrender in the Therapeutic Process," *Quarterly Journal of Studies on Alcohol* 10 (June 1949): 48-58.

48. Marc Galanter, "The 'Relief Effect': A Sociobiological Model for Neurotic Distress and Large-Group Therapy," *American Journal of Psychiatry* 135 (May 1978): 588-91.

49. Marc Galanter, Richard Rabkin, Judith Rabkin, and Alexander Deutsch, "The 'Moonies': A Psychological Study of Conversion and Membership in a Contemporary Religious Sect," *American Journal of Psychiatry* 136 (February 1979): 165-70.

extent are converts alienated from or reconciled to the wider world? Many contemporary scholars believe that authentic conversion is an ongoing process of transformation. The initial change, while important, is but the first step in a long process, a pilgrimage.

Consequences may be viewed from the convert's point of view or the outsider's. How does the convert experience the consequences? What experiences, ideas, relationships, and events are generated in the conversion process and what are the effects of these experiences on the person? These effects can convince the convert of the validity and value of the conversion, or they can serve to make the convert question the wisdom of her or his conversion. These changes also affect other people in the convert's life, eliciting both positive and negative reactions which will either facilitate or hinder the conversion process.[50]

The outsider seeks to make an assessment of the effects of conversion in terms of theological validity and value, and/or to make a psychological diagnosis as to the benefit and detriments to a person's psychological health.[51] In order to evaluate the consequences of conversion in this way, to make an assessment of what is progressive and what is regressive, the observer needs to be explicit about his or her own values, as our theological, intellectual, and personal stance will inevitably shape our interpretation of a person's conversion. For instance, can an agnostic or atheist affirm the validity and value of a conversion to fundamentalist Christianity? Can a devout, conservative Protestant scholar understand and affirm a conversion to the Church of Jesus Christ of Latter Day Saints?[52]

Beyond these obvious questions of religious orientation, scholars need to acknowledge the more subtle values inherent in their theoretical models and analytic tools. For instance, if psychologists are attempting to evaluate the mental health consequences of conversions, do they recognize the cultural values which shape their model of mental health? Do they recognize how their model might be differently constituted in other cultures? Do they acknowledge the underlying cultural, personal, and professional assumptions on which their work is based?[53]

Once biases and assumptions have been recognized a psychological evaluation of conversion must ask whether there has been progress, regression,

---

50. For an interesting discussion see Irwin R. Barker and Raymond F. Currie, "Do Converts Always Make the Most Committed Christians?" *Journal for the Scientific Study of Religion* 24 (1985): 305-13.

51. For examples of such diagnosis, see K. Bragan, "The Psychological Gains and Losses of Religious Conversion," *British Journal of Medical Psychology* 50 (June 1977): 177-80 and Gerda E. Allison, "Psychiatric Implications of Religious Conversion," *Canadian Psychiatric Association Journal* 12 (February 1976): 55-61.

52. For a fine examination of the problems involved in assessing what is progressive and regressive, see Ken Wilber, "The Pre/Trans Fallacy," *ReVision* 3 (Fall 1980): 51-72.

53. A good example of careful assessment is H. Newton Malony, "Conversion: The Sociodynamics of Change," *Fuller Theological Seminary Theology, News and Notes* (June 1986): 16-19, 24.

or fixation. One study which explores these questions was conducted by Robert Simmonds. He asked whether conversion to a Jesus movement was a genuine conversion or merely the replacement of an addiction to drugs with an addiction to Jesus. Given the emphasis on "dependence on Jesus" and obedience to group leaders and group norms, there seems to have been, in this case at least, no real change in personality, but merely a substitution of one addiction for another.[54]

David Gordon's study of a fundamentalist group is also instructive. Generally speaking, psychologists are very suspicious of notions of surrender, self-abandonment, and dependence upon a group because such notions often indicate immaturity. However, Gordon found that the people in his study had in fact made major positive changes in their lives because they had surrendered ways of functioning which were unproductive for new patterns of life. Thus the "dying to self" advocated by the group was psychologically effective in enabling the people to gain new ego control and strength. These studies demonstrate that assessment is a complicated process.[55]

Another possible approach to the assessment of conversion is the faith development perspective developed by James Fowler. The conversion process for a particular person can be described in terms based on criteria appropriate to the age and stage of the person involved. Conversion and developmental processes relate to each other in many different ways. For example, movement from one developmental stage to another can be the occasion for a conversion. Likewise, a conversion can foster a movement to a new stage of development. However, many conversions are merely reflections of the developmental stage of the person at the time. In other words, a person's developmental level serves as a filter through which the conversion is processed, setting the parameters for what can be accomplished through that conversion and influencing what is attractive to the potential convert.[56]

It is my hope that the drama of conversion will continue to draw the attention of psychologists. It is also my hope that psychologists will increasingly appreciate the complexity and dynamism of the phenomenon of conversion and will join with others in the human sciences and religious studies to develop research methods and theories worthy of the subject.

---

54. Robert B. Simmonds, "Conversion or Addiction: Consequences of Joining a Jesus Movement Group," *American Behavioral Scientist* 20 (July/August 1977): 909-24.

55. David F. Gordon, "Dying to Self: Self-Control Through Self-Abandonment," *Sociological Analysis* 45 (1984): 41-56.

56. James W. Fowler, *Stages of Faith: The Psychology of Human Development and the Quest for Meaning* (San Francisco: Harper & Row, 1981) and *Becoming Adult, Becoming Christian* (San Francisco: Harper & Row, 1984).

Chapter Twelve

The Sociology of Conversion

William Sims Bainbridge

Over a century ago, my great-grandfather set out on a world tour to collect data for what he called a *science of missions*.[1] By visiting the outposts of American Christianity that had been established in the farthest corners of the globe and by examining closely how each fitted into the exotic surrounding society, he hoped to learn general principles of successful evangelization, applicable at home as well as abroad. Today we might call his research sociology, although this academic discipline was not established in the United States until a decade after he published his book. His task is far from finished even today, and a sociological analysis of conversion remains incomplete and partial.

The sociologist, for example, must leave out the divine half of the equation. Social science has no tool to research the supernatural, and it must leave to theologians an analysis of how deity chooses to interact with humanity. And sociologists have not always done the best possible job in understanding the social side of conversion, either, occasionally projecting individual prejudices and political biases onto a topic that deserved objective scientific scrutiny. Still, there has been progress in my field, and I shall outline the chief debates in terms of the evidence collected to date.

At the present time, two alternative sociological theories compete to explain religious conversion. According to *strain theory*, persons join a religion in order to satisfy conventional desires that unusual personal or collective deprivations have frustrated. According to *social influence theory*, per-

---

1. William Folwell Bainbridge, *Around the World Tour of Christian Missions* (Boston: Lothrop, 1882).

sons join a religion because they have formed social attachments with persons who are already members and because their attachments to nonmembers are weak. Despite their great differences, there is scientific evidence in favor of both of these theories, and the best explanation is probably an informed combination of both.[2]

STRAIN THEORY

Variants of strain theory have been used to explain numerous different social phenomena,[3] and in some form many clergy accept its root idea, the hypothesis that religion has more to offer the poor and oppressed than the rich and powerful. People turn to religion, strain theory holds, because of their relative deprivation.

Sociologists distinguish between *absolute deprivation* and *relative deprivation*, and they have given the latter a far greater role to play in their theories.[4] A person suffering absolute deprivation lacks something he objectively needs. For instance, someone dying of a disease lacks good health. A person suffering relative deprivation lacks something that a person in a different status possesses. For example, the poor do not have the wealth and power of the elite in their society.

Several questions need to be answered about the standard against which deprivation is judged before one can apply the concept rigorously. Should relative deprivation be defined as having less than the average person in society? Less than a typical middle-class person? Less than a rich and powerful person? Or is the proper standard the kind of life that the individual in question could live if not beset by unusual calamity? If so, a poor person whose life was stable and trouble-free would not be deprived while a rich person beset by chaos and confusion would be.

The usual sociological solution to this problem is to focus on the factors that can make a person *feel* deprived. Among these is the perception that other people in society have more. Another factor is the experience of having had more in the past, oneself. Another is the images the culture presents of what a person could or should have. And an important role may also be played by social movements, often of a political or religious kind, that seek to convince people they deserve more than they currently have. Logically, some of these factors may produce a feeling of deprivation even among the rich and powerful in society, but sociologists have generally assumed that the most crucial factors in fostering a sense of deprivation were societal inequal-

2. Theodore E. Long and Jeffrey K. Hadden, "Religious Conversion and the Concept of Socialization," *Journal for the Scientific Study of Religion* 22 (1983): 1-14.

3. Robert K. Merton, "Social Structure and Anomie," in *Social Theory and Social Structure* (New York: Free Press, 1968), 185-214; Neil J. Smelser, *Theory of Collective Behavior* (New York: Free Press, 1962).

4. James C. Davies, "Toward a General Theory of Revolution," *American Sociological Review* 27 (1962): 5-19; Ted Robert Gurr, *Why Men Rebel* (Princeton, N.J.: Princeton University Press, 1970).

ities, causing whole classes of people to feel they have experienced a raw deal compared to more favored classes.

The natural response to relative deprivation is to seek to get what other people have, either through an individual career or political action. If the deprivation is extreme enough that the individual lacks the resources to achieve career success, or if the economic system is rigid enough to prevent it, then the person must turn to politics. According to some neo-Marxist sociologists, however, many people lack the advanced political awareness to see that political action is the solution, and thus they will turn to the supernatural "false consciousness" of religion.[5] But one does not have to agree with the Marxists to see that many people are unable to overcome their deprivations relative to more fortunate members of society and that these people will suffer continuing frustrations.

Religion offers a way to transcend and transvalue relative deprivation. In heaven, all will be equal and all will be fulfilled. Membership in the religion can be a private badge of status, compensating the individual for lack of status in secular society. From this perspective, those who claim to be born again may be guilty of the sin of pride, but the desire for positive self-esteem is a powerful motivator. In joining a religion, the person adopts an ideology about life that transforms deprivation into a virtue, or at least provides supernatural compensation for it.

The evidence in favor of strain theory mainly concerns radical religious movements, sects rather than mainstream denominations, and a good deal of it is historical. Norman Cohn showed that the millenarian movements of medieval Europe drew their support from deprived groups, often in response to a severe worsening of conditions.[6] The same was found true for traditional American sects.[7] Numerous questionnaire studies have also shown that sect members tend to be deprived relative to members of mainline churches.[8] A study by Rodney Stark and myself compared 110 adult converts to sects with 110 adults who had been born into the same groups, finding that the converts suffered greater deprivation than the lifelong members. For example, 39 percent of converts had attended college, compared with fully 57 percent of nonconverts; 46 percent of converts considered themselves to be of the working class, compared with 37 percent of nonconverts.[9]

Clearly, relative deprivation has something to do with religious affiliation. Sects recruit the relatively deprived. But there is no tendency for religious per-

5. E.J.Hobsbawm, *Primitive Rebels* (Manchester, England: Manchester University Press, 1959); Eric R. Wolf, *Peasant Wars of the Twentieth Century* (New York: Harper & Row, 1969).

6. Norman Cohn, *The Pursuit of the Millennium* (New York: Harper, 1961).

7. Liston Pope, *Millhands and Preachers* (New Haven, Conn.: Yale University Press, 1942); Elmer T. Clark, *The Small Sects in America* (Nashville: Cokesbury, 1948).

8. Nicholas J. Demerath, *Social Class in American Protestantism* (Chicago: Rand McNally, 1965).

9. Rodney Stark and William Sims Bainbridge, *The Future of Religion* (Berkeley: University of California Press, 1985), 160.

sons in general to be more deprived than the irreligious members of society, and some evidence exists that church members are actually better off than the average.[10] Therefore, relative deprivation cannot explain conversion in general, although it may explain why certain individuals join certain types of groups.

In their zeal to find class conflict and social inequality behind all social phenomena, many sociologists had ignored the possibility that it was absolute deprivation, not relative, that impelled people toward the churches. A recent analysis by Rodney Stark and myself showed how one could build a rigorous, formal theory of religious commitment based on the principle that all persons are severely deprived in an absolute sense, and thus everybody is a potential convert. Relative deprivation may merely steer individuals toward somewhat different forms of religion.[11]

Indeed, if one considers all the unfulfilled dreams and dashed hopes experienced by even the most fortunate of persons, deprivation seems the essence of the human condition. Logically, all individuals should have powerful motivations to find a faith that transcends the world. The problem thus becomes to explain why many people do not convert. Therefore, adding absolute deprivation to the relative deprivation that has been the key concept in strain theory does not entirely solve its problems, and we shall shortly look to social influence theory for help.

What are the lessons of strain theory for those seeking converts? If the community one wishes to convert is relatively deprived, then one should emphasize those aspects of religion stressed by sects, and several of them are compatible with most religious traditions: constant affirmation of salvation, open expression of emotion, informal services, strong fellowship within the congregation, and a continual sense of spiritual regeneration. Most churches could stand more of these qualities. But if the community to be evangelized is a cross-section of the society, then the traditional emphasis of strain theory on the relatively deprived offers bad advice. The rich and powerful face the same absolute deprivations as the poor and powerless. Individuals in every class will differ in their specific needs, and the evangelist must find a flexible manner of communicating to everybody that their greatest legitimate desires and gravest fears can find an answer in religion.

In consultations with individuals and families, spiritual attention must be given to their particular deprivations, whether absolute or relative. In the congregation or community as a whole, the absolute deprivations need emphasis. We all feel guilt, dread of death, sorrow at the pain of those we love. The Christian tradition has been particularly strong in bridging the gap between the relatively deprived and the advantaged classes. Through it, the fortunate can learn honest sympathy for those less fortunate, and the deprived can appreciate the humanness of those who possess what they lack.

---

10. Rodney Stark and Charles Y. Glock, *American Piety* (Berkeley: University of California Press, 1968).

11. Rodney Stark and William Sims Bainbridge, *A Theory of Religion* (New York: Peter Lang, 1987).

SOCIAL INFLUENCE THEORY

No one doubts that human beings can influence each other, but the job of formalizing this simple insight and determining scientifically exactly how the influence operates has proven a formidable task. Half a century ago, Edwin Sutherland argued that each individual is under the influence of competing cultural patterns, and the individual's behavior will tend to follow the culture from which he receives the most numerous, most powerful, earliest, and most enduring communications.[12] Subsequently, different aspects of this idea gave birth to separate schools of thought which deserve to be reunited: *control theory* and *subculture theory*.

Control theory holds that individuals will act in a conventional way, so long as they possess a powerful bond to the conventional social order. This bond consists of attachments to other individuals, investment in a career inside standard societal institutions, constant involvement in conventional activities, and belief in the correctness of the social order. Individuals who lack these ties to conformity will be free to experiment with novel alternatives. From this perspective, the persons most likely to convert to a new religious affiliation are those who have lost connectedness: newlyweds, the divorced, the widowed, freshly independent young adults, those who have just changed jobs, or persons experiencing any other major life disruption whether negative or positive in character.

Subculture theory stresses the role of a group of like-minded people in establishing a distinctive way of thinking and acting. In a group of close friends, if the majority think a particular way about an important matter, the others will soon come to agree with them. Through social interaction, persons repeatedly give each other information, emotions, and material rewards. Although sharp disagreements can cause a group to split in twain, so long as a group holds together powerful forces press members to become similar in thought and action.[13] In religious terms, the subculture is a congregation or a denomination. To accept the tenets of faith one must first become a member of the social group.

If we think of each church as a subculture, then people are not likely to leave one for another, unless for some reason they lack the bonds to make them solid members of the one they are in. If we combine both control theory and subculture theory, much about religious affiliation becomes clear. As control theory states, a person is socially free to join a new religious group only if he lacks strong ties to some other group. As subculture theory states, to convert to a new religion, such a person must develop strong social relations with persons who are already members.

While there are always exceptions to any rule of human behavior, the

---

12. Edwin H. Sutherland, *On Analyzing Crime* (Chicago: University of Chicago Press, 1973).

13. George C. Homans, *The Human Group* (New York: Harcourt, Brace and World, 1950); *Social Behavior: Its Elementary Forms* (New York: Harcourt Brace, 1974).

evidence in favor of these propositions is overwhelming. Studies of small, intense religious groups have repeatedly shown the importance of friendship relationships in drawing new converts.[14] Existing friendships with members draw people in, and friendless folk may be attracted to a group in the first place by the need for friends.[15] Many people convert to a new religion as a result of marrying a person who already has strong faith in it.[16]

Supportive evidence comes from research on two related topics: orthodoxy and apostasy. Data on a range of denominations show that persons whose friendships are primarily within their congregation accept their church's beliefs and practices more fully than do people with many outside friendships.[17] The factor that best explains why some communities have low rates of church membership is geographic mobility, because people who move lose social ties that would keep them within the church.[18]

I tested this last proposition recently in a statistical (multiple regression) study of the percent of the population who were members of churches or other religious organizations, in 288 American metropolitan areas. On average, about half of the residents of these cities were members, but there was great variation. Several competing theories were tested in competition with geographic mobility. For example, Wade Clark Roof had argued that cosmopolitan areas of the country, typically big cities and highly educated areas where the influence of secularization had most severely eroded traditional religious faith, would have the lowest rates of church membership. However, city size and level of education had only the weakest and most ambiguous associations with church membership, indicating that cosmopolitanism was not a significant cause of weakened church affiliation. In contrast, church membership was low where geographic mobility was high, as measured by the percent of residents who had moved in the previous five years.[19]

While the results of that study were quite clear, it had the defect that the data concerned rates for geographic areas rather than the characteristics of individual human beings. Another of my recent studies was based on the

14. James T. Richardson and Mary Stewart, "Conversion Process Models and the Jesus Movement," *American Behavioral Scientist* 20 (1977): 819-38; Stark and Bainbridge, *The Future of Religion.*

15. Bryan R. Roberts, "Protestant Groups and Coping with Urban Life in Guatemala City," *American Journal of Sociology* 73 (1968): 753-67.

16. Andrew M. Greeley, "Religious Musical Chairs," in *In Gods We Trust,* ed. Thomas Robbins and Dick Anthony (New Brunswick, N.J.: Transaction, 1981), 101-26.

17. Stan Gaede, "A Causal Model of Belief-Orthodoxy," *Sociological Analysis* 37 (1976): 205-17; Kevin Welch, "An Interpersonal Influence Model of Traditional Religious Commitment," *Sociological Quarterly* 22 (1981): 81-92.

18. Robert Wuthnow and Kevin Christiano, "The Effects of Residential Migration on Church Attendance in the United States," in *The Religious Dimension,* ed. Robert Wuthnow (New York: Academic Press, 1979), 257-76; William Sims Bainbridge and Rodney Stark, "Suicide, Homicide, and Religion," *Annual Review of the Social Sciences of Religion* 5 (1981): 33-56.

19. William Sims Bainbridge, "Explaining the Church Member Rate," *Social Forces* 68 (1990): 1287-96.

1911 census of Australia, reworking the data so that it was possible to examine the religion and mobility of individuals. Atheists were far more likely to have moved than were Christians. Thus, studies of different kinds using data from different nations and time periods, provide further support for social influence theory.[20]

What are the lessons of social influence theory for those seeking converts? Clearly there should be an emphasis upon fellowship—upon personal relationships linking members. Members of the group should be helped to share their commitment with nonmember friends and relatives. The church should welcome newcomers to the community and others whose social bonds have weakened.

As Dean Kelley has shown, however, it can be fatal to stress the social life of the church to the exclusion of its religious life.[21] Social influence is the medium of transmission of faith, and it can do much to sustain faith. But unless people have a religious yearning, and unless religion offers people something distinctively different from what any social club can give, faith will wither. Here social influence theory needs to borrow from strain theory.

A COMBINED ANALYSIS

Several studies have found evidence for both theories. When John Lofland and Rodney Stark reported that relative deprivation was an essential precondition for conversion to a radical sect, they noted that both development of social bonds with members and a weakness of bonds with outsiders were also required.[22] The model sketched by Lofland and Stark remains the most influential guide to research on the sociology of conversion.

To start with, Lofland and Stark said, a person must experience powerful, enduring frustrations. Also, the person must already believe that the best way to solve deep problems is through religion, but the nagging failure of his present religion to solve them places it under suspicion. The person becomes a religious seeker on a quest for a more satisfactory religious affiliation. The person then reaches a turning point in his/her life, when great changes are in order. At this moment of maximum vulnerability, the individual encounters people who already belong to the religious group. By developing attachments to them, and by losing attachments to others, the person becomes a member himself. Then, intensive interaction with group members brings him to accept the belief system, and thus to become completely converted.

In one set of principles, this model of conversion unites the traditions of strain theory and social influence theory, and its very eclecticism is undoubt-

---

20. William Sims Bainbridge, "Wandering Souls," in *Exploring the Paranormal*, ed. George K. Zollschan, John F. Schumaker, and Greg F. Walsh (Bridgeport, Dorset, England: Prism, 1989), 237-49.

21. Dean M. Kelley, *Why Conservative Churches Are Growing* (New York: Harper & Row, 1972).

22. John Lofland and Rodney Stark, "Becoming a World-Saver," *American Sociological Review* 30 (1966): 862-75.

edly greatly responsible for the influence it has held over later scholars. Another reason the Lofland-Stark model was so influential was that its authors offered vivid illustrations of how the process worked, in a number of brief life histories. These were drawn from their research on the radical, millenarian religious group called the Unification Church. The concept of strain is well illustrated by the case of Elmer, a frustrated fellow born in North Dakota but brought by his family to a farm near Eugene, Oregon, where the first, tiny branch of the Unification Church was struggling to attract converts.

After high school he flunked out of the university after one semester and spent the next two years in the Army, where he flunked medical technician school. After the Army he enrolled in a nearby state college and again lasted only one semester. He then returned to his parents' farm and took a job in the plywood factory. Elmer conceived of himself as an intellectual and aspired to be a learned man. He undertook to educate himself and collected a large library toward this end. Unfortunately he was virtually illiterate. In addition to more conventional books, he subscribed widely to occult periodicals, such as *Fate, Flying Saucers, Search*, and so on. He also viewed himself as a practical man of invention, a young Thomas Edison, and dreamed of constructing revolutionary gadgets. He actually began assembling materials for a tiny helicopter for use in herding the cows and a huge television antenna to bring in stations hundreds of miles away. Elmer also had severe interaction problems. He was unable to speak to others above a whisper and looked constantly at his feet while talking. He had great difficulty sustaining a conversation, often appearing to forget what he was talking about.[23]

The Unification Church seemed to provide Elmer with the sense of self-worth and intellectual status he longed for. After joining, he could consider himself the member of an elite, those chosen by God for a great mission, and he possessed knowledge that even university professors lacked—the divine principles of his church's doctrines. In consequence, his social awkwardness was to a great extent cured. He no longer stared at his feet while mumbling responses to what other people said to him; now he was able to look folk in the eye and proudly tell them the truth about God. His case is but one of many reported by Lofland and Stark that illustrate the role that psychological frustration can play in motivating people, and it shows further that membership in a supportive religious group can assuage the strains that impelled conversion, thus producing strong commitment to the church.

In the twenty-five years since Lofland and Stark wrote, many empirical studies and theoretical essays have cast doubt on the necessity of one or another step in their analysis, however. For example, my observational research on The Process Church of the Final Judgment showed that con-

---

23. John Lofland, *Doomsday Cult* (Englewood Cliffs, N.J.: Prentice-Hall, 1966) 38.

verts had not all suffered enduring frustrations or seen their problems in primarily religious terms.[24] Indeed many came to see their former life as unsatisfactory only after making contact with the Process, and the group did not begin with a religious conception of itself. Although some individuals may go through a series of stages in conversion exactly as outlined by Lofland and Stark, for other people the process may be far less smooth, and conversion may be achieved even when some elements are lacking, as the following case from my own research illustrates:

> Hathor was a student at an English art college where she met Christian, a young man who had been studying to be a concert pianist. His older brother was Lucius, a close friend of Micah, who was an intimate friend of Robert de Grimston, founder of The Process. Hathor was drawn into a psychotherapy group called Compulsions Analysis, which subsequently evolved into the Process Church, through this long chain of strong social ties. Robert brought in Micah, who brought in Lucius, who brought in Christian, who brought in Hathor. She had no particular intense life problems. In an interview, she told me, "Nothing dramatic was happening at that point in my life. I wasn't really going through a vast trauma, or anything like that. I was at a crossroads, really, in terms of a career. Would I do teaching? Which I didn't really look forward to with a great deal of pleasure, because with the qualifications I had it would have meant teaching art in grade school. It really didn't excite me terribly. Or should I go on and do further training in order to qualify for a different kind of teaching position? Or should I take up painting? It was a period of indecision. But nothing deep or wrenching."[25]

Clearly, Hathor was not suffering enduring, acutely felt tensions, when she joined the group, as the Lofland/Stark model said she must. Thus, her case does not support strain theory. However, we do see evidence of a turning point in her life, and the influence of social bonds is unmistakable. Enduring personal frustrations, the key idea in strain theory, certainly may facilitate conversion, but it is not essential. On the other hand, intensive interaction with group members may be essential for bringing the individual to trust the promises of faith and thus become a believer.[26] The need for an answer to life's questions is not enough; people require a reason to believe that a given answer is trustworthy. Thus, although every human being might be a potential convert, many people remain without faith.

To some extent, the faithless simply lack sufficient interaction with the

---

24. William Sims Bainbridge, *Satan's Power* (Berkeley: University of Calfornia Press, 1978).

25. Ibid., adapted from page 35, with all the original names substituted for the pseudonyms I employed in my book, which are no longer necessary.

26. C. David Gertrell and Zane K. Shannon, "Contacts, Cognitions, and Conversion: A Rational Choice Approach," *Review of Religious Research* 27 (1985): 32-48.

faithful. But one must also consider the opponents of religion and its competitors. Among them are some of the sciences and various academic disciplines that compete with religion in explaining the nature of things and in promoting solutions for human ills. Members of many learned professions are rewarded in their careers and social lives for being resolutely secular. People whose friends happen to be in highly secular careers will thus be pulled away from religion. By the principles of social influence theory, some individuals will be converted away from religion, just as others will be converted to it. Given that modern industrial economies need the highly secular professions, the tug of war between church and antichurch can never end, and complete conversion of the entire population is impossible.[27]

If one adds to the equation the non-Christian religions and such quasireligious phenomena as Marxism and psychotherapy, the Christian churches have a considerable amount of competition in their attempt to evangelize the world. Further, to the extent that strain theory explains conversion, frustrations can produce deconversion as well. An individual who joins a religious group in pursuit of solutions to life problems is very apt to drop out if the problems continue. Given sufficient fellowship and comfort, the individual may learn to live with the problems, and thus defection is not inevitable. but even lifelong members of the particular church may defect if severe problems arise in their lives. Thankfully, few of us experience all the calamities of Job, but few of us have his faithful endurance as well.

It would be too much to say that sociologists are convinced that the factors governing conversion balance off, and the evangelical labor invested in gaining converts merely offsets losses due to defection. But the combination of strain theory and social influence theory under consideration here does explain conversion in terms of counteracting forces which sometimes work against faith, as well as often for it.

THE MEANING OF CONVERSION

To convert means to transform, to change, to turn around. Thus it implies a radical change in the nature of the person undergoing religious conversion. But there is reason to doubt that people who convert are always, or even commonly, changed in an essential way. Social influence theory leaves quite open the question of how much the individual changes in personal behavior and inner feeling. It focuses on a shift in the person's attachments to others, and it conceptualizes conversion as simply the joining of a new religious fellowship. How much the person actually changes depends on the nature of the social influences after joining and on the degree of difference between the person's old affiliations and the new ones.

Strain theory accepts the full implications of the term conversion, and it assumes that the individual's beliefs undergo a radical change. The person was deeply frustrated with his former life and takes a leap of faith into a new

---

27. Dean R. Hoge, *Division in the Protestant House* (Philadelphia: Westminster, 1976).

way of thinking, feeling, and acting. But strain theory applies best when relatively deprived individuals join radical sects, and thus conversion to a liberal denomination may involve no substantial changes. Furthermore, because strain theory is based on an analysis of people's motivations it explains more about what people try to do than what they succeed in doing. That is, people may join religious sects hoping to transform themselves and their lives, but many will ultimately fail. And it is possible that religious conversion often means mere belief change—adoption of a new ideology without any concomitant change in feelings or behavior.

This possibility brings us to one of the hottest research topics in the sociology of religion at the present time: the behavioral differences between religious people and nonreligious people. Classical sociological theorists and clergy agreed that religion, through its rituals and teachings, encourages people to conform to the morals of the society, and perhaps to become better persons. But sixty years ago, Hartshorne and May discovered that young people who attended Sunday school were no less delinquent than those who did not.[28] Twenty years ago, in an extremely well-conducted and influential study, Hirschi and Stark similarly found no power of religion to make young people behave better.[29] This finding cast grave suspicion on the idea that conversion to a religion profoundly transforms the individual.

As good statistical studies mounted in number, sociological frustration also grew, because the results seemed quite contradictory. According to some research studies, religious people were more law-abiding and more respecting of others' rights, and according to other research studies, they were not.[30] Today, there is general agreement that religion does not have an intrinsic power to make people behave better, but that various social factors may temporarily give religion such power.[31] For example, in communities where most people are members of churches—where rates of geographic migration are low—religion supports the moral order; but in communities where only a minority belong to churches, religious folk are no less likely to commit crimes than are the irreligious.[32] Thus while conversion to a religion may

---

28. Hugh Hartshorne and Mark A. May, *Studies in Deceit* (New York: Macmillan, 1928).

29. Travis Hirschi and Rodney Stark, "Hellfire and Delinquency," *Social Problems* 17 (1969): 202-13.

30. Steven R. Burkett and Mervin White, "Hellfire and Delinquency: Another Look," *Journal for the Scientific Study of Religion* 13 (1974): 455-62; P.C. Higgins and G.L. Albrecht, "Hellfire and Delinquency Revisited," *Social Forces* 55 (1977): 952-58.

31. Stan L. Albrecht, Bruce A. Chadwick, and David S. Alcorn, "Religiosity and Deviance: Application of an Attitude-Behavior Contingent Consistency Model," *Journal for the Scientific Study of Religion* 16 (1977): 263-74; Charles R. Tittle and Michael R. Welch, "Religiosity and Deviance: Toward a Contingency Theory of Constraining Effects," *Social Forces* 61 (1983): 653-82; Dean R. Hoge and Ernesto De Zulueta, "Salience as a Condition for Various Social Consequences of Religious Commitment," *Journal for the Scientific Study of Religion* 24 (1985): 21-37.

32. Rodney Stark, Lori Kent, and Daniel P. Doyle, "Religion and Delinquency: The Ecology of a 'Lost' Relationship," *Journal of Research in Crime and Delinquency* 19 (1982): 4-24.

mean a more virtuous pattern of behavior, it need not, and nonreligious factors may determine whether it does.

Other evidence bringing the transformational interpretation of religious conversion into doubt has come from observational research. Many of the apparent conversions that take place in Protestant revivals, such as the Billy Graham "crusades," are ritual experiences repeated numerous times by the same individuals.[33] In contrast to Catholicism and the liberal Protestant denominations, evangelical Christianity places great stress on experiences of transformation. The effect is that equally religious people in different traditions use quite different language to describe their religiousness, some describing conversion experiences and others not. Many of the events commonly called conversions may better be termed confirmations or revivals. In any event, a substantial portion of the time when the word conversion is used, no real change of heart or behavior has actually occurred.

Social influence theory is entirely happy with these findings. It sees personal transformation as a quite different issue from a change in group affiliations. Once a person has joined a new religious group, intensive social interaction with members can gradually shape the individual's beliefs, behaviors, and feelings.

The implications for those interested in achieving conversion are clear. The process is not complete when the new convert acknowledges membership, even when he or she ritualistically expresses a deep transformation as some religious traditions require new members to do. The newcomer must become fully integrated into the fellowship of the congregation and share its spiritual life, perhaps for a long time, before such changes as can occur will be complete. If the particular religious tradition emphasizes swift and decisive conversion experiences, there is nothing wrong with encouraging such feelings despite the sociological evidence that real radical personal transformations are rare. The convert hopes for change, and the congregation has faith that a person can change. Joyful expressions are entirely appropriate. Indeed, social science should not intrude upon them.

It is well to be aware of how fragile such radical conversions can be and how disappointed the person can become—disillusioned and even guilt-ridden—when the conversion proves less complete than it at first appeared to be. Then the advice of sociology and common sense coincide: offer the comfort, fellowship, and spiritual regeneration that an inspired ministry can give.

CONCLUSION

While we have spoken of congregations, communities, and social classes, the emphasis has been on the conversion of single individuals. Yet much

---

33. Weldon T. Johnson, "The Religious Crusade: Revival or Ritual?" *American Journal of Sociology* 76 (1971): 873-90; David L. Altheide and John M. Johnson, "Counting Souls," *Pacific Sociological Review* 20 (1977): 323-48.

of the growth of religion comes through the conversion of families and friendship groups. Here the church faces a fresh challenge. An individual is most apt to join a new religion when his or her attachments to people outside the church are weak. At the extreme, the person will be what we call a social isolate, someone with no strong family and friendship ties. And such people can readily be gathered by the church, one by one. But isolates cannot provide a channel through which to recruit still more converts. A religious movement can spread most rapidly through an extended network of existing family and friendship ties, but the paradox is that persons already embedded in social relationships are least free to change affiliations.

The mirror image of this problem is that a religious congregation enjoying very high levels of fellowship within itself may become cut off from nonmembers and thus have no social avenues along which to convert. Apparently some high-fellowship groups get around this barrier by working through acquaintanceships with nonmembers, rather than friendships, using what Mark Granovetter called *weak ties* (weak but often extensive social bonds) to build membership.[34]

Another paradox is that it is easiest to build social bonds with an unbeliever if the beliefs are not emphasized, and yet the "good news" of that faith is precisely what the evangelist wants to share. The Mormons solve this by intentionally deemphasizing their special beliefs and religious practices while recruiting, stressing instead the benefits of family and community provided by their church. Conversion to the faith can wait until the person is a member of the Mormon community.

These are paradoxes of social influence theory, and the relative deprivation of strain theory provides its own dilemmas. Most crassly, if the church recruits only deprived persons, who will pay the bills? A little more subtly, can the church take upon itself all the problems of the surrounding society? If people join hoping that their secular conditions will be transformed, they may be disappointed. If the church invests its whole soul battling for improvement of the worldly conditions of deprived members, then it becomes a social service organization, prey to all the problems suffered by those in secular society.

There are two valid answers to these paradoxes, one religious and one sociological. In the Christian faith, ultimate success is not measured through worldly statistics. Although one can never be sure that a conversion is real and that a soul has been saved, still one must believe in the possibilities of conversion and salvation, and the final test is always on a higher spiritual plane. Sociologically, one must recognize that there are many styles of religion and many routes to conversion. Never in the history of the world has a single religious organization encompassed all believers. Far greater success can be achieved by a number of ministries, each with its own special qual-

---

34. Mark Granovetter, "The Strength of Weak Ties," *American Journal of Sociology* 78 (1973): 1360-80; Helen Rose Fuchs Ebaugh and Sharron Lee Vaughn, "Ideology and Recruitment in Religious Groups," *Review of Religious Research* 26 (1984): 148-57.

ities, recruiting particular sorts of people by particular means, than could be gained by a monolithic crusade.

If my great-grandfather's scientific questions of over a century ago remain incompletely answered, incomplete also is the evangelical work to which he devoted his life. Like science, conversion is a dynamic process, and neither may entirely complete its work so long as this world exists.

Chapter Thirteen

The Cultural Anthropology of Conversion

Alan R. Tippett

Berkhofer has demonstrated the possibility of reconstructing conversion patterns as acculturation studies on a framework of sequential analysis.[1] His patterns are sufficiently elastic to include resistance or fragmentation sequences. However, nothing has been done, to my knowledge, with respect to the general structure of *total* group movements into Christianity. This chapter will depict the dominant pattern of conversion among the peoples of Oceania, as experienced through the last century and currently in New Guinea.

The structure of this conversion pattern is fairly regular, whether it be conversion from animism to Christianity, or away from Christianity to some neopagan cargo cult. I shall attempt to provide a schematization of this process. It is an attempt to organize and interpret existing data.

Although the forces of acculturation at work in Oceania were considerable (planter, whaler, sandalwooder, *bêche-de-mer* trader, labor recruiter) and left marks of liquor, arms and ammunition, and venereal disease, and although missionaries also were strong acculturative agents, yet in one notable respect the Oceanic world differed from that discussed by Berkhofer. It was fragmented into thousands of small, isolated, island communities. To this day many have preserved their indigenous autonomy as social decision-making units. The agents of Western "civilization" were never fully able to impose

---

1. Robert F. Berkhofer Jr., "Protestants, Pagans and Sequences Among the North American Indians, 1760-1860," *Ethnohistory* 10, vol. 3 (1963):201-32.

their controls. The island people were never forced to "adapt to the reservation." Because they have preserved their decision-making mechanisms, some strong indigenous Christian churches have emerged in the Pacific.

Social anthropology has contributed to human knowledge by the study of small societies as total worlds in microcosm. These societies may be viewed whole. This does not mean that the complex way of Western life is reflected in simpler form in island communities. But it does mean that we are not bewildered by complexity, that many external impacting factors are eliminated, and that we do see a total community—a functioning, interacting, complete thing. We have no need to resort to sampling; or to set up experiments with selected persons for group study, persons who though they may fall into types, have yet no real cohesion as a group. By taking small island communities we are able to observe how the group reacts to such external stimuli as the advocacy of conversion, or the rejection of Christianity for a cargo cult. We see the significance of the group cohesion; we see how the innovation is advocated, how it is scrutinized, evaluated and accepted, rejected or modified, as the group determines.

Most of the Oceanic peoples who have become Christian have done so by group movements. I did not say "mass movements." They are multi-individual movements. We are concerned with individuals, not in isolation, but within groups and sub-groups. Oceanic conversion patterns reveal some remarkable regularities. There are some variables, but these may be accounted for by local and personal factors.

Definitions

We are concerned with the process of conversion. How are people 1) separated from the old context, and 2) incorporated into the new? We are not concerned here with motivation for, or occasions of conversion; or patterns of Christian application after conversion. We shall limit ourselves to the conversion experience itself, more particularly group conversion.

I accept Sherif's definition of *group* as "a social unit that consists of a number of individuals 1) who at a given time, have role and status relationships with each other, stabilized in some degree, and 2) who possess a set of values or norms regulating the attitude and behavior of the individual members."[2] Perhaps I should add that when we come to study communal societies there is bound to be a further specification that determines the group entity: viz., the affilial, consanguineal, or perhaps occupational tie between members. The need for this additional specification will be apparent when I explain that, although at times a whole village may become Christian at once, in other cases the deciding groups may be extended families, so that the village is converted over a period of time by a series of small group conversions. We must not lose sight of the fact that there are groups within groups.

---

2. Muzafer Sherif, *Group Conflict and Cooperation: Their Social Psychology* (London: Routledge & Kegan Paul, 1967), 12.

By *group conversion* I mean the process of multi-individual experience and action of a group, through its competent authority, whereby the group changes from one conceptual and behavioral context to another, within the operations of its own structure and decision-making mechanisms regardless of whether or not the external environment changes.[3]

When such group decision is specifically religious, if new elements are innovated, the group self-image may need restructuring, and a new set of norms may have to be fixed. The group may demand from each individual some ocular demonstration of separation from the old context.

The *schematization* is more a frame of reference within which to arrange, classify, and discuss data than a complete theory of conversion. It is not complete because it takes into account only observable data and events. It does not touch motivation; neither does it allow for the divine element in religious conversion. We are well aware of the existence of the spiritual factor, although we cannot measure it. We are asking what takes place in the *process* of group conversion. We are dealing purely with the human side of it. The tool we use could be applied to any changing religious or philosophical affiliation—animism to Christianity, Islam, or Communism; or from Christianity to neo-paganism. As Ferm points out, in spite of the great difference between Christian and non-Christian conversion a "universal psychological likeness" does exist. "Either the surrender of the self to the ideal occurs, or no conversion takes place.[4]

The questions before us, then, are: 1) What actually takes place in the communal group when it is converted? 2) What are the physical and psychological elements common to the individuals and the groups in the decision-making process? 3) Why do people behave as they do in cutting themselves off from a known stimulus field and confronting an unstructured one?

The value of this information to the missionary should be apparent, when we remember that the Christian mission assumes that God has chosen the *human agent* to be his advocate. The missionary who understands how people act and why they behave as they do should be the more effective advocate.

The study of group conversion involves a number of anthropological problems:

1. The problem of *advocacy*, with the possibility of either *acceptance* or *rejection* by the group.

2. The problem of *meaning*. (Even when a group is converted we may ask, *to what* is it converted? Is it necessarily converted to the precise idea advocated or does it assign its own meaning to the new faith?)

3. The problem of *incorporation*. (People move out of something, into something. This is the conversion process.)

---

3. Peter H. Rossi, "Community Decision Making," *Administrative Science Quarterly* 1 (1957): 417.

4. R.O. Ferm, *The Psychology of Christian Conversion* (London: Pickering & Ingliss, n.d.), 194.

Agents in Christian mission certainly need to understand these problems if they are to be held responsible for what they do. What anthropology has to say to the missionary is also said to the administrator, the educator, the social worker, and other reformer. If the gospel, or health, or educational program is worth advocating, it is worth the agents' time to understand the character of the process they are setting in motion.

Schematization of the Conversion Process

If we conceptualize the conversion process in units of time, although the length of time is variable, we find that there are three clearcut units. These I shall call the *Period of Awareness*, the *Period of Decision*, and the *Period of Incorporation*. As the experience proceeds with a mobility from left to right it passes from one unit into the next through a specific point which can be identified. I use the terms *Point of Realization* and *Point of Encounter*, indicated as R and E in the diagram.

Old Context (Pagan)   **New Context (Christian)**

| Period of Awareness | R | Period of Decision | E | Period of Incorporation |

It should be noted that the shape of the boxes has no significance and should not be so treated spatially. The model has been created to organize known data according to the processes of change which need to be identified and to pinpoint the dramatic moments in the total process. The model is purely processual, measuring periods and points. The length of time or "shape" of the period has nothing to do with it.

Exposition of the Conversion Process

Period of Awareness

Innovation (and conversion is innovation) is impossible without a period of awareness. This applies either to an individual or a group. It may be accidentally or intentionally stimulated. It may be clearly or vaguely felt. It may be of short or long duration, or of diminishing, accelerating, or irregular intensity. But somehow or another the individual and/or group must become aware of another way of life, another behavior pattern, or another set of values apart from the traditional context.

Individuals and groups are made aware of new contexts in any one of four ways. Any of these may lead to a change of philosophy or religion—i.e., conversion.

1. The awareness may be due to *natural development* as in the processes of education, experiment, interaction, cooperation, and even competition. This is the way of discovery. The biographical writings of Lin Yutang illustrate religious conversions of this type, as do also the many converts to the religions of Asia in our Western universities and in the armed forces.

2. The awareness may be due to *pressure from without*, forced conversion through military conquest or economic sanctions. Thus, for example, Olaf

Tryggveson is reported to have put in at the island of Rolandsa and found the pagan Earl had only one fighting ship. Olaf told him his time had come for baptism. The alternative was immediate execution. The Earl and his people were baptized, and the Earl's son was taken as a hostage for their good faith.[5] A recent writer has shown how social pressure and economic sanctions were applied to achieve the conversion of Zoroastrians to Islam in the seventh century.[6]

3. Awareness may be due to the *internal pressures of crisis situations*— personal tensions, epidemics, catastrophic experiences, and even tensions due to adaptation under migration. A good example of the advocacy and acceptance of new Hindu gods by the Kota under crisis situation pressures is well-known to anthropologists.[7] The structure of such crisis-situation innovation has been well-analyzed.[8]

4. Finally there is awareness due to *direct advocacy*. This is seen in the planned advertising campaign of the advocate, the evangelistic program of a Christian mission, the five-year plans of a government agency for education, sanitation, or agricultural improvements.

Awareness, then, may be due to any of a number of factors: natural causes, imposed pressures, or directed programs. We may say: natural, circumstantial, or stimulated; or it may be due to a complex of these; but without awareness of a possible context different from the old one, there can be no conversion—no "paradigm shift" as we might say today.

Period of Decision

The period of decision for a communal group may be a long road. It may spread over years of village or family discussion, as individuals, one by one, come to the position where they can at least say that they are of one mind— and when they can burn their fetishes as a total group. This is a *multi-individual decision*.

Decision does not necessarily mean *acceptance*. There are at least four quite different possibilities:

1. It may be an *act of rejection*. The whole community may decide against conversion, and register its feelings by specific organized opposition against Christianity in a manner that was not there before. In Christian missions we speak of *resistant areas*. A resistant area is one in which group conversions are regarded as unlikely. In point of fact, the resistance may be due to ineffective advocacy or to obstructive cultural factors. Whatever the reason, groups are not converted, and by this positive act of rejection they reinforce the traditional context, to resist the advocacy of any would-be converting

---

5. C.H. Robinson, *How the Gospel Spread Through Europe* (New York: Society for Promoting Christian Knowledge, 1919).

6. P.W. English, *City and Village in Iran* (Madison: University of Wisconsin Press, 1966), 23-24.

7. A.L. Kroeber, *Anthropology* (New York: Harcourt, Brace, 1948), 503-57.

8. Anthony F.C. Wallace, "Revitalization Movements," *American Anthropologist* 58 (1956): 264-81

agent(s). Such positive rejection may take any number of forms, from an intense nationalistic sentiment to an organized movement. It may even borrow foreign features to permit its claim to status and to validate its coexistence with the advocated religion. Hinduism, Islam, and Buddhism all have reform movements which have borrowed features of Christianity in order to resist Christianity—ethics, social service, medical work, and educational institutions, not to mention evangelism itself. Positive acts of rejection may also take the form of petty or serious persecution which may be spontaneous or organized. Frequently when *individuals* are converted *away from* the social group, that group feels its security is threatened and its entity is in danger. Organized persecution will result. The group rejects the way of conversion and innovates with persecution to prevent it.

2. It may be an *act of total acceptance*. The degree in which any acceptance is *total* will depend on circumstances. Acceptance due to pressure—military, political, or strong economic—or due to the prestige of the advocate(s), will probably mean that the advocate(s) dictate(s) the terms of the new structure. It will be foreign in character. All such conversion movements tend to create serious cultural voids that cause reactions in succeeding generations, as many Christian missions have learned to their sorrow. An imposed foreign religion is always an irritant. Its stability, at least for a time, will depend on the power or prestige of the body which imposed the conversion pattern. A certain mission in Melanesia established a foreign form of Christianity and maintained control by means of a monopoly of the copra market. After the best part of the century, the war brought an end to these economic controls, and thousands were converted overnight to a nativistic cult. If by *total* acceptance, we include the *meaning* of the innovation advocated, that conversion will be a foreign religion. It will be unstable unless the process of acculturation is extremely rapid and satisfying to the acceptors.

3. It may be an *act of modification*; i.e., acceptance with modifications. This has two well-known patterns. (a) The first leads to *syncretism*. Much of the folk-Catholicism of Latin America illustrates this type. Under the Catholic overlay of organization, worship, and saints will be found Indian mythology, magic, and belief. This is a new thing—i.e., not Christian; neither is it Maya nor Aztec. It has been called a "new kind of paganism." It is certainly not what the original advocates envisaged. (b) The second pattern of adjustment is that in which the basic advocated belief has been accepted, but molded *by the acceptors* into their own cultural structures, procedures, authority patterns and way of life. In Christian missions we speak of this as the *indigenous church*. Most of the data I have behind this article fits into this category. To cite one example here, the Batak Church of Western Sumatra is a good one to use as a model of conversion by acceptance of belief, with strong modifications of worship and organization to fit the cultural requirements; but note, the acceptors, and not the advocates determined the adjustments.

4. It may be an *act of fission*, or a division of the group. My experience has been that when a group is sufficiently large to have sub-groups, especially

if there are competitive values in the culture, it is always possible for one segment to respond with acceptance and the remainder with rejection. The point
to press here is that such acts of fission are invariably cleavages on a basis of
social structure—nuclear families within extended families, extended families within villages, status and craft segments, or perhaps culturally established factions or supporters of rival chieftaincies. There is room for more
research at this point, but meantime I record that where I have observed
Christian and animist groups co-existing, their religious differences have
been based on social cleavages. Furthermore, in the course of time, when the
animist group does eventually become ready for conversion, it will frequently elect a different denomination. Such conversion reinforces the cleav-
age in the social structure and the pagan segment does not lose face by the
conversion.

Period of Incorporation

Once the decision for conversion has been made and the group has separated itself from the old context, like the New Testament parable house
swept of the evil spirit, it is vulnerable unless it can quickly achieve its new
contextual entity. The new norms have to be fixed. The group entity has to
be established. After a certain amount of instruction and training the transition is ritually effected and finally completed by means of an *Act of
Incorporation*. This is usually an initiation into a neo-pagan cult or, in the case
of Christianity, usually baptism.

My period of incorporation may be fitted into van Gennep's frame of
reference for the classification of rites of passage.[9] To do this my point of
encounter would need to be equated with his Rites of Separation, my instruction and training with his Rites of Transition, and my act of incorporation with
his Rites of Incorporation. Van Gennep's hypothesis was posited on the
basis of much evidence from human societies over a wide area of the world,
and in all of my researches into primitive religion and ritual, I have continually found it a tenable frame of reference for most operating social structures.
It does not, however, provide for religious change—i.e., conversion. Where
a religion presents a stable and structured conceptual field, van Gennep's
scheme is adequate only as a starting point.

In the total process as I am presenting it, van Gennep's coincides only
with the phase I described as the period of incorporation. Yet this in itself is
interesting. If this is true, when Christianity is being accepted for the first time
by a new group of converts from paganism, especially when this is a spontaneous acceptance (i.e., without the presence of any missionary advocate),
then they *have already structured* their new conceptual field *in terms with
which they are familiar.* For the missionary advocate this signifies that *religious rites and forms which fit such a frame of reference have more likelihood
of finding permanent acceptance than those which are of foreign character.* This is partly because they are more symbolically meaningful and part-

9. Arnold van Gennep, *Les Rites de Passage* (Paris: Emile Nourry, 1909).

ly because they are accepted as functional substitutes. This need not necessarily have any bearing on the content of their religious belief. It does not follow that indigenous worship forms necessarily enshrine syncretistic faith—
though of course it may be that they do. I think we have a principle here: *For
any religious conversion to be permanent its new structure should both meet
the needs of the converts and operate in meaningful forms.* It is thus that
the new indigenous religion is born.

The duration of the transition from the point of encounter to the act of
incorporation—full incorporation at the end of that time unit—varies from
group to group. Under strong Puritan domination it can be drawn out for
years. Under intense religious experience as in the holiness movement in
Tonga it can be short but effective. The problem of how long a period of
training should precede baptism is one that missionaries have not yet solved.
The point of encounter is a dramatic experience for both individual and
group. The act of incorporation should be a confirmation and consummation
of the change of religious faith. It is likely to be a highly emotional and spiritually satisfying event, and will provide a sense of belonging to the individuals, and a sense of entity and satisfaction to the group.

The symbolism and meaning of the various ritual acts in the process vary
from society to society, because all societies do not feel exactly the same
needs; which may be influenced, for instance, by different environmental factors, or food patterns, or communal occupations, and so forth. Furthermore,
the structure of the society itself, the indigenous values, the authority patterns,
concepts of status and role, marriage, kinship, inheritance, all lead to different
concepts of needs. If a new religion is to be relevant it must meet the specific
needs the people feel. If it is to be accepted by the people, it must demonstrate
that it can meet those needs better than the old religion. This is why crisis situations are so open for religious change.

The Point of Realization and the Point of Encounter

The three time units of the process of conversion are separated into discrete periods by two points. These are specific realities. If I may use an analogy from biology, the impulse is transmitted from one nerve cell to the next.
The point of realization and the point of encounter may be likened to the
synapses. They have a reality, perhaps more than my analogy, because they
are conscious experiences. However, they represent the transmission of the
impulse of the conversion experience from one discrete unit to the next.

The point of realization terminates the period of awareness and com-
mences the period of decision. Either for the individual or for the group,
there comes a moment when it suddenly becomes apparent that the passage
from the old context to the new is not merely an idea. It is a possibility. A
vague notion becomes a clear truth. It came to the prodigal son, when, as he
sat among the pigs, he suddenly resolved "I will arise and go unto my father."
He realized the meaning of the old context to him. He saw his own predicament for what it really was. All along he had been vaguely aware of it, but
now it became suddenly *meaningful*. Observe that as yet he had not reached

the point of encounter. He had not yet really faced up to the implications of his discovery. He had not yet returned and made his confession. The period of decision stretched out over a long journey from the pigsty to the open gate of his father's farm.

The point of encounter is the climax of the period of decision. For the group, the individual differences have been ironed out by discussion and the group is ready to act in unison. The act itself must be an ocular demonstration with a manifest meaning to Christian and pagan alike. It must leave no room for doubt that the old context may still have some of their allegiance or still hold some power over them. This is as much a public testimony of conversion as an altar call in an evangelical church. The old way is terminated. Unless this is clear-cut, the group will be unstable in its new context and will be unable to fix its norms. I know one community where the ancestral images were not destroyed in the approved manner when the people were converted. Subsequently a neopagan movement claimed some 3,000 of those Christians, their prophet setting up similar images after the manner they had known before. Yet in nearby areas with kinship connections, this neopagan movement was rejected and the people remained true to Christianity. They gave the reason, "We rejected these things at our conversion." From this it follows that *there is clearly a relationship between the manifest form of encounter and the subsequent stability of the new religion*, or to state the principle the other way—*avoid the encounter and increase the reversions.*

In summary, this was the extent of the model as I earlier developed it. My emphasis was on the significance of the *point of encounter* where the precise decision is demonstrated, where the *period of decision making* is brought to a crisis with the converts giving ocular demonstration of their departure from paganism. This emphasis has been made with very good reason: the "missionary" theology of the 1960s being colored by interpretations of dialogue, Christian presence and co-existence which so frequently suggest there may be other ways to the Father but by Him (Jn 14:6).

Later it occurred to me that more emphasis should be placed on the significance of the *point of realization*. This is the point of time and experience, where, after a period of either vague or hostile awareness of the Christian option, the potential converts realize that the option has particular relevance for them. Hitherto we have regarded this rather objectively as the dividing point between two different mental states. A mere static awareness becomes dynamic, or a hostile opposition becomes an exciting possibility. In any case a fixed attitude has become a state of unrest, of conflict, of decision making. Obviously the potential converts are not going to make their decision without the experience of that point of realization.

Thrusts of Advocacy

The question now arises as to the precise part played by the advocate (evangelist) at that point, where potential converts realize that the option of becoming Christ's persons is real for them personally and calls for decision.

Can advocates do anything specific to bring that point of realization into focus? They most certainly can. For them it is a *point of advocacy*. In New Testament terms, they are witnesses; they have found a point of thrust, whether it is directed to an individual or a group. And we must not conceive of the advocate (evangelist) only in terms of an individual. In communal society the witness of one group to another is highly significant. One family influences another family, a sodality of young people may influence a whole village. Communal society has much to say to the West about corporate witness, especially in these days when many theologians denigrate the idea of the church and speak of churchless ministry.

During my research in the Solomon Islands I lived for six weeks in a village in the Tai Lagoon on the coast of Malaita. The most interesting feature of this coastline is a chain of artificial islands, built by the salt-water people to give them protection from their long-standing enemies. These are great architectural achievements and show how careful we should be before calling *pagan* people *primitive*. These people have learned a way of life which permits living close together in a confined space. They have adapted their communal organization and personal relationships to the physical limitations of an artificial island. Conversion to Christianity and the construction of a church for worship normally means enlarging the island, and this produces all kinds of innovations and demonstrations of cooperative endeavor, which show how significant the social group is as a multi-individual institution.

These islands are small and many of the inhabitants are related, even if distantly. Mechanisms have existed from earlier times for reconciling parties or social segments which fell into a state of discord. The ideas of unity and concord were regarded as necessary for security reasons—indeed for survival in the face of their enemies.

Many of these islands are now Christian, but some are still pagan and others half-Christian and half-pagan, divided on a basis of some element of social structure. When the processes of civilizing and nationalizing take over under government direction and the threat of enemy invasion is reduced, it is easy for people to settle down to a life of colorless co-existence because unity is no longer necessary for survival. This can operate against the planting and growth of the church.

I was perturbed by the fact that communities, which in pre-Christian times would have striven for unity and cohesion, were often divided into smaller segments on a basis of religion and were content to remain that way without doing anything about it. This meant that religion had become a mere compartment of life instead of the integrator of it; or perhaps that religion had become a thing of the small segment rather than of the total group. In the latter case this made them vulnerable to rival denominations. In terms of church growth theory we may say that people's movements had been sealed off after the winning of segments instead of the segment witnessing to its related segment. At this point the mission of the church had been terminated: The church in the segment had lost its outreach and sense of responsibility.

The Christian segment, whether an extended family on one of the smaller islands with relatives on the next, needed to realize its obligation to make *thrusts of advocacy*, urging the unconverted community to see that the gospel was speaking to them. Thus would they be brought to their point of realization.

I shared these things with the Church of England Melanesian priest of the locality, pointing out that the Christian groups had both a religious and sociological obligation to win the nearby pagans. I left him to answer for himself the question: Am I my brother's keeper? I noticed that after this he included more prayers for the conversion of the heathen in his morning and evening prayers with the village people—that was the Christian village where both he and I were living.

The missionary arm of the Church of England in Melanesia is an Order—the Melanesian Brotherhood. It does some splendid pioneering work and opens up the way in pagan communities as far away as New Britain, and also in the interior of Malaita among the bushmen. However, they have apparently been directed away from the nearby artificial islands, whose pagan residue has been left to the witness of the Christians of the area. Indeed, I was troubled that one village right next to us, whose daily life I could observe from my leaf house, was still pagan, and the Christian neighbors had resigned themselves to co-existence with it. They did not see that the existence of the Melanesian Brotherhood did not free them from the obligation to evangelize. They prayed for the Brotherhood but did no evangelistic work themselves. So my friend, the Melanesian priest added a new dimension to the morning and evening prayers, and reminded his people that there was still a missionary task at their door.

His prayers in this direction stimulated the Christian group, or at least one segment of the group. The young people began to consider some way in which they could draw the attention of their pagan friends to the relevance of the gospel. They saw themselves as advocates making a trust of advocacy in the hope of bringing a pagan group to the point of realization. The following Christmas they determined to present a nativity play, with an obvious evangelical purpose. Over a period of time they made elaborate preparations and invited their pagan relatives to see it. The content of the play and the sincerity of the participants effectively communicated to a number of the pagans the idea of the Lord coming into their lives.

Thus was set in motion a complex of the mechanisms of multi-individual social action. As individuals within the group on the pagan island the people discussed together the issue of their confrontation with the Christ who had come to mankind, and the possibility of their becoming Christian. This was the major theme for conversation on that island for the following four months and then, having reached a consensus, the whole population turned to the Lord as did those at Lydda and Saron (Acts 9:35)—eighty-seven adults, and between forty and fifty children with them. They asked for help and instruction and for a Sunday school for their children. They expected their evangelical friends who were older in the faith to teach them, that their corporate action of turning to the Lord might be consummated through teaching about, and fellowship with, that same Lord, that each person of the multi-individual group might truly know him. For four months these people were in the period of decision making as a corporate group. Under the guidance of the Spirit of God, they themselves came to the point of encounter and put aside their idolatry. Currently they are being incorporated into the Fellowship. The action has been group-oriented throughout, but never at any point has the individual been disregarded. It required four months of multi-individual deliberation to bring about unanimity and to permit the group action of decision making.

In terms of my model these people lived for years in the *period of awareness* without even thinking of the possibility of a break with paganism. In this case the *point of realization*, which made possible the transition from awareness to decision making, came with the nativity play presentation when the pagans first began to see that the gospel was *speaking to them.* This is a good example of the process of group conversion at work and here I describe it to emphasize the truth that the Christian group is responsible for thrusts of advocacy, presenting the gospel option to other groups with which they have some affinity or relationship. Here the initiative for evangelistic thrust came from the Christian young people's group and their means of communication was a play about the incarnation. It was effective, but the pagans themselves under the power of the Spirit had to make their own decision for Christ. The responsibility of the Christian group comes again later with the task of incorporation.

Thus is the Christian group responsible for bringing the pagan group from a state of awareness (static or hostile) to a state of decision making (dynamic) by thrusts of advocacy in meaningful forms so that the potential converts may see that the gospel does speak directly to them. "How shall they hear without a preacher?" Paul asks (Rom 10:14). Whether that preaching is from a pulpit or a play (and it is more likely to be the latter if directed to pagans outside the church) the church is called to be diligent in its gospel advocacy. I see no hope for a so-called mission based on resignation to co-existence. The very existence of an unconverted group charges the Christian group with responsibility.

Since my 1973 trip to Papua New Guinea where I encountered a great many cargo cult breakaways from Christian communities, thought to have been properly incorporated long ago into the church, I have come to realize that, although the model still stands as valid as far as it goes, it does need expansion.

In the model discussed above it will be recalled that "E" marked the *point of encounter* (or *commitment*) and represented the end of the struggle for decision, in one sense, and the beginning of incorporation into the fellowship group (the church), in another. This is marked by some such ocular demonstration as fetish-burning, eating the totem, burying the ancestral skulls, etc. Indeed, every acceptance of an innovation is simultaneously an act of rejection and an act of acceptance. This point is pressed by Homer Barnett in his major work on *innovation*.[10]

The value of the last box in the model (the *period of incorporation*) is to serve as a reminder that persons have not reached the end of the experiential road with a mere demonstration of conversion that the convert coming out of something must enter into something else. There are no vacuums here. Converts must be part of a group as participating beings. In dealing with national pastors and lay leaders (for the model first came out of my missionary experience as a field superintendent), I have found this third box profitable as a stimulant for dialogue and self-examination in pastoral workshops. Indeed, the whole model has served me well also in missionary research, for identifying elements of the Christian program which have been lost sight of or neglected. These discussions have often led to the correction of the oversight.

Beyond Incorporation

Now, both in the Western Solomons and in New Guinea, I have run into cases of large numbers of converts who long have been presumed properly incorporated into the church suddenly turning away as a body. In one area, twenty-two villages came within the orbit of my anthropological observation. They had developed a highly institutionalized and enthusiastic social pattern of their own—a rival program of incorporation—to serve as a functional substitute for the church, which, in point of fact, had brought them out of animism; and they had now their own ritual and some highly questionable theology, especially in their doctrine of the Godhead. This, I have described at length elsewhere.[11] I am not here concerned with its character but with the fact that for those villages the "period of incorporation" came to an abrupt end (as my original mode, in point of fact, also does). They passed outside, and beyond the model. The model, then, does not account for all the phenomena.

Although the arrows are calculated to make my model *dynamic* and not *static*, which is as it should be, nevertheless it is now proved to be a *terminal* model. I had thought to avoid the *danger of termination* at the point of encounter or commitment, but I failed to allow for it with the period of incorporation. The implications of the cargo cult breakaway phenomenon pressed me to expand this processual model in the following fashion:

Old Context (Pagan) **New Context (Christian)**

"C" is the *point of consummation* (or confirmation), where people, having been incorporated in the fellowship group and having learned to use the "means of grace" and to study scripture, and so forth, now pass on into a deep-

---

10. Homer G. Barnett, *Innovation: The Basis of Cultural Change* (New York: McGraw-Hill, 1953), 188.

11. Alan R. Tippett, *Solomon Islands Christianity* (London: Lutterworth Press, 1967), 212-66.

ening *experience of faith*, "growing in grace," or *sanctification*.[12]

I personally believe that the point "C" should be *a precise experience* of the work of the Spirit within man—and so did my spiritual father, John Wesley. The early mission records in the Wesleyan fields of the South Pacific speak of "two conversions," one from heathenism to Christianity as a system, a faith experience of *power encounter* as described at length elsewhere,[13] and the second, a little later, a faith experience leading to a positive *assurance of new birth*. In many cases still further "manifestations of grace" have been recorded, experiences of *sanctification*, associated with revivals rather than awakenings. The strongest and most indigenous church activity has come with these experiences. And because of these experiences, I have left the model open-ended.

I think the matter of greatest significance for us in the study of church-planting today about this new model is that it draws attention to the fact that "incorporation" and "growth in grace" are two quite different elements in the process, and one should not be taken for the other; also that it is possible for people to be incorporated formally into the church, to engage in its services and make use of its "means of grace" and yet never to "grow in grace" or mature (the word our Lord used when he said, "Be ye perfect . . ."). From the point of view of church growth field studies, therefore, I think this provides us with a point of reference for asking such questions as: How is it possible for so many village groups to abandon Christianity after, say, twenty years of post-baptismal Christian instruction?

This is one of the most serious questions of our day in Christian mission. All too often in our day we have in places like Papua New Guinea cases of rapid discipling (quantitative) without its essential qualitative concommitant. But both of these are part of the total conversion process in which God delivers his people from the dominion of darkness and transfers them to the kingdom of his beloved son (Col 1:13).

---

12. Alan R. Tippett, *People Movements in Southern Polynesia* (Chicago: Moody Press, 1971).

13. Alan R. Tippett, *The Christian* (Fiji 1835-67) (Auckland: Institute Printing & Publishing, 1954), 12-13,16,19-20.

Part IV

Conversion in Culture and Church

What are the ways in which we communicate our understanding of conversion? As Hudson noted in chapter seven, the reading of Augustine's *Confessions* was pivotal in Roman Catholicism. More than a thousand years later, Bunyan's *Pilgrims Progress* summarized and shaped the Christian life and the Puritan understanding of conversion. In chapter fourteen, Batson reviews the imaginative literature of poetry, fiction, and autobiography what has influenced American and English concepts of conversion from the time of Dante to the present.

Batson's survey is followed by a chapter on the phenomenology of conversion authored by Lewis Rambo and his assistant Lawrence Reh. Noting how William James intuitively utilized this type of analysis, Rambo and Reh extend this approach by utilizing the systematic procedures which have been developed during this century. They define phenomenology as going beyond bare facts to an indepth account of "facts-as-perceived." Through a perceptive account of one woman's religious experience over a decade, Rambo and Reh show how it is possible to transit through observation, description, empathy, understanding, interpretation, and, finally, explanation. They conclude their analysis by a discussion of how the phenomenologist's life-experience impacts the process of perception.

In chapter sixteen, Kraft focuses on the way in which group experience strongly influences the conversion experience. From a cross-cultural perspective, he discusses the worldview of societies where all decisions are group, rather individually, determined. He notes that even in contemporary Western society, group influences are much greater than has been supposed. From his experience in non-Western cultures, Kraft concludes that conversion in any society is strengthened where it accords with allegiance to family and clan.

In the final chapter, Gibbs portrays the ways in which the Christian church has sought to exercise its evangelistic mandate through mass appeals. He notes that presumptions that these endeavors inevitably involve quick, one-time decisions are erroneous. He encourages sensitive appreciation for the way in which conversion has been understood as a growth process which often depends on the evangelist to awaken a need for God.

Chapter Fourteen

Conversion in Literature

E. Beatrice Batson

To deal with the process of coming to belief is the story of conversion. What conversion entails as that experience is embodied in selected works of poetry, fiction, and autobiography is the special focus of this chapter. The selected works are representative, not exhaustive. Some are briefly examined; others are more thoroughly explicated in order to show how a given work (particularly selected poems) releases meaning. Except for Augustine, Dante, and Dostoyevsky, the study is limited to English and American authors.

AUGUSTINE
(345-430)

Aurelius Augustinus, whose scholarly influence insistently compels the attention of thinkers to this day, is the author of the first Christian autobiography, *Confessions* (397). Like a parable, this autobiography tells a metaphorical story; it is the story of a life and a metaphor of the self.

Augustine contends from the first chapter of his story and maintains throughout the remaining pages until the experience in the Milanese garden that there must be some kind of mysterious intertwining of divine grace and human belief before one can know God. In analyzing his life, Augustine discovers in the depth of his being the absence of God's power, the need for God's love, the visitation of God's forgiveness (in salvation), and the presence of God's strength in the life of grace as a Christian believer. After a long and circuitous route he brought the dignity of Christian learning and the majesty of the authority of the scriptures to the service of Christianity. Since he addresses the *Confessions* to God, it is no surprise that his various

209

questions are in the context of his own individual self's relationship to God. His urgent questions of God and torturous arguments with God are all part of his passionate quest for One beyond self. His quest took the form of a continual process.

In a garden in Milan in the company of his friend Alypius, he was meditating when he heard the voice of a child apparently saying, "Take and read!" He opened his Bible to Romans 13:13 and read, "Not in reveling and drunkenness, not in debauchery and licentiousness, not in quarreling and jealousy: but put on the Lord Jesus Christ, and make no provision for the flesh to gratify its desires." He read no further; instantly, a serenity infused his heart; the darkness of perplexing uncertainty vanished away; grace flooded his being. Augustine's radical discovery so transforms him that he later incarnates into a theology and a way of life what he has seen and heard as well as all that he would continue to learn.

DANTE ALIGHIERI
(1265-1321)

The author of the *Divine Comedy* (begun ca.1307, completed 1321), wrote one of the world's greatest allegorical works. It is referred to as the supreme expression of the Middle Ages. Conversion as theme and narrative mode form the basis of the Dante story.

In the opening lines of the *Divine Comedy*, the narrator finds himself lost and in darkness:

> Midway this way of life we're bound upon,
> I woke to find myself in a dark wood,
> Where the right road was wholly lost and gone.[1]

The first lines contain familiar allegorical devices, and no sensitive reader fails to understand that the "right road" has something to do with the "straight and narrow" way, that the "dark wood" has something to do with sin and loss of direction, and, by extension, that the right course must lie in finding the light which rescues the lost from darkness.

The journey, then, of the *Divine Comedy* includes the grim darkness of the "Inferno," the breaking light of the "Purgatorio," and finally the climactic vision of God in the "Paradiso." What the various categories mean for the sinner is a recognition of sin, the renunciation of sin, and an entrance into the rapturous presence of God.

By indirection and through his monumental metaphorical structure, Dante shows the way to God. Metaphorical language, never content with simply making a point in an argument, enables the reader to perceive reality beyond what may be conceptually stated. No serious reader can escape the signifi-

---

1. Dante Alighieri, *The Divine Comedy*, trans. Dorothy L. Sayers (Harmondsworth, Middlesex, England: Penguin Books, 1949), 71.

cant passages (Canto VII of "Paradiso," for example) which unmistakably reveal that one's redemption from guilt and sin is through the work of Christ. Grace pervades the human soul because of the substitutionary work at the cross. The entire allegory is a complex and vast metaphorical perception of the human condition and of humanity's need for God.

EDMUND SPENSER
(1552?-1599)

Edmund Spenser was the first great English Renaissance writer and *The Faerie Queene* (1593-1596) stands among the greatest narrative poems in English literary history. While one may think of its chivalric and allegorical aspects. *The Faerie Queene*, especially Book I, embodies the essentials of the Christian pattern of redemption. While admitting that the Christian emphasis varies from book to book, P.C. Bayley (editor of 1966 edition) holds that "*The Faerie Queene* is above all a Christian work." For him, the work is founded "upon an unquestioning acceptance of the primary relation of creature to Creator, the need for people to live in the light of and by the help of God's grace.[2]

What is obvious in the early cantos is the insufficiency of human beings to know salvation and that cleansing comes only by grace. One of the main characters, the Redcross Knight, receives education in the House of Holiness where he is "cleansed by repentance, taught by Faith, healed by Hope, led through the works of Charity to the hill of Contemplation.[3] On the level of spiritual allegory, the poem, particularly Book I, embodies concern for the attainment of holiness; in its broadest sense, holiness includes the Christian pattern of salvation, repentance, rebirth, and sanctification. In brief, Book I concentrates on human's relation to God, and the pilgrimage from error, doubt, sin, and despair culminating in the Knight's victory over Satan's power; and finally, the attainment of unveiled truth constitutes important stages of the conversion experience.

GEORGE HERBERT
(1593-1633)

George Herbert was a "metaphysical" poet whose theology and poetry are inseparable. He tremendously influenced his contemporaries as well as later writers of religious poetry. *The Temple* (published posthumously in 1633) consists of the poetical expression of Herbert's religious beliefs and experi

---

2. For a more complete discussion, see A.S.P. Woodhouse, "Nature and Grace in *The Faerie Queene*": *Essential Articles for the Study of Edmund Spenser*, ed. A.C. Hamilton (Hamden, Conn.: Archon Books, 1972), 58-83.

3. P.C. Bayley, ed., Conn. *Edmund Spenser: The Faerie Queene Book I* (Oxford: Oxford University Press, 1966), 9.

ences. Called a "fully Reformation poet,"[4] Herbert unmistakably embodies many features of Calvin and Luther's theology. Any number of his poems show a view of conversion, not unlike that of the Protestant Reformers, which insists on an essential Christian experience (and the assurance of it) as completely dependent upon God's nature and God's Word. God's grace alone is essential for salvation; human merit of any sort has nothing to do with it. The renunciation of merit abounds in Herbert's poetry. Poems like "Sighs and Grones," "Judgment," "Discipline," and "Miserie" are important examples. In the first stanza of "Judgment," Herbert writes:

> Almighty Judge, how shall poor wretches brook
> Thy dreadful look,
> Able a heart of iron to appall,
> When thou shalt call
> For ev'ry man's peculiar book?[5]

God's call is to each person—"ev'ry man"; not one is able to respond to this "Almighty Judge." The second stanza reveals that apparently "some" will give to God something "that they in merit shall excel." But Herbert will have nothing to do with such thinking. There is a wiser way for him:

> But I resolve, when thou shalt call for mine,
> That to decline,
> And thrust a testament into thy hand:
> Let that be scanned.
> There thou shalt find my faults are thine.[6]

Other Herbert poems show features of the new life following conversion. "The Dawning" embodies the necessity for joyous assurance of salvation *in the present*, not exclusively postponing the future to Christ's promises. Herbert chides the soul for lingering on the cross rather than on the significance of the cross in the plan of salvation. "Aaron" celebrates the manner in which the individual knows righteousness or justification.

"The Flower," one of the finest short poems in the English language, is complex in its metaphorical depiction of sin and grace. The familiar imagery and the extended metaphor of the flower permit readers to participate imaginatively in the realities of both sin and grace. "Love III," which appears as the final poem in "The Church" of *The Temple*, is a powerful dramatization of irresistible grace. In the opening lines, it would seem that the speaker assumes that to be the recipient of grace, one must have some assurance of

---

4. See Richard Strier's excellent study, *Love Known* (Chicago: University of Chicago Press, 1983). Chapter 5 focuses on Herbert's presentation of "the phenomenology of conversion."

5. C.A. Patrides, ed., *The English Poems of George Herbert* (London: J.M. Dent, 1974), 190.

6. Ibid., 191.

self-merit. As the poem develops from beginning to end, it becomes clear that redemption calls not for self-judgment, self evaluation. It calls for a willing acceptance of God's offer of grace. Few poems of Herbert's 170 works in *The Temple* lack allusions to the redemptive act of Christ and its significance for all individuals who believe by faith.

THOMAS SHEPARD
(1605-1649)

Thomas Shepard is the author of one of the best-known Puritan autobi-ographies in early America.[7] He calls the narrative "My Birth and Life" (first published in 1832). The conversion narrative dramatizes what the author called "God's great plot" of reformation and redemption. Shepard, a minis-ter of the first generation of settlers in Massachusetts, characterizes the strik-ing feature of his life as its unsettledness. Declaring that "first signs of grace are no indication that new life has begun," Shepard's conversion experience was long and painful; he describes various aspects of the experience as well as of his life in images of chaos. When he was a student at Cambridge University, he states that "the Lord began to call me home to the fellowship of his grace." This "call" came toward the end of his third year; the first two years were spent "in studying and in much neglect of God," as well as in enjoying the company of "loose" scholars. On occasion he would "light in godly company," and conversations with godly people awakened in him a desire for God, but in a short while he would again fall into his old habits.

For Shepard there was a period of prolonged introspection and self-anal-ysis—the analysis usually entailing a struggle to understand the revealed Word—which, in turn, led to an awakening of desire for grace. Although these stages are essential steps in the preparation of the heart prior to the acceptance of grace,[8] Shepard does not tarry on any one stage, and he gives little space to the conversion experience in the autobiography. His conversion experience, however, does include a conviction of sin, self-examination and analysis, a compunction for sin, interspersed with longing for deliverance from sin, self-attempts at finding peace followed by a severing from self-confi-dence, and finally an acceptance of grace.[9]

JOHN MILTON
(1608-1674)

John Milton belongs to the long tradition of Renaissance Christian human-ism. The author of numerous works in a variety of literary genres, Milton is

---

7. This is the only autobiography treated at length by Kenneth Murdock in *Literature and Theology in Colonial New England* (Cambridge, 1949), 99-117.

8. See Norman Pettit, *The Heart Prepared: Grace and Conversion in Puritan Spiritual Life* (New Haven, Conn.: Yale University Press, 1966), 2-17.

9. See Daniel B. Shea Jr., *Spiritual Autobiography in Early America* (Princeton, N.J.: Princeton University Press, 1968), 140-51, for an excellent discussion of Shepard's autobiography.

perhaps best remembered for his magnificent epic, *Paradise Lost* (1667). In this scholarly poem, Milton pursues "things unattempted yet in Prose or Rhyme," and embodies the story of humanity's disobedience and fall. By Book III there is promise of Christ's redemptive power and of humanity's justification before God through the sacrifice of Christ. In Book IX the Fall occurs; in Book X, the ensuing disorder, ranging from planetary changes through the "fierce antipathy" in animal life, culminates in Adam's mind. Adam sees growing disorder and reveals his own pain in a speech of despair. In this important speech (Book X), Adam begins the first stage of regeneration: He knows he is guilty before God. But he begins to waver and even retracts his guilt. To think of all the suffering that would fall on the human race is cause, in Adam's mind, for rebellion against the justice of his punishment. Following an intense argument with himself, he finally accepts his own guilt, but no peace immediately follows. To accept guilt is only the first step toward conversion: One must also repent of sin and turn to God through faith.

The last three complex books (X, XI, and XII) permit the reader to discover, among other significant matters, details of the conversion experience. In metaphorical language, not translatable into concepts, the mystery of the repentance and regeneration of both Adam and Eve unfolds. By no means in one-dimensional, univocal language, Milton unmistakably allows us to see a repentant Adam and Eve "in lowliest plight" asking for mercy and forgiveness. God the Son presents their prayers to God the Father, who mercifully forgives because of their faith in the son's sacrifice. Adam and Eve are reconciled to God and to one another, but God declares that they must no longer remain in the Garden of Eden.

HENRY VAUGHAN
(1621/22-1695)

Henry Vaughan is a Welsh poet in the Metaphysical tradition. His fame rests primarily on *Silex Scintillans: or Sacred Poems and Private Ejaculations* (Part I first appeared in 1650: Part II in 1655). The words of the title mean flashing or sparkling flint, an image of the sparks that fly when God strikes the heart. Part I unfolds the early stages of the private and personal qualities of Vaughan's sensibility to the Fall and resultant depravity of humanity, the decay of religion in the world, his experience of God's call, election, the need for reconciliation, and to the various vicissitudes as he seeks deepening faith and understanding.

RICHARD BAXTER
(1615-1691)

Richard Baxter, prolific author and minister, thought of his writings as yet another way of spreading the gospel. *Reliquiae Baxterianae* (1696) or *The*

Autobiography of Richard Baxter was published posthumously from manuscripts left at his death in 1691. In the early part of the book, Baxter writes most about his spiritual development. He contends that God made his father the instrument of his first convictions; in fact, his father's serious speeches about God and the life to come absorbed him with a fear of sinning. That a variety of sins appealed to him in his youth, including ambitious desires for literary glory, he readily admits. When he was fifteen, "an old torn book" which a local working man loaned his father had a tremendous influence on Baxter. *A Book of Christian Exercises Pertaining to Resolution*, Edmund Burney's adaptation of a manual by the Jesuit Robert Parsons, referred to as *Bunny's Resolution*, was the book. Reading this word awakened his soul to the folly of sinning and to the necessity of living a holy life. "Yet whether sincere conversion began now, or before, or later," declared Baxter, "I was never able to this day to know." In this statement there is the "fusion of his personal experience with the main Puritan tradition"; yet, articulate seventeenth-century Puritans were "reluctant to highlight the drama of conversion in a way that would oversimplify the experience."[10] But Baxter lacked assurance of his conversion. Ill-health, expectations of immediate death, and doubts about his salvation led to years of intense struggle. Even when he had decided to enter the ministry, he began to question the fundamentals of his faith; reassurances interspersed among his struggles finally led to a degree of peace. The experience of Baxter was similar in some respects to Bunyan, but unlike Bunyan, the reading of many books and thinking hard on what he had read played a crucial role in serious decisions.

JOHN BUNYAN
(1628-1688)

John Bunyan, born at Elstow, near Bedford, was the oldest son of a tinker. His formal education was slight, but he wrote more than sixty books and became a literary, religious, and historical figure of worldwide significance. He wrote his autobiography, *Grace Abounding* (1666) sometime during his imprisonment in Bedford Jail from 1666-1672. His strong beliefs in original sin and in Christ's atoning grace to release the individual from the power of sin are convictions that inform the autobiography. The attitude toward conversion unfolds through a study of the stages of the book. Four pivotal stages emerge: Stranger to Grace (sections 1-36), Movement toward Grace (sections 37-229), Advent of Grace (section 230), and Discoveries in Grace (sections 231-339). An intense struggle precedes his willingness to accept God's grace. The first stage shows agonizing concern over his eligibility for God's grace and concludes with his decision to "taste the sweetness" of any sin he had not yet experienced, simultaneously exploring attempts at legal righteousness.

Movement toward grace begins when he hears the conversation of "three

---

10. Owen C. Watkins, *The Puritan Experience* (New York: Schocken Books, 1972), 124.

or four poor women of Bedford" who speak of a "new birth" and the "work of God in their hearts." Their talk of free grace causes him to think that they had undoubtedly found a "new World," and he is temporarily encouraged to believe that he, too, might know such joy.

Soon, however, questions and doubts begin to overwhelm him: What if he is not among the elect? What if the day of grace has passed for him? Attacks of despair, a sense of dreadful guilt, and an awareness of inner pollution so plague him that he believes that the condition of his soul is unable to "stand with a state of grace." The intensity of his agony reaches a crashing climax in the moment when he feels he has yielded to the temptation to "sell" Christ. For him, the Tempter is the winner in a horrible battle, and Bunyan says "and down I fell as a bird that is shot from the top of a tree, into great guilt and fearful despair." What follows is a series of constant struggles between hope (with its possibility of salvation through grace) and despair (with its possibility of lostness and damnation). Unlike the climax of the first part, the climax of the second section ends with a vision of God and the redeeming Christ.

The Pilgrim's Progress (1678), John Bunyan's famous allegory, embodies the metaphor of the way to show the path one must take in order to enter the Celestial City. Simultaneously, the way also metaphorically shows the inner way of faith of the individual believer.

JOHN DONNE
(1573-1631)

John Donne, a distinguished scholar-poet, is the author of numerous works, including thirty-eight *Divine Poems*. "Holy Sonnets" (some appeared in 1633 edition; others were added in later editions) is the single largest subdivision of the *Divine Poems*. As all lyric poems, these nineteen sonnets are highly personal metaphorical expressions; and, as in the parable, each poem is a personal form which creates new contexts for old or traditional images, symbols, and stories. The "Holy Sonnets" may also be read as "the Protestant Paradigm of salvation in its . . . Pauline terms" and they also resemble the "Protestant exercises of self-analysis which involve a review of the soul's own state and the . . . evidence of God's action in it."[11] Allusions to Old Testament stories, the death of Christ, the letters of Paul, the new heaven as told in the book of Revelation, and to various scientific discoveries abound in the poems, but Donne sets these in a new context and generates fresh, rich meaning for familiar words. What the author does is to work metaphorically, and metaphor shows new connections and fresh resemblances. Metaphorical language, in brief, releases meaning by indirection. This embodied language *is* the meaning; it "makes" ontological and existential statements.

---

11. Barbara Kiefer Lewalski, *John Donne, Protestant Poetics and the Seventeenth-Century Religious Lyric* (Princeton, N.J.: Princeton University Press, 1979), 265.

INCREASE MATHER
(1639-1723)

Increase Mather contributed to the Puritan conversion narrative in America with the writing of *The Autobiography of Increase Mather* (1685). Lacking some of the usual components of autobiography, the first part is primarily in the convention of the seventeenth-century spiritual autobiography. In a probing self-analysis followed by conviction of conscience and a longing for grace, Mather narrates in this first part his conversion experience. God broke in upon his conscience "with terrible convictions and awakenings." For months in succession he would experience "anguish" and "horror." At one time, he shut himself up in his father's study and wrote down every sin of which he was guilty that came to his memory. Later he spread out before God the paper on which he named his sins, confessed each one, and cried for mercy. There occurred a transformation in his life; he was sensitive to his need for cleansing from sin, but anguish of soul persisted. His heart stirred toward Christ, his mind knew that God had accepted the sacrifice of Christ, and now his own will must accept Christ's sacrifice.

Once more he shut himself into a little room and prayed for mercy. At the close of a day in prayer, Mather records, "I gave my self up to Jesus Christ, declaring that I was now resolved to be his Servant, and his only, and his forever."[12] Following this resolute step, Mather knew "inward peace" in his "perplexed soul." The conversion experience is briefly described within a few lines without detailed descriptions of various stages.

Two additional sections complete *The Autobiography,* but it stretches a point to call them autobiographical. The second part is not introspective; the third section is in the form of a diary or journal.

EDWARD TAYLOR
(c. 1642-1729)

Edward Taylor served as minister, physician, and public servant in the town of Westfield, Massachusetts, for a large part of his adult life. In religious matters, he was a strict observer of the "old" New England way, demanding a public acknowledgment of a conversion experience before admission to church membership. A learned as well as a pious man, Taylor, like many Harvard ministers, knew Latin, Hebrew, and Greek. His work as a poet was generally unknown until in the 1930s, Thomas Johnson discovered that the Yale University Library held most of his poems.

"God's Determination" (not published until the twentieth century), Edward Taylor's lengthy poem, in the tradition of the Medieval "debate" consisting of a preface and thirty-five sequential lyrics, is a poetical story of Covenant Theology. It shows the working of grace through a framework

---

12. M.G. Hall, ed., "The Autobiography of Increase Mather" (1685), *Proceedings of the American Antiquarian Society* 71 (October 1961): 280.

similar to Medieval morality plays. The action of the drama-like poem centers upon "the difficulties experienced by the various classes of the elect, those who come early and rather easily to Christ and those who resist his call".[13] The Preface celebrates God as creator of a beautiful and perfect world. Man was also created, but he sinned and therefore marred the beauty and wholeness of the earth. Although man is "a Crumb of Earth," Taylor wants his pen to praise the Creator God and requests God's help in writing the praises for fear his "dull phancy" brings scorn rather than glory.

DANIEL DEFOE
(1660-1731)

Daniel Defoe, a representative of the middle-class dissenting Englishman, produced his first novel, *Robinson Crusoe* (1719) when he was almost sixty years old. The novel is a powerful depiction of man's struggle against nature as both physical and metaphysical. Through the adventurous episodes on the island, Defoe isolates, points up, and resolves conflicts within Crusoe. Raised by a "wise and grave" father, Crusoe is guided, nevertheless, by his natural tendencies in early life. One of his most obvious propensities was a spirit of restlessness, a plight which he calls his original sin. Despite the wise counsel of his father not to yield to his wandering inclinations, Crusoe continues to drift, rebels against his parents, ignores supernatural warnings, and breaks promises to God. After being shipwrecked on an island, he suffers through storms, earthquakes, and severe illness. Reaching the lowest point of his physical and spiritual condition, he experiences an unforgettable vision. He sees a "Man descend from a great black Cloud, in a bright Flame of Fire" and land upon the earth. Armed with "a long Spear or Weapon in his Hand," he moves toward Crusoe and speaks in a "Voice so terrible, that it is impossible to express the Terror of It" and says, "Seeing all these Things have not brought thee to Repentance, now thou shalt die."[14]

Crusoe's dream had a dramatic impact on his sensitivity to his spiritual condition. He acknowledges that the "Horrors" of his soul resulting from the vision are indescribable, but adds that his eight years of "Sea-faring Wickedness" and "a constant conversation with nothing" except those similar to him caused him to look neither upward to God nor inward toward his soul's needs. The result was a "certain Stupidity of Soul, without Desire of God, or Conscience of Evil."[15] As he continued to contemplate, "conscience that had slept so long" began to awaken; he cried out: "God's Justice has overtaken me."[16] He acknowledged his folly in rejecting the "Voice of Providence" and the counsel of his parents. His thoughts turn to the possibility of prayer and to the reading of the Bible.

Removing a Bible from his seaman's chest, he begins to read; the first

---

13. Lewalski, *John Donne*, 391.

14. Michael Shinagel, ed., *Robinson Crusoe*, Daniel Defoe, Norton Critical Edition (New York: Norton, 1975), 70.

words he comes upon are: "Call on me in the Day of Trouble, and I will deliver, and thou shalt glorify me" (Ps 50:15). Thinking the words to be appropriate to him, Crusoe could hardly get beyond his situation, for the reality of deliverance still seemed remote. Before he retires, however, he does what he never has done in his life: He kneels in prayer to God and asks him to fulfill his promise to him. After a few days, Crusoe reflects again upon the scripture and it occurs to his mind that he "pored so much" upon his "Deliverance from the main Affliction" that he "disregarded the Deliverance" he received. "God had delivered me," he now says, "but I had not glorify'd Him." He then offers a prayer of thanksgiving and later turns to Acts 5:31: "He is exalted a Prince and a Savior, to give repentance, and to give Remission." With his heart and hands lifted to heaven "in a Kind of Extasy of Joy," he cries out: "Jesus, thou Son of David, Jesus, thou exalted Prince and Savior, give me Repentance!"[17] What Crusoe now knows is deliverance from sin and his "Load of Guilt," a deliverance far greater than being removed from the Island and its solitariness.

Robinson Crusoe finally enjoys a radical transformation. He begins to know new life physically and spiritually. Marked characteristics of his spiritual awakening are reading the Bible, praying to God, and enjoying "a great deal of Comfort within."

JONATHAN EDWARDS
(1703-1758)

Jonathan Edwards is the author of one of the best known autobiographies of American literature. His *Personal Narrative* focuses exclusively on the work of divine grace in the soul. Although he frequently receives attention for his life of the mind, Edwards was convinced that an individual must do more than comprehend Christian ideas; one must know them *experientially*. Basic to this belief is the recognition that nothing the individual is able to do warrants the conversion experience. To know that one is totally dependent on God for salvation is imperative.

Edwards suggests that several convictions and various stages of thought preceded his conversion, or perhaps were steps toward his conversion, but his definite experience came when he could delight in God's sovereignty. Even as a child, Edwards was "full of objections" against the doctrine of God's sovereignty if it meant that God chose or rejected whom he pleased for salvation. But he finally achieved "a delight in that sovereignty." Also, when he read the words from scripture: "Now unto the King eternal, immortal, invisible, the only wise God, be honor and glory for ever and ever. Amen" (1 Tm 1:17), he experienced a rapturous "sense of the glory of the Divine Being." Edwards declares that from about that time he began to have new

15. Ibid., 71.
16. Ibid., 73.
17. Ibid., 77.

ideas of Christ "and the work of redemption, and the glory of salvation by Him."

At times, Edwards' work suggests that his pattern of conversion was a departure from that of other Puritans, a possibility apparently troubling to him. When he accepts the fact, however, that the Spirit's manifestations may not always follow the usual pattern, he left off his concerns over "particular steps" or stages essential to a conversion experience. Another aspect of Edwards' *Personal Narrative* is its emphasis on what salvation is *not*. Clearly obvious is the conviction that intentions, resolutions, and religious practices are not to be equated with salvation.

JOHN WOOLMAN
(1720-1772)

John Woolman, an eighteenth-century American Quaker, wrote works that are among the best literary expressions from the Quakers. Although the *Journal* is not an autobiography in the purest sense, it does, as does all autobiography, focus on the self as "an entity to which Truth must be related, not as personality . . . to be anatomized."[18] The overall pattern of the book is a recounting of his various journeys as a Quaker missionary.

The narrative covering the early years of Woolman's life presents the stages of childhood delights and musings on God's mercy as well as feelings of remorse for wicked acts. In adolescence, he became "estranged" from God and from "thinking on heavenly things"; "he knew," he said, that he "was going from the flock of Christ and had no resolution to return." Following a bout with illness, he was so humbled before God that he felt that the "Word which is as a fire and hammer" broke his rebellious spirit.

Despite his strong resolve to be obedient, he experienced several relapses into "youthful vanities." Later, he spends time alone, reads the scriptures, prays, and finds new strength. Failing to live in light of the new-found power, he loses "ground again." Finally, he confesses his sins to God, craves help, and becomes convinced that "true religion" consists of "an inward life, wherein the heart doth reverence God the Creator." In his words, he follows "the openings of truth" or direct messages from God to the soul, and as he ponders the change wrought in him, he is unable to find "language equal to it nor any means to convey to another a clear idea of it."[19] What is especially typical of Woolman's work is its lack of any self-exaltation; divine grace is the focus, not Woolman. To relate his understanding of divine love to an imperfect world—particularly one that condoned slavery—became a consuming desire of Woolman's life.

---

18. Shea, *Spiritual Autobiography*, 45.
19. All quotations are from *The Norton Anthology of American Literature*, 2nd. ed. (New York: Norton, 1985), 528-34.

FYODOR DOSTOYEVSKY
(1821-1881)

Fyodor Dostoyevsky explores the complex moral and spiritual condition of individuals in their particular world. Ultimate questions and concerns inform his major novels. *The Brothers Karamazov* (1878-80) is Dostoyevsky's compelling novel about human's search for God the Father, or their inquiry into the existence of God. Like his other novels, *The Brothers Karamazov* depicts a turbulent world in which Christianity encounters a challenge initiated by the positivist empiricism of contemporary society. To affirm the permanence of Christian values is not enough; proofs of negation receive thorough analysis, but Dostoyevsky is "impelled by a metaphysics, Christian in foundation and overview."[20] He permits one to comprehend unmistakably the enormous cost of humanity's estrangement from God.

The Russian monk, Father Zossima, a central character in the novel, is an image of believing faith and profound love. To the criticism that Father Zossima lacks convincing reality and offers unrealistic solutions to religious questions, George Panichas calls such views "part of the debased values and loyalties in modern society." Such misconceptions are "symptomatic of the crisis of faith that has gripped Western civilization since the middle of the nineteenth century."[21] It is Zossima who embodies the life of the spirit and firmly stands as an antithesis to the pervading stagnancy and decay of religious values. In notes, recorded by his most devoted disciple, Alyosha, Elder Zossima's own transformation from sin to faith unfolds. But it is Alyosha's conversion that receives the more dramatic treatment.

The death of Father Zossima, with the accompanying decomposition of his body, serves as a crisis and a turning point in Alyosha's life. It is a crisis because in his judgment the body of the saintly Father Zossima should know no decay; it is a turning point because "someone visited" his soul in "that hour." What Alyosha immediately thinks is that his brother (Ivan), who builds a rational argument against God's world and openly defies God, probably has taken a verifiable stance.

Following a brief period of disillusionment, Alyosha comes to the cell where Father Zossima's coffin stands. He falls on his knees and prays; he listens to another monk in the monastery as he reads the account of the Marriage at Cana where Christ works the miracle of turning water into wine. Although he listens, Alyosha falls asleep and dreams and has a vision of Father Zossima (this personification of miracle) counseling him to be reborn in Christ and informing him that "He is terrible in His greatness, awful in his sublimity, but

---

20. George A. Panichas, *The Burden of Vision* (Grand Rapids, Mich.: Eerdmans, 1977), 10.

21. Ibid., 166.

infinitely merciful."[22] When he awakens, he gazes first at the dead man in the coffin and then speaks one of the most majestic passages of the entire book, every line dramatizing a momentous transformation from doubt to belief. He makes a free, suprarational choice *alone* without knowing how few or how many would make a similar choice, and he does it without any promises that material needs would always be satisfied. He has no explanation in rational phrases for the transformation; he does know that someone visited his soul, and now wants only to go out into the world and live a life of love. Alyosha, the youngest of the Karamazov brothers, incarnates the acceptance of salvation in Christ. Dostoyevsky shapes into form a compelling novel with a Christian existentialist's worldview.

NATHANIEL HAWTHORNE
(1804-1864)

Nathaniel Hawthorne, one of America's most engaging authors, wrote numerous short works and several novels, including *The Scarlet Letter*, a classic set in Puritan New England.

In a short tale, "The Celestial Railroad," Hawthorne writes what might be called an inverted story of conversion. The work is a pastiche on Bunyan's *The Pilgrim's Progress*, with the caricature aimed not at Bunyan but at the religious pseudo-modernists of Hawthorne's era. With the accomplishments of applied science, the modern pilgrim finds everything—including salvation—much easier than Bunyan's pilgrim. Instead of trudging along on foot, with a burden on his back, the pilgrim rides on a railroad car, after checking his load of sins with the baggage man.

Hawthorne's sympathies obviously lie with Bunyan, not with nineteenth-century positivists or skeptics. The work clearly unfolds the need for repentance, for forgiveness, for the cross or redemption in Christ; salvation is not found in the easy planning of the religious modernist or with the "Giant Transcendentalist."

GERARD MANLEY HOPKINS
(1844-1889)

Gerard Manley Hopkins, popularly called the "Star of Balliol," became a convert to the Catholic Church during his undergraduate days at Oxford. To many readers, Hopkins' poetry is obscure and difficult, but painstaking care to understand his poetry will yield rich results. What is at once obvious is his celebration of God's glory in the world. The poem which Hopkins regarded as his best is "The Windhover," with its dedication "To Christ our Lord." An excellent example of metaphorical precision, the poem is a parabolic depiction of the Word at work in the cosmos. Further, the informing

---

22. Fyodor Dostoyevsky, *The Brothers Karamazov*, ed. Ralph E. Matlaw; trans. Constance Garnett, *Norton Critical Edition* (New York: Norton, 1976), 339.

metaphor is a bird in flight which embodies the glory of the knowledge of the Word experienced in the penitential, surrendering heart of the individual to Christ the Lord.[23]

FRANCIS THOMPSON
(1859-1907)

Francis Thompson frequently writes on the outcast in his poetry. "The Hound of Heaven" is, however, a splendid ode on the narrator's flight from the relentlessly pursuing "Hound." In words reminiscent of Augustine, Thompson says: "I fled him, down the nights and down the days;/I fled him, down the arches of the years." Fearful that love for God would exclude other kinds of love, the fleeing soul finds no rest in the natural world or in the imaginary world of poetry and song. What Thompson ultimately shows is not a picture of a guilty and repentant soul but rather an arresting figure of one unwilling to permit a foolish and blind wanderer not to know whom he really seeks: "Ah, fondest, blindest, weakest/I am he whom thou seekest!" God reaches down to man and extends his grace: "Rise, clasp my hand, and come!"

EDWIN MUIR
(1887-1959)

Edwin Muir, poet, critic, and translator was born in Orkney, Scotland. It is the collection of short poems under the title, "The Labyrinth" (1949) which show his journey through the labyrinth of despair and lostness to a return and inner peace. Harry Balmires comments on Muir's pilgrimage are especially perceptive: "Muir's imagination transfigures the mystery of his pilgrimage in parable. . . . The spiritual journey from a hyper-emotional evangelical conversion as a boy, through a long phase of religious indifference, to a realization that 'quite without knowing it, I was a Christian' and finally to a deep understanding of the Incarnation."[24]

C.S. LEWIS
(1898-1963)

C.S. Lewis, distinguished author and professor, describes his inability to run permanently from God in *Christian Reflections*: "God was the hunter (or

---

23. See James Finn Cotter, *Inscape: The Christology and Poetry of Gerard Manley Hopkins* (Pittsburgh: University of Pittsburgh Press, 1972), 182, who writes of the bird in flight as it is reborn from flames "a billion/Times lovelier" and adds: "So much greater is the uncreated presence of Christ in grace than the gift of himself as creating Word. For as Word-made-flesh he transforms man into himself, the servant whose obedience, humility, and suffering now bring him eternal glory."

24. Harry Balmires, ed., *A Guide to Twentieth Century Literature in English* (London: Methuen, 1983), 189.

so it seemed to me) and I was the deer. He stalked me like a redskin, took unerring aim, and fired." Lewis begins the first part with metaphors (hunter and deer) and moves to a simile (like a redskin) and closes with direct statement (took unerring aim, and fired). In all of the imaginative writings of C.S. Lewis, there are innumerable images, symbols, and metaphors that embody various aspects of the Christian story. In the Narnia stories: *The Lion, The Witch, and The Wardrobe*, and others, the symbol of unique salvation that is in Christ is unmistakable when Eustace, who futilely attempts to cast off his dragon-skin, submits to Aslan (Christ). Only when he surrenders to Aslan, with no faith in his own adequacy, does Aslan apply his Lion's claws and tears off his sinful nature down to his heart.

The Pilgrim's Regress is undoubtedly on one level Lewis's autobiography in fictional form. The character, John, eagerly desiring permanent satisfaction, wanders into the "hard" experiences and philosophies to the north of the main road and also among the "soft" ones to the south. Vertue, another important character, plods down the main road but without any comprehension of the goal to be reached.

The quest takes on special significance on John and Vertue's final visit to the great canyon. John finds himself clinging to a narrow ledge along the canyon wall. He is unable to go either forward or backward. In desperation, he begins to pray and "a Man" comes to offer him food. History, Reason, and Contemplation also converse with him. Then Death comes and commands that he go downward; Death also informs him of the descent of the Landlord's own Son.

What Lewis suggests here has not to do with eternal death but with the death of the self, for Death says that "the cure of death is dying." With fear, John begins his descent which is in reality an ascent; he starts his first steps toward the one for whom he has really searched from the beginning. He confesses: "I have come to give myself up." Mother Kirk tells him that his dirty rags must be stripped off. John's stripping is so radical that a piece of his skin comes off with his "righteous" rags. What follows the pain of stripping is joyous renewal. He now sees that his longing from the beginning had been not for "hard" or "soft" philosophies, but rather for the Lord Christ.

Reading C.S. Lewis's writings in their entirety rather than a random sampling of only a few fictional creations will lead readers to a deep respect for his distinctive contribution to an understanding of Christianity. Unbiased readers will also experience a new appreciation for imaginative writing.

T.S. ELIOT
(1888-1965)

T.S. Eliot was born in St. Louis, Missouri. He became a British citizen in 1927, the same year of his conversion to Christianity and baptism into the Church of England. Also in 1927, Eliot's excellent poem "The Journey of the Magi" was published which studies the paradox of birth through death that conversion itself embodies. One of the wise men in the poem recalls, in retrospect, his journey to Bethlehem:

> All this was a long time ago, I remember,
> And I would do it again, but set down
> This set down
> This: were we led all that way for
> Birth or Death? There was a Birth, certainly,
> We had evidence and no doubt. I had seen birth and death,
> But had thought they were different; this Birth was
> Hard and bitter agony for us, like Death, our death.
> We returned to our places, these kingdoms
> But no longer at ease here. . . .[25]

In the language of paradox, Eliot sees death as a prelude to birth. Death entails a stripping away of illusions; a self-negation precedes faith in God, or dying to self conjoined with faith are essential ingredients of salvation. "Ash-Wednesday" (1930) is a poem of penitence, cleansing, and self-surrender. The crowning work of his poetic endeavors, *Four Quartets*, embodies an extraordinary range, depth, and intensity of experience.

GRAHAM GREENE
(1904-1991)

Graham Greene, an English novelist whose religious ideology has been discussed and scrutinized by critics, offers a sacramental vision of reality, particularly in his serious or "Catholic" novels. In *The Power and the Glory* (1940) the surface story suggests an intricate thriller in which a priest says that he is a fugitive running from the pursuing forces of the state; but he later discovers that it is the everywhere-present power of Grace that is carrying on the most intense pursuit.[26]

The Heart of the Matter (1948) also shows Greene's sacramental vision of reality and further probes the mystery of God's grace and his relentless pursuit of man, his image bearer. Whether or not the rebellious ones are aware of him, God is still present, apparently eagerly waiting to answer if anyone calls upon him. Yet, how far does this grace extend? Greene tests the question and ends the novel with a paradoxical question: whether a man who has been a derelict, has committed adultery, has acknowledged his lack of trust in God and committed other sins—all out of love for others—is still the

---

25. T.S. Eliot, "Journey of the Magi," *The Complete Poems and Plays of T.S. Eliot* (London: Faber and Faber, 1969), 104.

26. George M.A. Gaston, *The Pursuit of Salvation, A Critical Guide to the Novels of Graham Greene* (Troy, N.Y.: Whitston, 1984), 29, believes that the structure and texture of the novel indicates that "salvation does not depend on formulas . . . or deeds, but on faith and ultimately on God's mercy."

object of God's saving Grace? The author seems to suggest that a response to such a question is a mystery hidden from individuals or the institutional church. Pervading the book, however, is the sure fact of the inscrutable nature of God.

The End of the Affair (1951) is another exploration of God's mysterious mercy and grace in lives. A character called Sarah appears to a novelist named Bendrix to be the source of a succession of miracles that drive him into an intense struggle with God. In an attempt to write a novel, Bendrix's proposed work actually becomes a diary of his spiritual quest. In humility, he recognizes his insufficiency to live (or to write) as he should, he accepts his guilt, confesses his dread of submitting to God, and reluctantly shows his belief in salvation by grace. What really matters is whether or not individuals experience a radical transformation, however reluctant the process.

W.H. AUDEN
(1907-1973)

W.H. Auden joins with other writers of the twentieth century such as T.S. Eliot in showing an awareness of humans' lostness, an understanding of their dilemma, and a belief in boundless love and unlimited grace offered in the midst of chaos. Auden also expresses a vast sacramental vision of reality: Redemption has not to do with pursuit but of surrender to One whose grace encircles humans and the cosmos.

When his early collections of verse were published, however, Auden became known as the leading figure in the new movement, the "poets of the thirties," who were outstanding poets frequently associated with "revolutionary clamor." But, Harry Balmires, for example, believes that "this strident, revolutionary clamor . . . is not often heard in Auden.[27] Balmires does contend that a "crucial development occurred when Auden was converted to Christianity in 1940," and records that Auden stated: "'It has taken Hitler to show us that liberalism is not self-supporting.'"[28] It is also of interest that the poet credited the Anglican layman, Charles Williams, for unknowingly exercising a remarkable influence on him.

Following his conversion, Auden's longer poems and the prolific output of shorter ones, show a poetic blending of moral, philosophical, and theological reflections. But in his poetry the matter of redemption ceases to be an "academic" matter (although it takes intellectual vigor to work through his poems) but becomes for lost man an imperative, experiential moment. In the poem, "For the Time Being": A Christmas Oratorio (1945), Auden states . . . redemption is no longer a question of pursuit but of surrender to him who is always and everywhere present.[29] Although humans are without abil-

---

27. Balmires, ed., *Guide to Twentieth Century Literature*, 10.
28. Ibid.
29. W.H. Auden, "For the Time Being," *Collected Longer Poems* (London: Faber and Faber, 1968), 183-84.

ity to earn God's grace, this does not mean that redemption comes without cost. Auden declares that grace is made possible only by Christ's willingness to suffer and die; to accept this grace, individuals must acknowledge their own insufficiency, surrender to the Incarnate Christ and die to self. Auden further writes:

> For the garden is the only place there is, but you
>   will not find it
> until you have looked for it everywhere and found
>   nowhere that is not a desert;
> The miracle is the only thing that happens, but to
>   you it will not be apparent,
>   until all events have been studied and nothing
>   happens that you cannot explain;
> And life is the destiny you are bound to refuse
>   until you have consented to die.[30]

FLANNERY O'CONNOR
(1925-1964)

Flannery O'Connor, a southern writer, who held that in the south the general conception of humanity was "Christ-haunted" if not "Christ-centered," found most of her primary subjects among "Christ-haunted characters." She develops her controlling images with wit and infuses them with biblical allusions. Figures of speech are tools of language for O'Connor with which to penetrate the heart of mystery, and her grotesque, parabolic stories dramatize essential theological truths that modern man either rejects or distorts. From time to time, O'Connor asserts that Christian theology is absolutely fundamental to an understanding of her writings. In the essay "The Fiction Writer and His Country," she specifically states that she sees from the standpoint of Christian orthodoxy. This means for her, she says, that "the meaning of life is centered in our Redemption by Christ." What she sees in the world she sees in its relation to that unique event.

O'Connor appears at her most characteristic in her short stories. In the best of them she developed the values which she considered essential and the Christian vision which informed every work she wrote.

Whether a life is superficially committed to Christianity or openly dedicated to wicked deeds, the explanation for both is the same: a disregard of a strong faith in Christ. In "A Good Man is Hard to Find," the Misfit cannot believe (even though he knows that Christ threw "everything off balance") and commits himself to "meanness" but he admits that if Christ does exist and can raise the dead, then "there is nothing for you to do but throw away everything and follow him," but if Christ does not exist, the only thing to do is to "enjoy the few minutes you got left the best way you can—by killing some-

---

30. Ibid., 138.

body or burning down his house." On the other hand, the grandmother in the story "talks" Christian, but face to face with the Misfit, she recognizes that her superficial commitment is without depth and meaning. At the moment, however, of the Misfit's privation from grace, the grandmother is given her moment of grace. What is particularly essential to see in this short work is that there is no middle way: Christ demands total commitment. In this O'Connor world, whether one commits himself to evil deeds or good works makes no difference ultimately; both are disobedient to the need for grace.

What O'Connor does is to show that no one is able to find salvation in any of the so-called "saviors" of the modern world.[31] Her various short stories and the novels (*The Violent Bear it Away* and *Wise Blood* are her only novels) all in their literary ways loudly declare that individuals are unable to justify themselves and that the only Savior is the Incarnate Christ. What especially troubled Flannery O'Connor was how to portray this radical transformation of divine grace for readers who seem not to have the vaguest sense of God and who lack understanding of the theological frame of reference which once provided meaning for Western culture.

FREDERICK BUECHNER
(1926-   )

Frederick Buechner, novelist, prose artist, and ordained minister, published his first novel, *A Long Day's Dying* in 1950. The number increased to seven novels by 1985, and by 1988 he had written some eight prose works. His fourth novel, *The Final Beast*, has as its focus the sin of adultery and the need for forgiveness. It is his novel *Godric* (1981), however, that is perhaps most timely for a study of conversion in literature. The entire work is a marvelous artistic depiction of the conversion story of an eleventh-century pirate into a saintly hermit. The controlling themes are the strangeness of life combined with the amazing grace of the God who sustains it. Buechner's graphic presentation of characters and subject matter may strike some readers as too earthy and secular; if so, some secular critics equally believe his work to be "too religious" to be taken seriously as literary art. For Buechner, Christianity is not a set of rigid rules for human beings to follow slavishly but the commitment to the person of Christ whose grace extends to all individuals.

---

31. See Harold Fickett's comments in Harold Fickett and Douglas Gilbert, *Flannery O'Connor: Images of Grace* (Grand Rapids, Mich.: Eerdmans, 1986). His excellent comments on some modern "saviors" should be noted. See particularly his view on "dark Romanticism" or "Nietzschean Romanticism" and "Logical Positivism," p. 47.

Chapter Fifteen

The Phenomenology of Conversion

Lewis R. Rambo, with Lawrence A. Reh

Esther Tenichev* was born in 1958, the only child of a mixed marriage. Her father was a non-observant Jew who died when she was sixteen; her mother, a lapsed Catholic who did not remarry. On rare occasions, in the company of the maternal grandmother, her mother took her to Catholic Mass.

She grew up in a west coast metropolis, attended a state university, then moved to another west coast metro area in 1981 to do graduate work at a prestigious medical school. She had entered counseling while still in college, and sought out a "spiritual teacher" in her adopted community, a university chaplain, concerning religious issues.

She began in 1983 to investigate the possibility of converting to Christianity, took formal Roman Catholic adult instruction in 1984, and was baptized in 1985. She subsequently left her initial graduate program and entered a Protestant seminary in the San Francisco Bay Area as a graduate student.

She became active and took training in nonviolent social protest, was employed at a Catholic-sponsored shelter and food program for the unemployed and homeless, and participated in civil disobedience for a number of peace causes.

---

* Names and other identifying information have been altered to preserve anonymity.

This is the skeletal outline of a personal faith journey that will supply the data for this chapter's exploration of the phenomenology of conversion. It is purposely drab, superficial, sketchy at this point, because it is meant to relate only the barest indisputable facts. It will be through the process of phenomenological inquiry that we* will put flesh on these bones, that we hope to gain a deep understanding of Esther's spiritual journey.

The heart of phenomenology[1] is to go beyond bare facts to the level of facts-as-perceived. It is the quest to discover and describe what a person actually experienced. The goal of phenomenology is elegantly simple to articulate, excruciatingly complex to accomplish. This chapter will explore the nature of the phenomenological enterprise** and offer a case study that illustrates some possibilities and problems with applying the method to the study of religious conversion. (Conversion itself, for the purposes of this discussion, will mean the personal adoption of and investment of faith in a particular set of religious rituals, relationships, roles, and rhetoric.[2])

My own approach as reflected in this chapter is informed by the work of Paul Colaizzi,[3] Donald Polkinghorne,[4] Kirk Farnsworth,[5] and H. Newton Malony.[6]

A Story of Conversion and Consequences

For the focus of this article, I selected Esther Tenichev's conversion to Roman Catholicism in order to examine both the strengths and limitations of the phenomenological method in the study of conversion.

Several years ago I interviewed Esther as part of the teaching process in

---

* In the text, "we" refers either to the authors jointly or to the authors and readers editorially—where important, context should make clear the difference. "I" and "my" always refers to Rambo (except in direct quotes from Tenichev and Snyder).

** For readers unfamiliar with phenomenology as a discipline, a brief overview has been provided as an "afterword" at the end of this chapter.

1. For an excellent overview of the field, see Richard Schmitt, "Phenomenology," in *The Encyclopedia of Philosophy*, ed. Paul Edwards (New York: Macmillan and The Free Press, 1967).

2. For a brief summation of my view of conversion, see "Conversion: Toward a Holistic Model of Religious Change," *Pastoral Psychology* 38 (1989): 47-63, and my chapter, "The Psychology of Conversion," in this volume.

3. Paul F. Colaizzi, "Psychological Research as the Phenomenologist Views It," in *Existential-Phenomenological Alternatives for Psychology*, ed. Ronald S. Valle and Mark King (New York: Oxford University Press, 1978), 48-71.

4. Donald E. Polkinghorne, "Phenomenological Research Methods," in *Existential-Phenomenological Perspectives in Psychology*, ed. Ronald S. Valle and Steen Halling (New York: Plenum Press, 1989), 41-60.

5. Kirk E. Farnsworth, *Whole-Hearted Integration* (Grand Rapids, Mich.: Baker, 1985); see especially pp. 36-47.

6. H. Newton Malony, "Religious Experiencing: A Phenomenological Analysis of a Unique Behavioral Event," *Journal of Psychology and Theology* 9 (1981): 326-34; and "An S-O-R Model of Religious Experience," in *Advances in the Psychology of Religion*, ed. L. B. Brown (New York: Pergamon Press, 1985), 113-28.

my graduate seminar on conversion at Berkeley's Graduate Theological Union. In doing so, I learned that during the process of her conversion, Esther had been working with a spiritual director, Cameron Snyder, and that both she and Snyder had kept written records of their experience. From the age of sixteen Esther had kept a very careful and extensive diary of her life, and Snyder followed his custom of keeping process notes of all his pastoral counseling and spiritual direction activities.

To find an individual case history so well-documented by the subject, and to have access in addition to the note-based recollections of a third party in close relationship to the subject during the conversion process, is extremely rare in the field. You will see, however, that there are minuses as well as pluses involved in examining and reporting on this case study.

This report is based on five interviews with Esther. After the initial classroom dialogue on September 27, 1990, each of the other interviews took place in Cameron Snyder's office, with his participation. They occurred on February 5 and 19, 1991; on March 5, 1991; and on April 29, 1991. All five were tape recorded and transcribed. The finished report itself was also read and commented on by the participants on January 28, 1992.

Methodology in the Study of Conversion

In a book currently in progress, *Conversion: A Dynamic Model of Religious Change*,[7] I briefly outlined six ingredients in a methodology for study of conversion: observation, description, empathy, understanding, interpretation, and explanation. These activities should not be seen as a neat sequential process but as interacting elements that synergistically can render the phenomena more completely. These six will be considered in greater detail, and their use in Esther's story will be demonstrated.

In addition to this methodology, however, a phenomenological study of conversion should also consider these factors: rigorous examination of potential researcher bias or presuppositions, candid disclosure of elements in the researcher's background that might bear on methodology and results, and incorporation into one's mental set the awareness of additional factors that may operate to influence researcher or subject, or both, as the study progresses. These additional factors are impossible to catalog exhaustively but may include the subject's motivation for submitting to study, the researcher's theoretical predilections, methodological quirks or patterns, constraints of a fixed model for investigation, contributions of other parties on either the subject's or researcher's side of the study, the presence of other forms of relationship between the two parties, the influence of parties outside the primary researcher/subject diad, and changes in life situation for either party during the study (such as major illness, loss of a significant other to death or divorce, other relationship upheaval, and so on).

My personal background and potential biases will be laid out below under

---

7. Lewis Rambo, *Conversion: A Dynamic Model of Religious Change* (New Haven: Yale University Press, forthcoming).

the heading, "The Phenomenologist as Person." Many of the above categories of additional factors are present to some degree in the study of Esther's
conversion experience. 1) The subject could be seen to have any number of
personal needs—satisfying perceived voids in her life, a desire to intensify,
salvage, or recapture her conversion experience, and so forth—thus a willingness to subject herself for study. 2) As an interviewer, I am often hesitant
to push for disclosure, prone to reveal even less. I am aware of a desire to protect subjects from themselves, and for them to *like* what I write about them.
To a degree, any disclosure from individual cases runs counter to my training and sensitivities as a pastor and therapist, in which confidentiality is of
prime importance. 3) The initial interaction in the study process was conducted
within the framework of a set interview protocol[8] which (it became apparent
as the interview progressed) was not very conducive to the needs and aims
of the study. I was conscious of a kind of free-form departure from the
model, even while trying to operate within it; it was abandoned for the
remainder of the study. 4) Third-party influences included seminar participants who witnessed and discussed the initial interview session; Esther's
spiritual director, who sat in on and participated in the dialogue of the subsequent four interviews; a transcriptionist whose identity became know to
Esther during the study period and to whom she introduced herself on an
occasion of chance meeting; and my research assistant, Lawrence Reh, who
contributed to the interpretation, analysis, and articulation of results but had
no role in the interview process. (Reh's involvement was chiefly in the organizing, co-writing, and editing of text.)

5) Besides being subject and researcher, Esther and I were also for a time
student and teacher, and I sat on the academic committee which reviewed and
approved her graduate work. Her spiritual advisor, Cameron Snyder, was
previously an acquaintance of mine in divinity school and to some degree a
role model. 6) This study was conducted while I was in the throes of a very
painful separation and divorce from my second wife. At one point in this
research, personal problems of my own reached such a pitch on a day scheduled for interview that I prevailed upon Esther to defer that appointment so
I might have benefit of emergency pastoral counseling from Snyder.

As reader, your reaction to all of this might well be that it is extraordinary—and atypical—in the number and degree of complications and "messiness." One might even suspect that the study example was simulated in
order to demonstrate as many potential complications as possible. It seems
extraordinary to *me*, though as an exemplar for potential varieties of research
contamination, it is particularly useful as a warning not to be lulled into
complacency, to think that such knotty complications certainly could not
happen to *you*. The study example is genuine; it is worth emphasizing that my
own awareness of the level of complication was not clear or complete until
well after the conclusion of the interviews. I am convinced from per-

---

8. Chana Ullman, *The Self Transformed: The Psychology of Religious Conversion* (New
York: Plenum Press, 1989), 199-213.

sonal experience that "messiness" is inherent in any phenomenological research which expects to deal seriously with the complexities of human experience.

Thus cautioned, we return to the case study and the six facets of conversion research. New and more detailed material from Esther's story will accompany each discussion. This material will consist of several types: direct quotes from the interview transcripts (setting forth comments of Esther, Cameron, or myself); in some instances, direct quotes from Esther's journal (only her voice figures here); and author comment, analysis, or interpretation in retrospect. All will be clearly identified.

I. "TO SEE AS IF FOR THE FIRST TIME": OBSERVATION

Observation is the basis of phenomenology. Seeing something "as if for the first time" (insofar as possible) is fundamental to the phenomenological method. The fact is that simple, accurate, fresh observation is extremely difficult, due to the biases, expectations, distortions, conditioning, and other handicaps with which we are all burdened, preventing us from seeing phenomena as fully and completely as possible. It is too easy to dismiss this as the first and foremost methodological factor; I am frequently amazed at studies which display little careful, objective, and systematic observation, with effort by the researcher to eschew presumption so that new perception and vision may be possible.

It should be noted, moreover, that observation refers not only to that of the researcher but also embraces that done by the subject of the investigation— the convert—especially research that is done primarily through the use of interviews. As with the "fact" of conversion, one generally takes at face value the self-reporting of the subject. It is the convert's experience(s), after all, that a phenomenological study aims to elucidate. (See discussion below of the researcher's awareness of shortcomings and complications in self-reporting.)

From Esther's interview dialogue: *"I didn't grow up with the sense that the world was a safe place or fair place." "I'd say both of my parents in their different ways were abandoned as children emotionally." "I learned at a very early age how to stuff feelings. My parents were free to rant and rave and dump their emotions, but there wasn't emotional room for me to express mine, so I just learned to clam up a lot."*

[When her father died] *"I actually tried to bargain with God at the time. 'God, please restore my father to full physical and mental health and I swear I'll do better in school.' I was very precise about this because I knew that some people who were resuscitated from heart attacks sustained brain damage, and I didn't want God to get around it by bringing my father back alive but leaving him brain-damaged. I was not exactly trusting of God when I put that petition out."*

[About the film, *A Man for All Seasons*] *"I found myself just fascinated, wondering what makes it possible for a person [Sir Thomas More] to maintain such a commitment in the face of such pressures . . . unconsciously I identified with More because I felt beleaguered, and I had had to give up some pretty essential parts of my own identity in order to survive in my family."*

[On moving for graduate school] *"It was the first time in my life I had ever lived away from home. That took me out of the family orbit, and I think that was crucial. I also made a friend, an intellectual Christian, the first one I'd ever known."*

[A crisis of identity] *"I was a grad student in this program that I really hated, but I couldn't admit that I hated it . . . I was in a terrible work block, which scared me because I wanted to be a hot-shot academic, and I was unable to. I had been busting my buns in therapy for the past year and a half . . . I realized I had been sabotaging my therapy in spite of my absolutely sincere desire to get well. That scared the hell out of me . . . there was something in me that was dragging me down . . . something I just had no control over."*

[An "aha" experience] *"In reading [an article by Gregory Bateson[9]] I realized my way of dealing with life resembled that of an alcoholic. . . . He pointed out that even believing in a power greater than oneself was an important first step. . . . I could respect Bateson, because this guy was an anthropologist. He was not someone who was engaged on a spiritual scalphunt."*

[On trying to pray] *"I felt like a total fool. . . . My train of thought would often be interrupted . . . I would suddenly not be able to speak at all, or I would have very severe stuttering. I'm usually very verbal, good with words, and finding myself at a loss was unusual. . . . There must be something out there; otherwise why would I be having all these weird reactions?"*

Researcher's summary observations, from study of transcripts: *In Esther's home life, religion was a subject of derision, when it was mentioned at all.*

She recalls her parents as distant—they were older than is common when she was born, her father 52, her mother 35. Esther describes them as "abandoned" and "lost" people, "badly hurt." She reports being closer to her father than to her mother, though the paternal relationship was a

---

9. Gregory Bateson, "The Cybernetics of 'Self': A Theory of Alcoholism," *Psychiatry* 34 (1971): 1-18.

very mixed lot, emotionally. She recalls him as having admirable qualities, but in failing health, both physically and psychologically—he had heart disease, required several operations, and at the same time was depressed and disillusioned over the way his life had played out. ("My father was a splendid ruin," Esther amplified when reading this text.)

Esther "hung around" her father a lot but never felt truly comfortable with him. He treated her as his confidante, a role she now sees as inappropriate in light of their ages and family relationship. She has no memory of being physically or sexually abused, but "had to live with the fear of that," and thinks that she responded emotionally as if she had in fact been abused. [These researcher observations are only meant to be representative, not exhaustive, of gleaning from the wealth of interview and journal material. A more definitive summation is presented near the close of this article.]

II. THE TEXTURE OF PERSONAL WITNESS: DESCRIPTION

Description is the method by which the observer records and relays observations. "Thick" description is advocated by Clifford Geertz,[10] a capturing of rich details of context, process, appearance, and sensation which is only possible with concentrated observation. Thick description is both wide-eyed and narrowly focused; it is complex, and as complete as the subject and researcher can make it without crossing the line into speculation.

Description has in common with observation that it is a process engaged in by both subject and investigator, and as in the prior case, where interviewing is the chief tool of the research, the preponderance of description will come from the subject, and be "taken on faith" by the researcher as genuinely experienced.

From Esther's interview dialogue: *"I got my first dose of unconditional love from Sophia, my mother's best friend. . . . When she visited, she really made an impression. . . . You got a feeling as if you'd suddenly come out of the cold and had a fireplace you could hunker down next to." "Unconsciously I must have been very angry at my parents, but I couldn't even allow myself to face that at the time. . . . I was very inept at school, and managed to keep my self-esteem intact by finding ways to have contempt for the other kids. I was really very insufferable." "In [my neighborhood] the early 1970s and on were rather crazy times. I was very much afraid of the sexuality and the rather rampant drug use that at least the media was emphasizing all the time, and I really didn't want to be an adolescent at all, and I didn't want to be part of the boy-girl scene.*

---

10. Clifford Geertz, "Thick Description: Toward an Interpretive Theory of Culture," in *The Interpretation of Cultures* (New York: Basic Books, 1973), 3-30.

Life at home had left me with enough anxieties, and it also seemed very phony."

[About early church-going] *"This is hazy. I think there was probably something about the atmosphere that one would encounter within Catholic churches when Mom and Grandma and I would get together and go to Mass, either when visiting my grandmother in the Midwest or she would come and visit us. . . . This was all due to the fact that my mother never had the courage to tell my grandmother that she had ditched the Catholic church, so when Grandma came to town, Mom and I would fake it and go to Mass with her, and I was acutely aware that this was dishonest, and it was all very anxiety-arousing. . . . I was terrified if I made one slip Grandma would catch on that Mom and I were fakes and . . . all hell would break loose, and it would be all my fault. . . . Aside from that though, and it's a miracle that this seeped through . . . you've got that absolutely jewel-like light that filters down from the windows, and the candles and the gleams of gold, and the well-developed sense of antici-pation and progression . . . and there's the building to that climax and that moment of tension at the consecration."*

[On relating to her father] *"It would be the equivalent of asking a child to take CPE [clinical pastoral education]. At that time I didn't even have God! I was afraid my father would die, and I also had to worry about getting inappropriate attention from him in a sexual manner. . . . I was not exact-ly happy being a woman, and I was even more unhappy when I found out women get discriminated against in the workplace. I was furious . . . that there was such a thing as sex discrimination because that exposed me to the possibility that you might not get what you want just because you're a woman. . . . And my father also had guns, and knew how to use them . . . down in the basement. I had a lot of fears that he just might misuse those guns at our expense or his own. . . . I found out later from my mother that she had the same fears. I couldn't even allow myself to be consciously afraid for fear that showing fear might actually precipitate the very things I dreaded."*

[On the world scene] *"[In 1980] I was just suddenly aware on a huge scale that failure was possible. It looked like the bad guys were going to win, and I was very much afraid of the Moral Majority, because I had grown up with a tremendous fear of religiously oriented bigotry, and here they were coming to power. . . . I was just terrified that the world could end in a nuclear exchange. . . . What got to me was you could do your very best and it still might not be enough, might be too late. . . . I was just paralyzed . . . suppose we destroy ourselves—is there going to be anyone out there who will even care? That was a heck of question, and I began to wonder about God; I'd been kind of curious anyway off and on over the years. I found myself wondering why I believed in God."*

"There was lots of evangelizing going on at the campus, and there were these people I considered rather ridiculous who would do their hell-fire and brimstone preaching. I had very much grown to detest this. . . . If I were God and had basic common sense, I would want people to hang around me because they enjoyed my company, not because they were afraid of me. . . . Now why do you believe in God, Tenichev? If it's because you're afraid of facing some kind of void, that is just as dishonest and fear-ridden as believing in God because you're terrified of getting your ass roasted in hell. . . . I finally decided that God made sense simply because I couldn't see how the universe could have started from nothing. . . . Theologically, it wasn't very sophisticated. . . . I tried to talk about it to my mother, but she just blew up and told me to talk to my therapist. And I didn't do it because I was afraid my therapist would assume that all of these concerns were pathological. . . . I felt very ashamed and just shut up."

[On finding a spiritual teacher] *"I realized that I was in this prayer business because of very self-interested motives. . . . I realized I needed a teacher, and I identified myself as Jewish so I thought, maybe I should go to a rabbi, but this little voice in my gut said 'no.' . . . I finally was referred to a university chaplain. . . . I didn't even think of ever being a Christian, I was just praying to God, OK? I didn't let myself ponder why I had gone traipsing into a Catholic church, you know, (as if at) random. . . . I said to him, I don't think I can ever be a Christian, but I believe in God, and I need some help in praying. Could you teach me how to pray?"*

[On deciding for Christ] *"I started getting more and more anxious because Christianity just started to look like a burr under the saddle. . . . It was November 11, 1983, Martin Luther's birthday . . . and it suddenly hit me—OK, kid, why are you so anxious? If you're a monotheist or a functional unitarian, you don't have a thing to worry about because that isn't going to get you into hot water with your family, and it's not really going to change your life much. . . . If you want to be a Christian, then you have a lot to be anxious about. You're going to get into hot water with your family, it's going to involve serious commitments, your life's not going to be the same. . . . Then I realized, I was anxious not because I didn't know what I was but because deep down in my heart I did know, and was scared to death of the implications."*

Cameron Snyder's interview dialogue: *"I remember very distinctly your saying at one of our first meetings that Jesus had in some way made an impact—you were living with Jesus. You weren't particularly happy about it . . . you wanted to know some way how to do that. . . . I felt a kind of fascination with the right-up-front Jesus talk, but it wasn't talk . . . it was a real kind of confession, almost, that this is what's going on with me, and I need some help. I need some support."*

*"You presented yourself as somebody with more affinity to the Jewish
tradition than the Christian. . . . That presented a conflict within me. . . .
It put me in the position of saying, I'm not too sure I want to be the one who
leads her to Jesus, if she's going to Jesus, because my purpose is to deep-
en her spiritual life and her own faith, and I'm going to be very cautious
about this Christian stuff."*

III. THE DELICACY OF "FEELING WITH": EMPATHY

Empathy in phenomenological research determines the extent to which an
investigator can experience the world as another person experiences it, and
may be seen as the point at which the investigator's responsibility first out-
weighs the subject's. It is obvious that one's level of empathy directly influences the quality of observation and the content and style of description.
While observation and description may seem to proceed from the perspective of the researcher, it is empathy which should impose the framework
for them: assessing the researcher's point of view as much as possible and
engaging the experiences, thoughts, feelings, and actions of the subject
through the window of that person's perspective. Empathy is never perfect,
of course, but should be no less a goal.

Rambo's interview dialogue: *"This is a kind of blend of therapy research,
psychology of religion research, but also a kind of anthropology research
where you have more than one informant. I hope you can feel comfortable
kind of living on the edge here,without clear definitions. This is going to
be an experiment for all of us." "One of the thoughts that has come to me
is that in class we rarely talk about how one would pastor someone
through the journey in a way that is significant and helpful." "The truth
is, not everyone can be altruistic and strong and courageous in every situation, and it's nice to hear stories of when people succeed . . . and it's nice
to be reminded that other people fall off the wagon." "Your talk about
wanting a second conversion, or an intensification—it seems to me that's
one thing we're doing, in a way." "One of the things I find striking is
that you talk slower, you are so articulate, that there is a sense of very deep
and profound feeling. . . . No wonder you sometimes need to find dis-
tractions when the feelings are so powerful and genuinely awesome."*

Snyder's interview dialogue: *"I was a little off balance. . . . I would
have much rather worked with you in the framework of the Jewish faith and
not crossed over, but as I remember your persistent interest . . . it was a
sense of obligation—she's brought this up, and if Jesus is leading her,
what am I going to do about that? . . . I said, finally, I'll see where the Spirit
is leading." "It almost seems like what gets to you has to get through the
lives of other people first, people in the past." "A lot of people go back to
square one and they have no perception, no concern about it. . . . You're
disappointed, you're angry because you've got a real struggle there. . . .*

There have been times when you've been about ready to throw in the towel: 'If this is what the Christian life is all about, then I don't want it, I'm going to escape, I'm not going to do anything,' but you haven't allowed yourself to do that."

IV. A PARTNERSHIP OF DEDUCTION: UNDERSTANDING

Empathy also promotes understanding, which is essential to the notion of studying conversion holistically. Understanding involves grasping the world-view, cognitive experience, and relational systems of the people one is studying, utilizing *their* orientation as much as possible in reporting the phenomena of their history. Understanding deepens empathy; they richen and reinforce each other.

Esther's interview dialogue: *"I hadn't yet faced the fact that I wanted to be a Catholic, and a week later I realized that's what I wanted to be. That really scared the hell out of me, because I knew that was going to put me on a collision course [with my family], and I also wasn't terribly crazy about some of the things the Vatican does. . . . Part of me was relieved to know at least where I stood, but 75 percent of me was scared to death and rather resentful. I remember asking God, why couldn't you make me want to be a Quaker? . . . Why does it have to be the one denominational choice that's going to put me in a world of shit? I think that's why it had to be that—psychologically I was still an extension of my family. I had never had an adolescence. Some family therapist once wrote that strong circuits require even stronger circuit breakers, and I needed a very strong circuit breaker. Nothing but the strongest medicine would have done it. So God went ahead and prescribed castor oil."*

[On social activism] *"I was waking up as a peace activist at the same time I was taking formal instruction. . . . In some ways I think there were some problems for me. . . . At the very beginning, my reasons for starting to go to church, to pray, were very simple. . . . I think that pursuing the activism at the same time as formal instruction in Catholicism got me distracted from Christ. . . . I've done a lot of peace work for what I thought were Christian reasons, but I've been very prone to burn-out . . . to get angry at people when they act human . . . to be very hard on myself and get much too wrapped up in works righteousness." "You know, a life of good works can become just as much a crummy rat race as working at Rockwell or IBM."*

[On changed behavior] *"I don't have to worry too much about my parents anymore [but] I still get crabby, I still get tired all the time, and I'm still prone to burn-out. . . . I'm rather ashamed that I continue to be so self-centered." "There are a lot of things that I can't let pass, that I was able to blow off before the conversion. It doesn't mean I behave in such a ter-*

ribly virtuous manner, but at least where I continue to sin I don't enjoy it so much." "You have to think about what kind of example you may be presenting. Are you behaving in a way that might make Christ or Christianity look bad to people who are vulnerable and who might misunderstand?" "It's been incredibly difficult for me to begin to understand that I can't do this as a Lone Ranger, and I'm really not happy that the Christian life can't be lived by a loner." "[In our family] we didn't have a lot of recognition that to be a human being was to be interdependent with others. We were socially very isolated, and it was literally a revelation to me when I began going to church . . . started confiding in Cameron . . . in other friends. . . . What an incredible thing it is when you finally dare to tell people what's really going on with you and give them a chance to respond."

Snyder's interview dialogue: *"This isn't about being a budding Christian, it's like you were Jacob and had come back and said, I've wrestled with somebody at the bank of the Jordan and I have to know who this person is." "Symbolically, some people carry Bibles. Sometimes I've seen you carry a Bible, too, or other books, but this [journal] is some form of religious expression. I remember Henri Nouwen saying 'this is one of the ways I cultivate my own spiritual life, by writing.' I think it's a spiritual discipline with you."*

Rambo's interview dialogue: *"We keep coming back to your being sixteen. The turning point of your father's death, the beginning of writing the journal,* A Man For All Seasons—*sixteen was a very crucial turning point, and it was framed somewhat as a preparation for what came later." "It seems to me that there are two things: causation, and a lot of people I've talked to who have been converted have been marginalized to start with—in your case, Esther, with a Jewish father and a Catholic mother who identified with Judaism, with a difficult childhood, etc. Or there are people who, through conversion, or the process that leads to conversion, become marginalized, so they see the world differently. It takes a lot of energy to do that, because you're spitting against the wind. It's hard to sustain without a community; it's an alternate reality of sorts."*

V. KEEPING FAITH WITH THE PROCESS: INTERPRETATION

Interpretation should not emerge before the previous activities are completed with integrity. Interpretation makes the process and content of conversion more fully understandable in terms of the scholar's, as opposed to the subject's, frame of reference. It is important that the scholar recognize, be alert to, even deliberately cultivate a shift of perspective from that of the convert to that of the scholar, a viewpoint which is presumed to be valuable but is not intrinsically superior to the one studied.

Rambo's interview dialogue: *"To me the word narcissism is more like saying you have diabetes, that you're a diabetic, rather than you have a case of intentional selfishness." "What else is conversion about . . . if God isn't working with our brokenness, our narcissism, whatever it is we've got, because it's not just an intellectual exercise." "In a way it seems to me it can be rather noble [to admit we have our own needs and motives in ministry, in healing professions], because it's dealing directly with the profound conundrum of our lives. A lot of people do it destructively, but a lot do it in ways that really engage the issues and help fellow strugglers. Psychoanalysis cannot fill the void—maybe God can, or help us begin working on it. It's a burden too heavy for another human being to take alone. That's why we need community to bolster us."*

Snyder's interview dialogue: *"There's a kind of way in which [Esther's] journal is a substitute, something that is written down as if it would pass away were it not written down. I've never really understood that, and I've not always been easy with it. . . . It's got its uses and abuses." "Going back to Sir Thomas More, I want to ask what was so fascinating about a guy who said no to everybody and was willing to die? You couldn't put that down. . . . You know, it certainly prefigured the crucifixion, or reflected the crucifixion. . . . You've always been struggling with what I see as a command of Jesus to let your life go so that you can live; 'don't sweat it, there's something higher than life itself.' Here is More, a historical character—he wasn't Jesus, because that was too hot to handle at the time— but calling you right into Christianity. You're being called to live that life, and that's what you came here for, to find out how it was to live the life and have some support doing that."*

"When you first convert, there's a kind of enthusiasm. . . . You set for yourself very high standards . . . a part of you really believes you can just be living like that. . . . Then after you fall on your face five or six times, you begin to think either I'm not a Christian or something else is going on here that I need to address. . . . What you go through is called a second conversion: I can fail, I can be narcissistic, I can be selfish, I can be less than I want to be and still be a Christian because I have some apprehension of God's love and forgiveness."

Esther's interview dialogue: *"Instead of good versus evil, I like to think of certain acts being sacramental in that they reveal God, reveal grace, reward trust, instead of being antisacramental actions that punish people for trusting, for living, that hide God, that make God seem absurd rather than a friend and leader." "It makes living a lot different when you see each day as an opportunity to go out there on a detective hunt and at least try to look for some signs of grace here and there. I think a very big part of Christianity is trying to make a commitment. . . . This is a world that would, in its distorted way, distract us from God, from grace,* *and get us to value things that are side issues. I think a very big part of being a Christian is resisting that gravitation." "In some ways being a Christian can actually expose you to stress rather than alleviate it, because you have to take evil seriously . . . deal with the brute reality of death . . . face your own human finitude. . . . Resurrection is just a very pleasant fairy story if you don't have the courage to face that body on the cross. . . . Being Christian means living in tension, because you're simultaneously given a vision of just how wonderful a thing a God-saturated world really can be, and made brutally aware of the fact that it hasn't happened yet."*

VI. KEEPING FAITH WITH THE AUDIENCE: EXPLANATION

Explanation is the last procedure that may occur in conversion study, a systematic application of still another frame of reference that is even further removed from the experiential world of the convert. It is technically *not* a part of phenomenology, but an approach that might build on phenomenology. As used in this text, explanation is the application of theories from other disciplines (the perspectives of other windows) to the subject's experiential phenomena to see what other forms of sense or order might arise from them. Ideally, explanation is tentative, respectful, subtle.

Interpretation and explanation are closely related, but in my opinion, interpretation is closer in spirit to the humanistic viewpoints of religious studies, history, and theology. Explanation tends more to the analytical, critical, and reductionist attitudes of the social sciences. Explanatory models tend to be more secular and demanding of logic and proof, less amenable to dimensions of mystery, emotion, inspiration, and spiritual effect.

Snyder's interview dialogue: *"Sartre had a student once who presented an ethical problem. Sartre asked, What do you want me to say? You already know the answer. The student said, I came to you for your insight, and Sartre responded, But you know how I am. You wouldn't have come here unless you wanted to hear the answer you knew I was going to give."* [Esther's reaction: *"You don't go to the poodle store to buy a cat."*] *"You see what the religious situation is all about from the point of view not of being on the mountaintop, but being in the valley, knowing that you don't have the power, finally, to protect yourself, to become like Christ or whatever, and that you must ask God's mercy. . . . It's a matter of indirection, not direction. Not, there's a goal here and here I am climbing the mountain, but rather, I'm slipping back, and I know I'm slipping back, and I have some concern but not tremendous concern; I'm not beating up on myself."*

Rambo's interview dialogue: *"Some of the lines in these interviews could have come right out of Alice Miller,*[11]*— of killing a part of oneself*

11. Alice Miller, *The Drama of the Gifted Child*, trans. Ruth Ward (New York: Basic Books, 1981).

*in order to be loved, or maybe, in order not to be hated. The cup of life, in
terms of nourishment, just got a few drops." "My trouble with [the film]*
The Last Temptation of Christ *is that it seems to me that being crucified
is quite easy in comparison to raising a family. You have five or six hours
of pain and suffering, whereas those who raise families have forty or fifty
years, and you don't become a hero to anybody." "I want to get back to
the point of [conversion]—instead of using the word 'conversion' I'm
thinking of always using 'converting.' . . . It seems to me that it's ongoing,
and that if it stops, it's no longer conversion. It's sort of like a plant that
grew but at some point died. The water never kept flowing into the roots
so it could keep growing and changing."*

Esther's interview dialogue: *"It became very important when I learned
the concept of coming out of the closet. Anytime you are made to feel
radically ashamed of who you are, that's a closet. The first step is admitting, hey! that's what I am; the next step is admitting to some very trusted others—widening the circle of risk." "T. S. Eliot has a phrase in one
of the Quartets: The work of the poet consists of making raids on the
inarticulate with equipment that's always breaking down . . . and when you
are able to find words to grasp an experience, the experience has passed
and is no longer an immediate and living thing. You can only conquer
an experience in the retrospective."*

It may certainly be charged that there is a degree of fuzziness, of arbi-
trariness, in the assignment of snippets of dialogue to one or another category
of process. The point is, surely, that one builds a richer and more rounded
appreciation and understanding of experience as the wealth of material accu-
mulates. I think it also fair to say that, as the above recitals demonstrate,
the more nearly equal the level of discourse between participants, the better
the resultant material is likely to be.

The Phenomenologist as Person

From the above recitals, one might conclude that phenomenology is an
exacting but orderly research process. Exacting, yes; orderly, no. Indeed,
as suggested earlier, the "messiness" and disordered complexity of a study
may be directly proportional to the degree of effort one makes to cover all
bases, to be thorough, methodical, and exacting. One's sense of obligation,
of fairness to the subject, and one's determination to be thorough build up ever
more layers of knotted experience into a huge tangle that eventually seems
impossible to unravel.

For instance, in order to do phenomenological research, one must be willing and able to set aside one's own theological position. Theological objectivity, of course, does not exist in any pure, unadulterated form, but I do
believe that a student of conversion can recognize his or her own assumptions
and beliefs and guard as much as humanly possible against one's own
demands for theological "correctness." In other words, a scholar must sus-

pend his or her own theological framework so as to be open to what is experienced by the convert/subject. This chapter's focus on a woman who converts to Catholicism might seem objectionable to those Protestant Christians whose beliefs deny the validity of such a conversion. Setting aside one's own biases is clearly very difficult but is just as clearly necessary.

I grew up in the Church of Christ,[12] which promotes very strong theological beliefs, rejecting Catholicism outright as not "biblical," in some cases even identifying it with the "anti-Christ." I do not currently embrace those assumptions, but I am nevertheless conscious of residual anti-Catholic bias which could, and probably does, shape my interpretation of the Roman Catholic church. I have a hard time with Catholic positions on the authority of the pope, severe limitations on the role of women, theology of the Virgin Mary, and so on.

I am not proud to admit such bias, but I am convinced that exposure of such bias is essential for anything so subject to variability as phenomenological study. Acknowledging conscious biases alerts one to the filters which may distort perception and prompts recognition that there are probably still more unconscious biases at work. Recognition of bias is one way of refining a more objective approach, so that one might do the best possible phenomenological analysis. Moreover, articulating one's own bias is salutary in an enterprise which will be read, analyzed, and evaluated by others.

Another major issue in phenomenological research is the degree to which one can actually find, describe, and reproduce original experience and the extent to which the experience is "pure." Eugene Gallagher, in his book, *Expectation and Experience*,[13] argues that just applying the term "conversion" to a particular experience or constellation of experiences is itself an act of interpretation. Gallagher argues that a person's theological context shapes the nature of experience and also provides criteria by which a person would apply the label "conversion" to a particular experience.

Is there such a thing as raw or pure experience? I personally doubt it. All human experience is formed within the matrix of a person's own history, community, culture, society, and personality. It is produced by the confluence of people, expectations, forces, and institutions, an almost infinite amalgam of pressures. As people live and move at the center of the vortex, they nevertheless experience their lives as an ongoing parade of phenomena: Think of

---

12. For an excellent historical perspective on the Churches of Christ and other "primitivist" denominations, see Richard T. Hughes and C. Leonard Allen, *Illusions of Innocence: Protestant Primitivism in America, 1630-1875* (Chicago: University of Chicago Press, 1988) and Richard T. Hughes, ed., *The American Quest for the Primitive Church* (Urbana and Chicago: University of Illinois Press, 1988). For "insider" critique of the Churches of Christ, see Allen and Hughes, *Discovering Our Roots: The Ancestry of Churches of Christ* (Abilene: Abilene Christian University Press, 1988) and C. Leonard Allen, Richard T. Hughes, and Michael R. Weed, *The Worldly Church: A Call for Biblical Renewal* (Abilene: Abilene Christian University Press, 1988).

13. Eugene V. Gallagher, *Expectation and Experience: Explaining Religious Conversion* (Atlanta: Scholar's Press, 1990).

them, if you will, as pictures, pages, or chapters in a book, scenes in a play or film. Phenomenology does not aim at discovering something that does not exist but at uncovering, describing, and articulating as well as possible what is experienced by an individual.

Braving the Waters of Self-Disclosure

Most scholars are reluctant to reveal much of their personal lives. In fact, the more "scientific" a researcher claims to be, the more he or she is apt to consider intrusion of personal material a detriment to the value of one's research. I do not necessarily disagree but rather believe that self-disclosure is a potential servant of and contributor to "scientific" objectivity. Moreover, I believe that such revelation is vital to the task of so malleable a process as phenomenology. Unless the phenomenologist is keenly aware of his or her own assumptions, methods, values, and goals, the phenomenologist cannot pretend to the capacity to see, articulate, interpret, and clarify what is distinctive about someone else's experience. To be sure, no researcher can attain perfect, detached objectivity, but the aspiration must be present and the attempt evident to keep trust with one's audience.

The following personal background is an example of what I believe needs to be mined by phenomenologists from their own history and conditioning and also exposed to the scrutiny of colleagues and others if one seeks a high level of objectivity.

Growing up in the Churches of Christ, an "exclusivist" denomination (believing only its own adherents can achieve salvation), I was taught that the only way to be a "true" Christian was to follow the precepts found in the "divinely inspired" New Testament; to be "saved" arose out of hearing the gospel in a receptive manner, acknowledging one's sinful condition, repenting, confessing (professing belief in) Christ as both son of God and savior, and being baptized by total immersion. Thereafter, the "new" Christian would participate regularly in church attendance, prayer, and Bible study in addition to living as much as possible in accordance with God's will and law. The emphasis throughout was obtaining Bible knowledge and altering one's behavior to conform to what is considered characteristic of a good Christian life. Sinful temptation abounded, and rigorous efforts were required to grow into a mature Christian. Failure to do so was directly attributable to personal weakness or insufficient effort in living the strict requirements of a faithful life.

Some time in 1956 or 1957, when I was thirteen or fourteen years old, I was baptized at the Church of Christ in Comanche, Texas. Church of Christ preachers emphasized the necessity of a "conviction of sin" for the conversion process to be initiated—a personal sense of a sinful self and acute need for salvation. I had no doubt that my cursing, masturbation, laziness, and other "sins" were repulsive in the eyes of God. I sensed God's judgment and had a vivid conception of eternal damnation for those who rejected the commandments of a holy God. God's wrath was portrayed in sermons and hymns at church, but the grace of God was also envisioned for those who were obedient to proscriptions and prescriptions of the Bible.

I remember thinking constantly about these issues. I also remember telling my father about my desire to be saved—an awkward conversation because, even though *he* believed he had been saved by a teenage conversion at a Southern Baptist revival meeting, he had never been active in church, and, given the exclusivist approach of the Churches of Christ, he was not considered a "real" Christian by my mother or me, or anyone in our congregation. (As with Esther, and no doubt many others, the "family sense" of religion could be very isolating.) Still, I wanted him to be aware of my intentions. He didn't say much, but encouraged me to do whatever I thought was right. After the event, I told him I had been baptized, and he expressed some dismay that he had not been present. This took me by surprise: I had assumed that he didn't want anything to do with church for any reason (on the rare occasions when he had attended, he was targeted by other members for persuasion to convert). I was chagrined that I had misread his wishes, and felt bad for a long time that he did not have the opportunity to attend my baptism.

As I look back on the experience, I still feel some guilt for not including my father. I also feel some anger at him for not introducing any critical edge to my religious life in that denomination and possibly "saving" me from the rigid grip of the Churches of Christ. Aside from the misunderstanding with my father, what I remember most was the sense of heaviness of sin and a subsequent sense of lifting of the burden after baptism. My baptism *was* my conversion, in the eyes of the Church of Christ. In the denominational view, it was the crucial turning point, the mandatory ritual for inclusion in the Body of Christ and access to the saving blood of Jesus. An ontological transformation was asserted in the event of baptism. I was taught by the church that, being baptized into Christ, I now had real hope of heaven for the first time.

The overall assumption was that God's action was evidenced in the "plan for salvation," which made deliverance available in exchange for obeying the rules. There was no sense of God being involved in the actual conversion process—human agency was responsible for conveying the message, informing the potential convert of what was expected, and supplying encouragement that would help persuade a person to do what was right. There was scant sense of divine agency or intervention beyond the initial authorship of the "plan." In the Churches of Christ, God was (is?) seen as a being who created the world and redeemed it through Jesus Christ, and continues to make salvation available through the Bible and the church, but who does not *directly* touch peoples' lives.

That point of view, I think, contributes to a human sciences perspective on my part. I can easily see human activity in the conversion process but am less inclined to seek or discover the mysterious or supernatural. My conditioning makes it easy for me to recognize the "natural" elements in a conversion history but probably less inclined to attribute actions, experiences, or events to the direct intervention of God or the Holy Spirit. It is also probable that, as a person with an exclusivist conditioning, I am able to bring a sense of distance and detachment to the study of other traditions, while paying a certain price in empathy.

Layered over my small town, rural Texas, Churches of Christ background is my subsequent socialization at Yale University and University of Chicago Divinity Schools. From those institutions, with their learned professors, broad spectrum of students, and massive resources of books and classroom opportunities, I was both encouraged and required (and I relished the regimen) to delve into psychology, the history of religions, hermeneutics, anthropology, and sociology on top of my earlier college education in the Bible.

My approach to phenomenology can be characterized by acknowledgement that it is informed by field work methodology of anthropology, institutional analysis, the sociology of knowledge, and the comparative approach from the history of religions. Underlying each of these approaches is the primacy of seeking out insofar as possible what actually happened, and the subsequent intricacy of interpretation, both by the experiencer and the researcher. Hermeneutics is thus foundational to my enterprise.

The Subject as Phenomenologist

If it is difficult for a trained and practiced investigator to be aware of and account for personal background, conditioning, presumption, and bias in the process of phenomenology, it is customarily far more difficult for the subject. At least partly for that reason, a phenomenological study proceeds on the "given" that the subject's reports of observation and experience and description, and the subject's interpretations, valuations, and analyses of such reports, will be taken pretty much at face value, as stated above. That does not mean the researcher will not apply critical faculties to the material—indeed, that is the crucial shift which is expected, and should be evident, in the stages of interpretation and explanation detailed above.

Still, the researcher must also be aware that the subject is undergoing his or her own phenomenological journey (as many people do informally, either at various important junctures of their lives or on a more or less continuing basis) while the study is in progress. The investigator should never lose sight of the distinction between observations, descriptions, interpretations, and evaluations which are presented by the subject and those which are the result of analysis by and reflections of the investigator.

James Beckford,[14] Bryan Taylor,[15] and other researchers, especially in the field of sociology of religion, have noted that the conversion researcher is not dealing with pure experience, but with experience as it is reported by a person *after* the event. Beckford and Taylor have shown how such reporting is shaped by a person's ideological orientation and institutional constraints.

---

14. James Beckford, "Accounting for Conversion," *British Journal of Sociology* 29 (1978): 249-62.

15. Bryan Taylor, "Conversion and Cognition," *Social Compass* 23 (1976): 5-22, and "Recollections and Membership: Converts' Talk and the Ratiocination of Commonality," *Sociology* 12 (1978): 316-24.

Other shaping factors include the subject's susceptibility to the opinions of others, capacity for self-criticism, openness to differing viewpoints and interpretations, and conscious or unconscious self-image.

Seven Levels of Complexity and Distance

Perhaps the single most important potential impediment to phenomenological enterprise is retrospective reinterpretation—altering one's perception of experience as time and reflection distance one from the "nowness" of experience. As with Esther's case study, most phenomenological research in the human sciences is based on interviews of people and consists mostly of self-reportage. Unless the subject has comprehensive diaries, annotated appointment calendars, or some other form of recording events and experiences as they happen, the researcher is dependent upon the subject's memory of an event.

Even when journals or other memory aids exist to bolster the record, however, the researcher must be wary of assuming that they are complete, completely "true" to the facts of an event, or completely "faithful" to the experience of an event. It is rare for a personal record to be created in the midst of experience; more commonly, such a record is (as Wordsworth said of poetry) "emotion recollected in tranquility." The richest, most detailed journals are especially likely to be produced after the fact and are saturated with the benefit of subsequent reaction, mental and emotional churning, reflection, analysis, and interpretation. The veracity of what is set down on a page, in relation to "objective" experience of an event, depends in large measure on the ability of the diarist to be (first) ruthlessly frank and (second) simultaneously engaged in and uncommonly distanced from an experience, even as it happens.

With the intervening passage of time, influence of other persons, or adjustment of attitude and values by the person who is self-reporting, there is further potential for the "account" of an event to differ from the "experience" of that event. Steps in this process are summarized in Table 1.

Theory, Distortion, and Community of Discourse

One of the most perplexing problems in phenomenological studies is the use of theory in the selection process of research. Whatever one's intentions, it is virtually impossible for any researcher to be totally objective (as it is also for the subject) in his or her perception of reality. As you read even direct quotations from the case study of Esther, for instance, you may detect ways in which my own bias concerning the nature of personal relationships and, some might say, even my psychodynamic orientation, shape the sort of questions I ask (or do not ask) and the sorts of things I am particularly looking for or alert to in her conversion report. An excellent example is the use of Chana Ullman's interview protocol in the classroom setting which initiated this study. Ullman's orientation is noticeably informed by psychoanalysis and object relations theory; hence, many questions concern important relationships with family members and other significant figures in one's life.

Theory can both distort the phenomenological process and illuminate facets of the experience. In the case of psychodynamic factors, the phenomenologist can be alert to the personal dimension in ways that might not be possible for someone whose primary orientation is theological. Conversely, theological orientation can disclose specifically religious and/or spiritual factors that might be glossed over or missed entirely by one whose framework is chiefly psychological or sociological.

For these reasons, I believe the task of phenomenology should always involve a "community of discourse." Nothing should be ruled out of the discussion. Description of the conversion experience should be as detailed as possible and ideally the convert subject should be available to scholars with points of view differing from the primary researcher. What I advocate is a kind of team effort in phenomenology, an approach so atypical and disregarded to date that the inclusion of my subject's spiritual director in Esther's interviews can be viewed as distinctive, even radical, while to me it seems a rather modest approach to the ideal. Inclusion of the convert herself in the process—right up to the moment of finalized manuscript—is also atypical of phenomenological research to date, but in my opinion is highly to be recommended.

The advantage of the community of discourse study type is its greater richness, complexity, and completeness of data (though completeness, like objectivity, should be acknowledged as a never-to-be-achieved ideal). The disadvantage is that it adds to the messiness factor. Paul Pruyser[16] states that one of the contributions of what he calls a clinical approach to the psychology of religion is that it captures well the messiness of the human predicament—and I agree. In fact, I regard phenomenology as a form of "clinical" study of religion. In other words, real human beings are far more complex, messy, and resistant to reduction and simplification than any of our theories so far either admit or are capable of taking into account.

One thing that did occur in the study of Esther bears noting because it should have been anticipated as a theoretical possibility and wasn't. There was a kind of evolution of the interview process from an originally fairly strict focus on the experiences (the phenomena) of Esther's conversion, to an exploration on an almost psychotherapeutic level (there being room for some confusion as to which party was the "client"), of the interpersonal dynamics operating between Esther, Cameron, and myself. As the later interviews progressed, there was a subtle but detectable shift from observation, description, interpretation, and explanation, to what my colleague Reh, in his close examination of the transcripts, felt was a tendency toward justification and defensiveness in reportage and commentary by the participants.

It may be that there is a "natural" optimum length of such an interview process before it begins to lose focus; it may be that diversion is just another factor that a skilled researcher must be alert for, guard against, and take into

---

16. Paul Pruyser, "Where Do We Go From Here? Scenarios for the Psychology of Religion," *Journal for the Scientific Study of Religion* 26 (1987): 173-81.

account if it appears. It may be that this kind of deterioration is less likely to develop in a study team of greater numbers, where personal dynamics involving the subject might be diluted; it is also possible that greater numbers might accelerate or intensify the deterioration. Without more experience in using a community of discourse model (and this was only a rough approximation), I cannot say if this is an inevitable further "messiness" inherent in the model. It did provide a few uncomfortable moments for each of the participants, especially in recognizing it in hindsight. This is not necessarily a bad thing, but perhaps simply not necessary, once we learn more about how best to employ the model.

The Phenomena of Esther's Experience

It is the degree to which a researcher reduces the tangle and finds a thread of continuity through the maze which may determine the end value of the exercise. There is, hypothetically, a "Gordian knot" approach, by which the researcher wields his or her own theoretical or theological bias like a sword, reducing the intricacies of the individual study to irrelevant shreds before the "truth" of the researcher's presuppositions. (Theological bias or insistence on psychotherapeutic perspective, for example, might lead one to state that Esther never experienced religious conversion at all, but merely went through the motions, ultimately unsuccessful, of trying to fill anxious voids in her psyche. I would consider this presumptuous and dishonoring the complexity of the material.) Another possibility is the bulldozer approach, by which complications are explained away, ignored, or melded into a formula by such gross over-simplification that once again the study's individuality becomes meaningless. (One might say Esther found a need for and a recognition of God, was attracted by exposure and example to Roman Catholicism, became disillusioned by its inability to be her ultimate answer, and continues her search. I find that bland, a poor representation of the complexity of the subject's experience, and virtually useless.)

What, then, shall we enumerate as phenomena of Esther's conversion experience?*

As a child, Esther received "messages" from her parents that religion was of dubious, if any, value. Both parents were "fall-aways" from the faith traditions of their families, the father from Judaic worship and practice, the mother from Roman Catholicism. At the same time, she learned from her mother that one shouldn't rock the boat in which significant others are riding; when visiting or being visited by her maternal grandmother, Esther's mother accompanied grandmother to Mass and took Esther along. The need to "fake" familiarity with strange rituals, and the anxiety that she would be found out, combined to cause stomach pains whenever she went to church. Other than on these occasions, religion was always a kind of *eminence grise*,

---

* It should be understood that any enumeration of phenomena (as experiences or events in another's life process) is somewhat arbitrary, both in the number, the mode of expression, and the degree of breakdown or detail recited for each "phenomenon."

a kind of background shadow of unresolved—and undiscussed—issues.

Having married into a Jewish family tree that gave much lip service to its traditions, Esther's mother did her best to fit in, to the extent of trying to keep kosher for one relative who professed that lifestyle, only to discover that practice did not live up to profession. The Jewish influence on Esther was primarily sociological, not spiritual, and Esther came to regard the Jewish side of her family as somewhat hypocritical.

In what she perceived as a cold and lonely home, Esther received many conditioning messages that kept her from a normally self-involved, expansive, and exploratory childhood, that treated her as a little adult and demanded from her forms of behavior beyond her years (as therapeutic confidante to her father, as long-suffering co-conspirator with her mother), and taught her not to express her true feelings, not to question the words or worlds of others, not to be different in any way that could be interpreted as challenging to the family's "values." All of this left her somewhat socially stunted and inept, a loner, lonely, and alone. [The reader should appreciate that those three words carry very different freight.]

Esther recalls as her first experience of unconditional love the exposure to one of her mother's closest friends, a Jewish woman who, though not a frequent presence, impressed Esther in a deep and lasting way—so much so that to this day Esther refers to that kind of interpersonal warmth as "the Sophia factor." She also reports admiring, as she grew up, persons who took risks for their beliefs and values, e.g., civil rights workers, but indicates she had difficulty actively emulating them. Those views, however, are likely to have helped nudge her toward peace activism and civil disobedience in her adult life.

As early as sixteen, "God" was sufficiently a presence in Esther's life (though the family discouraged religion) for her to appeal to the deity as her father lay dying. The "bargain" that she wished to strike at that time did not turn in her favor, yet there is no conclusive evidence that this experience deferred or altered her later attraction to Christianity. She had a broad-ranging, voracious appetite for books, films, even television when they helped her address personal concerns and suggested possible ways of life that met her needs; when she couldn't muster will, energy, or courage to embody or act them out at the time, they often saturated her consciousness, stuck in her awareness, and influenced her future development. She cites *A Man for All Seasons,* Robert Bolt's film treatment of Sir Thomas More; Aldous Huxley's biography of religious struggle, *Grey Eminence;* and *The Colloquies* of Erasmus. She attributes her college major in psychology to her early fascination with More, and the question of how one can maintain commitment, follow conscience, in spite of tremendous pressure to the contrary.

Esther grew up "gun-shy" of overt professions of religiosity, especially the active evangelism which she encountered on her college campus (she called it "scalp-hunting"), and the ministries of televangelists. Later she was wary of "cults" which flourished in California and received much publicity. She grew to value "scientific" attitudes above "religious" ones, demanding clarity, accuracy, and factual consistency in her life, her studies, and her relationships. While seeing herself as rigorously "scientific," however, she turned her studies toward areas of less certitude, e.g., psychology. She admits that all the while, from childhood to adolescence to young adulthood, she was obsessed with what might be called the "what if?" of religion, and the conviction that there must be "someone [God?] out there."

That she was uncomfortable and confused and at a loss for how to deal with conflicting attitudes, pressures, and attractions in her self and her life, and recognized her discomfiture, is shown by her seeking counseling while yet in college and continuing therapy through a succession of different professionals. She had a particularly stressful time nearing her last year in college when America failed in an attempt to rescue hostages in Iran, Reagan seemed a shoo-in to become the next president, there was much media coverage of the Moral Majority, and the U.S. seemed to be swamped by foreign policy problems. That period, she reports, made her aware of the extent to which failure was possible on the global, national, and personal scales.

Esther took what might be labeled her first real step toward her own life, her individuation from her family, when she moved away from her home community to do graduate study. However, she eventually found herself hating her graduate program and afraid to admit it might be a mistake, conscious for the first time that her ambition to be a "hot-shot" scientist might not work out. Anxiety increased, and she realized at the same time that her counseling wasn't helping, that in fact, she seemed somehow to be sabotaging both her academic program and her therapy.

Esther's fear coincided with a quandary about religion, but she was impressed by an article on mindsets and lifestyles of typical alcoholics (by a "scientist," so it was all right) to regard herself, an abstainer, as having problems of a similar nature which particularly manifested themselves, she believed, in self-sabotage. She was attracted by the potential value in acknowledging and surrendering to a "higher power," as described in the 12-Step Program of Alcoholics Anonymous. She felt an attraction toward prayer as a method of reaching out to God, but was unsure how to go about it. Warily, she sought feedback from friends known to her to be Christians and was given a copy of Henri Nouwen's book *With Open Hands*. She began to try to pray regularly, but felt even more the need for a spiritual teacher of some sort. She wrote to a campus chaplain whom she knew of from news reports on protest activities. That person had just moved out of the Bay Area, however, but responded warmly, referring Esther to her successor, with whom Esther began regular dialogue, first about prayer and then an expanding circle of "Christian" issues.

What might be considered a turning point occurred during a Sunday walk when Esther felt moved to visit a church. First she went to a Russian orthodox cathedral, and was turned away for not being properly dressed. Walking on, she found herself in front of a Catholic church, and conceded that this was the experience that was drawing her. She was surprised but also pleased that she no longer reacted with stomach pains, and she retained a memory, after ten to fifteen years lapse, for something like 75 percent of the content of the Mass. She also recalled a sense of awe and mystery felt as a child in Catholic churches, an atmosphere of stained glass light, candles, gleams of gold and incense—an atmosphere of the numinous.

Esther began to read the New Testament and the Psalms, along with other spiritual writings. She felt a desire to visit church again, tried different denominations, and before long was attending Roman Catholic Mass on a regular basis. On November 11, 1983 (she remembers it as Martin Luther's birthday), she says she consciously realized and admitted to herself that she wanted to be a Christian, and she identifies that as her major turning point. She was still riddled with anxiety, unresolved questions and fear, but chose the costs of becoming a Christian over the costs of the status quo.

Esther "came out" to her mother about her desire for conversion over Thanksgiving 1983. There was some disgust and resistance from her mother, some anger and mild argumentation, but the decision was accepted fairly easily. Esther was warned, however, that she should take care not to put her mother at odds with the rest of the family (the Jewish side—the maternal Christian background was left behind, both geographically and chronologically). Esther's acceptance of the idea of conversion at first had been powerfully countered by feelings that such a step constituted rebellion and challenge to her family (particularly her mother) and would precipitate anger and disapproval that she was not sure she could handle. Even after the revelation was accomplished, Esther reported feeling hurt, loneliness, guilt, and alienation with respect to her mother. She identified very strongly, however, with an article she read about this time concerning difficulties gay and lesbian people have coming out of the closet. Coming out as a Christian seemed to involve the same degree of difficulty for her, though she knew she did not face violent assault, legal discrimination, or exposure to fatal disease just for being a Catholic, and she was inspired by the coping and even celebrating she saw in the gay community.

Though she had misgivings about institutional Roman Catholicism, she was encouraged by the direction taken by and subsequent fallout from Vatican II. She felt more attracted to it than to any other form of communal religion, and she had become convinced that true faith must be practiced in company with others, in a community of like values and support. By late 1983, she regarded her regular attendance at Mass and involvement in other church activities, plus her ongoing study with her spiritual director, as informal preparation for conversion; in 1984 she began inquiry classes, took formal RCIA classes (Rite of Christian Initiation for Adults), and in 1985 was baptized a Roman Catholic.

Concurrently, she was learning from her mentor about his experiences of faith put into practice in peace demonstrations and acts of civil disobedience. She took training in nonviolent resistance and ultimately began participating in protests—some in the company of her spiritual advisor and some on her own. This activity she recalls as sometimes feeling like distraction from a concentration on faith building, and also the possible cause of burnout feelings. Neither conversion nor baptism ended her personal struggles, and she is candid about Christianity not being an overnight cure for everything difficult in her life. She has had concerns about personal motivation and "pay-offs" for activism and volunteer work, including some two years of service at a Catholic charity.

Feeling a need for renewed focus on faith, Esther enrolled as a graduate student at seminary, continued her involvement in social activism and explored an ongoing need for regular company of committed Christians. Except for a self-imposed six-month hiatus in 1989, she also continued meeting with her spiritual director every two to three weeks, a practice of some eight years.

Esther confesses to ongoing anger with God, with the way the world is created—that some people have a much more difficult time surviving, both in the physical and the psychological and spiritual senses, and that God gives humans the freedom to do terrible things to each other. She finds it hard to be a Catholic today and says she has "tried" twice to leave the church. She worries that she is "complicit with an institution that's riddled with structural sin," but sticks it out because no other community of faith makes as much room for human eccentricities.

"The rock of my faith," she declares at the end of the first interview, "is Jesus Christ, not the hierarchy." Her bottom line by the time of the last interview, seven months later, is that her Christian identity has begun to seem phony. She wonders if her life and behavior are significantly different than they would have been without conversion. "I still am a Christian," she says at one point; "I'm not sure why." In the next sentence she asserts, "I can't call myself a Christian, but I can call myself a wanna-be Christian." Her summation? "Let's just say the conversion saga continues."

The phenomenological challenge to "go to the things themselves" and take into account the life experiences of the convert demands great effort from the scholar. The payoff is also great in richness and complexity of understanding, however. I see the phenomenological approach to conversion as radical and subversive, demanding as it does that scholars take seriously the self-reported experience of converts, in whatever context they find them. Future development requires phenomenological study of larger numbers of converts from different cultures, backgrounds, and life histories. The richness and diversity of conversion experience itself points to the mystery of God.

There are limitations to phenomenological method. That it is subjective is not disputed; rather, the approach tries to make the factor into a plus. It is also true that the method works best in the human sciences (anthropology, psychology, and sociology). It cannot be applied as successfully to documentary data as to living beings with whom one can explore, question, corroborate, or clarify.

The worst development would be outright rejection of phenomenology, rather than additional training, research, and refinement of the method as one of a kit of tools with which human religious experience is studied. The mystery and majesty of spiritual activity in our lives deserves no less.

TABLE 1. COMPLICATIONS OF SELF-REPORTING

Self-reporting is self-censoring: selective, discriminating (and discriminatory), judgmental, and subject to internal and external influences.

Tracing the "7th remove" (level of distance/complication) in the phenomenology of a soldier's story:

Level 1: **Direct research access to subject's own experience ("subject-in-event").** *A reporter accompanies soldier into battle, encounters the "same" experiences, but is trained and focused on being an observer of the experience.*

Level 2: **Direct research access to subject's immediate reactions to experience (immediate self-reporting).** *A reporter interviews a soldier about experience and reactions immediately during/after battle.*

Level 3: **Direct research access to subject's own record of reactions to experience (reflective journal).** *A reporter reads for himself the battle diary of a soldier who wrote daily (or more often) of ongoing experiences and reactions.*

Level 4: **Subject's self-reporting of "representative" excerpts from record (self-reporting from a subsequent perspective—content censorship).** *A surviving soldier shares verbatim portions of a diary, selected only on personal criteria, with a reporter.*

Level 5: **How the subject chooses to report selected contents of the record ("cast" or "spin" applied).** *Surviving soldier, instead of simply reading/sharing portions of the diary, retells the stories in light of intervening reflection and assessment.*

Level 6: **How the researcher conducts the exploration interview (nature/style/content of interviewer's questions and comments).** *Which diary portions are revealed and in what manner is influenced to some degree by which questions are asked by the reporter, how much interest, understanding, empathy is noted by the soldier.*

Level 7: **Influence of presence of other observers and/or participants during self-reporting (selectivity, self-censorship, is affected by presence of varieties of significant others during the interview).** *Soldier omits or plays down horrors of killing, personal fear, and danger to own survival in mother's presence, for instance; for a male, sexual escapades or preoccupations might be played up among male peers.*

–Lawrence A. Reh

Afterword: Overview of Phenomenology as Discipline

One of my goals in this chapter is to indicate a way for anyone to approach one's own or another's religious experience so that its fullness, complexity, and sacredness can be appreciated and understood. "Phenomenology" used above means an orientation and methodology which, practiced with rigor and integrity, renders human experience with richness and depth. Phenomenology is not to be seen as the ultimate or only discipline; the panorama of approaches represented in this book is extremely valuable. No approach should be eliminated except for that which insists there is only one way to study conversion, or that only one form of conversion is valid.

Phenomenology can mean many different things. Generally, the term refers to a descriptive approach to a phenomenon or a specific form of philosophical methodology. Philosophical phenomenology was developed primarily by Edmund Husserl and a group of scholars at Gottingen and Munich, Germany, before World War I.[1] Since then many philosophers, such as Martin Heidegger, Maurice Merleau-Ponty, and Paul Ricoeur, have expanded and enriched the field of phenomenology. While riddled by conflicting views of phenomenology, philosophers have striven to attain precise definitions, rigorous methods, and intricate examples of the field.

Phenomenology has extensively influenced the history of religions, or as it is also called, comparative religions. Formative figures include Rudolf Otto, Gerardus van der Leeuw,[2] Friedrich Heiler, and Mircea Eliade.[3]

Douglas Allen has summarized the characteristics common to philosophical phenomenology and the phenomenology of religion.[4] First and most important, phenomenology is descriptive. Consonant with the meaning of phenomenology, "that which shows itself" or "that which appears," careful and systematic attempts to describe what is in immediate experience is foundational and phenomenology. A common slogan is "to the things themselves." That which is actually experienced by a person in his or her consciousness is the subject matter of sociology.

Second, phenomenology is opposed to reductionism. Throughout the history of the phenomenological movement, attempts to explain away important human experiences have been vigorously rejected by phenomenologists. A

---

1. Richard Schmitt, "Phenomenology," in *Encyclopedia of Philosophy,* ed. Paul Edwards (New York: Macmillan and The Free Press, 1967). This article provides an overview of philosophical phenomenology and is itself an example of Husserl's orientation.

2. Gerardus van der Leeuw, *Religion in Essence and Manifestation: A Study in Phenomenology,* trans. J. E. Turner (New York: Harper & Row, 1963).

3. For an overview of Eliade's life and work, see Joseph M. Kitagawa, "Mircea Eliade," in *The Encyclopedia of Religion,* ed. Mircea Eliade (New York: Macmillan, 1989).

4. Douglas Allen, "Phenomenology of Religion," in *The Encyclopedia of Religion,* ed. Mircea Eliade (New York: Macmillan, 1989).

popular target of phenomenology has been "psychologism." In the religious field, psychologism might be illustrated by various projective theories of God, *e.g.*, Freud's notion that "god" is nothing but our projections of the ideal parent.

Third, phenomenology has insisted that human consciousness is intentional; that is, it is the human experience of consciousness actively engaging the world around us. Consciousness is not merely some internal process, but a vital intersection of the human person with his or her environment, composed of people, objects, and a multitude of experiences.

Fourth, phenomenology involves "bracketing" (the technical term is "epoche"). A phenomenologist is to set aside assumptions, biases, and theories in order to grasp as fully as possible the nature of immediate experience as it appears in human consciousness.

Fifth, phenomenology seeks what is known as the "eidetic reduction." This strategy involves seeking out the necessary or invariant features of phenomena. Phenomenologists speak of essential structure or the invariant core of various phenemon. "Eidetic reduction" also attempts to separate these structures and features from particular instances.

In addition to these five characteristics of phenomenology, Eric Sharpe reports[5] that phenomenologically oriented historians of religion approach the study of religion with deep respect for the religious believer and appreciate the "sacred" or the "holy" as fundamental, irreducible elements of religious experience. While some might legitimately argue that such an attitude biases a scholar in the direction of affirming religion, I feel that the position is defensible, given the prevailing tendency in society at large and among many secular scholars either to denigrate religion or to reduce it to explanatory systems alien to and reductionistic of religious experience.[6]

Phenomenology has also influenced psychology. Though there were harsh criticisms of "psychologism" in the early development of phenomenology, those assessments were based largely on atomistic and reductionist forms of "scientific" psychology that emerged in Europe and the United States. Although technically not a phenomenologist, William James can be seen as a major bridge figure between philosophy and psychology.[7] James's own contribution to the study of religion in general and conversion in particular is especially noteworthy. *The Varieties of Religious Experience,* James's Gifford Lectures at the University of Edinburgh in 1901-02,[8] embodies many

5. Eric J. Sharpe, *Comparative Religion: A History,* 2d ed. (La Salle, Ill.: Open Court, 1986). Note especially Sharpe's Chapter 10: "The Phenomenology of Religion," pp. 220-250.

6. For more extensive discussion and examples of the phenomenology of religion, see Joseph Dabney Bettis, ed., *Phenomenology of Religion* (New York: Harper & Row, 1969).

7. Ash Gobar, "The Phenomenology of William James," in *Proceedings of the American Philosophical Society,* 114:294-309 (August 1970); Henry Samuel Levinson, *The Religious Investigations of William James* (Chapel Hill: University of North Carolina, 1981); Don S. Browning, *Pluralism and Personality: William James and Some Contemporary Cultures of Psychology* (Cranbury, N.J.: Associated University Presses, 1980).

8. William James, *The Varieties of Religious Experience* (New York: Vintage Books, 1990).

characteristics of phenomenology: profound respect for the experience of the convert, extensive descriptions of conversions, and deep appreciation for the effects of conversion.

Phenomenological psychology[9] as it has evolved under the leadership of A. van Kaam, Amedeo Giorgi, Paul Collaizi, Donald Polkinghorne, and C. T. Fischer continues the critique of scientific psychology as rooted in positivistic assumptions and pursued with manipulative methods. The fundamental contention of phenomenologists is that any psychology that does not take human experience and consciousness seriously is fatally flawed.

—Lewis R. Rambo

---

9. For general overviews of this approach, see Amedeo Giorgi, "Phenomenological Psychology," in *International Encyclopedia of Psychiatry, Psychology, Psychoanalysis and Neurology*, ed. Benjamin B. Wolman (New York: Aesculapius Publishers, 1977); and M. S. Lindauer, "Phenomenological Method," in *Encyclopedia of Psychology*, Raymond J. Corsini, ed. (New York: Wiley, 1984). Two collections of essays provide splendid explorations of dimensions of phenomenological psychology: Ronald S. Valle and Mark King, eds., *Existential-Phenomenological Alternatives in Psychology* (New York: Oxford University Press, 1978); and Ronald S. Valle and Steen Halling, eds., *Existential-Phenomenological Perspectives in Psychology* (New York: Plenum Press, 1989).

Chapter Sixteen

Conversion in Group Settings

Charles H. Kraft

As the references of the various chapters in this volume attest, by now there are hundreds of studies of religious conversion. The vast majority of them have been written by Western academics. As discussed below, this fact has led to the neglect of at least certain aspects of the topic here in view.

It is my intent to deal with one of those neglected areas, that of the place of the group in Christian conversion. Though the group of which a convert is a part is important in any society, I will focus especially on group issues in conversion to Christianity in what we call "group-oriented" (as opposed to individual oriented or individualistic) societies.

LITERATURE

The concerns of those who have researched conversion have a strong academic and individualistic bent to them. This is not surprising, given the academic involvement of scholars and the worldview (see below) within which they operate. This means, though, that a search of the literature on group issues in conversion tends to be disappointing.

A fairly comprehensive bibliography of current (largely since 1950) research on religious conversion was published by Lewis Rambo in 1982. This includes sections on anthropology (63 listings) and sociology (104 listings). Of these about half of the anthropology listings and another thirty in the sociology list plus about three in the psychology list would have some relevance to our topic. Even most of these are, however, disappointing for those looking for a solid theoretical understanding of the relationships of groupness to conversion.

A recent literature search of articles and dissertations since 1982 resulted in the discovery of but eight more relevant items. Rambo's conclusion to
the anthropology section provides an apt summary of the situation:

> The overall impression one gets from reading the anthropological litera-
> ture is that cultural factors are extremely important in the conversion pro-
> cess, but the exact role of culture is not yet understood in such a way that
> would permit precise elucidation. Furthermore, the complexity of cul-
> ture and the difficulty of systematically relating personality and culture pre-
> vent consensus at this time.[1]

Nevertheless, several of the articles surveyed provide useful insights into
the way conversion proceeds in group-oriented societies. Among those coming from a theoretical perspective, I have found several to be helpful.
Sociologists such as Heirich, Lofland and Stark, and Straus probe the nature
and validity of current theories within their field. Though the data they work
with is from American society, there are some insights that would seem to be
cross-culturally testable.

Max Heirich's is the most comprehensive of these articles. He sets himself to test conventional social-science wisdom concerning the nature and con-
comitants of conversion. He then suggests an alternative set of questions to
ask designed to "probe the circumstances and procedures by which a sense
of ultimate grounding is affirmed or changed, at both an individual and a
social level."[2] His questions are two: "1) What circumstances destroy clarity about root reality?" and "2) How is an alternative sense of grounding
asserted in ways that lead observers to take it seriously?"[3]

In answering the first question, he points to the need to enlarge the conventional approach that identifies stress and a sense of impending doom as
sources of change. Without denying the effects of such factors, Heirich
focuses on the need to factor in the reactions of persons who have experiences
"that cannot be encompassed within current explanatory schemes, yet cannot be ignored" and who feel that "quite unacceptable outcomes appear
imminent" who then notice that "respected leaders publicly abandon some
part of past grounding assumptions."[4] When such reactions take place, what
I refer to below as "felt needs" develop, setting the stage for seeking answers
to his second question: How to effectively communicate "an alternative
sense of grounding."

Robert Conkling studied an Algonkian case in which "between 1610 and
1750 the missionaries provided the Indians with alternative forms of belief

---

1. Lewis R. Rambo, "Bibliography: Current Research on Religious Conversion," *Religious
Studies Review* 8, vol. 2 (April 1982): 147.
2. Max Heirich, "Change of Heart: A Test of Some Widely Held Theories about Religious
Conversion," *American Journal of Sociology* 83 (1977): 653.
3. Ibid., 674-75.
4. Ibid.

and social organization, which the Indians adopted."[5] He finds the disruption of the Indian social system sufficient to explain the "disappearance of an old order, but it cannot account for the emergence and acceptance of a new one or the deep commitment to it."[6] He feels the mere presence of an alternative cannot explain such commitment and points to the "charismatic authority" of the missionaries "proved through cures and their power as middlemen" as crucial. The shamans failed in competition with the missionaries both in healing and in trade, making them "of much less use than the missionaries to their fellow band members."[7] In the midst of social disruption and demoralization, then, the shamans found themselves without the authority to bring about the necessary changes.

The decisions concerning who to follow and how far to follow them were made by the insiders. And they were made on the basis of pragmatic considerations. In keeping with what we will say below about worldview, not everything was changed in their perception of reality. Nor were the changes total. They accepted the fact that Christian prayer was more useful than their former customs, and changed many of their traditional customs. But, though "converted" and having rejected many of the old customs, they remained emotionally attached to them since "there had not yet been an inner revolution in their worldview."[8]

Alan Tippett chronicles the conversion of the Samoans in a chapter entitled, "Cultural Determinants and the Acceptance of Christianity." He finds that in Samoa the acceptance of Christianity took place with comparatively little social disruption "despite the dramatic changes in basic theology."[9] He quotes Keesing, "The chiefs and orators merely rejected one set of interpretations and functions and took over the other without any vital blow being struck at the fundamentals of the existing order."[10]

Tippett, like Conkling, focuses on the strategies of the cultural insiders who saw the acceptance of Christianity as advantageous. Without questioning the genuineness of their "multi-individual" (i.e., group) conversion decision, however, he is critical of "the church's failure to follow up these decisions to spiritual maturity"[11] resulting in widespread nominalism.

Crucial to the initial acceptance of Christianity by the Samoans (as with most of the peoples of the South Pacific) were "power encounters." These were occasions when the attention of the people came to be fixed on whether the old gods or the Christian God would win in a contest over which was the

---

5. Robert Conkling, "Legitimacy and Conversion in Social Change: The Case of French Missionaries and the Northeastern Algonkian," *Ethnohistory* 21 (1974):1.

6. Ibid., 19.

7. Ibid., 20.

8. Ibid., 21.

9. Alan R. Tippett, *People Movements in Southern Polynesia* (Chicago: Moody Press, 1971), 139.

10. Felix M. Keesing, *Modern Samoa: Its Government and Changing Life* (London: Allen and Unwin, 1934), 400.

11. Tippett, *People Movements*, 146.

most powerful. Tippett observes, "In a power-oriented society, change of faith had to be power-demonstrated."[12] The multi-individual conversion decision was thus made after the priest of the clan totem, claiming the protection of the Christian God, had desecrated the totem (e.g., by eating a sacred fish or turtle, burning a fetish, burying the ancestral skull, or destroying the sacred grove) and walked away unharmed.

One of the more helpful presentations in the literature surveyed is that by Jacob Loewen published in three parts in 1968-1969.[13] He likens conversion to socialization, referring to it as "resocialization." In the first article, he surveyed the processes of socialization, social control, and resocialization. In the second and third articles, then, he applied the insights derived from this perspective on conversion to the ongoing ministries of the church.

Theoretically, these articles break new ground both in defining conversion as a process of resocialization and in detailing the steps the Christian community has to take to bring that process to fruition. In relation to our topic, the place of the Christian group in the process of conversion is constantly in focus. The presentations seem to assume, however, that those in the conversion process will ordinarily be individuals or small groups.

Two older presentations that could usefully be used in conjunction with Loewen to enlarge the scope of what could happen in the resocialization as conversion model are those of J.W. Pickett and colleagues. In 1933, Pickett published a study of mass movements into Christianity in India that details both the fact of such movements and the pluses and minuses of the kind of conversion involved in them.[14] In a second volume, most of which was first published in 1936, several shorter studies are collected describing and analyzing this group (multi-individual) conversion phenomenon.[15]

Though such problems as nominalism and syncretism are recognized as endemic to multi-individual movements into Christianity, the overall perspective is well-summarized by A.L. Warnshuis as follows:

> Briefly summarized, the wrong way to try to build up the church in a non-Christian land is by the conversion of individuals extracted from dozens of different families, clans, villages and social groups. Such converts are promptly ostracized, separated from their relations and cut off from their roots in the past of their own peoples. . . .
> The better way is by recognition of the principle that the church grows along [social] lines. . . . The right and natural growth of the church is by

12. Ibid., 81.

13. Jacob A. Loewen, "Socialization and Social Control: A Resume of Processes," *Practical Anthropology* 15 (1968): 145-56; "The Indigenous Church and Resocialization, *Practical Anthropology* 15 (1968): 193-204; "Socialization and Conversion in the Ongoing Church," *Practical Anthropology* 16 (1969): 1-17.

14. J. Wascom Pickett, *Christian Mass Movements in India* (Lucknow,India: Lucknow Publishing House, 1933; 2nd Indian ed., 1969).

15. J. Wascom Pickett et al., *Church Growth and Group Conversion*, rev. and enlarged 1956; 5th edition published 1973, Pasadena, Calif.: William Carey.

the conversion of groups, where Christian forces help some group reconstruct its life, individual and corporate, around Jesus Christ.[16]

CHRISTIAN CONVERSION: SOCIAL AS WELL AS SPIRITUAL

The Bible shows God meeting and interacting with people where they are, within their own sociocultural structures. Though there are cosmic-level events going on in heavenly places (e.g., Jb 1:6f), at the earthly level it is in human language that he speaks; it is according to human patterns that God's people are governed and in terms of human structures that battles are won or lost. God's people marry, raise their children, perform their various activities, die and are buried according to the patterns of the cultures in which they live.

It is not surprising, then, that when people commit themselves to God in what we have come to call a "conversion experience," they do so in ways amenable to cultural and psychological analysis. In God's sight a convert may move "from death to life" (Jn 5:24). But on earth, that movement may or may not be a remarkable experience. And it may take place when the person is alone or when he or she is with others.

For those who are temperamentally more emotional than others or for whom a turning to God involves a radical change of life, the experience may be quite emotional (e.g., the apostle Paul, Acts 9:1-19). For others there may be little or no emotion. In either case, those who study the relation of emotion to life-changing decisions can analyze the human side of the conversion experience quite helpfully. Culturally, then, those participating in individualistic societies are likely to convert individualistically, while those participating in group-oriented societies are predisposed to convert in groups. And those who study such phenomena can analyze such differences quite helpfully. For conversion is a human process, even though Christians believe something cosmic takes place behind the scenes.

For most of the faithful whose stories are recorded in the Bible, their relationship with God was the result of their growing up in the covenant community and at some point committing themselves to the God whose convenants they had learned as children. Often, however, such commitment was in contrast to the rejection of God on the part of most of the community around them. Those who came into such a relationship with God, therefore, often had to go through a "turning" or "returning" (Hebrew, *shuv*; Greek, *epistrepho*).[17] Since Hebrew society was "group oriented", such returns to God and his covenants usually occurred as group experiences rather than individually (e.g., Jas 3:9, 15; 4:3; 6:7; 10:10, etc.; 2 Kgs 23:4; Ez 9:1-10:3; Jon 3:5-9). In New Testament times, this conversion as a group is pointed to among Jews in such passages as Acts 2:41; 4:4 and among

---

16. A.L. Warnshuis, "Group Conversion," *Religious Life* 11, vol 5 (1942):21-22.

17. See George Bertram, "*Epistrepho*," in *Theological Dictionary of the New Testament*, ed., Gerhard Friedrich (1971), 7: 714-29.

gentiles (Romans) in passages such as Acts 10:44; 16:31. (See Kraft for more on this subject.[18])

Thus even a phenomenon as intensely spiritual and personal as Christian conversion should take place within the "rules" of the society in which it occurs. If, then, in group-oriented societies such as those portrayed in scripture, conversion takes place largely as a group phenomenon, we should expect those living today in group-oriented societies to experience conversion according to the similar sociocultural guidelines in operation in their societies.

The assumptions underlying the worldviews of those who seek to study and/or advocate conversion from Western perspectives, however, tend to intrude into the way they/we analyze and interpret such a "sociospiritual" phenomenon. Thus it is often assumed by Westerners, in spite of the biblical evidence, that whenever conversion is discussed, we are thinking only of an individual act. Theological understandings are then predicated on that basis and individualistic conversion taken to be the norm. Such should not be the case.

WORLDVIEW AND CONVERSION

Underlying all cultural behavior are a sizable number of basic assumptions concerning reality and how to respond to it. We call such assumptions worldview. These assumptions provide the guidance people ordinarily follow when they engage in activities such as interpreting, evaluating, explaining, making commitments, relating, and adapting. In terms of these guidelines people organize reality into categories; perceive and relate to time, space, and other people; and explain and deal with causation. (See Kraft[19] for more complete treatments.)

Both in the approach of various peoples to conversion and in the view taken of conversion by those who analyze it, worldview assumptions play a crucial part. This fact leads me to first state my own worldview biases, then to make three important points concerning the influence of worldview on analysts and advocates of conversion. First, my own position.

To be up front with my own worldview biases, I am aware that they center around several foci rooted in my own training and life experience. First of all, I am a Western academic myself. But I am trained in both cultural anthropology and Christian theology (as well as in linguistics with a focus on language pedagogy). I have, however, unlike many academics, worked in a non-Western (African) field situation for several years (as a missionary) where one of my primary concerns was to bring about the change in a group-oriented society that I here attempt to analyze academically. Beyond that, I have functioned for over twenty years as one who seeks to train missionar-

---

18. Charles H. Kraft, *Christianity in Culture* (Maryknoll, N.Y.: Orbis, 1979), 328-44.

19. Charles H. Kraft, *Christianity with Power* (Ann Arbor, Mich.: Servant Books, 1989) and Kraft, *Christianity in Culture*.

ies and international church leaders to focus on the anthropological aspects of the conversion process they seek to bring about. In addition, I would claim a greater measure of experience with the more supernaturalistic dimensions of Christianity than characterizes most of those with a Christian commitment similar to mine.

I am, therefore, biased both in favor of a Christian supernaturalistic perspective and of the validity of conversion to a relationship with God in terms of that perspective. I am, however, also committed to analyzing such conversion experiences from a crosscultural anthropological perspective.

With regard to the three points concerning the worldview of analysts and advocates, I will treat the first two of them together. The third is discussed below.

1. *In dealing with conversion (as in all areas of life), we who analyze are influenced by our own worldview assumptions, and*

2. *Those who have advocated Christian conversion have usually worked from a Western worldview.*

These first two points tend to link those who analyze conversion with those who advocate it—at least with respect to their approach to non-Western, group-oriented peoples. I have mentioned the individualism of Western worldviews and the influence of such a perspective on Western academic analyses. Those who advocate conversion in non-Western contexts, however, can be no less individualistic. Indeed, they often assume that all conversion must be individualistic to be valid and that any individual, regardless of his or her position in society can and must make a conversion decision as an individual, even if all other major decisions in the society require consultation resulting in either consensus or permission of the leadership.

Naturalism is another Western worldview value that infects both analysts and the advocates of conversion. Most Westerners, including theologians and those who seek to convert, are quite naturalistic in comparison to most of the non-Western peoples of the world. In addition, we can expect a certain lack of sympathy for the process they are analyzing on the part of those researchers not devoted to the religion they are studying.

Cultural bias, then, stemming from Western attitudes toward other societies, has often figured in the ways in which Christians have approached non-Westerners in attempting to convert them. This has probably not been so much of an influence on researchers, at least recently.

The high value put on rationality in Western societies also tends to intrude both into the studies of conversion in non-Western societies and into the approaches made by the advocates of conversion. Western academia has since the so-called "Enlightenment" been mind-focused. Western advocates of conversion, then, have tended to see rational belief in certain doctrinal propositions as a major precondition to conversion, focusing more on the ability of converts to digest information than on their ability to integrate Christian principles into their everyday lives.

When the focus does turn to less rational behavior, academic analyses will usually tend to highlight emotion while neglecting or questioning the reality of the spiritual dimensions of the experience. Western advocates of conversion, then, though attempting to focus on the spiritual dimensions, are often found to be advocating a degree of spirituality far less vital than that already known to the prospective converts from their pre-Christian experience.

3. *The worldview assumptions of those considering conversion, then, play a major role in whether and how they respond to invitations to convert.* The majority of the societies of the world, unlike Western societies, are characterized by what we have called a "group orientation." This means that the members of the group tend to be much more interdependent in their interrelationships than most Westerners can even imagine. Hierarchical authority structures tend to be strong and decision making, even on matters of apparently minor importance, tends to be done in concert with others and in accordance with the authority patterns dictated by a communal worldview.

Other things being equal, such decision-making patterns would have mitigated against the movement of such peoples into an individualistic style of Christianity. The sociocultural prestige of Western advocates, coupled on the one hand with the attractiveness of the message and on the other with the perceived benefits (both material and nonmaterial) of association with Westerners has, however, led many from non-Western societies to convert to individualistic Christianity.

The apparent material wealth of the Western advocates of Christianity and their followers has done much to overcome non-Western bias against individualistic religion. Though the comparative naturalism of Western Christianity eventually proves disappointing to many non-Westerners, the fact that many of their worldviews assume that greater material wealth is a sure sign of greater spiritual power has often delayed the disappointment for a generation or two. It is the promise of greater supernatural power that has often provided the "bait" to which they responded.

It is unfortunate that taking advantage of the opportunity to obtain these perceived benefits has often been contingent on acquiescing to such a disruptive approach to decision making. Westerners, due to their/our prestige, could both offer the benefits and control the means by which they were to be attained. And the primary means was via individualistic conversion, often closely tied to attendance at Western schools. Those in charge have usually not allowed those of group-oriented societies to come into Christianity in groups.

One result of this process, especially in the pioneer periods of Christian witness, was the encouragement of low status persons to convert as individuals. This has resulted in churches full of youth, women, and marginal men. Often, therefore, the Christian movement as a whole is viewed as marginal to the society, largely because of its approach to conversion.

To summarize, though individualistic conversion patterns fit Western worldviews, they seldom fit non-Western custom. In fact, those who follow an individualistic path to conversion tend to be seen as challenging the authority of their leaders and are, therefore, marginalized. This has often cost them and the Christian movement dearly in traditional society—a cost often only partially compensated for by the gain in global awareness and contacts.

Such a situation can be quite culturally disruptive. It is disturbing, therefore, to those positive toward Christian advocacy to note that a message intended to bring maximum benefit to the peoples of the world has often resulted in considerable social disruption. Though there are other factors involved, the Western monolithic approach to conversion coupled with the willingness of many of the peoples of the world to embrace the messages brought by people they consider prestigious has played an important part in bringing about such disruption.

REASONS WHY THIS TOPIC IS IMPORTANT FOR CHRISTIANS

There are several reasons why a discussion of group issues in Christian conversion is important, at least for Christians:

1. In the Christian scriptures, notably in the book of Acts, we find several instances in which conversions took place in groups. Note, for example, the accounts in Acts 2 (see especially v. 41) and Acts 3-4 (see especially 4:4). In Acts 10, then (especially v. 44), we find all of those in Cornelius' household responding to the Christian message at one time and in Acts 16 (especially v. 31) we find Paul promising the Philippian jailer that his response to the gospel message will result in the salvation of his whole household.

Western biases have led to widespread ignoring of the significance of these passages to the way conversion ought to be advocated in non-Western contexts. Indeed, some seem to think that things were different enough in biblical times that such group conversions were all right then but are not to be encouraged now.

2. The history of Christian missions in many parts of the non-Western world (and even the ancient Western world), however, is dotted with examples of what Donald McGavran[20] has termed "people movements" in which sizable numbers of people came into Christianity at one time. The conversion of 8,000 Dani tribesmen in Irian Jaya is one famous recent example.[21]

3. Western individualistic assumptions have influenced Western theological thinking on the subject of conversion to such an extent (especially among conservatives) that examples such as those cited above have not been well understood. They have, therefore, ordinarily been either ignored, explained away or interpreted in such a way as to cast aspersions on the reality of the step taken to the people who took it and to the social context in which they took it.

---

20. Donald A. McGavran, *Understanding Church Growth* (Grand Rapids, Mich.: Eerdmans, 1970).

21. James Sunda, *Church Growth in West New Guinea* (Lucknow, India: Lucknow Publishing House, 1963).

4. Even when an individualistic Westerner makes conversion decisions, he or she is not alone. It is likely that every such decision is accompanied by questions in the mind of the one converting relating to the attitude of the members of that person's reference group concerning the change. Questions such as, "What will my family think?" or "What will my friends think?" can be powerful deterrents (or encouragements) to any change in attitude or behavior for even the most individualistic among us. Such considerations are even more powerful in more group-oriented societies.

ANTHROPOLOGICAL INSIGHT INTO GROUP MOVEMENTS

Though we may never be able to claim absolute understanding of group movements, a crosscultural or anthropological perspective can be of great assistance in enabling us to see beyond the individualistic biases of a Western mindset. Anthropological analyses, for example, make it clear that groupness is always a factor in human behavior. We should expect, therefore, that any person who seeks to change his/her belief, allegiance or behavior will be answerable to some group for that decision. The dynamics of such account-ability will, however, differ from society to society, especially with respect to the degree of freedom allowed to individuals to make choices that differ from those of his or her reference group.

To attempt to understand those dynamics in relation to Christian conversion, we will highlight several relevant sociocultural factors.

1. The first factor to discuss is *the phenomenon of groupness*. Humans always exist in sociocultural relationships with other humans. We are born into relationships with other members of our families. These families are, in turn, in relationships with other families, communities, clans, tribes, nations, and the like.

People are taught within the community into which they were born to think and behave according to the cultural patterning of their society. They learn the assumptions, values, and allegiances of the worldview of that society. They learn to value what their society values and commit themselves to what their group commits itself to. They learn to behave according to the status and role patterning appropriate to those assumptions and values. They learn to view the world largely the way their reference group views it and to use their powers of choice (wills) largely in ways approved by the members of that reference group.

2. *Decision-making patterns, then, will accord with the guidelines followed by the society as a whole*. As noted, that group may allow greater or lesser leeway for any given individual to choose an alternative belief or practice that differs from that of the other members of the reference group. In individualistic societies such as those of Euroamerica we have been taught that anyone of age may replace almost any pattern of life learned from his or her parents, including religion, if he or she so chooses.

Though we have considerably less freedom of choice than we like to believe, most of the societies of the world allow much less than ours does. For in our society, as in those that are structured more tightly, the allowed leeway is typically keyed to (a) the person's status in the society and (b) the relative importance the society attaches to the choice to be made.

a) *In many societies, at least in their traditional state, an ordinary person would expect to have little say in such decisions* as those concerning whom he or she would marry, where they would live, and what occupation the husband would engage in. Any thought of an ordinary person changing his/her religious allegiance, then, would be completely unheard of. Those of very high prestige are often even more restricted in their ability to make such changes since they are looked upon as the preservers of traditional values. Lower class people, especially the disaffected and marginalized, however, would likely be able to claim much more leeway in many areas of life—either out of rebellion or because they no longer care.

b) A second major consideration with respect to social guidelines for change is *the relative importance attached to the choice to be made.* Choices to adopt a new household or farming implement, for example, are usually not penalized (though with groups like the Amish even such material implements may be labeled "sinful" and disallowed). Those sociocultural practices perceived as more closely related to a people's self-identify, however, are likely to be much more difficult for a people to change. Religious commitments often fall into this category. Specific religious practices, though, may not.

For example, though the idea of changing from traditional religion to Christianity may be disallowed by the elders, the adopting and adapting of some Christian practice (e.g., the use of holy water or of sacred writing to bring blessing) may be readily embraced. In many societies, furthermore, their religious allegiance is seen as so integral to their overall identity that they regard religious defection as social treason (e.g., Muslims, Jews). A person who converts to Christianity is, therefore, likely to be treated as dead by his or her society.

Nevertheless, there is at least one major condition that counters both religious conservatism and the expectation that ordinary people are not allowed to innovate. It is the fact that for many (probably most) of the peoples of the world, the felt need for more spiritual power seems to be more important to them than the mere perpetuating of their traditional religious practices. People from all walks of life will, therefore, often gladly incorporate into their lives techniques for gaining additional spiritual power derived from other religious traditions while feeling no compulsion to convert to that other tradition.

3. Whatever the society and however tight the decision-making structures, however, *the steps involved in any consideration of a change of attitude or behavior* would seem to be as follows:[22]

a) *Some stimulus starts the process.* This may come from within the society or be introduced from outside. It will often be brought by an outsider or by someone from the society who has traveled and returned. Often

---

22. Kraft, *Christianity in Culture*, 335-38, after Alan R. Tippett, *Verdict Theology in Missionary Theory*, 2nd ed. (Pasadena, Calif.: William Carey, 1973).

the person bringing the idea has already adopted it at least tentatively. This is the way technological ideas, often encapsulated in gadgets move into new social groups. Religious ideas are transmitted in the same way.[23] The chances of acceptance of the idea are, of course higher if the one who brings it is prestigious.

b) The introduction of the idea issues in a *growing awareness* of the idea. If the idea involves a material object, people observe those using it. Whether or not such an item is involved, the idea is discussed and word of it moves through some important segment of the society.

c) Through this process, a people may come to a kind of *realization that it might indeed be possible for them to adopt the idea.* Not all ideas appear immediately to be compatible with prevailing practices. So at this point, many ideas are rejected.

d) If people accept the possibility of adopting an idea, they may begin a *consideration of what the innovation could mean in their lives.* Though all of the implications are seldom, if ever, obvious, the group attempts to assess the pluses and minuses to weigh the potential gain against the social cost of adoption. Though this stage may be quite short for many technological innovations, much discussion over considerable periods of time often accompanies the consideration of potential changes in worldview, including the assumptions underlying religion. This process preceded the Dani people movement.[24]

e) Eventually, though, *some decision is reached.* The decision may be to reject, to delay further consideration, to accept tentatively, or to accept completely—though any decision can be reevaluated and possibly changed later. In tight-knit societies, consideration of major decisions is typically initiated by the leaders, though the idea itself may have been suggested by others, whether social insiders or outsiders. The matter will then ordinarily be discussed widely throughout the society before a decision is agreed upon and announced by the leaders.

f) If the decision is to accept the innovation, *the people will give themselves to the incorporation of the idea into the life of the society.* Once the decision is made to adopt a new idea or allegiance (e.g., a new religion) by the leaders of a tight-knit society, all are expected to accept or to leave the society. Such would have been the options facing the members of Terah's family when he decided to leave Ur (Gn 11:31) and Abraham's family when he decided to leave Haran (Gn 12).

g) *The decision to incorporate a new belief or practice issues in a new habit or set of habits.* People "empower" their customs by following them habitually. Customs would not be particularly difficult to change if it weren't for the habit factor. New ideas, then, have to become new habits, added to or replacing old habits, if they are to become new customs.

---

23. Homer G. Barnett, *Innovation: The Basis of Cultural Change* (New York: McGraw-Hill, 1953).

24. Sunda, *Church Growth.*

4. Understanding such decision-making processes takes us a long way toward understanding *the dynamics of change in any society, especially those that are group-oriented.* There are, however, a few additional factors to be highlighted.

a) The first is the fact that *real, thoroughgoing change needs to register at both deep (worldview) and surface levels of a culture.* That is, the assumptions, values, and allegiances that lie deeply embedded beneath the surface of cultural behavior need to be changed to support whatever changes are made in behavior if the change is to be pervasive. But surface and deep-level changes often take place at different speeds. Surface-level behavior is often much more easily changed than are the deep-level assumptions supporting it.

In religious change, if changes are made on the surface without corresponding changes at the deep level, the result is the condition that Tippett has called "submersion.[25] This is a situation in which new surface behavior is combined with essentially unchanged deep-level assumptions to produce a syncretistic brand of religion in which the new surface-level forms make it look as though the people have converted. Underneath, however, the meanings attached to those new forms remain pretty much the same as the meanings attached to the older, now discarded forms. Much Latin American Roman Catholicism has long suffered from this problem. Many of the saints, for example, though possessing Roman Catholic names really represent traditional gods. And many of the rituals, though appearing to be orthodox, are in fact understood by the people more as their ancestors understood the rituals these Catholic rituals supposedly replaced.

The ideal, then, in sociocultural change is for conversion to take place at both surface and deep levels. Indeed, if people converting to Christianity are to be genuinely Christian, it is to the conversion of their assumptions, values, and allegiances (their worldview) that primary attention must be given. As we see in scripture, God is far more willing to allow diversity in the surface-level forms practiced by his followers than in the deep-level meanings and commitments.

b) A second important factor to consider in dealing with the dynamics of change is the *importance of felt needs* in the change process. The members of every society learn to focus on certain things and to ignore others. As a part of this process they learn to feel the need for certain things. Americans, for example, learn to "need" physical comforts such as sit-down toilets, private bedrooms, frequently washed clothes and bodies, soft chairs, firm beds, and good health. To attain such comforts our society sees to it that certain of our people exercise power over *material* entities to produce these things for us.

In many societies, most of these physical comforts are not so important. Having good health and good relationships between those who share living

---

25. Alan R. Tippett, *Introduction to Missiology* (Pasadena, Calif.: William Carey, 1987), 168-74.

quarters is, however, supremely important. Attaining these felt needs, though, may be seen as primarily a matter of exerting influence with *spiritual* entities rather than seeking control over any part of the physical universe. Whereas in the West we develop material means such as physical medicines, physical,and spatial privacy to attempt to deal with disease, comfort, and interpersonal relationships, in many other societies it is to the spiritual dimensions of human experience that they would look for their primary solutions to such problems.

In addition to the differential in the definition of felt needs accompanying such differences in sociocultural focus, it appears that no cultural way of life provides completely satisfying answers to every question or problem faced by the social groups who live by it. There are, therefore, additional unmet needs felt by a people that provide points of contact that can be used by outsiders who seek to introduce new ideas into a society.

c) A third dynamic to be taken seriously is the fact that *in every segment of a society there are "opinion leaders" whose example is followed when they make changes in their behavior*. Even in tight-knit, group-oriented societies, all major culture change is rooted in changes made by individuals. The locus of all sociocultural change is in the minds of individuals.[26] But everything depends on which individual makes the change. When marginal individuals change their behavior, few, if any, follow them. But when someone with a following makes a change, those who follow him or her often also make that change.

People with followings are termed "opinion leaders."[27] Such individuals exist in every segment of a society. They are not necessarily prestigious in the society at large. But they carry enough prestige in whatever segment they function to attract others to their ideas, opinions, and behavior. For example, Jesus' disciples were not prestigious in Israel as a whole (especially not in Jerusalem). They were, however, prestigious and, therefore, able to influence opinions within Galilee where being expert at occupations such as fishing, politics, and tax collecting was highly respected.

An opinion leader may have influence within a greater or smaller segment of society. Some opinion leaders are only able to sway their own immediate families. Others may have little influence over their families but be followed carefully by those of their occupational group. Some opinion leaders are followed by their group in many or all areas of life. Some, however, are only influential in specific areas. For example, some will be followed when they deal with technological things but not when they deal with how to raise children. Others will be listened to attentively on any subject.

Opinion leaders may influence people either for or against change. Those in official positions (e.g., politicians, appointed or elected leaders), in fact, often stand against change, lest their own positions be threatened. Those outside the establishment, however, often favor any change they

---

26. Barnett, *Innovation*.
27. Everett Rogers, *Diffusion of Innovations* (New York: Free Press, 1983).

feel could give them an advantage over those in power.

When the members of a group decide to follow an opinion leader, a kind of "multi-individual, mutually interdependent" decision,[28] is made that may result in a social movement into a new type of social commitment. Because such a movement takes place according to socially expected processes, it can be every bit as binding and involve every bit as much individual commitment as would be true of an individual conversion in a Western(ized) society. (See L.P. Gerlach and V.H. Hine for a study of such a factor in two Western movements.[29])

d) A fourth dynamic at work in group oriented societies is *the process of consultation that goes on between the members of such societies prior to major decisions*. Though the specifics of this process will differ considerably from society to society, they will ordinarily involve discussions among the leaders designed to examine the potential effects of such a decision on the society as a whole. In small-scale, kinship-based, patriarchal societies, the oldest male leader from each of the families in the society will typically function with his counterparts on the leadership council. When that group considers major decisions those men consult with the heads of the families under their authority (usually their sons and grandsons). Not infrequently, even in strongly patriarchal societies, the leaders will also engage in informal discussions with their wives and the younger men to solicit their input and to win their agreement to any eventual decision for change. This is the probable process that preceded Abraham's decision to obey God by leaving his home territory.

Outsiders are often unaware of this process and of the sometimes significant power of veto wielded by women and younger men in such societies. It is, however, this factor that leads knowledgeable anthropologists such as Barnett[30] to refer to such decision making as "multi-individual" rather than as "group." Whenever this process goes on, the statement of the leader concerning the decision should be regarded more as an announcement of what the group leaders have decided than as an autocratic decision that he has made on his own.

One interesting variant of such decision-making patterns occurs in Japanese companies. Reportedly, at least certain of the ordinary workers are regularly invited by their supervisors to spend time with them socially after business hours. This time is spent drinking and talking quite informally in a way not permitted in the formal work setting during working hours. While together in this way, the supervisors can "float" new ideas to get the reactions of the workers. The workers, for their part, are permitted to freely make suggestions directly to their bosses concerning how business activities are conducted. Certain of these suggestions get implemented at a later time as if they were

---

28. McGavran, *Understanding Church Growth*.

29. L.P. Gerlach and V.H. Hine, *People, Power, Change: Movements of Social Transformation* (New York: Bobbs-Merrill, 1970).

30. Barnett, *Innovation*.

originated only by the bosses themselves. In addition, though participating in a rigidly hierarchical system without obvious formal opportunities to be heard, the workers get to be an important part of the decision-making process.

e) When someone within a group-oriented society seeks to make a decision (such as conversion to Christianity) not authorized by the leaders (e.g., family heads), *there are potentially three courses available to him or her*. The person may (1) influence the leaders to make it a group decision, (2) gain permission from the leaders to make that decision by himself or herself, or (3) go ahead and make the decision and become marginalized (or even banished) by the rest of the society.

If the person is an opinion leader, he or she may be able to follow the first course quite successfully. Others would be wise to attempt to win over opinion leaders before they lock themselves into anything as radical as Christian conversion. In many situations, even more conservative leaders are willing to allow younger people and women to make individual decisions apart from the majority of the society. In other situations, such an individualistic decision results in the person being ostracized from the society. Either of the last two options results in the segregation of those who convert and should be avoided by those who advocate changes such as Christian conversion if they seek to gain any significant coverage in the society as a whole.

f) Finally, it should be pointed out that *even in individualistic societies (whether Western or not), most of these principles and dynamics are also operative*. As pointed out above, even Westerners ask questions such as, "What will my family/friends think if I make this choice?" We too are not alone when we make decisions, even when we are by ourselves. Whether it is in asking this kind of question or in participating with groups in mass situations or in business meetings, groupness plays an important part in much (most?) of our decision making, especially when we are considering potentially life-changing decisions such as that to convert to Christianity.

As the literature points out, there are important psychological factors at work in group situations, even in individualistic societies. These combine with a strong recognition, whether conscious or unconscious, of our need to be part of a group. We all have "significant others" in our lives, people whose opinions we value whether or not they are present with us at any given decision-making time. We consider ourselves a part of their group, seeking to please them and to continue in relationship with those others who also seek to please them.

The major difference between individualistic peoples and group-oriented peoples may be in the way each group prioritizes its allegiances. In a group-oriented society, allegiance to family and clan is usually much higher than allegiance to oneself as an individual. One's personal security and hopes for the present and the future are felt to be inextricable from that social matrix. This dictates that one not stray far from what that group approves. Any thought of straying raises in a person's mind the specter of social abandonment in time of need. He or she then usually snaps quickly back into line unless given specific permission by the leaders of the group linked with assurances that he or she will not be abandoned or banished.

In an individualistic society, however, one's allegiance to self may be much higher on the list. For some that allegiance will be above allegiance to the family/reference group. For others it may be below. But even if self-allegiance is below that to the family/reference group, the potential is much greater of elevating it above the latter allegiance in situations where one's own interests may conflict with the perceived interests of one's group. So reference group considerations need to be taken very seriously in individualistic societies as well as in group-oriented societies in attempting to analyze and/or advocate Christian conversion (or any other type).

Chapter Seventeen

Conversion in Evangelistic Practice

Eddie Gibbs

The purpose of this chapter is to describe and evaluate the range of procedures which are most commonly followed in accordance with the nature of the evangelistic situation. Evangelistic encounters range from one-on-one, through small groups, to the evangelistic "crusade" meeting with crowds of tens of thousands. It is evident that the procedures adopted in inviting individuals to respond to the Good News will need to be designed for each specific context. But evangelistic procedures are influenced by other considerations than pragmatism. They are also shaped by theological and cultural factors.

In the first part of this chapter I will examine the relationship between theological and cultural factors bearing on evangelistic strategies in conversion and in the second part I will address the practical issues related to the fostering of lasting and significant conversions in personal, small group, local church, and crusade evangelism.

PRINCIPLES WHICH INFLUENCE PROCEDURES

The procedures adopted will arise directly from the evangelist's understanding of the nature of evangelism and of conversion. For some, evangelism consists essentially in winning souls for eternity and rescuing them from eternal damnation. Dwight Moody represented this position when he proclaimed, "I look upon this world as a wrecked vessel. God has given me a lifeboat and said to me, 'Moody, save all you can.'"[1] From this standpoint, the task consists of pulling as many individuals out of the water as quickly as possible, before they disappear beneath the waves.

Those who broaden the concept of evangelism to include the whole person—rather than an exclusive preoccupation with the soul; and who extend the relevance of the evangel to abundant life in this world—in addition to eternal life in the next; and who emphasize the corporate dimensions of the gospel—not just the reconciled individual but the reconciled and reconciling community, are likely to be less crisis and more process oriented. This broader understanding of evangelism is defined by South African missiologist David Bosch as, "that dimension and activity of the church's mission which seeks to offer every person, everywhere, a valid opportunity to be directly challenged by the gospel of explicit faith in Jesus Christ, with a view to embracing him as Savior, becoming a living member of his community, and being enlisted in his service of reconciliation, peace, and justice on earth."[2]

For the sake of greater clarity I will identify the principal theological and cultural issues in a series of propositions.

1. *Conversion represents a divine initiative as well as a human decision.* The Lutheran and Calvinistic traditions stand in sharp contrast to the Arminian and Wesleyan traditions in this regard. Lutheran theologian Robert Kolb sees the conversion process as a series of steps. As the Spirit of God works in the life of individuals they move from becoming "secure sinners" to the "semi-pelagian" stage in which they confess that they need some help from God's grace in Jesus to assist them in righting their own slightly skewed lives, then through the "synergistic" stage, in which sinners recognize that they are so sinful that God's grace alone can save, but at the same time they still insist that grace is only available if the sinner exercises some responsibility, makes some contribution, by reaching out a hand to grasp God's favor. The final stage which must be reached in order for genuine conversion to take place is for persons to become "broken sinners," by which we mean a profound recognition that they have nothing to offer to bring about their salvation. It is only in coming as broken sinners that they can know eventual security in Christ.[3]

Within the strict Calvinist tradition one of the cardinal points of doctrine is that of "irresistible grace," which in practice means that the preacher's task consists of proclaiming the truths of the gospel and leaving the Spirit to do the work of converting. Martin Lloyd-Jones, who for many years occupied the pulpit of Westminster Chapel, London, and was widely regarded as

---

1. Quoted in G.M. Marsden, *Fundamentalism and American Culture: The Shaping of Twentieth-century Evangelicalism: 1870-1925* (New York: Oxford University Press, 1980), 38.

2. David J. Bosch, "Evangelism: Theological Currents and Cross-currents Today," *International Bulletin of Missionary Research* 11, no. 3 (July 1987): 103.

3. Robert Kolb, *Speaking the Gospel Today* (St. Louis: Concordia, 1984), 174, 175.

the last of the Puritan preachers, would never call for a decision.[4] Yet week by week he had a stream of people who came to him for counseling after hearing his sermons wanting to know how to get right with God.

By contrast, churches within the Arminian and Wesleyan traditions, such as certain brands of Baptist, Methodist, Salvation Army, Nazarene, and Pentecostal churches will call people to make a public response week by week, inviting them to walk the aisle to the communion rail or penitents' bench. They are not unduly perturbed when the same people come forward to receive salvation on a regular basis because they do not hold to the position of "once saved always saved." If salvation can be lost there must be opportunity for it to be regained.

Between this polarity many evangelist-theologians try to avoid an exclusive emphasis either on divine sovereignty or human responsibility by recognizing the validity of both positions as equally logical and necessary. Divine sovereignty is necessary because only God can bring about regeneration, and humans are held responsible for communicating the good News and for their response to that communication. James Packer, who writes from a Reformed Evangelical Anglican position, draws attention to the use of the word "convert" (*epistrepho*) in the New Testament. "We think of conversion as a work of God, and so from one standpoint it is; but it is striking to observe that in the three New Testament passages where *epistrepho* is used transitively, of 'converting' someone to God, the subject of the verb is not God, as we might have expected, but a preacher (Lk 1:16; Jas 5:19f; Acts 26:17f)."[5] Packer observes that these passages highlight the responsibility of God's people in summoning men and women to turn to God in repentance and faith. The task of the preacher is not simply to inform their hearers but to invite them to respond.

2. *Conversion represents a long-term process as well as a one-time decision.* Some people can name a time and place when they were suddenly, and sometimes, dramatically converted. The classic biblical example is the conversion of Saul on the Damascus Road. But on further reflection there was a sequence of events leading to that transforming experience. Saul had been instructed in the scriptures by Gamaliel and he had been face to face with believers in the course of making arrests and interrogating them. Furthermore, he had been present to hear the testimony of Stephen and to witness his death by stoning. Although he had approved of his murder, the words of the Risen Lord as reported by Paul in bearing witness to King Agrippa indicate that the Lord had awakened his conscience during the period when he was persecuting the followers of Christ, and that for some time Paul had been kicking against the goads (Acts 26:14).

---

4. Martin Lloyd-Jones, *Preaching and Preachers* (London: Hodder and Stoughton, 1971), Ch.4 "Calling for Decision."

5. James I. Packer, *Evangelism and the Sovereignty of God* (London: InterVarsity Fellowship, 1961), 49.

James Engel has applied his marketing skills to assist in a greater understanding of the decision-making process in drawing up the Engel's Scale.[6] This
describes eight steps by which people come to faith:

-8 Awareness of a Supreme Being, but no effective knowledge of the
    gospel
-7 Initial awareness of the gospel
-6 Awareness of the fundamentals of the gospel
-5 Grasp of the implications of the gospel
-4 Positive attitude toward the gospel
-3 Personal problem recognition
-2 Decision to act
-1 Repentance and faith in Christ
-0 A new disciple is born
+1 Postdecision evaluation
+2 Incorporation into the Body

This scale must be viewed with caution on two counts. First, most people
do not in reality come to Christian commitment by passing through this
sequence step-by-step. They may leap-frog, or bounce back and forth.
Second, the scale is one-dimensional, based exclusively in the cognitive.
This has led the Danish communication specialist Viggo Sogaard (who
worked for Engel on the original scale) to produce a two-dimensional model
which combines the attitudinal with the cognitive.[7] The value of the scale is
twofold. First it challenges the evangelist to communicate the gospel at a
level appropriate to the knowledge level and degree of responsiveness of
the audience. Second, it encourages greater realism in terms of anticipated
results, especially for people in the minus eight to minus five range. Such persons may need an extended period of time and a number of exposures to
the gospel before they have sufficient knowledge of the message and contact
with the human messengers to make a meaningful decision.

This point particularly needs to be kept in mind when considering evangelistic procedures to bring about conversions in the context of "crusade
evangelism." In the Western world, and more particularly in the United
States, this method has arisen out of the Revival meetings designed to restore
lapsed churchgoers who had a considerable amount of prior knowledge of the
person of Jesus Christ and lived as "black sheep" in the midst of the faithful
flock of regular churchgoers. The annual, week-long "revival" provided an
appropriate opportunity for "backsliders" to mend their ways. As society
becomes increasingly secular and religiously pluralistic, the short-sharp-
shock approach adopted in the "crusade" setting becomes less and less effec-

---

6. James F. Engel and Wilbert Norton, *What's Gone Wrong with the Harvest?* (Grand
Rapids, Mich.: Zondervan, 1975).
7. Viggo Sogaard, *Applying Christian Communication* (Ph.D. diss., Fuller Theological
Seminary, 1986), 248.

tive. This is due to the fact that the target audience no longer has a background of biblical knowledge and churchly associations to provide a context for an informed decision to be made followed by social integration into a Christian congregation. Later in the chapter some suggestions will be made as to how the traditional "crusade evangelism" approach could be adapted to meet changing conditions.

Not only is there a lengthy process leading up to a conversion, there is also a process following the conversion. As a person continues in the Christian life he comes to realize that there are still unyielded areas in his life which need "converting."[8]

An undue emphasis on crisis conversion as the norm of entry into the kingdom may cause unnecessary anxieties on two counts for those who are unable to name a specific date and place when they turned from darkness to light and were transformed from death to life. Many people nurtured in a Christian home by godly parents who prayed for their children from before their conception cannot recall a time when they did not love Jesus. Although there may have been times of growing awareness of Christ, of the demands and promises of the gospel, and of the need to make their faith their own outside of the supportive environment of the home, it would be inappropriate to term any of these moments of realization as a conversion experience. Those Christian traditions which stress a covenant theology by which the covenant promises extend to the children of believers, regard sudden conversions of such children as an exception rather than the norm. Then there are other individuals, who were not raised in a Christian home, who are unable to recall a single crisis experience, but they are deeply aware of the hand of God on their lives during a period of time to bring about a gradual, but no less significant, transformation. Will Metzger testifies regarding his own experience, "I now understand my initial interest in Jesus Christ as the beginning of my awakening and not my conversion. I find myself dating my conversion much later, though I still don't know the day. I now think of my conversion as closer to a time when I began to understand who Jesus was. As my life slowly took on a new direction, I had assurance of salvation."[9]

In the course of my travels I have crossed the equator on a number of occasions. One time I was on a steamship when the event was recorded with traditional ceremonies performed by King Neptune. On other occasions, when traveling by airplane, I have been totally unaware of crossing the boundary between the northern and southern hemispheres. Arrival at my destination was proof that I had made the crossing. To change the analogy, the important thing is that I know that I am alive, rather than know the day when I was born.

When conversion is regarded as both *process* as well as *crisis* evangelists are sensitized to the fact that God may already have been at work in the

---

8. Keith Miller, *Taste of New Wine* (Waco, Tex.: Word Books, 1965), 83, 84.

9. Will Metzger, *Tell the Truth*, 2nd ed. (Downers Grove, Ill.: InterVarsity Press, 1984), 104.

lives of those with whom they are seeking to communicate the gospel. When numbers are small enough to make it feasible, time should be taken to discover in what ways God has been making himself known and what stage people have reached in their spiritual pilgrimage. Furthermore, the process dimension safeguards the evangelists from operating as those who know it all and have spiritually arrived. David Bosch, cites the example of Peter's encounter with Cornelius as being as much the conversion of the evangelist from his racial prejudice as of the God-fearing centurion to Christ. He also points out how the incident illustrates the fact every evangelist must be prepared to run a risk of getting changed in the course of evangelistic outreach."[10] When in dialogue with the world, especially in a cross-cultural situation, evangelists are challenged regarding their own understanding of, and response to, the gospel which they are charged to proclaim.

3. *Conversion has corporate ramifications as well as an individual focus.* The corporate dimension of conversion is frequently overlooked by Western Christians in the evangelical tradition who have such a strong individualistic emphasis. One of Donald McGavran's greatest contributions to missiological thinking has been his insights into the decision-making process on the part of first generation converts to Christ out of non-Christian societies. He observed that the majority of new believers from the Third World became Christians as a consequence of a group decision-making process. He described such turnings as "People Movements" which he defined as a "multi-individual, mutually-dependent decision making."[11] Everyone may participate in the debate and the decision-making process and in so doing a chain-reaction is set in motion. People Movements may take various forms: follow-my-leader, crowd conversions (Acts 2:37-41; 4:4); household conversions (Acts 10, 16); community response (Acts 9:35); web movement (Jn 1:40-42,45); to which list we might add the contemporary phenomenon of a media movement as evidenced in the electronic church.[12]

Particularly in societies where the tribal and extended family network still exerts a powerful influence, evangelistic procedures must take account of this network of relationships and the communication directed to the group rather than to vulnerable individuals. Sometimes it is advisable to hold back the response of the enthusiastic one or two in the interest of winning substantial numbers within the total group. This insight is equally applicable in the Western world among communities with a strong sense of solidarity. Examples would include, youth gangs in the inner city, shift workers in heavy industry, particular professions which entail a distinctive lifestyle, such as long-distance truck drivers, race-track workers, as well as ethnic minorities and counter-culture groups.

---

10. Bosch, "Evangelism," 101.

11. Donald McGavran, *Understanding Church Growth* (Grand Rapids, Mich.: Eerdmans, 1980), 340.

12. Eddie Gibbs, *I Believe in Church Growth* (Grand Rapids, Mich.: Eerdmans, 1981), 118,119.

The approach advocated by Donald McGavran is in contrast to the "one-by-one against the tide" method, which can easily result in isolated converts becoming dispossessed through being rejected by the group they have left behind.

Conversion means more than entering into a personal relationship with the Lord Jesus Christ. It also entails belonging to the new community of the family of God. The convert is baptized not only into Christ but into his body, "For by one Spirit we were all baptized into one body—Jews or Greeks, slaves or free—and all were made to drink of one Spirit" (1 Cor 12:13). The church is not only a herald of the message, it embodies that message. Therefore it is advantageous for potential converts already to be in contact with a community of believers prior to making a decision to "convert," because they will then have a demonstration model of what the Christian life is meant to entail, and they will immediately receive support from people they already know.

The early church seems to have welcomed all-comers. Anglican missiologist Robert Brow observes of the early church that it seemed to take in anybody, since all baptisms were immediate with no probationary period to weed out the good from the bad.[13] Their readiness indicates their tremendous faith in the transforming power of the Holy Spirit. But for such expectations to be realized the church itself must be living in the fullness and power of the Holy Spirit. Brow likens the discipling function of the church to the role of the good driving instructor, contrasting it with the role of the government driving examiner. The former patiently works with the trainee, providing advice and correcting errors until the person gets it right through practice. By contrast the latter sits by the driver with a checklist at the ready to record every mistake and pronounce a pass or fail verdict. If Brow is correct in his emphasis, then the church's evangelistic procedures must take account of the quality of life which the church has to offer the new convert (cf. 1 Jn 1:3). They must show that they are themselves still under instruction in the lifelong school of discipleship.

Like that of the Lord, the church's witness is incarnational in nature. The "body of Christ" language militates against overspiritualization of the church, which refuses to deal with the empirical and practical realities of historical existence.[14] Thus the church must itself become a sacrament of the gospel—a visible word, which partially and imperfectly embodies that which it proclaims, both containing within itself and pointing beyond itself to the One who is the source of its life. Alongside the work of heralding the gospel to the world is the equally important task of internalizing the gospel so that the community has the credibility of progressive conformity to its public declarations and exhortations. Darrell Guder observes that "only through its pilgrimage through time can the church discover the vast dimensions of the meaning and application of the gospel."[15]

---

13. Robert Brow, *Go Make Learners* (Wheaton, Ill.: Harold Shaw Publishers, 1981), 31.
14. Darrell L. Guder, *Be My Witnesses* (Grand Rapids, Mich.: Eerdmans, 1985), 28.
15. Ibid., 39.

4. *Conversion has cultural ramifications as well as a theological basis.*
By virtue of the fact that the gospel is communicated by human agents it is
inevitably both filtered and colored by culture. It is filtered due to cultural biases and blind spots, and colored through being translated into a particular
cultural milieu. Not only is such a process inevitable, it is also to a degree
desirable in that the God of the Bible communicates incarnationally, as is
supremely demonstrated in the ministry of Jesus who came as a Jew to
express the Good News within that cultural context.

The contextualized approach, is not without problems, however. One
problem is the tendency for culture to predominate over gospel to such an
extent that an emphasis is placed only on those aspects of the gospel which
affirm culture, while suppressing the radical demands of Christ which run
against culturally accepted norms. When such a complete identification
occurs, the church functions as a mirror rather than a light in society. This state
of affairs is more accurately termed "enculturation."

The other problem occurs in the cross-cultural communication of the
gospel. Those seeking to convert people of other cultures sometimes fail to
realize the extent to which their embodiment and verbal expression of the
gospel has been shaped by their own culture. Thus, the emphases they bring,
the assumptions they make and the vocabulary they use may make the gospel
seem an irrelevant foreign import. In regard to conversion, the two basic
questions faced by the persons being invited to respond to the gospel message
are: "What is it that I am committing myself to?" and, "If I decide to take this
step, what will I have to turn away from?" In other words, how does God
relate to culture? The missionary task is not to make converts who will conform to their cultural expression of the Christian faith, but to help the people
among whom they are working to see how the gospel relates to their own culture. Some aspects it will affirm, some aspirations it will fulfill, and some elements it will pass judgment upon. The gospel works redemptively in a variety of ways on all cultures.

Saint Paul, as a missionary to the Gentiles, did not seek to bring about a
cultural conformity to Judaism among his converts. One the contrary, he
himself lived as a Gentile among Gentiles in order to help them appreciate
how they could place their lives under the management of Christ without the
prerequisite of conformity to the Jewish ceremonial law (1 Cor 9:9f).

Missionary anthropologist Paul Hiebert observes that "a call for contextualization without an equal call for preserving the gospel without compro-
mise opens the door to syncretism."[16] He argues for a communicational
model which he describes as "critical contextualization," which involves a
three step approach. Step one is the exegesis of the culture, uncritically gathering and analyzing the traditional beliefs and customs. Step two is the exegesis of scripture and the translation of the biblical message into the cognitive, affective, and evaluative dimensions of another culture. And the third

---

16. Paul Hiebert, "Critical Contextualization," *International Bulletin of Missionary
Research* 11, no. 3 (July 1987).

step is one of critical response in which people corporately evaluate critically their own past customs in the light of their new biblical understanding, and make decisions regarding their response to their new-found faith.

In regard to evangelistic procedures, it must be recognized that the decision-making process varies from culture to culture. Westerners are accustomed to individuals making up their own minds. However, in other cultures specific individuals or groups need to be consulted prior to making any significant decision. For instance, missionaries working among young people in a traditional African tribal setting would be unwise to encourage the teenagers to make a decision to follow Christ without consulting with the village elders. For them to make an independent decision would signal to everybody in their cultural setting that the decision could not be of any great significance.

Another aspect of decision making which Westerners need to bear in mind is that not infrequently first-generation converts to Christ from other religions such as Islam, Hinduism, Animism, etc., step over the threshold from one faith position to another, through the impact of a power encounter and not simply because they have been intellectually convinced by the propositional truths of Christianity. Missionary accounts reveal numerous illustrations of healings, deliverance from demonic power, and supernatural protection in dangerous situations as occasions in which God revealed his presence and created receptivity to the gospel message.[17]

5. *Conversion has a psychological as well as a spiritual dimension.* "Conversions" from one ideology to another as well as dramatic personality changes can be induced by psychotherapy, brain surgery, or mind-changing drugs. William Sargent's popular treatment of the physiological basis of conversion in *Battle for the Mind* presents a classical reductionist explanation.[18] Other contributors to this volume are more competent than I to address these issues. My concern is to point out the dangers of undue psychological pressure which may be present in a one-on-one evangelistic encounter when the evangelist is the dominant personality; in a small group situation when there is strong peer-group pressure on an individual to conform or experience rejection by the group; or in a highly charged emotional atmosphere generated by a speaker who has the ability to sway the crowd.

As Christian conversion is a human response to the love of God expressed in Christ, it must be entered into voluntarily. Second, it is advisable that the decision be taken with an awareness of alternatives. Third, the decision needs to be accompanied by appropriate action. And, fourth, the decision once taken is acted upon with a fair degree of consistency.

17. For a source book of responsibly written personal experiences see Paul B. Long's *The Man in the Leather Hat* (Grand Rapids, Mich.: Baker Book House, 1986). The author was a Presbyterian missionary in the Congo and Brazil.

18. William W. Sargent, *Battle for the Mind* (London: Heinemann, 1957).

6. *Conversion often occurs in response to invitation or even persuasion but must never be induced by manipulation.* The communicating of the gospel entails more than the dumping of information. It is proclaimed with a view to eliciting a response. Thus, on the day of Pentecost Peter preached to the crowds in Jerusalem to answer their question, *"What does this mean?"* so puzzled were they by the phenomenon of Galileans speaking their home languages as though they were their native tongues. At the conclusion of his address, those who had been impacted by his message were asking, *"What shall we do?"* (Acts 2:12,37). Frequently Paul entered into dialogue, arguing and persuading, in the course of the addresses he delivered in the synagogues (Acts 18:4; 19:8; 28:23,24). Motivated by his reverential fear of the Lord, as well as the love of Christ, he did all in his power to persuade men and women (2 Cor 5:1).

In exercising the ministry of persuasion evangelists must ensure that they have given sufficient information to form the basis of a meaningful decision. Appeals must be preceded by biblical content. Will Metzger perceptively comments, "It is possible to encourage unbelievers to arrive at decisions from false motives. They 'become Christians' for what they can get out of it, such as coveting the speaker's experience or happiness or success in life. The true reason for becoming a Christian is not that we may have a wonderful life but that we may be in a right relationship to God. Too many of our evangelistic methods are benefit oriented."[19] First the issues must be clarified, and then any attempts at persuasion must be characterized by integrity and sensitivity. Is the evangelist's motivation of paramount importance? Are we trying to win the person to Christ or to our group and cause? Mark McCloskey asks, "Are we asking others to change outward, sociological or cultural allegiances without a corresponding inner change? Do we merely want to see our group get larger and more powerful, or do we want to see the kingdom of God grow? Do we want nonbelievers to decide for Christ for our benefit or for theirs?"[20]

We now turn from an examination of how principles influence the adoption of particular procedures and the way the chosen method is applied to a consideration of the different contexts in which conversions might take place.

ADOPTING EVANGELISTIC PROCEDURES WHICH ARE APPROPRIATE TO EACH CONTEXT

Evangelism may take place in widely differing situations, ranging from a discussion between two friends, to a small group situation, through the congregational level, to the city-wide crusade attracting tens of thousands of people. The method adopted will relate to the size of the occasion. It will also

---

19. Metzger, *Tell the Truth*, 98.
20. Mark McCloskey, *Tell It Often—Tell It Well* (San Bernardino, Calif.: Here's Life Publishers, 1985), 60.

depend on the target person's or group's level of responsiveness and the extent to which the potential convert is known personally to the evangelist.

Personal Evangelism—The One-on-One Context

Sometimes the occasion is no more than a chance and brief contact between people who were strangers up to that point. If there is little likelihood of those two individuals meeting again, as with persons who have met on an airplane flight, then the evangelist might work for sudden closure or consider that the encounter was one in a chain of such encounters and, therefore, commit the individual to the further leading of the Lord until the appropriate time for that individual to make a commitment.

On other occasions the meeting is deliberate in the sense that the evangelist sets out with the specific intention of confronting individuals in order to present them with a brief presentation of the core of the gospel message and invite them to make an immediate response. Sometimes the point of closure is couched in such phrase as, "Can you think of any good reason why you cannot now make a commitment to Christ?"

There are a number of problems associated with such a confrontational approach. First, it can appear programatic and "pre-canned," with the person approached made to feel that the evangelist is after their soul rather than having a genuine concern for them. Second, if a decision is elicited, it may be as a device to terminate the interview. Third, the person who has prayed a prayer of acceptance is left high-and-dry, for there was an adequate basis for an ongoing relationship with the person who made the approach, and the decision was taken in isolation from any community of believers on hand to provide ongoing support. It is not surprising, therefore, to discover how small is the percentage of those who are reported as converts through such methods that have an ongoing relationship with Christ or who are incorporated into any local church.[21]

The most productive form of personal evangelism occurs in situations where the individuals have established a prior relationship. They may be relatives, neighbors, or work colleagues. The Institute of American Church Growth studied 14,000 lay people who were asked to respond to the question, "What or who was responsible for your coming to Christ and your church?" Choosing between eight possible reasons, over 75 percent stated the primary influence was a friend or relative.[22]

One further consideration to be taken into account in personal evangelism is the value of the person being brought to the point of conversion to meet other Christians to provide alternative role models other than the evangelist. It is particularly valuable for the person to meet people in the same line of business as themselves or facing similar family situations, in order to provide

---

21. See C. Peter Wagner's comments on "Key '73" and "Here's Life" in *Your Church Can Grow* (Ventura, Calif.: Regal Books, 1976), 165-168, and *Your Church Can Be Healthy* (Nashville: Abingdon, 1979), 70-72.

22. Win Arn and Charles Arn, *The Master's Plan for Making Disciples* (Pasadena: Church Growth Press, 1982), 43.

opportunity to discuss how another Christian has applied his or her faith to everyday problems.

In summarizing these reflections on personal evangelism we draw attention to the important considerations detailed by Eddie Fox and George Morris which underlie every one-on-one relationship with evangelistic potential.

In the process of sharing faith the closure of an encounter with another person depends on four factors: the leadership of the Holy Spirit, the faith-sharer's assessment of the quality of the relationship, the degree of receptivity on the part of the other person, and the context. These four variables seems to be present in every faith-sharing situation. The context or arena has a great influence upon the manner of closure.[23]

Evangelism through Small Groups

Small groups, whether home-based or located on neutral turf can provide a nonthreatening environment in which the gospel can be shared effectively. They have the advantage of providing a homey environment in which people can quickly relax. The setting is informal so that in the hands of a capable leader there is plenty of opportunity for participation and honest questioning. People are known individually and are in personal contact with one or more of the group members so that issues can be further pursued outside of the context of the meeting. Most small groups are fairly homogeneous in nature so that a topic can be chosen which will be of immediate relevance to all present.

Dialogue evangelism has been modeled and advocated by Richard Peace[24] here in the United States and John Chapman, the Diocesan Evangelist in the Anglican Diocese of Sydney, Australia.[25] In some situations the group meeting is related to a topic of general interest—i.e., "How do we bring up our children to face the challenges of tomorrow's world?" At other times a guest speaker will be invited to open up the agenda. Some might speak of how their faith has helped them in their professional life or through a domestic crisis. Others will adopt a more direct approach. Other groups are set up as Bible study groups for those interested in the Christian faith. Rebecca Manley Pippert has described this approach in her InterVarsity student work. She intrigued students with the statement, "We had an interesting study this week on how Jesus related to women. He sure was ahead of the culture of his day in his attitude toward women."[26] And then waited to see if their curiosity was aroused sufficiently to want to be present at the next meeting.

---

23. H. Eddie Fox and George E. Morris, *Faith-Sharing* (Grand Rapids, Mich.: Francis Asbury Press, Zondervan, 1986), 101.

24. Richard Peace, *Small Group Evangelism* (Downers Grove, Ill.: InterVarsity Press, 1985).

25. John C. Chapman, *Know and Tell the Gospel* (London: Hodder and Stoughton, 1981).

26. Rebecca Manley Pippert, *Out of the Saltshaker* (Downers Grove, Ill.: InterVarsity Press, 1979), 130.

A number of considerations need to be borne in mind in organizing such groups. People need to be invited to bring their doubts. One famous London church has one such group for skeptics and honest seekers called "Agnostics Anonymous."

Second, when the Bible is being used, Christians present need to be cautioned to keep to the passage under discussion and to refrain from using the occasion to display their encyclopedic knowledge of the scriptures. It is preferable to keep to one version and the same edition so that people unfamiliar with the Bible are not confused by other people reading a different text, or embarrassed at not being able to find the references cited. When everyone has the same edition then page numbers can be announced.

Third, ensure that the meetings begin and end on time. Unbelievers seldom made a commitment within the context of the meeting. Therefore it is important to conclude promptly to give opportunity for those who want to remain to engage in personal conversation.

Fourth, people are seldom converted at the first meeting. This is especially true of those who have never been church attenders or who have lapsed for a number of years. A series of meetings need to be planned, on a monthly basis, but only one announced at a time. If people think that their agreeing to attend one meeting commits them for the next six months they may not be prepared to take the risk or accept the commitment.

Fifth, it is important only to take people as far as they are prepared to go. One of the secrets of effective communication is to tell people a little less than they want to know, rather than to keep on talking and pressing a point after the person has stopped listening!

Sixth, a presenter who is skillful in small-group evangelism will involve the members of the group, calling on individual Christians to speak from their experience to emphasize and illustrate a point. Frequently, an individual who comes to faith is as impressed with the stumbling and nervous response of the ordinary Christian as they are with the polished communication of the evangelist. The role of the evangelist is to make the message clear and to present it in a winsome manner, while the task of the Christians present is to tell their story which provides a point of identification for those who are considering the truth and relevance of the gospel. The unbelievers present should always outnumber the Christians to ensure that they are not made to feel on the defensive. Furthermore, honest sharing by all concerned will help to dispel any feeling of "us" and "them," for all present are on a spiritual pilgrimage with their lives still very much in process.

Seventh, frequently there will be at least one argumentative person present, who to everyone's surprise is among the first to show interest in a further meeting. Sometimes people are aggressive as a cover for their own loneliness and vulnerability. At other times they launch a verbal attack as a ploy, either to test the sincerity of those who have organized the occasion, or their acceptance by the group. It is their way of discovering whether the Christians present are really concerned for them and ready to accept them as they are, or whether they are only interested in them as long as they seem hopeful prospects.

Crusade Evangelism

As previously noted, modern, city-wide crusade evangelism had its roots in small-town revivalism, where its purpose was to restore the wandering and lost sheep to the fold of the faithful. In today's increasingly urbanized and pluralistic society, crusade evangelism had to be adapted and organized with a high degree of sophistication to be an effective means of bringing significant numbers of non-believers and notional Christians to an active faith. The problem is not how to gather the crowds to fill the stadium. This can be achieved without too much difficulty in areas which are heavily churched and where Christians appreciate the thrill of a big occasion and media attention to give them a sense of significant corporate identity.

A study of a Billy Graham Crusade audience in Knoxville, Tennessee, in 1970 revealed that 78 percent of the respondents to a questionnaire sample of 1 percent of the seats reported attending church the previous week, and fully half of the respondents were officers in their church.[27] The sight of the great crowds helps them appreciate that there are more Christians in the area than they previously believed. When churches which have participated in such a crusade meet to describe the benefits, this aspect features prominently in their reports. As significant as this reason may be for the morale of existing Christians it is not the primary reason for holding the crusade.

A strategy must be developed which ensures that the stadium is not just filled with the faithful but includes significant numbers of those to be invited to come to Christ for the first time or be restored to faith. One of the main obstacles to the achievement of this goal can be those enthusiastic, supportive church leaders who have unrealistic expectations regarding the outcome of a crusade. Some think that the importing of a famous name combined with city-wide publicity and media exposure will provide sufficient attraction for nonbelievers to make their own way to the stadium, driven by curiosity or spiritual hunger. There are sufficient anecdotes to give credence to such expectations. But statistically the numbers of such individuals do not represent a significant percentage.

There is strong evidence from the experience of the Billy Graham Evangelistic Association's work in the United States and Europe that 80 percent of those who respond to Graham's invitation to decide for Christ have been personally invited and accompanied to the meeting by church members. John Corts, the director of the Crusades in Cincinnati and Tampa (1977), reported, "from surveys administered in both cities, approximately 80 percent of all unchurched inquirers stated that they were personally brought to the Crusade by someone."[28] The same figure emerged from the 1984-1985 Mission England meetings, which consisted of seven regional

---

27. Donald A. Clelland and Thomas C. Hood, "In The Company of the Converted: Characteristics of a Billy Graham Crusade Audience," A paper presented at the Association for the Sociology of Religion meeting, New York, August, 1973.

28. Lewis A. Drummond, *The Impact of Billy Graham Crusades: Are They Effective?* (Minneapolis: World Wide, 1982), 11.

crusades, attracting a total audience of 1,026,000 with 123,113 inquirers.[29]

Sterling Huston, Billy Graham's Director of Crusades for North America summarizes the benefits of mass media coverage of a crusade in that it helps establish its significance in the minds of people in the community. It reinforces the supporters, making it easier for them to invite their non-Christian friends. It serves as a conversation starter and raises the spiritual consciousness of the community and may plant the idea of attending in the minds of people. "Briefly stated, mass media helps plant the idea, interpersonal contact prompts the person to act on that idea. The two are an effective combination."[30]

One of the limitations of the city-wide crusade approach is the small amount of immediate counseling which can be provided for the inquirer who has stepped to the front of the crowd at the invitation of the evangelist. Within the Billy Graham and Luis Pallau crusade setting, these persons are paired with trained counselors who are strategically placed in the audience to walk forward with them. They are trained in how to introduce themselves and to quickly discover the reason why the person has made their response, for in addition to making a first-time commitment, between 40 and 60 percent may have responded for other reasons: That is, they lacked assurance of salvation, wanted to rededicate their lives to Christ, or came forward to seek counsel regarding a personal problem. The counselor has to work quickly because most people will have to rejoin their parties and be returning home within half-an-hour.

Additional problems include the fact that the inquirer will most likely be a complete stranger to the counselor, they will probably not meet again, and the inquirer may be too distracted by the unfamiliar surroundings and the emotion of the moment to take in what the counselor is trying to say. Recognizing the restrictions under which they operate, the two evangelistic organizations mentioned above recognize that the on-site counseling is just a small element in the total follow-up strategy.

The key question is, who has the primary responsibility for the follow-up inquirers—the evangelistic organization, the local committees, or the local churches? A survey conducted by Vanderbilt sociologist Glen Firebaugh in 1979 on the Billy Graham Crusade revealed that "an overwhelming majority (90 percent) of the local church leaders feel that the local church, not BGEA or the crusade committee, has primary responsibility for follow-up. Yet only one minister in three said his church was 'involved' or 'very involved' in follow-up."[31] For their part the BGEA undertakes to inform the ministers of the churches identified by the inquirers of the name of the person and nature of the commitment within seventy-two hours.

Those persons counseled at Billy Graham meetings who state that they

---

29. Gavin Reid, *To Reach a Nation* (London: Hodder and Stoughton, 1987), 56,61.

30. Sterling W. Huston, *Crusade Evangelism and the Local Church* (Minneapolis: World Wide, 1984), 106.

31. Glen Firebaugh, "How Effective Are City-Wide Crusades?" *Christianity Today*, 27 March 1981.

have a church are referred back to the minister of their church. Those who have no previous church contact are assigned to a church in their area of town by a Designations Committee consisting of church leaders supportive of the crusade. They handle only about 5-20 percent of the total number of inquirers. Their task is admittedly a hit-and-miss affair, rather like arranging a blind date! Those churches which have not been effective in taking unbelievers to the Crusade meetings and are relying entirely on a windfall of referrals to justify their involvement in the project are likely to be disappointed by the outcome and to be most negative in their assessment. The general rule is that those churches which take most non-Christians and lapsed churchgoers to the Crusade meetings receive the most fruitful follow-up opportunities, for the obvious reason that they are not following up strangers but individuals with whom they are already in contact.

The secret to bridging the follow-up gap is to solve the problem before the Crusade meetings, rather than chasing up the inquirers afterwards. The most effective Crusades are those in which the unbelievers, the nominal Christians and lapsed churchgoers are personally invited in significant numbers and accompanied by Christians with whom they have already established a personal relationship. These same Christians need to have been trained in the counseling procedures so that they can accompany those they have invited who respond when the evangelistic invitation is given. The inquirer is then talking to a friend rather than a stranger, and the counseling can continue on the way home from the meeting and into the following weeks.

In areas of the United States where a high proportion of the population claim to be church members it is evident that many of those who respond as inquirers will already be church members who may be nonattenders, irregular attenders, or not even in church most weeks. Therefore their response will not be reflected in increased church membership following the Crusade.[32]

Both the Billy Graham Evangelistic Association and the Luis Palau Evangelistic Association place great importance on the establishing of "nurture groups" by local churches and groups of Christians in which the inquirers can be helped to a deeper and clearer commitment. Special basic Bible studies and discipleship training materials have been prepared for use in these contexts. The "nurture group" strategy is of particular importance where there is a wide cultural gap between the churches and the bulk of the population, as in Australia and England. John Mallison, a small-group specialist in the Uniting Church, and John Chapman, Director for Evangelism for the Sydney Diocese of the Anglican Church, trained 2,500 nurture group leaders in preparation for the 1979 Billy Graham Sydney Crusade. Some 22,500 inquirers recorded their decisions at the meetings held at the race course. "According to Bishop Dain, 11,000 to 12,000 of these were Anglicans. A thorough survey by the diocese revealed that 72.6 percent of these were in full church membership one year later, not including those who had moved

---

32. See Firebaugh's response to Win Arn's article, "Mass Evangelism, The Bottom Line," in *Church Growth: America* (January/February 1979).

away from the city and could not be counted. Bishop Dain went on to state that although hard data were not available on all inquirers, he reliably estimates that 70 percent of the 22,500 had been brought into the life of the church and were continuing in their commitment to Christ."[33]

A sample research of incorporation of inquirers in three of the Mission England regions three months to a year following the 1984 and 1985 meetings reveal that over 60 percent of the inquirers had completed the six-week nurture group course in Luke's gospel and were continuing in the fellowship of the church. Unfortunately, neither study indicated the proportion of these who were church members prior to their attendance at the Crusade meetings.

The studies reveal that the great majority of those who respond at Crusade meetings are already in contact with a local church to a greater or lesser extent. With this in mind the Mission England organizers planned for a more extensive Crusade preparation of two years duration to encourage the widening of networks of contacts and the renewal of local church life. In preparation for the 1984 missions some 5,000 church leaders attended a course provocatively entitled, *Is My Church Worth Joining?* Thirty thousand attended a training course, *Caring for New Christians*, which was a requirement for any nurture group leader.[34] Churches were encouraged to focus on small-group evangelism prior to the main crusade meeting and to run their nurture groups on a pilot basis to gain experience prior to the big events.

A further innovation was to establish groups of three who would pray together on a regular basis for nine persons they already knew whom they would like to see come to faith in Christ. These groups were known as "Prayer Triplets." Over 90,000 Prayer Triplets cards were requested for the six 1984 crusades; and the following year 150,000 were distributed in connection with the Sheffield Crusade.[35] This element has been introduced by both Graham and Palau in their United States crusade preparations.

In the more secular environment of England, where church attendance is down to around 9 percent and only 13 percent claim church membership, it was important that the nonchurchgoers invited to crusade meetings should have had opportunities prior to receiving their invitations to become familiar with the gospel and to dialogue with committed Christians. Such contacts would provide them with a background knowledge on which to make a more meaningful decision at the evangelistic meeting. In order to equip Christians to articulate their faith more clearly a workbook entitled *Care To Say Something?* was published by Scripture Union. In addition, small-group and local church evangelism was encouraged in the months leading to the arrival of Billy Graham. Crusade evangelism is most effective in areas where

---

33. Huston, *Crusade Evangelism*, 147,148.

34. Derek Williams, *One In A Million: Billy Graham with Mission England* (Berkhamstead, England: Word Books), 52,53.

35. For a detailed account of the Prayer Triplets concept see Brian Mill, *Three Times Three Equals Twelve* (Eastbourne, England: Kingsway, 1986).

local churches are already proving their effectiveness in ongoing congregational evangelism. It is these elements which contributed to the impact of Mission England, which represented the largest combined evangelistic effort ever to be undertaken in the country. Six thousand churches were involved, with the backing of church leaders from most of the mainline denominations.

Local Church Evangelism

Evangelism must take place within the context of the local church as a continuous congregational activity if anything of lasting significance is to happen in terms of large numbers of lasting conversions. The ministry emphasis of the church must strike the right balance between the pastoral care of those who are already incorporated into the flock and searching and bringing into the fold the sheep wandering on the hills. Karl Barth expressed these two aspects of ministry in terms of "intensive growth" and "extensive growth."[36] Neither should be pursued to the neglect of the other.

Evangelism represents a dimension of the church's life which should permeate its programs rather than be considered as a departmental concern of a few individuals. Furthermore, churches which are sustaining an impressive growth rate through conversions regard evangelism as an ongoing activity and not a spasmodic effort.

As in crusade evangelism, the local church must have trained counselors who can assist those individuals who are being challenged to a first-time step of faith or to a deeper commitment through the regular ministry of the church. In addition to one-on-one counseling, beginners groups are also a valuable help in Christian growth and church incorporation.

Conversions take place on a regular basis in those churches where the congregation feels confident enough to invite their non-Christian friends to attend and culturally appropriate response opportunities are provided. In some traditions it is appropriate to invite inquirers to come to the altar or communion rail. In other situations the response may be less public, with inquirers invited to meet afterward in a side chapel, or to take a booklet on the way out of church with the opportunity to return a card requesting further counsel.

But what of those churches where the pastor does not have the evangelistic gift? In such situations, the pastor may appoint a staff person with the gift to work alongside, or invite visiting ministers to preach evangelistically. In addition, the principal evangelistic strategy might be through outreach groups, led by lay members of the congregation who do have an evangelistic gift. Peter Wagner postulates that about 10 percent of church members have the gift and need to be identified, trained, and deployed.[37]

---

36. Karl Barth, "The Growth of the Community," in *Theological Foundations for Ministry*, ed. Ray Anderson (Grand Rapids, Mich.: Eerdmans, 1979), 267.

37. C. Peter Wagner, *Spiritual Gifts Can Help Your Church Grow* (Ventura, Calif.: Regal, 1979), 177.

Furthermore, the congregation's awareness that conversions are taking place in their midst may be enhanced by interviewing people regarding their spiritual pilgrimage. This may take place within the context of a baptismal service or during a normal Sunday worship service in which visitors are present. Churches in a liturgical tradition will find that interviews can be scheduled either immediately preceding or following the congregation's recital of the Apostle's or Nicene Creed. By whatever means, evangelism must be shown to be an essential characteristic and not an eccentricity in the life of the church, and that conversions are the expected outcome.

In the course of this chapter it has been argued that the evangelistic approach and message must encompass the whole person and therefore the gospel presentation needs to be contextualized. We have also noted that conversion is as much process as crisis, which means that the task must be viewed in long term and not merely as an event. It consists of preparatory stages and subsequent steps as individuals and groups are first led to Christ and then deepen their ongoing commitment to him as they recognize his lordship over every area of life. As Christians engage in evangelism they must be prepared for their own understanding of the gospel and level of commitment to be challenged and extended. They must also recognize that conversion is but the human response in the divine action of regeneration, which realization places a restraint on persuasion, for biblically valid conversions cannot be induced by human manipulation of the emotions. Such considerations have an important bearing on conversion strategies at every level, whether the evangelistic context be one-on-one, small group, local church, or city-wide crusade.

Contributors

WILLIAM SIMS BAINBRIDGE is Professor and Chairman of the Department of Sociology and Anthropology, Towson State University (Maryland). He earned his doctorate from Harvard University in 1975. Dr. Bainbridge's many books include *The Future of Religion* (1985), written in collaboration with Rodney Stark. His articles have appeared in *American Sociological Review, American Journal of Sociology*, and *Review of Religious Research*.

E. BEATRICE BATSON, Chair of the English Department from 1975-88, now serves as Kilby Professor of Shakespeare and Coordinator of the Shakespeare Collection at Wheaton College. The author of several books, Professor Batson's latest work is a literary study of John Bunyan's *The Pilgrim's Progress,* written for the schools of England and published by Macmillan of London. She is also the author of essays and articles on various literary figures and has written numerous book reviews, especially for literary journals. In addition to her teaching and writing, she lectures at various colleges and universities in North America.

WARREN S. BROWN JR. is Professor of Psychology in the Graduate School of Psychology at Fuller Theological Seminary, and Director of the Lee Edward Travis Institute of Biopsychosocial Research, Adjunct Associate Professor of Psychiatry and Biobehavioral Sciences, UCLA, and a member of the UCLA Brain Research Institute. He received his doctorate from the University of Southern California. His areas of research include neuropsychology of human cognition and cognitive disorders and psychoneuroimmunology. Dr. Brown has contributed articles to such scholarly journals as *Neuropsychologia, Psychophysiology, Neurobiology of Aging, Biological Psychiatry*, and *Electroencephalography and Clinical Neurophysiology*. He has been the recipient of a National Institute of Mental Health Research Career Development Award and a National Science Foundation Exchange of Scientists and Engineers Grant, as well as various research grants. He is listed in *Who's Who in California* and *Who's Who in Behavioral Sciences*.

CARLA CAETANO is a doctoral candidate in the Graduate School of Phychology, Fuller Theological Seminary. A native of South Africa, she is

295

preparing to be a clinical psychologist with special skills and interests in the area of neuropsychology. She is a graduate assistant to Professor Warren Brown.

FREDERICK J. GAISER is Professor and Chair of the Department of Old Testament at Luther Northwestern Theological Seminary in St. Paul. He was born in West Alexandria, Ohio, and is an ordained pastor in the Evangelical Lutheran Church in America. Professor Gaiser served a rural parish in South Dakota for five years prior to teaching. He began his career as a research chemist before entering seminary. He earned his doctorate in theology at the University of Heidelberg, Germany. In addition to publishing many articles and sermons, Professor Gaiser has written extensively on the Psalms, especially for lay readers. He contributed the unit on Psalms for Augsburg's SEARCH Bible Study series. Dr. Gaiser is the editor of *Word & World*, a journal of theology for Christian ministry.

BEVERLY ROBERTS GAVENTA is Professor of New Testament at Columbia Theological Seminary in Decatur, Georgia. A native of Tennessee, she is a laywoman in the Christian Church (Disciples of Christ). She holds a Ph.D. from Duke University and a D.D. from Kalamazoo College *honoris causa*. The author of numerous articles and reviews, Dr. Gaventa has written *From Darkness to Light: Aspects of Conversion in the New Testament* (1986) and has edited, with Robert Fortna, *The Conversation Continues: Studies in Paul and John in Honor of J. Louis Martyn* (1990). She is the founding editor of *Critical Review of Books in Religion*, serves on the editorial board of the *Journal of the American Academy of Religion*, and chairs the Society of Biblical Literature's committee on Research and Publication. She represents the Christian Church (Disciples of Christ) on the Plenary Commission on Faith and Order of the World Council of Churches.

EDDIE GIBBS is the Robert Boyd Munger Associate Professor of Evangelism and Church Renewal at Fuller Theological Seminary. He was born in Nottingham, England, is a priest in the Church of England and served as a missionary in Chile. He is author of *I Believe in Church Growth* (1982), *The God Who Communicates* (Hodder and Stoughton), and *Followed or Pushed* (MARC Europe). He has led seminars for church leaders on Church Growth and Evangelism for the Billy Graham Evangelistic Association, and for mainline denominations in Europe, Australia, and across North America.

ARTHUR FREDERICK GLASSER is Professor and Dean Emeritus of the School of World Mission at Fuller Theological Seminary. Born in Patterson, New Jersey, he is an ordained minister of the Presbyterian Church (U.S.A.). He took his doctorate at the University of South Africa. A former missionary to China and U.S. Navy chaplain, he co-authored *Missions in Crisis* and also *Contemporary Theologies of Mission* (1983). His scholarly articles have appeared in numerous journals including *Religion and Intellectual*

Life, International Bulletin of Missionary Research, and *Evangelical Missions Quarterly*. For many years he served as the director of the Overseas Missionary Fellowship and as editor of *Missiology*.

PAUL G. HIEBERT is Professor of Anthropology and South Asian Studies and Chair of the Department of Missions and Evangelism at Trinity Evangelical Divinity School. He was born in Andhra Pradesh, India. He received his doctorate from the University of Minnesota. He and his wife served in India as missionaries and later taught at Kansas State University, University of Washington, and Fuller Theological Seminary. Among his books are: *Konduru: Structure and Integration in a South Indian Village* (1971). *Anthropological Insights for Missionaries* (1985), and *Case Studies in Missions* (1987). His articles have appeared in important scholarly journals including the *American Anthropologist, Journal of Anthropological Research, International Bulletin*, and *Missiology*. Reverend Hiebert has been a Fulbright Professor in India and served as consultant to the Mennonite Brethren Board of Missions and Services.

DEAL W. HUDSON is Associate Professor of Philosophy at Fordham University. Raised in Fort Worth, he received his doctorate from Emory University. Dr. Hudson received his license to preach from the Southern Baptist Convention. He has taught at Mercer University (Georgia). He has co-edited *Understanding Maritain: Philosopher and Friend* (1987) and also *The Future of Thomism* (University of Notre Dame Press). Dr. Hudson's articles have appeared in *International Philosophical Quarterly, Notes et Documents*, and *Crisis*. He serves on the Board of Directors of the Yves R. Simon Institute, the International "Jacques Maritain," and is a four-term Vice-President of the American Maritain Association. Dr. Hudson is a convert to Roman Catholicism.

CHARLES H. KRAFT is Professor of Anthropology and Intercultural Communication at Fuller Theological Seminary. Born in Waterbury (Connecticut), he received his doctorate from Hartford Seminary Foundation. An ordained minister of the Brethren Church (Ashland, Ohio), Dr. Kraft served as a missionary to Africa, then taught at Michigan State University and UCLA. Among Professor Kraft's books are *Christianity in Culture* (1979), *Christianity with Power* (1989), *Communication Theory for Christian Witness* (1991) and *Introductory Hausa* (University of California Press).

H. NEWTON MALONY is Professor in the Graduate School of Psychology, Fuller Theological Seminary. He is the author/editor of twenty-seven books, the latest of which is *Religion in Psychodynamic Perspective: The Contributions of Paul W. Pruyser* (1991) which he co-edited with Bernard Spilka. He is a Diplomate in Clinical Psychology, American Board of Professional Psychology, and the former president of the Christian Association for Psychological Studies and Psychologists Interested in Religious Issues,

Division 26, American Psychological Association. He is the co-editor of *The International Journal for the Psychology of Religion.*

DONALD K. McKIM is Interim Pastor of Trinity Presbyterian Church in Berwyn, Pennsylvania. He formerly served as Professor of Theology at the University of Dubuque Theological Seminary. Dr. McKim was raised in Wampum, Pennsylvania. He received his Ph.D. from the University of Pittsburgh. In addition to numerous articles, Dr. McKim has written: (with Jack B. Rogers), *The Authority and Interpretation of the Bible: A Historical Approach* (1979); *Ramism in William Perkins' Theology* (1987) and *Theological Turning Points* (1988). Dr. McKim has served as President of the Calvin Studies Society and is listed in the *International Authors and Writers Who's Who* (1981), *Historians of Early Modern Europe* (1983-1991), and *Who's Who in Religion* (1985; 1991-1992).

LEWIS R. RAMBO is Professor of Psychology and Religion at San Francisco Theological Seminary and the Graduate Theological Union in Berkeley. He was born in Texas and is a minister in the Churches of Christ. He received his doctorate from the University of Chicago Divinity School. Prior to joining the SFTS/GTU faculty, he taught at Trinity College, Deerfield, Illinois. In addition, Professor Rambo has served as a visiting professor at Fuller Theological Seminary and the University of California in Berkeley. In 1986 he was a Lady Davis Fellow and Visiting Professor of Comparative Religions at the Hebrew University of Jerusalem in Israel and a Fellow at the Ecumenical Institute, Tantur. He is the editor of *Pastoral Psychology* and is the author of *The Divorcing Christian* and the co-editor (with Donald Capps and Paul Ransohoff) of *Psychology of Religion: A Guide to Information Resources* (1976).

DAVID H. C. READ, Minister Emeritus of the Madison Avenue Presbyterian Church (NYC) was born in Cupar, Scotland. He received his terminal degree from Edinburgh University. An active parish minister at various times throughout his career, Reverend Reid also served as chaplain to the University of Edinburgh and chaplain to Her Majesty the Queen. He is the author of numerous books including *The Christian Faith, The Faith Is Still There,* and *Go and Make Disciples.* A preacher of international renown, the Reverend Read also developed the movement in preaching known as The Living Pulpit.

LAWRENCE A. REH, a native Illinoisan, earned a B.A. with honors at Bradley University and continued with master's study in adolescent psychology at Western Illinois University. He is currently an M.Div. student at San Francisco Theological Seminary. A veteran journalist and free-lance writer, he has written extensively on human rights, environmental and religious issues, and is the recipient of a number of awards for excellence from the Associated Press adn the Inland Daily Press Association. he has published one book of poetry, *If I Could Crown Your Hills With Gold* (1978).

JAMES T. RICHARDSON is Professor of Sociology and Judicial Studies at the University of Nevada, Reno. He earned his doctorate in sociology from Washington State University and his doctorate in law from the Nevada School of Law. Among his books are *Conversion Careers: In and Out of the New Religions, The Brainwashing/Deprogramming Controversy* (with David Bromley), and *Money and Power in the New Religions*. Professor Richardson has been the recipient of a Fulbright grant to the Catholic University of Nijmegan (The Netherlands), and has served as Departmental Visitor at the London School of Economics. He has also consulted and served as an expert witness in a number of legal actions involving new religions.

SAMUEL SOUTHARD received a Ph.D. from Southern Baptist Seminary, Louisville, Kentucky, and is a visiting scholar at that school while writing a pastoral theology of the gospels. He is also senior professor of pastoral theology at Fuller Theological Seminary, Pasadena, California. His latest books are *Theology and Therapy* (1989) and *Death and Dying, a Bibliographic Survey* (1991). His current pastoral project is the development of lay ministry teams at the Versailles Baptist Church, Kentucky, where he serves part-time as minister of pastoral care.

ALAN R. TIPPETT (1911-1988) was Professor of Missionary Anthropology and Oceanic Studies in the School of World Mission, Fuller Theological Seminary until his retirement in 1977. A native Australian, Dr. Tippett was a Methodist minister and missionary to the Figi Islands for twenty years prior to receiving an MA in history from American University and a PhD in anthropology from the University of Oregon. He was the founding editor of the journal *Missiology* and the author of *Solomon Island Christianity, People Movements in Southern Polynesia*, and *Introduction to Missiology*, as well as numerous presentations and published articles. St. Mark's Seminary in Canberra, Australia, houses his extensive library holdings and his writings.

J. DUDLEY WOODBERRY is Associate Professor of Islamic Studies at Fuller Theological Seminary. He was born in Ichowfu, Shandung, China, and is an ordained minister in the Presbyterian Church (U.S.A.). He received his doctorate from Harvard University and has edited *Muslims and Christians on the Emmaus Road* (1989). He has pastored churches in Riyadh, Saudi Arabia, and Kabul, Afghanistan, and lectured at universities in Lebanon, Pakistan, and Indonesia.

Index of Names

Index of Subjects

RELATED BOOKS OF INTEREST FROM RELIGIOUS EDUCATION PRESS

THE DYNAMICS OF RELIGIOUS CONVERSION
by *V. Bailey Gillespie*

In many respects this book is a companion piece to *Handbook of Religious Conversion*. This volume examines the nature and structure of conversion as a major transformational change which brings about wholeness and identity in a person's life. It shows how and why persons change before and during conversion. And it views conversion, not only as a change from one faith group to another, but even more importantly as a change from superficiality to depth within or outside one's present faith commitment. It includes three helpful chapters on conversion in pastoral and educational ministry.
261 pages   ISBN 0-89135-084-5

RELIGIOUS JUDGEMENT
by *Fritz Oser and Paul Gmünder*

There are two contemporary leading schools of thought about the cognitive-psychology basis of religion: the American school associated with James Fowler and the Swiss school associated with Fritz Oser. This book is Oser's magnum opus. Its unique feature lies in Oser's attempt to prove the existence of a distinct domain of religious cognitive deep-structure, namely a sphere of knowing which is distinctly religious. Though related to moral cognition, this intellectual "religious mother structure" is independent of moral knowledge and other forms of cognition.
235 pages   ISBN 0-89135-081-0

HANDBOOK OF FAITH
edited by *James Michael Lee*

An especially comprehensive and ecumenical treatment of faith. Part I contains chapters on the history of faith, the psychology of faith, the philosophy of faith, and the way various major world religions regard faith. Part II has two chapters on the biblical view of faith (one by a Catholic and one by a Protestant) and two other chapters on the theology of faith (one by by a Catholic and one by a Protestant). Part III shows how faith development can be facilitated by worship, pastoral counseling, social ministry, and religious instruction. Chapter authors include Monika Hellwig, John Carmody, Louis Dupré, H. Newton

Malony, Carroll Stuhlmueller, James L. Price Jr., Avery Dulles, Alexander McKelway, Louis Weil, Randolph Nelson, Melvin Blanchette, and James Michael Lee.
328 pages   ISBN 0-89135-075-6

THE EXPERIENCE OF FAITH
by *V. Bailey Gillespie*

Goes beyond Fowler in that it shows how faith develops not in abstract stages but in concrete situations. It interweaves psychological, theological, and biblical foundations of faith. A special feature of this book is that it shows how faith develops and how it can be facilitated over the entire life cycle from childhood to old age. Merton P. Strommen, author of *Five Cries of Parents,* writes: *"This is the finest book I have read on the experience of faith. Gillespie's book organizes faith around situations (not stages) and hence serves an important useful purpose in all ministry."*
263 pages   ISBN 0-89135-065-9

THE PSYCHOLOGICAL DYNAMICS
OF RELIGIOUS EXPERIENCE
by *André Godin*

An internationally acclaimed book written by one of Europe's leading psychologists of religion. The subtitle of this book on religious experience is: "It Doesn't Fall Down From Heaven." It treats a wide range of topics ranging from sudden conversion, types of privileged religious experience, fusional joy as an experience of the Spirit (charismatic groups), conflict as a religious experience of hope (sociopolitical groups), intense religious experience and mysticism, and a psychological interpretation of the Christian experience. Orlo Strunk Jr., author of *Mature Religion: A Psychological Perspective,* call this book *"a refreshing European perspective on the nature and workings of religious experience.*
279 pages   ISBN 0-89135-039-X

LONELINESS AND SPIRITUAL GROWTH
by *Samuel M. Natale*

The basic theme of this book is that loneliness can directly lead to deeper personal and spiritual growth. It examines the main forms of loneliness and delineates the eight major theories which explain the nature and structure of loneliness. An important feature of this book is that it deals with loneliness over the life cycle— loneliness in children, in youths, in mid-life adults, and in older adults. Bernard Groeschel, author of *Spiritual Passages,* writes: *"This clearly written volume offers a wealth of research-based ideas and practical procedures for effectively dealing with loneliness and isolation in others as well as in oneself."*
171 pages   ISBN 0-89135-055-1

FAITH DEVELOPMENT AND FOWLER
edited by *Craig Dykstra and Sharon Parks*

A comprehensive examination of Fowler's research, giving the pros and cons of his position. Main sections include: 1) an overview of faith development theory; 2) a critical examination and evaluation of faith development theory; 3) ways to enhance the development of faith in persons; 4) faith development and ministry; and 5) a response by James Fowler. Walter Brueggemann, author of *Genesis*, states: *"This is an uncommonly valuable volume."* Wayne Oates, author of *Psychology of Religion*, writes: *"This book is a definitive one for exploring the development of faith."*

322 pages   ISBN 0-89135-056-X

MORAL DEVELOPMENT, MORAL EDUCATION, AND KOHLBERG
edited by *Brenda Munsey*

An especially comprehensive and thorough multidisciplinary analysis of Kohlberg's work. This penetrating volume examines Kohlberg's theory and research from the standpoints of psychology, religion, theology, and education. It probes the strengths and weaknesses of Kohlberg's theory and gives concrete applications of his work to various areas. A reviewer writing in the journal of the Christian Association of Psychological Studies calls this book *"one of the really crucial books on the subject of moral development."*

457 pages   ISBN 0-89135-020-9

THE KOHLBERG LEGACY FOR THE HELPING PROFESSIONS
by *Lisa Kuhmerker*

This volume places the enduring riches of Kohlberg's work at the direct disposal of practitioners in counseling, clinical psychology, and education. F. Clark Power, co-editor of *Self, Ego, and Identity*, writes: *"I know of no better source of practical suggestions for persons wishing to bring the moral dimensions into their professional activities in a variety of settings."* Ann Higgins, co-author of *Lawrence Kohlberg's Approach to Moral Education*, states: *"It is the only book which lays out Kohlberg's overall vision as distinct from what he actually wrote because his life was cut short prematurely."*

234 pages   ISBN 0-89135-078-0